Dorothy Heathcote, a pioneer of Drama in Education: At last, a collection of finely honed papers ... sufficient to provide the reader with a variety of ideas and practical examples of work in progress, with clear theoretical frameworks explained. The common core of *dramatic engagement* emerges consistently. I shall continue to keep this book by me, using it rather like a box of interesting jewels. It's a gem of a book, subtle, and demanding careful reading and thinking about.

Eric Booth, author of *The Everyday Work of Art*: If you believe in art for the sake of community building, come get your bible—33 essays from those who know from the inside out about the ways that theater can bring people together in a time when we begin far apart. Ancient truths discovered afresh to transform our times.

Robert Barton, author of *Acting: Onstage and Off*: This is the book many of us have been waiting for, offering us ways to take theatre out of elitist art form and into a vital means by which we can improve lives. I very much look forward to using it as the text for a new course, Theatre for Change, that will greatly expand my students' awareness of what theatre can do.

Milton Polsky, author of *Let's Improvise* and *The Improv Workshop Handbook*. In its breadth and depth of information and insights regarding improvisation, this book is simply the best in the field! The range of subjects ... is amazing. What a joy to read! Whether you are a teacher, actor, therapist or someone who wants to explore drama in your life, you will find this book hard to put down and so useful in your work, study and play.

Michael Rohd, author of *Hope is Vital: Theatre for Community, Conflict and Dialogue*: Applied Theater is a growing field. This book is a map to help the reader sort through the ever-evolving geography of who is doing it and how. Part spark, part guide, part encyclopedia, it should quench your thirst even as it whets your appetite for more.

INTERACTIVE AND IMPROVISATIONAL DRAMA

This book is dedicated to
the Source of inspiration, enthusiasm, creativity and spontaneity

INTERACTIVE AND IMPROVISATIONAL DRAMA

VARIETIES OF APPLIED THEATRE AND PERFORMANCE

Adam Blatner, Editor

with *Daniel J. Wiener*

iUniverse, Inc.

New York Lincoln Shanghai

INTERACTIVE AND IMPROVISATIONAL DRAMA
VARIETIES OF APPLIED THEATRE AND PERFORMANCE

iUniverse books may be ordered through booksellers or by contacting:

iUniverse
2021 Pine Lake Road, Suite 100
Lincoln, NE 68512
www.iuniverse.com
1-800-Authors (1-800-288-4677)

The information, ideas, and suggestions in this book are not intended as a substitute for professional advice. Before following any suggestions contained in this book, you should consult your personal physician or mental health professional. Neither the author nor the publisher shall be liable or responsible for any loss or damage allegedly arising as a consequence of your use or application of any information or suggestions in this book.

ISBN-13: 978-0-595-41750-6 (pbk)
ISBN-13: 978-0-595-86090-6 (ebk)
ISBN-10: 0-595-41750-7 (pbk)
ISBN-10: 0-595-86090-7 (ebk)

Printed in the United States of America

Contents

Adam Blatner presents an overview of two significant traditions in education. Creative drama has been (in the USA) the main approach to introducing the basic elements of imagination and spontaneity training in schools. Role playing is often used to promote social and emotional learning in both elementary and secondary education.

Gustave J. Weltsek-Medina notes the potential of teachers to educate students through designing and facilitating improvised classroom enactments of relevant situations.

Allison Downey describes a form of theatre that combines theatrical elements, including scenes performed by actors about socially relevant issues, with interactive moments to emotionally engage the audience in addressing a particular social or curricular issue.

Daniel Kelin II shares his process for students learning English as a Second Language. Students tell their own culture's stories and develop performances from them, thereby strengthening their cultural identity while also exercising language skills.

Muriel Gold reports on her improvised dramatic format for helping drama students, educators, and professionals learn to deepen their understanding of various social roles by experiencing in family settings

ACKNOWLEDGMENTS

My path into this exciting and diverse arena began with training in psychodrama. As a young psychiatric resident, I became fascinated with the psychotherapeutic application of this method, developed by J. L. Moreno, M.D. I soon learned it also had been applied in education and that Moreno had instituted the first improvisational theatre in Vienna in 1921. (His troupe was called "The Theater of Spontaneity," and he offered some of the first "Living Newspaper" programs. The 1940s Hollywood star, Peter Lorre, started in that troupe.) With a vision of the importance of spontaneity and creativity as a deep psychological and even cosmic principle, Moreno's effort was aimed at revitalizing and redeeming drama from its crystallized format as scripted theatre. His ideas and influence have been seminal to the work addressed in this book.

Another influence on my development was the Human Potential Movement of the late 1960s, Esalen Institute, and workshops with Will Schutz (a pioneer in the encounter group movement), James F. T. Bugental (a pioneer in the field of Humanistic Psychology), Fritz Perls, and others during my life in England and Northern California.

Jonathan Fox, Jo Salas, and others in the Playback Theatre troupe impressed me strongly at a weeklong training my wife and I took in New Paltz, New York, in 1982. Fox's 1987 book, *Acts of Service* had as its second chapter a discussion of yet further forms of nonscripted theatre. This planted a seed that those other forms should be described more fully in a book. The result, these many years later, is being read by you right now!

I became aware of Joel Plotkin's work in sociodrama, which led to our corresponding. I even suggested that he write this survey, but he tossed the ball back to me. Around 2003, I began to have a sufficient number of resources and a sense of the format for this book. I talked with Daniel Wiener, who had edited other books, regarding the challenge of trying to gather together a number of authors and create an overview-anthology of the many approaches that used both interactivity and improvisation in drama. His help has been most meaningful.

During the period of gathering the authors' writings and rewritings of chapters, and editing, the various contributors have been remarkably patient as I asked them to describe their work in detail and set limits on the lengths of the chapters. I wish to especially thank a few authors who offered help above and beyond the work on their own chapters—especially Anne Curtis, Joel Gluck, Mecca Burns, and Clark Baim.

Many thanks are due to the editorial help by Beverly Lane Lorenz and Frances Danis. I especially want to express appreciation for the time and support given by my wife, Allee Blatner.

FOREWORD
David Shepherd

What impresses me about many of the approaches in this book is the way their inventors have had to try different things before they evolved their final methods. I learned a similar lesson as a young man, around 1953. I'd become dissatisfied with the mainstream, hard ticket tradition of theatre, and thought that a cabaret format would better serve most Americans. I wanted plays to relate to ordinary people, not be just about those wealthy enough to afford tickets. I wanted the audience to move around, eat and smoke and have some say about what was on stage. We began in Chicago. The scripts that fit our prescription, however, were flat. My business partner at that time, Paul Sills, suggested that we get help from his mother, Viola Spolin, who had been developing "theater games" in the training of actors. She came and trained our troupe, and the outcome was *COMPASS Theatre*, the first improvisational theatre in America. This led to *Second City*, also in Chicago, and that in turn led to many other spin-offs. Over the next fifteen years, I helped form several other COMPASS companies, and these, too, served as professional nurseries for actors who learned to integrate a different kind of personal authenticity into their work—actors such as Alan Alda, Alan Arkin, Jerry Stiller and Ann Meara.

Once the idea of improvisational and interactive theatre had caught on— and it is continuing to grow!—it occurred to me around 1973 that another way to keep theatre vital was to design it like a sport. So Howard Jerome and I developed the ImprovOlympix. Beginning in New York, it spread to other cities, and up into Canada, where Canadian Improv Games planted it in 300 high schools. (In another part of Canada, Keith Johnstone was developing a similar approach, TheatreSports, but at the time we didn't know about each other's work.) In Chicago, around 1981, Charna Halpern and I planted IO with 25 affinity groups (e.g., rabbis, cops, therapists, lawyers, inmates). With Del Close, Charna then spun off to produce a complex of short form, long form and news formats. (More history is available on the webpage supplement to this Foreword: <www.interactiveimprov.com/forewordwb.html>)

In the 1990s, I found myself considering how the new technology of inexpensive video recorders could make it possible for more people, amateurs, to make movies. I've stayed with this approach, as have some colleagues, such as Nancy Fletcher, working with teenage girls. (See Chapter 31).

More recently, I've begun to experiment with a kind of playshop, exploring with friends in groups ways to "stretch" physical movement, emotion and the skills of improvising songs and stories. The chapters in this book reflect a similar process on the part of many others at the cutting edge of the theatre arts.

One lesson I want to endorse is willingness to explore the edges of the field, new applications, working with populations that haven't in the past been thought to be reachable, integrating new technologies. Blatner's idea for a website that supplements this book is a good example, and other possibilities may arise. The very recent development of the internet site, "YouTube," as a place to share homemade videos offers a further venue for my MOVIExperience format.

Another lesson: Be willing even to change the identity of a format! For example, Second City was asked to teach improvisation to businesses that needed employees as quick and creative as the players they admired on stage. As a result, interestingly, Second City's main income shifted from box office to fees—for workshops! This move led to a widespread expansion of this component in what is now the evolving field of applied theatre. Today, most improv companies offer corporate training as well as programs for children and other special populations.

Our culture nowadays cries out for a theatre that counters tendencies towards regulation and repetitious tasks. Improvisation cuts through the barrier of conventional verbal thought and unleashes the imagination. I'm 82 now, and occasionally I connect with the idealism of fifty years ago, when we were jumping out of our skins with excitement about people connecting, recognizing stories on stage as being like their own, tentatively reaching out through people they empathized with to control and shape the show. Those vibrant ideals are reflected in the pages of this anthology.

I'm excited to see others who have shared my vision taking improvisational and interactive drama into senior recreation programs and nursing homes, prisons and personal development workshops, teen programs and schools, counseling and even the home.

As hinted at in the chapter on playmaking for Pacific Island students, these approaches may be used to help immigrants in assimilation and adjustment as well as in learning English.

Extending the chapter on Healing the Wounds of History, I also envision leaders of nations, churches and international organizations, participating in sociodramas and programs that integrate role reversal and other creative improvisations in the service of understanding, cooperation, and peace.

Colleges could be teaching history as a living story running on a broad scenario in which students improvise the very moment at which a crucial political decision is made.

As conference-call technology embraces television, and as the internet expands our ability to communicate, improv teams may play without having to travel from home base, so that, as with some present games, literally millions of people in many countries may participate.

Mainline movies and regular theatre are beginning to incorporate fresh levels of improvisation, which will also reduce the staggering cost of making movies.

It looks like today's improvisers will have their hands full.

INTRODUCTION

Adam Blatner

Over the last fifty years, beside the mainstream tradition of scripted and rehearsed theatre, interactive and improvisational drama methods have been increasingly used in education, business, and therapy, and for social action, recreation, community building and personal empowerment. Recognizing the common denominator in all these endeavors, beginning around 1990, the term "applied theatre" began to be used as a general term for this emerging field. This book is unique in offering descriptions of over 32 of these methods.

Interactive and improvisational dramatic approaches differ from mainstream drama in which actors perform for a relatively passive audience, memorize a script, and rehearse their parts. That kind of scripted theatre is what most books on drama talk about. However, the actual roots of drama are more inclusive and spontaneous, closer to the types of approaches described in these pages.

Historically, some of the more dynamic traditions in theatre include the late Renaissance form of commedia dell'arte, which was partly improvised, as were some of the early performances of Shakespeare's plays. In less technologized cultures, many tribal ceremonies, healing rituals, and story-telling activities were similarly partly or fully improvised. From the viewpoint of developmental psychology, the real root of drama is the make-believe play of middle childhood, a lively, imaginative, interactive process that most people wish they could recapture. (Using my Art of Play method, described in Chapter 21, they can!)

There are many advantages to learning about these drama approaches. First, you can enjoy many of the elements of drama, especially the fun of taking on and living through a role, without having to spend a lot of time and effort memorizing a part. Second, you don't have to audition or feel that you must be especially talented or have a lot of experience. Most of the activities in this book are aimed at ordinary people—applied theatre is more inclusive. If you're a theatre artist, you can allocate some or most of your professional efforts to the enjoyment of turning people on to the richness of drama and empowering their imagination and spontaneity.

Another advantage is that production and rehearsal costs are little or none at all.

Playing with the Parameters of Drama

There are a number of variables in thinking about different types of drama.

- The activity might involve carefully memorized scripts; it might be loosely scripted, the actors just agreeing on a general plot line; or the event is fully improvised.

- Rehearsal could be done carefully and extensively; lightly, just to block out general positions of key actors and the progress of the main sub-scenes; or engaged impromptu.

- Audience involvement may be passive throughout; passive initially, but brought into a level of interactivity towards the middle or end; or there may be no audience—everyone present is a co-player.

- Enactment may take place on a raised stage apart from the audience; in a designated stage area on the same level with the group; or in the midst of the group.

- The stories presented may be fictional; somewhat fictional but based on real issues in the actors' or audience's life; or arise spontaneously in enactments of past or anticipated events in the lives of those participating.

- Goals of the event may be purely for entertainment; to evoke concern and thought about a specific issue; to provide information or modeling on a topic; to explore an area in order to provide insight for the participants; and/or opportunities for practice within simulated psycho-social predicaments.

Who Will Enjoy This Book?

If you are a drama student who is wondering about a wider range of opportunities available to you as a result of your training, we want to inform you about the surprising and successful alternatives to the competitive professional environment of Broadway and Hollywood. Maybe you already realize you don't want to engage in a highly competitive system, yet you love drama and feel frustrated.

Are you a teacher of this drama student, whether in high school or in college, and yearn for a book that shows the larger field of drama as an occupation/avocation in society? You might share some of the ideals presented in these pages, and want your students to be aware of a contemporary world of activity that utilizes drama as its core discipline. Even though the approaches in this book are becoming increasingly popular all over the world, most theatre textbooks hardly mention them.

You're an actor and committed to the demands of becoming successful. You want to supplement your income by doing work that keeps you in the field. The approaches in this book offer ideas for extending your skills into alternative theatre or ways to specialize in teaching not just acting, but improvisation and its related forms in the community, privately, or through college extension courses.

Perhaps you're not a student, actor, teacher, or theatre artist—just an individual who likes drama! Did you once play a role in community theatre, participate in a church pageant, or put on skits at camp? Maybe you just took a class on improvisational comedy or acting and felt inspired and expanded! Here are ways you can still be involved.

In any of these roles, perhaps you already sense the broader potential of drama. Maybe you have experienced in your own life that it is a force for psychological growth, spiritual realization, or political consciousness-raising. You have wished that this incredibly vitalizing activity could be brought to help others.

Type-casting can feel like a dead-end street. You want to expand and explore your rich reservoir of instincts and interests. The alternative formats described in this book show you places where you can be freer because the players in roles can even change gender, age, and in other ways don't have to "look" the part.

Including drama as an avocation is important to you. Other life goals require the focus of your time and you cannot devote yourself to the great demands of memorization and rehearsals. Here are a variety of contexts within which you can engage in your interest in simpler ways.

Do you want to be a teacher (maybe you are one!) and enjoy doing activities with students—bringing subjects alive for them? The approaches mentioned in the section on education offer you a rich range of techniques to help you flourish in your classroom. Remember that a number of states have recognized the value of creative drama and arts education by including these activities in their school curricula.

The following readers will also benefit from this book:

- teachers as well as teachers of teachers, i.e., faculty in departments of education

- religious educators who want more meaningful activities at spiritual retreats
- human resources professionals who are asked to help develop emotional intelligence, "people skills," and management training
- people seeking personal growth, attending human potential holistic learning programs, workshops, and the like
- recreation workers, group workers for social groups of all kinds—youth, the elderly, the disabled
- administrators in agencies that seek to educate people about health and social issues
- creative arts therapists, drama therapists, and others who mix creative and trans-rational approaches, play, imagination, body movement into their healing and coaching approaches
- creative artists who are into performance art and who integrate dramatic elements
- folks seeking more involvement in recreation instead of just being a spectator
- community leaders who want to use a common modality to build a sense of community and address issues
- public health educators who want an engaging way of reaching people of all ages

Professionals, researchers, scholars and practitioners in related fields will also find this anthology useful. Some of those fields, discussed further in Chapter 33, include performance studies, the study of play from the viewpoint of anthropology or child development, study and promotion of humor, story-telling, social and emotional learning and character education, occupational and recreational therapy, leisure studies, expressive dancing and movement programs, communications studies, human relations training, the impromptu speaking of Toastmasters' clubs, and others.

This book may also be used to support efforts to develop and establish programs in communities, obtain grants, and seek funding. Finally, our hope is that you may be stimulated to follow up, to learn more about this or that approach. We've asked the chapter authors to make some comments to readers regarding the skills you might need to learn as well as where you can begin to learn them, in order to adapt what they've been doing for your own purposes.

We have avoided theory in order to inform you, with simple descriptions, about each approach, how it's done, and some vignettes so that you can picture the process. Of course, actually doing drama evokes a certain magic. Just as you can't really know what swimming is from any written description—you need to get into the water and learn the skills. Drama is like that, too.

How to Use This Book

The topics selected for inclusion in this book reflect samples of the breadth of this field. Although the chapters have been grouped in five sections—Community Building, Education, Therapy, Empowerment, and Entertainment—these placements should not be taken as a clear differentiation of types. In fact, many of the approaches presented serve several functions.

Each chapter is an introduction to the method, an overview designed to orient you to that approach. The chapters are written in a non-academic style without a lot of philosophy and theory. References have been designed so that readers interested in a given subject can more readily follow up on it.

A special advantage of this book is that we have established an associated website: <*www.interactiveimprov</*>. There you will find supplementary webpages for each chapter as well as other supplementary essays. The supplements offer references, anecdotes of methods contributed by others doing similar kinds of work, further examples of techniques, and explanations of the psychological and other theoretical foundations of applied theatre. For example, I've written an essay titled "Why Drama" that notes twenty ways that drama can be useful in everyday life (<www.interactiveimprov.com/whydrama. html>).

The advantage of a website is that it can be updated as new books or articles are published and authors can integrate new revisions, including your suggestions for additions or corrections! Since promoting interactivity is one of the goals of this book, a website also offers this dynamic. This website significantly enhances the value of the book and helps it to keep current with an evolving field. There is such a wealth of approaches and activities going on around the world that we highly encourage your interest by using the references and our website to develop a better understanding of specific topics in this book.

Summary

Drama is a broader and deeper process than traditional theatre. Drama methods are a new kind of tool, a psychological-social tool, just like the computer is a kind of tool. These methods are made available here in more "user-friendly" forms so that drama can be naturally woven into many aspects of life. This book may inspire your own exploration and participation in alternative drama. In addition, thanks to the associated website, you can share your own co-creative responses.

[A note about the spelling of *theater* versus *theatre*. For much of the general public the terms are interchangeable. For most people in the theatre arts, though, the term theater with an "er" refers to the building or setting where the performance happens, while theatre with an "re", refers more to the general endeavor of producing and acting—and such will be our usage in this book.]

SECTION I

COMMUNITY BUILDING

Adam Blatner

As a psychiatrist with over 35 years of clinical experience, I've been impressed with the importance of vibrant social networks in the maintenance of mental health. I am concerned that there are current social and cultural forces that offer a kind of psycho-social drug, and I am referring especially to the mass media which, while offering intensive vicarious experiences, provide a kind of connectedness and involvement that is rather illusory. In fact, though, without their "fix," they become more empty and dependent on these external sources. In contrast, I think interactive drama in the many forms presented in this book offer a more authentic kind of involvement, one that draws people to connect their inner vitality with real encounters with others. These types of social and community building experiences seem to me to be far more wholesome.

That improvisation is experienced as somewhat challenging operates initially as an inhibition, but once one gets the knack—and it's not harder than learning to swim or ride a bicycle—spontaneity is invigorating. Sure, there's a little risk—improvisation means you don't know the answer, it's not in the books. Placed in the fail-safe matrix of play, though, it's a pleasant thrill, leading to a slight catharsis of delight: "Say, I didn't know I had that in me!"

The more people use dramatic methods to become aware of their own vitality and capacity for improvisation, exploration, and self-expression, the more they can feel their inner being as active and connected. There is a potential for substantive personal psychological and spiritual growth in these endeavors. Also, gesture, movement, breath, and the other physical elements in drama makes for an expanded body-energy exercise. The playful element adds a further component: a redemption of the joyous and innocent inner child.

Finally, people need to be seen, heard, known. We're not talking about excessive vanity here, but the ordinary optimal balance of social belonging, the give and take of recognition. Again, drama offers a vehicle whereby people can discover their own ways of adding to the group's enjoyment. There is a special added element that is provided by people operating at the level of art (in the broadest sense)—style, emotional expressiveness, story, empathy. When people share the products of their imaginations it generates an amusing kind of pleasant intimacy.

The chapters in this section speak to these dynamics. Some involve more serious dimensions of the soul and the social fabric, while others invite more celebrations. The point here is that integrating the tools of applied theatre can serve these varied purposes.

Chapter 1

PLAYBACK THEATRE

Hannah Fox

Playback Theatre is an improvisational, interactive theatre method which uses personal stories as its source material. In Playback Theatre, life stories are volunteered by audience members and then enacted on the spot by a team of actors and a musician. Conceived in 1973 by Jonathan Fox in the USA, the technique is now practiced world-wide in over fifty countries in a variety of settings, such as schools, social service organizations, prisons, hospitals, conferences, and public theaters. Whereas Playback Theatre grew from therapeutic and artistic arenas, it is now used widely as a vehicle for social change. As the method is being applied in many cultures, it is necessary for the contours of the form to remain flexible so that it can adapt to each community's specific needs. The fundamental components of Playback Theatre, however, remain consistent across geographical lines.

How it Works

The setting is a small conference room, rather than a theater, and the audience consists of forty residents in a lock down drug-treatment program, many of who are ex-offenders and are living with full-blown AIDS. The five members of the Big Apple Playback Theatre troupe arrive an hour before the audience and transform the room. They push back the tables, arrange the chairs in one half of the room, and clear a space for a stage area in the other half. Colorful pieces of fabric are hung upstage left and percussion instruments for the musician are placed downstage left. Four empty chairs for the actors are put upstage center, and two chairs, for the conductor and teller, are positioned at an angle downstage right. As the audience-participants file in for today's performance, the atmosphere is charged with anticipation. The body language of the residents shows curiosity and hesitancy: What kind of show is this? Will I have to say something or can I just watch? Am I going to be safe?

The performers begin the performance with a "doo-wop" song and then introduce themselves theatrically by sharing their names and recalling a recent personal experience, dramatized physically. After each actor has spoken, one of the players (who now becomes the *conductor* or master of ceremonies) turns to the audience and asks, "And how has your day been?" After a couple moments of silence, an audience member raises his hand and says, "Sad." The conductor asks why. "Because today is my birthday and instead of celebrating it out there with my friends, I'm in here, alone and sober." "And your name?" the conductor asks. "Marco," the teller replies. "Let's watch," says the conductor, glancing at the actors who begin to make a moving-sounding sculpture with their bodies, capturing different aspects and the essence of Marco's feeling. As Marco watches his story enacted on stage, he laughs, and nods when it is finished. The performance continues in this fashion, with audience members sharing feelings and experiences and the actors and musician playing them back.

Gradually rapport builds between the audience members and the actors and there are many enthusiastic hands waving in the air. Eventually, someone is invited to come up on stage, sit in the "teller's chair," next to the conductor, and share a fuller story from her/his life. A woman resident tells of being stabbed twelve times in her elevator and riding in the ambulance to the hospital. Her story is not about anger or even resentment; instead, it is about survival and finding the inspiration to go on, in spite of hardship. Her story is told, cast, and then enacted on stage. The next teller is a cross-dresser called Candy. She shares a memory of when she was six years old, living in Tennessee, and was beaten by her father after spending all the food stamp money on candy across the street at the store. There are tears in Candy's eyes when the enactment is finished. Not all playback stories are about grief and trauma—there is in fact a wide range in the kinds of stories told. However, when people do find the courage to tell these kinds of deep stories, the healing effects are not just felt by the teller alone, but shared by the whole room.

When the hour is up, the actors recount moments from all the stories, using storytelling language and mirrored movements. They end the show by returning to the original song and inviting the residents to sing along. Many stand up to sing and even dance. Afterward the room is filled with warmth and cheer. In only one hour's time, a quiet room pregnant with tension has been filled with *communitas,* a term coined by anthropologist Victor Turner. his wife, Edith, defined it as "… the sense of fellow feeling, person to person, a sense of human kindness and the joy of being together.") Playback is considered to be a "theatre of neighbors, not strangers," as Jonathan Fox likes to say. It is creating this sense of community connection that is at the core of this theatre technique.

History

Playback Theatre was conceived in the early 1970s in upstate New York by Jonathan Fox, and developed by Fox with his wife, Jo Salas, and his team of actors, the "original company." Influenced by the American experimental theatre movement, psychodrama, and the oral tradition of indigenous cultures, Fox created Playback Theatre as an informal community theatre, which held the art and vulnerability of being human at its core. When asked where his inspiration came from, Fox recalls his dream "of a new kind of theatre that brought theatre back from the domain of entertainment to its earlier purpose of preserving memory and holding the tribe together."

For centuries, performance has existed not only for entertainment, but also as a medium for personal and societal transformation. Anthropologists describe how theatrical performances of early societies often functioned as "ceremonial centers" at which groups would gather to exchange dances, songs, and dramas. These gatherings used performance to incite certain actions, such as dancing for rain, such as dancing for rain, praying for a good harvest, healing the sick, or celebrating a birth or a death. Fox wanted to find a way to "recapture that kind of ceremonial enactment in which there is no distinction between art and healing," and to "embody a transformational ritual that could be a source for hope without whitewashing what is wrong with the world" (Fox & Dauber, 1999:14).

When living in a pre-industrial village in Nepal, Fox was drawn to a living oral tradition and drawn to the folk art of storytelling. Along with theatre and ritual, storytelling has been used for centuries as a means to make sense of life's mysteries, as well as a way to pass on cultural knowledge from one generation to the next. Before the age of computers, cinema, television, video, radio, and even literature, people assembled to share stories for the evening's entertainment. Indigenous cultures which still function without these technologies continue to practice this ritual. In modern Western society formal storytelling is, to a large extent, channeled through technological media. Although it may be becoming more obscure, live storytelling manages to survive as an art form. Jo Salas, co-creator of Playback Theatre, writes: "People *need* to tell their stories. It's a basic human imperative. From the telling of our stories comes our sense of identity, our place in the world, and our compass of the world itself" (Salas, 1993).

In the late 1960s and early 1970s the American experimental theatre movement was in full swing. Fox was inspired by Antonin Artaud's idea of "immediate theatre" and Jerzy Grotowski's idea of theatre as a process. He was interested in performance that didn't camouflage, or distort life experience but, instead, illuminated it. He envisioned a kind of spontaneous theatre in which the members of the audience weren't mere spectators watching the play, but co-creators. Fox and his company members were intrigued by the possibility that the simple act of telling and listening to peoples' stories could generate understanding and compassion. From 1975 to 1986, Fox and the original company experimented with their ideas. They rehearsed weekly (plus one Sunday per month), performed one Friday a month for the public, and traveled around the Hudson Valley in New York State to outdoor festivals, hospitals, prisons, conferences and schools. The company wore bright overalls and hauled around milk crates for stage boxes. Although much of the work was unpaid, the adventure of trying a new kind of theatre, along with the positive response from audiences, moved them forward. Through trial and error, the team began to define the standard Playback Theatre forms used across the world today.

In 1980, four members of the original company were invited to teach and perform overseas in New Zealand and Australia. The idea caught on abroad. It was after this tour that other Playback companies around the world began to sprout: first in New Zealand and Australia and then a few years later in Switzerland, Sweden, Japan, and subsequently, England, the USA, Germany, Russia, Hungary, Finland, Italy, France, Argentina, and Brazil. By 1993 there were Playback Theatre companies practicing in seventeen countries; by 1999, thirty countries. Currently, in 2006, there are an estimated 100,000 people using Playback Theatre, including performers and audience members, in over fifty countries, including India, Hong Kong, Singapore, Cuba, and countries in Africa. Playback Theatre has grown from a local theatre to an international movement with great velocity, which points to the accessible and inclusive nature of the form and to the obvious need for creating community in the modern world. Although each company brings its unique cultural and artistic style to the form, the basic technique remains consistent. The Playback ritual of spontaneously playing back citizen stories is reaching to include more and more people from diverse racial and economic backgrounds.

Since 1990 an organization called the International Playback Theatre Network (IPTN) has existed to support and oversee playback activity around the globe. The IPTN also supports whichever local company has volunteered to organize the international Playback Theatre conference. The international conferences occur every few years in different countries. The first was in Finland

(1993), then the USA (1995), Australia (1997), England (2001), Japan (2004), and Brazil (2007).

The School of Playback Theatre, an affiliated yet separate entity from the IPTN, was established in New Paltz, New York in 1993. The School offers a diploma program for training in the technique as well as support for company projects, and is a meeting ground for Playback practitioners from all over the world. There are also affiliate schools set up in Japan, Israel, Hungary, Italy, and Germany. It is necessary to receive proper training in order to do Playback Theatre skillfully and effectively.

Methods

Five ways of portraying the stories told by audience members are most often used in Playback Theatre. The first three, *Fluid Sculptures, Pairs,* and *Stories,* were developed by the original company. The fourth form, *Chorus,* was developed sometime later by practitioners in New Zealand and Australia. The fifth form, *Three Part Story,* a relatively new form, was created by Eugene Playback Theatre in 1994. There is now a common vocabulary of forms used by playback companies worldwide, although variations and new forms are in constant generation.

Fluid Sculptures. Typically, a performance begins with short forms in order to warm up both the actors and the audience to the Playback ritual. After a theatrical opening (i.e. a song, movement, poetry, music) in which the actors introduce themselves, the first form most frequently presented is called *fluid sculptures.* These are *dancing tableaux* that aim to represent a feeling an audience member has about a particular experience, such as the weather, a moment from the day, a general mood, or about the theme of the performance, if one has been designated. After the audience member shares, the actors step out one at a time to the center of the stage with a repetitive sound and movement that reflects one aspect of the teller's experience. The next actor joins the first, connecting physically as one would in a three dimensional sculpture, adding a different sound and movement (a different texture) and embodying another aspect to the feeling or experience. This action continues until all the actors on stage are contributing to the sculpture. Once the last actor has joined, the sculpture continues moving for another couple of beats and then ends by all the actors stopping together and then acknowledging the teller with a glance. Fluid sculptures resemble the traditional theatre game, *machine,* in structure, although in form and content they appear much more fluid and organic, and are based on personal stories. A fluid sculpture lasts for about one minute and sometimes contains words/phrases apropos to the theme of the story, in addition to sounds.

Pairs. Another staple short form is called *pairs.* Pairs offer us the opportunity to reflect on those situations or relationships in our lives which pull us in opposite directions between conflicting emotions, such as love and hate, excited and nervous, resentful and grateful, eager and hesitant. Actors pair up on center stage, one standing behind another. Often there are three sets of pairs or six actors lined up in twos. After an audience member has shared her pair of emotions, the pair positioned on stage right begins the action. Generally, the front actor begins with movement and non-repetitive sound/words representing *one* of the teller's feelings. Once the second actor is clear on which emotion is being depicted, he embodies the other. Pairs are expressive and physical; however, for the most part, the actors remain stationary, i.e. both actors continue to face front and do not travel the stage. The actors should work to create a gestalt—as both these emotions supposedly co-exist in the teller's psyche—by connecting physically and even possibly thematically in their words or sounds. After the first pair is performed, the first actors bring their bodies back to neutral (or freeze in an image), and the next two actors begin their own version of the same internal struggle. Then the final team shows a third depiction. After each pair has performed, the whole ensemble acknowledges the teller with a glance. Ideally, there is contrast between each pair of actors. Pairs last for approximately thirty seconds each.

Stories. The main form in Playback Theatre is called *stories.* This is what we are warming up to do together. The short forms familiarize audience members with the custom of telling stories and then watching them replayed on stage. They also serve to stir the "story soup," as it were, helping people to recall their lives as well as build *communitas* and trust in the room. In stories or "scenes" as they traditionally were called, an audience member is invited on to the stage to sit in the "teller's chair" and share a longer experience from his life. The story may be recent or one from childhood, one that is humorous, serious, simple or complex. Some stories have been told before in other contexts, others are being heard for the first time. The story may not have happened yet and might be a vision or a dream. As long as it is autobiographical, it is welcome. There are five designated steps to a Playback story (Salas, 1993, pp. 33–36). I will describe them in sequence:

The first step is the *Interview,* in which the conductor (who sits next to the teller) asks the teller to share her experience, sometimes asking questions to clarify points or to help move the story forward. During this process, the conductor asks the teller to cast the key characters in the story. After the teller has chosen actors and has finished his narration, the conductor passes the story over to the actors with the ceremonial words, "Let's watch!" This signature line is commonly said by the conductor in each of the Playback forms to launch the actors into action.

These words take us into the second stage of story called the *set-up*. They also cue the musician to play music that invokes the mood of the story. While the musician plays or sings, the actors prepare for the scene by placing boxes (or chairs), choosing fabric if needed (in Playback Theatre, fabric is used symbolically rather than for costumes), and positioning themselves for the beginning stage picture. This stage preparation is done ceremoniously without talking or planning.

The *Enactment* is next. Through improvisation, the actors and musician work together as an ensemble to bring the story to life, not only literally, but also metaphorically, and not necessarily playing back every detail. Instead, they try to find a way to illuminate the key moments and essence of the story in a creative and efficient way.

When the story has been enacted, the actors freeze in a final stage picture and then dissolve back into to neutral again, sending the story off—as if it were a gift—, back to the teller with a glance. This is called the *Acknowledgement*, the fourth stage in a playback story.

In the *Check-Back*, the final step, the focus comes back to the teller who has been sitting on stage watching. The conductor checks back with the teller, not so much to see if the actors "got it right," but more so to find out how the experience of watching the story might have been. "What was it like to see your story?" the conductor might ask, or "Is there anything you would like to say now?" Often a teller is moved to share an insight or a revelation; other times the teller is too emotional or just simply does not have any more words and doesn't need to make a final comment. In either case, when the conductor feels that the teller is ready to integrate back into the audience, the conductor thanks the teller for his story, gesturing or walking him back to his original seat, and waits for the next story to come. (At this point, the actors replace the scarves and return to the boxes.) Typically, there are three to five of these longer stories told in an evening's performance. Each story, from the interview through the check-back, takes approximately ten to fifteen minutes, although given the great range of stories, this time frame can vary. It is always interesting to notice how the string of stories that are told are linked. Often a theme emerges on its own—if one wasn't established beforehand—over the course of the performance or workshop. We call this emergent theme the *red thread*.

At this point, I have described the three basic forms in Playback Theatre: *fluid sculptures, pairs,* and *stories.* I will now explain two other common Playback Theatre forms:

Chorus. The Playback chorus was created in Australia by the late British practitioner Francis Batten and is inspired by the Greek Chorus. It is used in Stories, either as a way to play back the story in its entirety (instead of choosing actors and assigning characters) or as a mood sculpture in the background of a story that has been cast and is being acted out. In a full-story chorus three to seven actors begin by standing in a clump upstage center. They breathe together and then one actor offers a sound and movement that the rest of the group follows. Another actor offers the next gesture, and then another. The gestures illustrate the various dynamics (or *beats*) of the story. The story is played back as a series of unison sounds and movements by the team of actors. Unlike a fluid sculpture or a pair, a chorus has the freedom to travel all over the stage. It is important for the actors to synchronize their movements, create contrast between the gestures, and, ideally, to share leadership. A full-story chorus usually lasts around four or five minutes.

Three Part Story. Three part story is a less common form than chorus. I include it here because it is a form that I (and my company at the time, Eugene Playback Theatre) created, and because it is being used more and more. It is a short form, generally used as a warm-up to stories, yet is capable of holding great meaning. The form was originally called *three sentence story* because the story solicited from an audience member was told in only three sentences, resembling a haiku poem. Today the conductor will ask either for a three sentence story or a short story (told from the audience) which the actors will divide, or "chunk," into three parts. This form was derived from a storytelling exercise which emphasized finding the essence of the beginning, middle and end of a story. Three actors stand in a line in neutral upstage. After the story has been shared, the first actor steps forward into the playing space and, using the whole stage, embodies the first sentence or part, using words, sound, dance, song, poetry, mime—whatever mode of expression the actor discovers in that moment. After thirty seconds or so, the first actor freezes in an image and the second actor enters the stage acting out the second part, again using whatever medium he is inspired to use and playing from the perspective of any character in the story. The second actor freezes and the third comes forward, picking up wherever the second actor left off and finishing the story. The final moment is a frozen *tableau*, or stage picture, made by the three actors in their respective frozen shapes. Although an actor may use the other actors as props or characters to interact with, the actors do not react to one another once they are frozen.

The full enactment of a *three part story* generally takes about one minute and a half. A *three sentence story* follows the same acting sequence only it is told in three sentences (which the conductor repeats) instead of as a short story.

Conclusion

All over the world, there are interesting Playback Theatre projects currently underway. In Hong Kong, of the several Playback Theatre companies, one of the oldest, called Chosen Power, is comprised of practitioners with mental and physical disabilities. This company is active and well-respected in the community. Cuba, which also has a handful of companies, may soon have a national Playback Theatre company, endorsed by the Ministry of Culture. There has also been a strong effort in Cuba to use the form to hear and see stories about HIV/AIDS. In Burundi, Africa, a company called Tubiyage, combines Playback Theatre with Theatre of the Oppressed to train ethnically mixed teams to work in harmony and reach communities devastated by civil war. In the USA, Hudson River Playback Theatre works in schools across the region to address issues of bullying and diversity. In New York City, Playback Theatre NYC brings a unique blend of Hip Hop and playback to communities of color. In Auckland, New Zealand, Playback Theatre is being used as a medium to empower the Maori culture. Composite Playback Theatre groups made two separate trips to New Orleans last year in response to Hurricane Katrina.

Playback Theatre recognizes the need for *communitas*, this need for gathering, listening, dialogue and understanding. It uses art as a means to this end. Theatre over the centuries has brought people together to explore and affirm collective ideas and values. Whereas Playback Theatre begins with the personal, it reaches beyond, toward universal human experience. When I tell my story, it is not only mine, but a reflection of your own.

References

School of Playback Theatre: <www.playbackschool.org>

International Playback Theatre Network: <www.playbacknet.org> (And especially note that there are many other articles about Playback Theatre at: <playbacknet.org/interplay/journal/index.html> as well as related resources!

Toni Sant's AITG also has good links: <www.tonisant.com/aitg/Playback_Theatre/

Fox, Jonathan. (1986). *Acts of service: Spontaneity, commitment, and tradition in the nonscripted theatre.* New Paltz, NY: Tusitala Publishing (These and other books from this publisher may be obtained by going to the playbacknet.org/tusitala/website.)

Fox, Jonathan, & Dauber, Heinrich (Eds.). (1999). *Gathering voices: Essays on Playback Theatre.* New Paltz, NY: Tusitala.

Grotowsky, Jerzy. (1968). *Towards a poor theatre.* New York: Simon and Schuster.

Salas, Jo. (1993). *Improvising real life: Personal story in Playback Theatre.* New Paltz, NY: Tusitala. This book illustrates and defines Playback Theatre, discussing its historical and cultural effects as well as personal impacts

Chapter 2

BIBLIODRAMA: EXPLORING THE WRITTEN WORD THROUGH ACTION

Linda Condon

In bibliodrama, group members explore the stories that are found in the Bible or other well-known written works in order to discover psychological and cultural insights that lend relevance to those stories. The characters and issues chosen are based on stories in sacred texts or legends that are generally familiar to most of the group members. Techniques derived from psychodrama and sociodrama help to deepen the group process and experience.

While bibliodrama generally involves stories in the Bible, the method can also be applied in exploring well-known stories from many cultures, or even the myths and stories from secular culture, such as a Greek myth or a fairy tale. For example, in improvising the enactment of a scene from the classic children's story of "Hansel & Gretel," some group members might confront the children's neglectful parents. The method can be extended to imagining historical events, such as a dialogue between Anne Frank and a Nazi soldier or between Julius Caesar and Brutus. Modern popular stories in the Disney animated movies also may be explored: Thus, involving younger participants in "The Little Mermaid" story, one student steps into the shoes of the villainess, Ursula the Sea Witch; in the story of Cinderella, another might introduce an interesting twist in the way Prince Charming is played. The possibilities are endless. That said, most of the examples in this chapter will be stories in the Old and New Testament.

The roles taken in these stories need not be limited to people. In drama, animals also can be imagined to have feelings and thoughts, and so can inanimate objects or places (as is true in doing dream work in psychodrama). For example, if we are exploring the story of Jesus' birth, a piece of hay in the manger or a lamb in the scene may have something just as meaningful to say to us as one of the shepherds or wise men.

One of the principles of sociodrama is that every role expresses both personal and socio-cultural elements, and this makes a connection between a story and audience member possible. For instance, the 'father' in the Biblical story of the prodigal son, implies those qualities that most fathers in general have in common (e.g., they provide for their family, deal with sibling rivalry, love their children, etc.), and there are also particular ways in which the father in this story played out his role.

Bibliodrama has been developing in Europe since the mid-late 1970s, and since the mid-1990s, there has been a growing interest in it in the United States. Peter Pitzele, who has presented widely and written about bibliodrama in his book, *Scripture Windows*, notes that the process of bibliodrama shares some similar elements with the tradition within Judaism called "midrash," in which rabbis made up stories to illustrate the implications of a text. They recognized that the challenge of understanding the deeper meanings may require going beyond what is actually written. An old Jewish commentary says that the Bible is made up of 'black' and 'white' fire. Pitzele explains, "The black fire is the form of the printed or handwritten words on the page or scroll; the white fire is found in the *spaces between* and around the black." This white fire, the figurative "space between the words" might better be expressed as that which is ordinarily not explicitly written or read aloud, sometimes almost not even to oneself. The equivalent of the white fire in movies is the device of the "voice over," and in sociodrama, it is expressed through the "double" technique. Working with what is implied, not spelled out, the "white fire," is the extra dimension of psychological depth in a Bibliodrama group.

Seeking the implied elements of a story might involve identifying relevant characters who are not actually mentioned in the story. For example, in the New Testament episode about the threatened stoning of the adulteress, the text mentions the crowd, the adulteress, Jesus, and even the stones—but not the man, the adulterer! Is he off at the edge of the crowd? His thoughts and feelings would be the "white fire," and usually someone in the group will make use of the opportunity to explore this rich role.

The purpose of bibliodrama is not to push any officially approved or presumed correct doctrines, nor does it imply that there is a "right" way to interpret a Scripture passage. The method seeks no converts. Rather bibliodrama provides an opportunity for us to recognize that our own personal and spiritual journey today is perhaps not so different from that of the many spiritual sojourners who have come before us. It is very important for the director to beware of any group members' starting to assert specific dogmas or creeds. Because that kind of talk tends to create divisions and interferes with the group dynamic, the director should gently steer the discussion in a different direction.

Warming-Up

A bibliodrama director will utilize many of the techniques, as well as the same three-step process of warming up, enactment, and sharing found in psychodrama or sociodrama. The warm up begins as soon as people agreeing to join in a bibliodrama session. The director's role is to facilitate the warm-up once the group forms, and this includes communicating how the participants will be kept safe if they share ideas or experiences that they fear may not be within the expected norm. (Of course, most people do have at least a few such ideas, and bringing out the capacity of the group to include all these is part of the art.) Nothing affects the outcome of the bibliodrama session more than the director's attention to the warm-up of the group. A group's warm-up may be imagined as having different layers. Other techniques are described on the webpage supplement to this chapter.

The second phase of warming up prepares group members to be drawn gradually into the enactment. Often it may begin with a brief mini-lecture about what bibliodrama is and is not. Other times it can take a more active form. One of my favorite warm-ups evokes the participants' imaginations: Group members are invited to imagine a richly illustrated Bible and watch the pages opening up to pictures of different stories that they recognize. The pages continue turning until eventually they stop on one particular story. They are then directed to focus on that story and identify the various characters in it. Finally, they decide on one character that intrigues them or that they would like to know more about today.

Once everyone indicates they have made a choice, they are asked to imagine themselves to be that character. There are two different ways to proceed. If the group is large and warming up slowly, they can be invited to write down five statements about their character beginning with "I am...." Alternatively, they might write on a notebook or in a journal a short soliloquy of their character's thoughts and then move into smaller groups or dyads for sharing. Participants often need to be reminded to stay in role, speak as the character, as they share their statements. After small group sharing, each group picks one of their number to share in the larger group. Time is then spent interviewing these characters and encouraging greater spontaneity in their roles. The benefit of this method is that even the more reticent group members are thus given the opportunity to warm up without having to express themselves in the larger group. They may become more involved later.

The third phase of warm-up involves the choice of which story the group wants to explore in more detail. Bibliodrama enactments tend to be chosen in two ways. The first is when the story is chosen before the group meets together. Perhaps a retreat is planned around a specific season of the year (i.e., Advent, Hanukah, Passover, Easter, etc.), or maybe a congregation wants to utilize the readings of their liturgical calendar, or it might be a Bible study group delving into a certain book or passage. If a group is larger than 40 and a story hasn't already been designated, it is usually wise for the director to pick one ahead of time and design a warm-up to move group members in the direction of it. The pre-determined focus will help the group move into action quicker. The second way of choosing an enactment is through a process of the group choosing which character seems most interesting or relevant to most of the group members.

Enactment

If a story has been chosen ahead of time, the director can plan the second layer of warm-up to be directly connected with the story instead of using the more generic exercises described above to warm the group up. For example, if the group will be exploring "The Sower and The Seed" parable, first the Scripture passage may be read, then the group can be asked to identify the characters that are present in the story and an empty chair can be set up to represent each character (e.g., the seed, sower, path, sun, weeds, rocks, etc.). Group members can then be invited to spontaneously give voice to each character as they begin to warm-up to the story. For example, "I am the seed and I am full of potential. But there are so many things that can affect my growth …" The director's role in this exercise is to ask questions which encourage a variety of perspectives from different group members as they explore the roles that are present.

During this interaction, the director may find it useful to use the technique of "echoing," which is a mixture of doubling and amplification. In the example above, the director might echo the one who spoke up in the role of "the seed," "There can be lots of things that prevent me from growing." Then group members might continue by identifying some of the blocks to growth such as being thrown in an uninviting place, not enough resources, etc. and in the echoing the director might begin to add in how it feels to have growth determined by these factors to deepen the group's exploration and connection with the roles.

As each of the roles has been given a voice, the transition into the enactment will occur when a group member is warmed up to a certain role more than another and agrees to remain in that particular role for a dialogue between roles to develop. Sometimes the participant might come up and sit in an empty chair or take the character's posture. Occasionally, it's helpful to have a group of participants agree to take on a particular role and sit in a certain part of the room together. Whenever possible, it is wise to encourage group members to physically move into the role and take on the posture and gestures of the character. The non-verbal aspects of the role can provide as much insight during the enactment as the verbal aspects.

Once the story has been chosen and the characters identified and cast, a variety of different techniques can be utilized by the director to deepen and/or broaden the enactment. One of the most useful techniques is the aforementioned "doubling," which involves standing behind the character and verbalizing unexpressed thoughts or feelings that the character might be experiencing. The person then has the choice of either repeating what has just been said or modifying it to be more accurate. It is somewhat similar to the "echoing" or "voicing" used during the warm-up phase; however, now that the scene has begun, it takes place within the scene from the position of one of the characters.

The director or other group members may double for any role in the drama at any time. Doubling provides opportunity for many different viewpoints and possible interpretations to be expressed. For example, during an enactment of the story of the Prodigal Son, the father and older son were having an encounter after the return of the younger son. Group members were invited by the director to think of something that they would want to express in this scene and to line up behind either the father or the older son. As group members proceeded to double for each of the characters, the father and son began to openly express feelings of discouragement, jealousy, misunderstanding, regret, anger, sadness, forgiveness, unconditional acceptance and love. Without the group's willingness to double, the scene would never have reached the depth of expression it was able to reach.

Another technique used during the enactment phase is role reversal, although it is not used as frequently as it is in a psychodrama. In a role reversal, two characters will switch roles with one another and respond from the other role position. Sometimes when a person is locked into one particular way of viewing the character's position, or the action seems stuck, or when a very heartfelt question has been asked, it can be powerful to ask for a role reversal. For example, Amy Clarkson, a bibliodramatist from New Jersey, was directing an encounter between Jesus and Martha when Martha asked Jesus "Who will take care of everyone if I don't do it? Don't you appreciate all the things I've done for you?" A role reversal was called for and the person playing the role of Martha moved into Jesus' role and responded very powerfully to the questions of her own heart. It's important for the director to remember that if a role reversal has been used, the characters need to be reversed back to their original position. Otherwise the action can become very chaotic; no one knows who is who; and, the drama comes to a standstill. (Other examples are described on the webpage supplement.)

There are many other psychodramatic techniques, which can be modified for use in bibliodrama. The use of an "empty chair" can be a tool that facilitates action, especially when group members are initially reluctant to step into a role. Sometimes they will agree to stand behind a "chair" and speak from a more distanced position as they warm up to the action. At other times, they can be asked to move from the chair to stand behind it to express a deeper, more internal truth. For example, once a group was exploring Mary's experience after the Angel Gabriel spoke to her. Initially she expressed "honor at being chosen to play such an important role in human history." When directed to move behind the chair and speak from a deeper place within her heart, she began to express her confusion ("I didn't realize what I was being asked to do"), doubt ("Maybe I just imagined it all"), fear ("Joseph will never believe me and what will I tell my mother), and terror ("They'll kill me when they find out").

Another valuable technique is the "soliloquy." This occurs when one character gives a monologue about what he/she is thinking or feeling without having someone else listening in the scene. For example, in a scene set a few days after the Crucifixion, Jesus' mother, Mary, is kneading bread as she expressed her feelings about her son's death and what she would do next. Another group of teenagers explored the Crucifixion, and one of the boys did a soliloquy from the role of the nail used to crucify Jesus, which led to a lively discussion about how members of the group still hurt Jesus today.

Being able to "freeze" a scene and let the group decide how they might want to change it or end it is another directorial choice. At times, it's possible to "rewind" a scene and replay it, trying out different action options. Once a group of women were enacting the story of Abraham and Sarah's trip to Egypt and trying to gain insight into Abraham's request that Sarah tell Pharaoh she was his sister instead of his wife. They replayed the scene several times with Sarah responding differently to Abraham's request each time until they ran out of responses. The action yielded a great deal of insight and connection to the choices within their own relationships.

Instead of a person or animal, an abstract concept can be played by a person. (Moreno called this slight variation of sociodrama "axiodrama.") Sometimes in the course of a bibliodrama, it may be useful to have people explore their understanding of certain ideas such as "truth," "justice," "love," "time," "beauty," "peace," or "freedom," by imagining this as kind of a person or spirit, then take that role and speak as if one embodied that principle. For example, a group chose to explore "the armor of God" mentioned in Ephesians. The armor pieces included a belt of truth, a breastplate of integrity, shoes of eagerness to spread the gospel, a shield of faith, a helmet of salvation, and a sword of God's word. Each armor piece was assigned an empty chair and group members were asked to move to the piece to which they felt most drawn or connected. They were then asked to create a moving sculpture that showed how that piece of armor worked or protected its wearer. Once the sculpture was created, they added sound to it and the armor pieces spoke to the group of their value and importance.

Sharing

Whichever type of enactment is done or whatever techniques are used to bring a scene alive, it is absolutely critical that the director structure the group's time so that sharing, the third part of the bibliodrama session, be given enough time. Sharing allows the group members to identify what they have learned from the enactment and/or how their story is connected to the story. A good rule of thumb is to spend 25% of the bibliodrama session doing warm-up, 50% of the time doing the enactment, and the remaining 25% doing sharing. How the director structures the sharing depends upon a few factors: how large the group is, how much room is available, what type of group is gathered, how much time is left, and what type of drama was enacted.

The director should remind the group that sharing is not analyzing, criticizing or giving advice to other group members; rather, group members are asked to share something new they discovered about the story that was enacted or some way in which they experienced their own life as connecting with the characters in the drama. The director might ask, "What stood out to you in the drama?" "What in your life is similar to the story told here?" "What is something new you discovered during our imagining this story together?"

Some sharing may be a bit intellectual as the individual seeks to clarify a concept or a fresh understanding of the story. The director must ensure the safety of each group member by having the group make an agreement about confidentiality, as well as, cautioning group members to not exceed their comfort level when sharing. Never is anyone to be pressured to share anything they do not wish to disclose.

Occasionally, the group will move deeply very quickly. For example, once a group of women had just completed a living sculpture of "The Pieta" (Mary holding her son's dead body in her lap). At the end of the enactment, there was a tremendous amount of grief present in the room that was not expressed adequately in the enactment. Many women were present who had lost children or spouses, and it was essential that the director provide a safe environment for group members to process their experience. Obviously, the choice of this type of drama being explored is only with great discretion and in a group that knows one another well enough to be supportive of each other.

It is important for all group members to be given an opportunity to share their experience before leaving the room, especially if the enactment has involved intense expression of feeling. This applies even if the group is fairly large. At a time like this, the director may choose to divide the group into dyads having each person find someone in the group with whom they feel comfortable sharing and to do an initial sharing in dyads. Just as the warm-up process moves the group into action layer by layer, the sharing process similarly moves gently away from the action. Often, after an intense enactment, it's important to help participants 'de-role' from the part they have played. Sharing how their life is similar and different from the role they played usually accomplishes this task.

Sharing in dyads is also useful if time is limited. After this, it sometimes helps to have a few people share again some of their experience/insights in the larger group. If the room is large enough and the group is bigger than 25 people, small groupings might be another option for a sharing structure. Each group summarizing its learning and presenting it to the larger group can follow this.

Although finding group closure can often times be reached through the group's sharing process, there are other instances when it is useful to close a bibliodrama session with some type of communal ritual—a formal group action that marks and brings together the group's learning and experience. The ritual may be as simple as forming a circle and having group members spend a few minutes silently, vividly imagining themselves retaining what they have learned and experienced in the session. It could also be effective to provide group members with the opportunity to verbalize in a statement what has been most valuable for them. For some sessions, closure might include a spoken prayer, poem, maybe even a meaningful song that the experience evokes. (See related ideas in Chapter 5 on Ritual in this book.)

Summary

The technique of bibliodrama makes it possible for participants to experience stories from the Bible in a new way. Imagining these episodes as happening in the here-and-now, they become more "alive," relevant, and open to fresh interpretations and understandings. Bibliodrama is also a relatively untapped and exciting resource that can be used to explore all varieties of story, whether from other religious traditions, myths or legends from our ancient past or more contemporary written works. Creating together can be a powerful vehicle for learning.

References

See the webpage supplement: <www.interactiveimprov.com/bibliodrwb.html> for other references. More can be found by a websearch keyword bibliodrama.

Condon, Linda. (2003). *The warm-up ring: keys for energizing your group.* Provides over 100 action warm-ups that can be easily adapted for use in bibliodrama groups. Can be purchased for $35.00 plus postage from the author. See links below for address.

Garcia, Antonina, & Sternberg, Pat. (1994) *Sociodrama: who's in your shoes?* (2nd ed.). Westport, CT: Praeger. (A chapter on bibliodrama is included at the end of this book.)

Kellermann, Peter F. (2007). *Sociodrama and collective trauma.* London: Jessica Kingsley.

Krondorfer, Bjorn. (Ed.). (1992). *Body & Bible: interpreting and experiencing biblical narratives.* Philadephia, PA: Trinity Press, 1992. (Also material on his website: <www.smcm.edu/users/bhkrondorfer/biblio.htm>)

Pitzele, Peter. (1998). *Scripture windows: toward a practice of bibliodrama.* Los Angeles, CA: Torah Aura Productions, 1998. (One of the most thorough sources for learning about how to facilitate a bibliodramatic session. Provides excellent examples of various techniques. Also, Pitzele's website, <www.bibliodrama.com>, has other papers on it that illustrate bibliodrama further.)

Pitzele, Peter. (1995). *Our fathers' wells: a personal encounter with the myths of Genesis.* Harper Collins Publishers. (Examples of bibliodrama as applied to stories from the Biblical Book of Genesis.)

Further references on Bibliodrama, most in German: <www.bibliodrama-gesellschaft.de/html>/bucher_uber_bibliodrama.html>

Chapter 3

LIFEDRAMA WITH ELDERS

Rosilyn Wilder

LifeDrama uses interactive and improvisational drama with elderly people in a variety of ways: care facilities with patients in wheelchairs; county geriatric homes for indigent elders; dementia and Alzheimer units with diverse patients; or in community centers with healthy and active elders who live independently. At every age we each have stories. As poet Muriel Rukeyser wrote: "The Universe is made of stories, not of atoms."

Our stories remind us how we experience and exist. I use drama to stimulate the stories: We begin by helping people simply tell their stories, and then extend these narratives into active improvisation. We stage life stories of simple, even daily, routine moments within the cultures and experiences of each group. Feelings of empathy and bonding come through stepping into roles in each other's life stories.

Life Drama, as a method, draws from a range of approaches: creative drama, drama therapy, psychodrama, group dynamics, Stanislavski's sensory method, and other art forms. The aim is to help elders to affirm themselves, acknowledge how they've been ingenious in adapting to the great changes of this last century. In aging, the loss of active roles often leads to a corresponding loss of self-significance; drama can help counter this tendency. Each person can become a storyteller who passes history to the young. He or she can help the present generation imagine what it was like before processed baby food, disposable diapers, television and TV dinners; before unions and Social Security; before cordless telephones, electric drills and refrigerators; and certainly before cell phones and birth control pills. These developments can thus be brought into consciousness as both a blessing as well as a burden, because each "advance" introduces new complexities and unintended cultural impacts.

This kind of review also helps elders realize how much they have changed and adjusted. Many have survived four wars, immigration to the US without a word of English, illness without hospitals and doctors within easy reach, and a devastating Depression which forced an exodus from rural America into cities in search of work. They often finish a review with a mixture of wonder and pride, exclaiming, "How did we manage?" "Did we really do all that?!"

The Facilitator's Role

A major task of Life Drama leaders is to listen closely, to respect the ethnic, cultural and socioeconomic backgrounds of people whose lives have differed greatly from their own. Avoid a patronizing tone or manner and suppress inappropriate amusement.

A bit of inquiry of the nursing staff or from others on the medical team before meeting the group may be in order. Find out who has problems with hearing or seeing and what other physical limitations exist among the group members. Be aware that some may need extra emotional support. The leader maintains an active role, subtle and consistent where needed, never overbearing. Groups need to be warmed up to drama and reminded that this is not "just silly stuff;" mature adults can also enjoy the pretend and play—that this is part of what creative artists do.

A Basic Workshop Format

The basic Life Drama structure is fairly consistent, but also capable of being adapted to the dynamics of the group and the needs of the individuals involved. The progression of activities is maintained from week to week, offering group members a reassuringly comfortable and predictable framework. Typically, a session begins with simple name games; this is followed by breathing and movement warms-ups; then the session moves into an appropriately selected theme for the session.

It helps to introduce the theme with a short story, poem, myth, prop, or a physical motion. Often. just a question will serve well as the lead-in. For example: "Without refrigeration, how did you keep your food?" Stories of the iceman or icehouse will emerge.

"Food? We *enjoyed*!" prompted a thin man bent over a walker, shifting into role as a waiter in a restaurant. Miming, he took an imaginary towel and placed it over his arm. Two women fell into the improvisation, becoming customers, and ordered the soup of the day. His reply, "I have to warn you, it isn't so good" evoked laughter all round. It turned out that, in fact, he had been headwaiter in a Jewish restaurant in New York City.

As trust grows within the group and with the leader, serious stories also emerge: a long factory strike, the worries and sacrifices of the war years, children sick and medical help far away. Balancing this, there are also stories of Sunday picnics, "made from scratch, not like today's prepared stuff." There are stories of sewing circles, gatherings around an early radio, and Friday night dances.

A 90-year old man remembers, "Everyone pulled together, fixing a roof: All the men in town were up there singing and laughing."

A lady reminisces, "My father found me on the back porch necking with a boy from school—don't even remember his name—, I got the belt that night."

These stories are then enacted: The leader says, "Let's do it. Come on, who'll be the father?" The enactment brings it all to life.

With Alert Handicapped Patients

The group was made up of many foreign-born men and women who emigrated from other countries in the early 1900s; the setting was a 700-bed County Geriatric Center for Medicaid patients. It was late morning, the ninth month of weekly workshops, and the theme was "Growing up." Everyone was full of stories beginning with the sentence fragment, "In my mother's home …"

Martha, a thin, older woman sitting hunched in her wheelchair, remained silent. A group member asked where she had grown up. Gradually bits of her story emerged:

"I remember my mother waving at me as the boat left Bulgaria in 1916 taking me to the USA. A family in Connecticut brought me here to be an indentured servant. Seven years I worked for them to pay back my passage!" she wept as she spoke. On impulse, the leader adapted a psychodrama exercise. "Martha, may I push your wheelchair into our circle?"

She placed an empty chair 5 feet in front of Martha and asked that she describe her mother, as if she were sitting in that chair. Martha began hesitantly. "I remember she had brown hair."

The leader led her with gentle questioning: "Yes, was she tall or tiny like you?"

Slowly, Martha pulled forth from memory, "Bigger than me. She had a kind face—a tired face. I know she was worried because I was her youngest daughter. When the ship pulled out, I saw her standing there, crying." Martha continued, "I never saw her again."

A gasp went through the group. The leader asked softly, "What do you want to tell her you learned from her?"

Martha answered, holding back her tears, "I want … I want to tell her. I still love her." "Anything else you think would make her proud of you?" the leader urged.

"I always remember, she was kind to everyone. I try to be kind too."

The leader turned to the group, "Please tell Martha's mother what you think of her daughter." There was no moment of self-consciousness.

"She is a kind lady."

"She is a very nice lady."

"I am getting to know Martha. I like her. You should be proud of her."

Wheel chairs surrounded her then. Women who had barely known each other after years in this nursing home were taking turns hugging her.

Resistances

"Life Drama" doesn't attract everyone. There are those who resist participation in activities as their right. Such a person was Mr. Chase in a residence for the elderly. He was always sitting in the hall staring out the window. A lean, lanky man, missing one leg, chain smoking, Mr. Chase was unreachable. Often the laughter from the Life Drama workshop drew his gaze. An invitation to join us was rejected by a nod of his head. One day, for the warm up, the group was circling crocheted balls, patient to patient. On an impulse, I, as leader, moved to the doorway and tossed a ball to him. A tremendous hand raised to catch it in mid-air. This was repeated week by week with balls varying from tennis and handball to baseball borrowed from a school's sport coach. Each time he reached that long arm with that enormous hand into the air timed just right to make the catch. Occasionally, a half smile began on his face.

Finally, I addressed him: "I think …" I started tentatively, "I think you've done a lot of ball playing in your life."

He nodded and looked away. "Where are you from?" I persevered.

"Baltimore," he answered without looking up.

"Did you play there?"

A long silence until he mumbled, "Yep."

"Semi-professionally?" I was edging in slowly.

"Yep."

"Professionally?"

"Yep," he looked me in the eye suddenly as though expecting me to doubt him, "Baltimore Orioles, some years."

That night we checked his name on the Worldwide Web: He was the first famous African-American pitcher of the 1920s! Even the home administrators knew none of this. He'd avoided saying more than "yes" or "no" most of the time he'd been there. The next week he was waiting in the sunroom when others arrived. The staff was excited.

Drama with Patients with Mild Dementia

The cognitive memory may be fading, but tapping into the sensory and muscle memories can often release untold life stories. Responses are unpredictable. Dementia patients have moved into their own realities and these are not ours, but we accept them and move with them. Do not fear them. They can often be more imaginative and less inhibited than more alert, frail elders.

The warm-up itself may be unruly. Building a sense of group will take longer if it happens at all; it will not be sustained for the next session. Warmth and gentle assurance from the leader will nourish responses and some remarkable sessions may happen. Patients who may react violently are not included in group work of this kind. It is important to check with staff regarding these potentials.

For example, in a locked ward of a western Massachusetts facility, a drama therapy group was begun with twelve patients. In time, others emerged from their doorways to join in. There were three leaders and a participating nurse. Five aides stayed by the wall, shouting reprimands to patients, which we, as leaders needed to mediate. For props, we used a number of non-specific articles, such as a World War II parachute, two top hats, long scarves, several old neck fur pieces, and miscellaneous other items, all contained in a large wicker basket. For musical background, we had a cassette recorder and a variety of cassettes.

We started with the group assembled in a circle. "Let's all breathe from the bottom of our stomachs," said the first leader, stretching her arms upward at the same time. Some followed her lead. Others just stood still, looking bewildered. All leaders stood in front of patients, demonstrating, careful not to touch or invade their personal space. Most patients imitated mechanically.

Next, the parachute was opened. Everyone took hold of the fabric's edges. "Let's raise it slowly."

It rose, but unevenly. "Now, lower the parachute, slowly."

Suddenly, one woman grabbed the entire nylon parachute to drape about her, including a train. "She's getting married," a voice called out.

The "bride" began to parade down the hall. The leaders got into role immediately: "Let's go to the wedding. Where's the groom? Are you the groom? Here's a hat for you, Mr. Groom."

Thus encouraged, other patients jumped into roles as though pre-assigned. A cadaverous-looking man took her arm as her father. Another man, once a Methodist preacher, took his position as the preacher, holding an imaginary book. The procession began. The boom box was turned on to marching music. Along the way several patients turned to the leaders to explain who they were and why they approved or didn't approve of this marriage. "She's a very naughty daughter to get married at only sixteen," spoke a tiny, wrinkled woman.

A very large woman grabbed a basket on the prop table to be the flower girl. One person rushed up to kiss the groom. Others just stood along the hall clapping in time with the music. The leaders remained in role, helping further shape a scene that so involved the elders.

The marriage ceremony was a combination of the real and the absurd, but it worked for the patients. They were flushed with enjoyment. What spurred all this from their pasts? Which memory systems were reactivated? While there is no real substitute for the intellect, expressive drama activities of this kind stimulate sensory memory. This allows comfortable interaction and pleasure, temporarily relieves panic, and fosters communication within a community of people.

Enriching the Lives of Vital Elderly

We recruited a group of elders with no previous experience in the theatre. This would become an unusual theatre troupe. Named *Autumn Stages*, it was described as an "Older Adult Lifestory Theatre." These active elders, between sixty and eighty-five years of age, toured for ten years (with some inevitable turn-over). Members initially answered a newspaper call for elders interested in a new kind of service activity. (The County Office on Aging and a Federal grant supported the project.) For months they did not realize that the activities in workshop equaled acting. It was not until we began to perform for our first audiences did it sink in that this was indeed theatre.

What they did have in common was a most needed quality of rich playfulness and a lack of self-consciousness in stepping into the roles of animals, people or things. They did it because it was fun! During the years on tour, they sometimes squabbled on our Autumn Stages bus (donated by a major pharmaceutical company), but they worked harmoniously with each other in workshop and interactively with audiences.

Training workshops were held every week for three hours throughout those ten years. I, as a Gerontologist/Drama Therapist, directed the workshops and led each tour. We also had a dance/movement leader and a Music Therapist. The members grew, week by week, in their ability to spontaneously and imaginatively bring life stories into action. Workshops included chair exercise, pantomime, voice projection and improvised role-play. The telling of life experiences led to small group improvisations, generating potential themes for use on tour. Improvisational skits were planned by small groups using the five "W's": *Who* are you in the story? *What* do you want? *Why? Where* are you, and *When* is the story taking place? No scripts. No pre-assigned roles.

One afternoon each week, September to June, Autumn Stages toured to elder sites or middle and high schools within a three-hour radius. They became adept at quickly improvising life stories that became bait for stories drawn from members of the audience. Then troupe members ranged through the audience, catching someone with their left hand, another by the right to come up and improvise a life story with them. Rarely did anyone refuse. There were warm-up songs and other activities. Stirred by old songs, tales emerged, about planting Victory gardens; women taking over men's jobs; a doorbell ringing, followed by a handing over of a telegram announcing "Missing in Action," or "Wounded in Action."

Youth and Elders Interact

Another program brought together teenagers and the active elderly, with a view to rebuilding a sense of community between generations, and offering a forum for people to look beyond societal stereotypes. For nine years, Youth and Elders InterACT involved classes of students in middle and high schools throughout New Jersey and some towns in Western Massachusetts. (Indeed, our various intergenerational programs have involved over 10,000 people over the years!)

Non-trained elders who lived in each school district were also recruited to participate. Participants had no drama background. Principals asked the teachers in their schools who might be interested in the project. Sadly, we found that a number of drama teachers considered improvisation detrimental to acting! We found greater welcome from teachers of Social Studies, Visual or Language Arts, and Health and Family Living.

Our project's Educational Director recruited elders by visiting senior clubs, centers, Y's, and AARP meetings, where she explained the intent of the program: "We want to involve youth and elders in collaborating together in Life Drama, to find out about each other's lives, and discover similarities as well as respect differences." Elders often questioned, "Isn't this oral history? Will the students interview us to learn about us?"

The answer: "Yes and No. You will also be learning about their lives, understanding how different life is today for young people." Very few will turn away due to a disinterest in learning about kids. Adventurous, caring elders are intrigued with the idea.

A questionnaire was issued asking how students see elders, and how elders see youth. Responses, often quite funny, always indicated prevalent stereotypes. "All elders wear striped pants and talk loud," or, conversely, "Youth today are impolite and must be watched out for. They can carry knives or guns." It was rare for a student to praise a grandparent, or an elder to feel really close and accepting of a teenager.

At a first joint workshop, a long rope is stretched from one wall to a far wall. It is quickly recognized as a "Century Line." As the youth take positions near the far end, 1980–?, according to their birth year, Elders hold on at the near end, 1900–1950.

Questions are thrown out, such as: What games have you played?

Responses will often be met with "Hopscotch, hey, we've played that."

Or, "Were you ever mischievous?" which evokes stories of pranks played.

This is the beginning: similarities; differences; just enough to set the tone. Finally, "Are you really different? In what ways are you the same?"

It's often a student who answers, "We're kinda similar, just born in different times. I guess we just know different ... well, it's different for us today."

Here's an example of a workshop in action: In a middle school classroom, twenty-five students, ages 13–14 years, fifteen elders, and one teacher meet together with two of the program's facilitators. The students are seated in a circle with an elder between each of them. Today's theme is: In hard times, do parents and children pull together?

A typical workshop always begins with a movement warm-up, (mirror is a favorite), the introduction of the week's theme, short activities to stimulate lifestory telling, and then, as the core activity, improvisation. We move towards closure with "rap time" (i.e., a discussion of the improvisations), and then finish with a lively game or chant. The final activity is that of standing in a circle and having the group affirm each person's contributions to the workshop.

Today's theme is met with silence by both youth and elders, their faces thoughtful. Mr. H., a man in his late seventies, starts waving his hand. He stands up, very formally, to tell how his family survived the Great Depression, how he and his siblings, aged nine to sixteen, pitched in to earn money when his father lost his job in a factory. His life story is next improvised with both youth and elders assuming roles: Three elders and three students volunteer to 'be' the children, while another elder and a student play mother and father. They decide they will begin sitting at the supper table waiting for father.

Mother: I'm getting worried. Sit still, children. We won't eat until your father is here. You know that.

A child (played by an elder): I'm hungry.

The other five children chant: Mom, we're hungry. We're hungry.

Mother: Shame on you. Shame on you. Here, take a bite of bread. That's all until your father comes.

(Father arrives; his face and his bent body express deep anxiety. All watch him until he speaks): I apologize, mother, children, for being late. Today, (sigh), today, I lost my job. Thirty-five years! The notice was up, the company is closing. I don't know how we'll meet the rent next month.

This improvised scene continues with the "children" volunteering ways they can help earn money, helping the family survive the "Great Depression."

In the rap time discussion, we compare the 1930s with 2000. What is similar; what is different? Have people's feelings or behaviors changed? After working together for several months, the youth, who may have initially balked at working with "old people," now see them as active people. Age differences gradually diminish. Friendships are made which endure. And most important, stereotypes are replaced with the realization that people of all ages can be valued.

Elders write us, "I get up happy on the days I meet with these kids. They make me feel hopeful about the future." Another: "I learn what it's like growing up today. I'm learning stuff I never understood about my grandchildren." A fourteen-year old girl wrote, "I really like these elders. They're fun. And I'm learning from them, stuff not in history books. You know, they don't act so old." And improvisation? "It's like living," said an elder. "My day never works out as I planned. Don't we always have to improvise?"

Attributes of Successful Leaders

The most useful attributes that mark our more successful leaders include:

- They are caring and accepting of people, young and old, well, ill or handicapped. They are able to encourage group members to participate, and they listen, really listen.

- They are playful and imaginative; they are flexible enough to accept members' ideas, then change direction when something isn't working or doesn't catch on. They have a reservoir of possibilities.
- They speak clearly and give clear directives.
- Finally, supporting all of the above, they have experience with drama and improvisation as a *process*. All that happens in a workshop emerges from this. The shapes it takes, the product, is not significant. We can never expect to know exactly how a workshop will evolve. In itself, the workshop is an improvisation determined by group members and the leaders, so "let's play along with it."

Summary

There is a hunger to remember, to assemble the threads of one's life, to see that there was a purpose, significance, and meaning to one's life. Many programs working with seniors or with intergenerational troupes are working to restore the historic role of elders. Drama offers an especially valid way of passing on their lifestories, values, and dreams. Over the years, our various intergenerational programs have involved over 10,000 people.

References

The webpage supplement to this chapter: <www.interactiveimprov.com/ elderwb.html> has other references, anecdotes of others who also use interactive drama with elders.

Perlstein, Susan, & Bliss, Jeff. (1994) *Generating community: Intergenerational partnerships through the Arts.* New York: Elders Share the Arts. 57 Willoughby Street, Brooklyn, NY 11201. (Describes projects that focus on the social history of elders, increasingly combined with youth to explore the social problems and realities of the century.)

Weisberg, Naida, & Wilder, Rosilyn (Eds.). (2001). *Expressive arts with elders: A resource.*(2nd ed.) New York & London: Jessica Kingsley. (Anthology in which five drama therapists describe their work. London: Jessica Kingsley.)

Wilder, Rosilyn. (1996). *The lifestory re-play circle.* State College, PA: Venture Publishing. Describes spontaneous "Life Drama" workshops as used with

ill, handicapped and dementia patients in health care facilities. <www.
venturepublish.com>

Wilder, Rosilyn. (1996). *Come, step into my life: "Life Drama" with youth and
elders*. Charlottesville, VA: New Plays for Children. (A first in the field of
intergenerational drama as psychosocial education and therapy. Presents
six teams of artist-educators in workshops with youth, collaborating
with community elders, inner city, suburban and rural districts.)

Chapter 4

HEALING THE WOUNDS OF HISTORY

Ronald Miller & Armand Volkas

Healing the Wounds of History is a group process in which drama techniques are used to work with participants from two cultures who share a common legacy of violent conflict and historical trauma. First used with sons and daughters of Holocaust survivors and Nazis, the process has subsequently been applied to the conflicts between other cultures. The process was developed by Armand Volkas, a drama therapist from Oakland, California. Volkas, the son of Holocaust survivors and resistance fighters from World War II, was moved by his personal struggle with this legacy of historical trauma to address the issues that arose from it: issues around identity, victimization and perpetration (i.e., being hurt by and hurting others), meaning, and personal and collective grief.

After graduating with an MFA in theatre from UCLA, he created a theatre piece with other post-War Jews of his generation about the legacy of the Holocaust. Subsequently, he created an experimental theatre company in Los Angeles to explore Jewish culture and values. In 1989, he invited seven children of Holocaust survivors and seven children of the Third Reich to spend several days together exploring their legacies from the War. This was the beginning of a series of workshops—in the United States, France, Germany and Canada—which sought to "heal the wounds of history", working with the legacy not only of Nazism and the Holocaust, but also the French and Algerians; Palestinians and Israelis; Japanese, Chinese and Koreans (on the legacy of WWII); Americans of both African and European descent (on the legacy of Slavery); Blacks and Jews; Bosnian Serbs and Muslims; as well as Deaf and Hearing cultures.

This work has led to three related processes. The first is a workshop open to persons of diverse cultures who wish to explore their legacy of historical trauma. This is a workshop that is usually led by Volkas, alone or with co-facilitators. The second process brings together participants from two cultures with a shared legacy of conflict and trauma (i.e. 'enemies') to work intensively for several days. Volkas directs these workshops with a co-therapist, and sometimes with assistants. The third process is a *playback theatre* performance that follows an intensive workshop of either kind. At these performances, participants from the workshop and volunteers from the audience share personal stories of historical trauma and healing which are performed impromptu for the audience, using traditional playback techniques, as well as techniques derived from sociodrama, Theatre of the Oppressed and creative ritual.

Purposes

The work has four important purposes: The first is *recognizing cultural or national identity*. Participants are encouraged to reflect upon and publicly identify their cultural identity or identities (sometimes a set of complex variations), and to experience and reveal to other participants the emotions and attitudes that each identity evokes in them. (See comments on nature of the phenomenon of "identity" on website reference.) The goal here is to encounter the obstacles to cultural self-esteem. In cultures with a history of trauma, some members of the culture have been designated, consciously or unconsciously, as 'carriers' of the legacy of violence and perpetration. In others, the legacy of trauma is hidden; it has gone 'underground.' This breaking down the elements of cultural and national identity into their component parts helps participants uncover the "collective story" they may be carrying and allows them to integrate their legacies in a more positive and generative way.

A second purpose of these workshops is *to open and enhance intercultural communication*. Often there is a taboo against speaking to 'the others', those from another culture regarded as perpetrators or aggressors. This taboo may be spoken or unspoken, and may sometimes carry an implicit threat of violence against those who violate it. Simply to speak to 'the other' is a first step in healing. Ultimately, the goal is to teach communications skills that can help participants make cultural adaptations in intercultural contexts.

A third function is *to experience collective grief and mourning*. Often there is a well of grief, present but not displayed or even acknowledged, held within the participants' parents or grandparents, and in the culture as a whole. This grief may be related to victimization or to perpetration, or both. Each cultural group needs to experience this culturally received pain, and to understand it—and have it understood by others—as unique. Participants, as representatives of their cultures, are given the rare opportunity to give shape and expression to this collective grief.

Finally, the workshops seek *to create a culture of empathy*. While initially the representatives of one conflicting culture may seek to outdo the other culture in suffering and victimization, ultimately the work seeks to teach compassion for the pain of others which transcends the tendency to embrace one's own suffering as superior. Instead of 'dueling dramas', one may then find empathic acceptance of the uniqueness of another's historical pain.

Phases of the Process

In a multi-day workshop, the work moves through several phases of development: The first phase involves *breaking the taboo against speaking to one another*. Often, when two cultures have a history of conflict and violence, there is an invisible barrier preventing contact. Speaking to the 'enemy' is perceived as an act of betrayal. When two polarized groups break the taboo and engage in honest dialogue, they can begin to work through the layers of unresolved feelings each carries about the other. Those who dare to speak despite the taboo are referred to by therapists in this method as the *emotional pioneers*, who pave the way for others.

The second phase is that of *humanizing one another through sharing personal stories*. When members of different cultures in conflict listen to each other's stories and hear each other's pain, they begin to care for one another. These feelings of empathy become more powerful than the historical imperative to hate one another. Friendships are created. This creates a *double bind* which participants must resolve. How can I hate this person and have empathy for him at the same time? This phase begins the process of *role reversal*, a psychodramatic process in which one participant begins to experience in an embodied and affective way the reality of another.

Third, participants are helped to explore and own the potential perpetrator in themselves. This phase requires a sense of trust, and begins the process of reconciliation. People need to acknowledge that, under extreme circumstances, we all have the capacity for cruelty. Accepting this truth is the great equalizer. It levels the playing field.

Phase Four involves *moving deeply into grief*. It is crucial that collective grieving take place. Participants often are carrying not only their own pain, but that of parents, grandparents, ancestors and the cultural collective. Permission must be given to grieve: by the therapist, by the community, by the individual himself. If their pain is not fully grieved, participants will pass it on to the next generation, and that legacy will have the potential to perpetuate continued violence and depression.

In the fifth phase, group members create rituals or performances *in memoriam*, to acknowledge publicly the difficult history they share. Here feelings are channeled into an aesthetic form. The public nature of these ceremonies of reconciliation extends its healing effects into society, touching the awareness of others who did not participate in the workshops.

Finally, in Phase Six, the goal is *making commitments to acts of creation and acts of service*. One of the ways to master a legacy of historical trauma is to focus emotional energy into acts of creation, such as telling stories or creating poetry, art, theatre or dance, thereby transforming the history of pain into beauty. Another pathway of commitment is that of service: working with political refugees or survivors of violence, for example, or political action to end injustice.

Methods

Workshops often begin simply, in a sitting circle, with participants introducing themselves and self-defining roles and objectives. The talking circle provides an opportunity to clarify the therapeutic nature of the process. In other words, the process invites individuals to bring forward their personal stories and feelings, and to do so in a private, sequestered space. Facilitators in *Healing the Wounds* make it clear that this process is fundamentally emotional, depending on the willingness of those *emotional pioneers* who 'hold the collective story' to come forward and express their grief and anger as representatives of their culture. It is this commitment to emotional self-sacrifice that creates the potential to 'change the emotional landscape'.

The talking circle is generally followed by playful warm-ups. In this phase, participants are asked to engage in structured, spontaneous and imaginative exercises which are embodied and affective rather than cognitive. The functions of this play are several. Primarily, it serves as a warm-up to the dramatic processes which follow. It also allows the participants to engage with each other as human beings in a state of play, rather than as representatives of the 'other' culture. In addition, as in all drama therapy processes, each individual will confront during this playful warm-up his or her own limitations in terms of spontaneity, embodiment, and expression of affect. The participants also begin to work together as a group, and to communicate with each other in non-threatening contexts.

As a beginning warm-up, participants are asked to introduce themselves with a *sound-and-movement*; another warm up has the group pass one or two imaginary objects around the circle of participants. These playful exercises can be followed by something more *sociodramatic*, in which participants take roles in spontaneous dramas that unfold between *role types*, such as a police officer and a driver. Often these are done as dyadic exercises—that is, breaking the group into pairs of people and having them interact. That way participants are not observed by spectators, thus reducing performance anxiety. Feeling the pulse of the group and the readiness of participants to engage emotionally and thematically, the facilitator might begin introducing role pairs more directly related to the conflict, in scenes such as an Israeli soldier and Palestinian encounter at a checkpoint; a Japanese tourist encountering an elderly Korean woman who remembers the Japanese atrocities in her country during World War II, or two adolescent daughters of Holocaust survivors speaking to each other in the middle of the night because their survivor mother has had yet another nightm>are about her experience in a concentration camp.

Other exercises and techniques for developing group cohesion are noted on the webpage supplement to this chapter: <www.interactiveimprov.com/healhistwb.html>.

A final exercise begins the transition from *warm-up* to *storytelling*. This is a verbal, embodied ritual in which each participant stands alone, in front of the group, and speaks his or her name, both in English (in English-language settings) and in the language of origin. Then, each person names his cultural identity, which may include elements of nationality, ethnicity, religion, gender, sexual preference and other factors. Obviously, in some cases, these are complex. Different kinds of statements evoke different feelings. 'I am an American' has a different resonance for a participant than 'I am an Israeli-American' or 'I am a Jew' or 'I am a Jewish-American of Austrian descent'. Each participant is questioned by a facilitator, asked to speak different options, and to express feelings or images related to each 'identity'. These feelings may range from pride to guilt, to ambivalence, to pain, to an absence of affect or feeling. Often, there are stories underneath each feeling (or denial of feeling) which reveal a person's relationship to their cultural identity and self-esteem.

Sharing Stories

The second phase of helping participants to humanize each other is also rich in possibilities. Often the storytelling begins with an invitation to describe a brief incident about the *transmission of the legacy of historical trauma*. The story might be considered *formative* (a story from childhood or adolescence) or *transformative* (an adult story around a moment of personal discovery or recognition). Usually the facilitator asks other participants to 'step in' to the story, either into a *fluid sculpture* or into a more developed *playback theatre* enactment (See Chapter 1). In either case, the key components are physical distance (for the storyteller) and emotional and physical engagement (for the other participants). This helps establish a balance. The courage demonstrated by the storyteller in bringing forward the story, and her willingness to self-disclose and re-experience the remembered event, needs to be met by the group's willingness to empathize and reenact.

Stepping forward into others' stories requires risk-taking by participants. On the one hand, there is a risk for those without theatre experience or training. But this is usually secondary to that of stepping authentically into the story of a member of an 'enemy culture'. Because of this risk, the teller of the story needs be coached to restrain his natural impulses to correct or critique the enactment in favor of the larger good: building trust, intuition, and empathy. Facilitators also need to concern themselves with the safety and emotional needs of the teller. Stories that are told at this early stage often take on archetypal significance for the group. There is a kind of self-sacrifice taking place, in which personal (*psychodramatic*) needs are set aside in the (*sociodramatic*) interests of the group.

Sometimes the first story creates a *choice-point* for the director. The first volunteer is often an *emotional pioneer*, and sometimes this initial offering can serve as an opportunity to open up into the next stage of the workshop. One possibility is to move directly into *psychodrama* with this storyteller, asking her to participate in a second story with a stronger content of perpetration and violence. The director needs to consider whether the rest of the group is ready to follow at this point, however, and engage their own legacies of perpetration. If not, the leader can invite further stories.

One sociodramatic warmup which is sometimes used is an improvised performance by each national or ethnic group, entitled 'The History of my People (in five minutes)'. Each ethnic group is given only a few minutes to prepare. Always spontaneous and often lighthearted, this exercise allows each group to enact an 'auto-history', including their view of stereotypes about themselves. Other warm-ups that stimulate stories and/or psychodramas are conversations between victims and perpetrators, or improvisations with a master/slave or victim/perpetrator motif.

Third Phase: Exploring and owning the potential perpetrator in each of us

An exercise which opens up the issue of perpetration in a powerful way is one in which a collection of historical photographs is displayed, and then reenacted first as a series of sculptures, then as living figures with voices. The photographs are those of victims, perpetrators and bystanders: sometimes taken before historical acts of perpetration, sometimes after. This exercise is part of an important shift in the process, one which moves beyond *witnessing* and towards *retrieving, reclaiming* and, ultimately, *resolving*.

This phase begins where there is impatience with the relatively passive stance of *witnessing*, and an emerging urgency about bringing the past forward into the present in an active way, so as to work with it and begin to change it. Often this comes forward as a powerful need to speak directly to *the other*, to reveal one's own suffering in a way that holds members of the opposing group accountable. In this way, participants are forced to confront their own complicity as well as their victimization.

Fourth Phase: Moving deeply into grief

In a two-day workshop, the second day often begins with this issue in the forefront: Will the group be willing to go deeper, into the more vulnerable feelings beneath the anger? Some groups may not be ready to do so. It may have been enough for them to genuinely listen to the stories of the opposing group, and perhaps to double or role-reverse their 'adversaries'. This in itself begins the healing, and there is no shame in the resistance that may arise among group members to going deeper into emotions that expose their vulnerabilities. Other groups, however, may yearn for a deeper healing, and a richer sense of shared humanity. In the opening hour of the second day, the facilitator begins to sense whether there is an opportunity to go deeper. If not, then the facilitator begins to consider the nature of the closing ritual which will bring the experience to an end. (See *Fifth Phase* below.)

Each day may begin with a talking circle, with participants sharing their experiences, and stating or restating their personal goals. On the last day, this is especially important, because the goals identified by the participants give clues about the nature of the culminating enactment. The talking circle is then followed by embodied warm-ups, often ones more advanced or challenging than on earlier days.

If there is potential for emotional depth, the group may move again into stories. Participants may be asked to share their experiences of aggression, violence, fear and humiliation, especially when these had formative or transformative impact on their lives. These are then mirrored back by the group through fluid sculptures or playback performances. An Israeli woman may share a story of her father lying down in front of a tank in the 1948 conflict, or a Palestinian woman may speak of the humiliation of her family in an immigration line in a Paris airport. These stories intensify the emotional learning and empathy of the group. Sometimes a collage of historical photographs is used to bring the deeper emotions to the surface. These can be supplemented by personal photographs brought in by participants, family images before, during and after cultural traumas. Images from the Holocaust, for example, or of the aftermath of massacres of American Indians, can bring up collective and personal grief.

Another option is a *person-to-person talk* between participants of different cultures. Unlike the conversation described in the third phase, here each individual speaks for himself or herself. In such a conversation, the goal is authentic emotional communication. The facilitator coaches for phrasing such as: "What I need to hear from you is ..." or "I deeply apologize for...." This process is enhanced by role reversal, in which each participant is given a chance to say (to oneself) what one wishes to hear from the other, and then, in turn, to hear it. Sometimes participants cannot give fully what the other needs, because they remain separated by disagreements. Nevertheless, they can hear and acknowledge those needs. Throughout this process, participants are coached to make their statements 'feeling' and personal. There is a difference between 'I can see that you might feel that my people have taken your land' and 'I am deeply saddened to see your pain. I am so sorry that I have hurt you'. While the first statement represents a step towards empathy, the latter creates the potential for genuine healing.

Often such a confrontation will create the emotional space for a story which requires great courage to tell, one which is 'closer to the bone'. Stories that emerge towards the end of the process tend to be more cathartic. On the one hand, they allow each group to feel the uniqueness of their own historical pain. But they also have the potential to transcend the paradigm of 'dueling victimizations' and move towards recognition of the universal nature of suffering.

Fifth Phase: Creating performances and rituals of remembrance

Usually the final phase takes the form of a *ritual of commemoration*, one which includes elements of *memory, celebration* and *transcendence*. Group members collaborate in the creation of a final performance which may consist of a series of vignettes or images, or some deeper ritualized process. In this phase, the participants should be given wide latitude to create what is most meaningful to them. Facilitators often bring stones or other symbolic objects which can be used as commemoration when placed significantly on an 'altar' or other sacred space. Participants sometimes use fluid sculptures or *future projections*, scenes taking place in the future. Scarves, often present where the facilitators use playback techniques, can be used to create mandalas or other configurations on the floor.

Sixth Phase: Making commitments to acts of creation or acts of service

Often this phase takes the form of a playback performance to which members of the larger community are invited. The audience may consist of friends and family of the participants. In other cases, a professional playback troupe may be invited to respond to stories arising from the workshop in a performance advertised in the wider community. In this case, audience members may bring with them some of the same unresolved emotions initially felt by participants in the workshop. This renews the process of healing from the beginning, as participants consciously put forward their own stories a second time, before a larger audience, as a service to the community. Then, in playback tradition, members of the audience will be asked to bring forward their own stories for performance.

Certain group members may prefer to move forward in less public ways, by committing to ongoing meetings with members of the group with whom they share the common legacy of historical trauma. They may commit collectively to political action, social engagement, and community service. Other individuals feel more comfortable expressing themselves privately through writing, poetry, music and art. They may continue their engagement through the creation, rehearsal and (sometimes) performance of dance, theatre, music and performance art.

Training

Facilitation of this kind of work requires an expertise in the dramatic process, and sensitivity both to group dynamics and the emotional psychology of trauma. Generally facilitators are drama therapists or psychodramatists with a background in playback theatre or some other form of theatrical performance or improvisation. Assistants are sometimes used to help facilitate the process by participating in exercises and improvisations, and by taking roles in enactments. These assistants are usually drama therapy students or members of playback theatre companies. In other words, participating in this kind of work requires an ability to be emotionally present, and to respond authentically, spontaneously and therapeutically in dramatic forms. Because of the focus on supporting the emotional healing the participants, facilitators and assistants alike must be confident of their theatrical skills and able to use these skills to make therapeutic interventions effectively and creatively.

Drama therapy and psychodrama require graduate-level training and certification. Playback theatre training programs are also available to interested persons.

Conclusion

Healing the Wounds of History is a workshop process which brings together participants from cultures with shared histories of perpetration and victimization. Dramatic techniques from various sources are used to develop in each participant a clear sense of cultural identity, an ability to speak and listen to members of other cultures, a willingness to enter into the collective grief created by their histories, and an emerging empathy for their historical adversaries. Techniques are drawn from various sources, including drama therapy, psychodrama, sociodrama, playback theatre and theatre of the oppressed.

The form of the process follows from its intention to heal, as well as from the emotional spontaneity of the participants, and their willingness to 'play' dramatically with the shared history of violence. In this sense, it is a structured improvisational process. Often, in its final stages, it moves from dramatic improvisation into theatrical presentation, in the form of playback theatre performances or other public enactments.

The ultimate intention of the work is to change the emotional landscape of cultural conflict by sharing with others one's stories, feelings and yearning for apology and forgiveness. The chosen form of the work is dramatic improvisation because drama is a holistic form of human expression, which allows individuals to express themselves completely—in a fully present, spontaneous and integrated way—through body, voice, feeling, intellect and spirit. It is this affective engagement of one's whole being with that of the 'enemy' which makes possible the experience of healing.

Further information may be found at <www.interactiveimprov.com/healhistwb.html>

Chapter 5

DESIGNING AND CONDUCTING RITUALS, CEREMONIES AND CELEBRATIONS

Adam Blatner

The theme running through this book is that more people want to feel a greater involvement and interactivity in public events—not just to be passive spectators. Similarly, people often complain of feelings of alienation at traditional ceremonies. It is as if these events were almost a scripted process, superficial, and held nothing that was really personal. This has become true for some experiences with traditional theatre, also. New, more interactive rituals are being designed and conducted in response to this felt need.

Dramatists and theatre artists are in a perfect position to cross-train in order to apply their skills in designing and conducting rituals. Names for practitioners in this relatively new cultural niche might be "celebrant" or "master of ceremonies" (Blatner, 2000). The need for this trans-denominational social role has arisen because many people have become dissatisfied with traditional rituals, finding them insufficiently relevant and involving. People are seeking to experience their life transitions, weddings, funerals, and other events in ways that are more vivid and meaningful. While many still prefer traditional ceremonies, an increasing number of people wish these occasions could include the guests who attend. Also, there are other life-transitions that don't have a widespread tradition for their celebration, so rituals for these events are an opportunity for an exercise of a mixture of psychology, theatre art, group dynamics, and spiritual sensitivity.

Roots of this interest became more prevalent in the 1960s as people began revitalizing conventional rituals in churches, adding new types of music, poetry, dance, and other forms. Modern Jewish subgroups have sought to develop innovations in domestic rituals and in small study groups. The growing popularity of the neo-pagan movement (e.g., Wicca) and forms of earth-based feminist spirituality have more interest in the power of creating interesting and more meaningful rituals. Rituals for more active involvement in death, dying and grieving as well as celebrations for promoting family life have been described by various journalists. In the academic world, there has been more research on comparative religion, mythology, and ritual as studies of other cultures have become more available. Searching for rituals, ceremonies, celebrations on the World Wide Web turns up thousands of websites!

There are numerous books that have been published in the last few decades that address this new socio-cultural trend (see the references at the end for some examples, and others on the webpage supplement to this chapter: <www.interactiveimprov.com/ritualswb.html>).

Who becomes a Master of Ceremonies?

Another factor supporting this emergent field is that there is an increasing number of people who seem to be interested in assuming the role of master of ceremonies. Because spirituality has become a more prominent element in the fields related to psychotherapy—and this includes the creative arts and expressive therapies, such as drama therapy—professionals are moving beyond the clinical context, into coaching, spiritual direction, and celebration facilitation. Indeed, there are now actual programs for training as a "celebrant," drawing students from a range of backgrounds.

A "master of ceremonies" (MC) role, in which a person helps others design and then conducts the ritual, requires that the celebrant has a genuine interest in spirituality and individual and group psychology, as well as experience in improvisational and interactive drama. Such a person would not simply be the one who narrates the event, but more, one who truly aspires to master "the art of ceremony." The role includes a capacity for being sensitive to the needs not only of the key celebrants, but also of the group and its dynamics. A key skill an MC should develop is an ability to discover and create "meaning" as part of the dramatic process.

Those who might be motivated to help in co-creating new forms of commemorations may share a number of factors:

- they aren't affiliated with a mainstream religion
- they are religiously affiliated, but the traditional liturgy isn't satisfactory or supplemental elements are desired
- they perceive a need for rituals that are generally not performed by more traditional clergy (e.g., retirement, divorce, and others to be mentioned below)
- they are more in sympathy with an interfaith orientation, or the key participants have different religious backgrounds, or elements of other cultural spiritual traditions are desired.

Common issues need to be addressed in creating rituals:

- More people need to be involved, and the MC should helping others to feel acknowledged and appreciated
- The MC should design a ritual that expresses elements of the individuality, the personal life-style, tastes, special interests, and spiritual orientations of the key celebrants
- Communicating a sense of the "story" of the people involved is helpful.
- The MC allows for a mixture of positive, playful, and serious elements

The goal is to have participants leave feeling that this wedding, funeral, baby-welcoming, or other rite of passage/commemoration/celebration was meaningful; equally important, the participants should feel closer to the key people in the ceremony, and perhaps to each other.

Types of Ceremonies

The main ceremonies in our culture increasingly call for new adaptations. Marriages are often inter-religious, interracial, or intercultural. Sometimes they involve re-commitment for a couple that had been living together for some years and are now making it official—and sometimes there are the children of this couple present. Often there are re-marriages for one or both parties. A commitment ceremony may involve a same-sex couple. Such occasions are ripe for creative adaptations that speak not only to the uniqueness of the relationship, but also to some of the individual qualities and requirements of the people involved.

The grief experienced at funerals may be compounded by the loss being addressed indirectly or inadequately. The bereaved may feel that the lost one's unique qualities are being overlooked, they are not getting a chance to have their say in making their goodbyes, they don't know how to express these goodbyes, and/or are given no direction nor invited to consider how they might like to do this.

The point of this chapter is to not only encourage people to help design and conduct meaningful ceremonies, but to develop an integrated set of skills including

- a capacity to generate a sense of spirituality that is inclusive of the full range of the beliefs of those participating

- an aesthetic sense that can bring out the intrinsic drama in the situation and make it relevant and emotionally meaningful

- a psychological sensitivity that takes into consideration group dynamics and the personal needs of both the primary celebrants and the others who have been invited

Other types of ceremonies include:

- Pre-birth blessing. While a "baby shower" tends to involve practical gifts for the mother-to-be, this ceremony would be a bit more spiritual, sharing supportive wishes and envisioning a healthy and positive future.

- Welcoming a newborn child into a community of friends, family, and spiritual guardians is recognized within various religious traditions, and may also be enjoyed by families not affiliated with any particular religion.

- Birthdays, especially when they are associated with some perceived milestone or shift in status, can be dramatically enhanced by creative ceremony design.

- Coming-of-Age rituals offer opportunities for adding elements that might also have a growth-stimulating impact on the teenager involved.

- Weddings have become more personal than ever and the designing of such events should ideally include a consideration of the invited group's dynamics and the psychology of all concerned in addition to the spiritual tone and message to be created.

- Mid-life ceremonies. A variety of rituals can be generated for various purposes:

healing	letting go of a dream	retirement
divorce	starting over	forgiving and releasing
adoption	re-uniting	other major life transitions

- Elder-ing. What about a ceremony to honor the establishment of a certain measure of wisdom and empowerment? The preparation for such a ceremony could take years, and thinking about the appropriate prerequisites might constitute part of the preparation. Already there are such "sage-ing" ceremonies for women who have entered a path of developing wisdom. Suggs & Suggs (2000) suggest other possibilities of new rituals for this age group. At a conference of older adults, they explored this challenge by dividing those attending into five small subgroups and asking each to develop a ritual associated with the elder years. The following ceremonies were suggested:

- Ritual of Hands. Designed for long-term care workers and caregivers, this ritual is a ceremony to bless and empower their work.

- Memory Bridge. A ceremony for people with Alzheimer's disease and their families to mark the move into a care facility. The ritual builds a sacred connection between the elders with Alzheimer's and their new homes.

- Ritual Toward Freedom. Designed specifically for prisoners about to be released, this ceremony celebrates their transitions into their new lives and helps them build a sense of confidence that they are valued members of the community.

- Grandparents Day Celebration. Designed as an initiation into the order of wisdom, the ceremony honors elders and the wisdom and love they share with younger generations.

- Ritual of Passage: Crossing the Threshold. Designed for anyone moving to another level of care or another stage in life. This ceremony helps participants feel that there is hope in change and that change brings possibilities for living.

More meaningful funerals, wakes, and associated rituals are sorely needed so that the bereaved can feel a more vivid sense of closure. It's good to consider how various people in the social network can make whatever contributions seem most appropriate. One of the problems with the traditional funeral is that it is generally held at a time when it is a financial and life-disrupting hardship for family members and friends to break away and attend, and this is because so many are scattered around the country or the world. It might be better to inform people that a memorial will be held—and perhaps in the not-too-distant future, this may happen in real time via web-cameras and the internet—an extension of teleconferencing.

Even better is the idea of a person holding an appreciation ceremony before one dies. This would be a review of one's life and an opportunity to thank the key participants, to tell family and friends what they've meant, and to allow them to respond. (A relative of mine did just this and that's what started me thinking about the whole subject of creative ceremonies.)

Those who design rituals, integrating drama, psychology, and spirituality, will also be encouraging folks to use more rituals in their everyday lives. Masters of Ceremony might teach people to create for themselves a variety of family rituals, small rituals with children, deepening their social and spiritual connections. While some ceremonies may be directed by officially ordained clergy and held in special buildings, there are so many more that can be performed by ordinary people in their homes, in parks, and other settings (Biziou, 1999).

Planning

Too often ceremonies are designed and performed with a minimum of preparation. They may hire a ceremonial consultant for the planning who attends primarily to the administrative functions, and certain affiliated clergy are called in for an adjunctive function. Instead, what if the ceremony would be anticipated with an eye towards heightening the psychological, spiritual, and aesthetic impact. (A simple and practical definition of "spiritual" is that it is an activity of developing a relationship or deepening a sense of connectedness with the broader system of meaning, the Greater Wholeness also given many other names, such as Transcendent Being, God, Higher Power, Tao, and so forth.)

In other cultures, significant rituals might have weeks or even years for people to gather certain materials, achieve certain ordeals, fulfill goals, master skills, or rehearse songs, prayers, or dances. There may be masks or costumes to be constructed, bowers or special houses to be built. In modern ceremonies, planners might consider budgets, time, and also what is to be achieved.

Nina Strongylou, in San Francisco, offers the service of designing and conducting rituals under her business title, "Mysteria." She writes, "Since every ceremony reflects its participants, in order to maximize the experience of the celebration as really meaningful, we ask the following questions so as to better understand the celebrant's beliefs and needs: (1) What inspired you to make this commitment now? (2) What aspects of your life do you want to celebrate/honor/mark? (3) What, if any, is your philosophy of life or spiritual orientation?

(4) What is the mood you want to create? and (5) Who will be involved and how active will they be?"

As part of the planning, consider that those invited can be sent instructions, requests, or suggestions for what they can prepare such as some words to say or a meaningful object. These may be enclosed with the invitation. Such requests could also be individualized with various people being asked to prepare to participate according to each individual's talents or relationship with the main celebrants.

For those ceremonies that really need the active participation of a priest, rabbi, or other ordained clergy, part of the challenge involves finding ones who are also skilled in the aforementioned role components of a master of ceremonies—and there are some who are!—or collaborating with ones who will share the design of the process.

Another variable is that of recognizing key participants because such acknowledgments communicate a reverence for the point of a ceremony as an implied request for the community to validate a role transition. In most guest lists, for example, there are certain people who have a greater status in some respect: respected elders or key family members; having been a mentor or teacher of the key players; those who have exerted special efforts, expense, or other sacrifice to attend; or those who, in other ways, have been special for the primary actors. It becomes meaningful for the whole group to see and hear these people being recognized.

A useful technique is to arrange ahead of time for key elders or other significant community participants to give a blessing—something like a toast. Envisioning a positive future for the key players, affirming a belief in their potentials—such actions have a deep and powerful impact.

Components of Rituals

First there is the *invocation*, the activity of speaking to the unseen audience. This is a device that assumes an audience, the spirits, ancestors, small-g gods or goddesses. It could be very secular: Imagine that all our teachers were present. Or: Imagine that our grandparents and great grandparents, and all who have loved us, are here with us now.

The invocation is a calling, from the Latin word, *vocare*, to call. It establishes a kind of context of performance, of stage and audience, and that which happens becomes experienced as a bit more significant because we imagine that audience's witness. Invocation also is a kind of prayer, an affirmation of intention, which, by saying aloud, carries more weight. It penetrates the layers of subtle tendency to withhold commitment and vulnerability that is served by low-grade inhibition, and stands forth as if to say, "*Here I am and here's what I stand for.*"

On the other hand, *silence* can be a useful techniques. It helps if the master of ceremonies suggests a task the participants can do for focusing their mind during the silence, such as contemplating what they can feel grateful for in this gathering, or noticing the sense of connectedness with the present community.

During a ceremony or ritual, *prayer* is also used, and, as noted, is simply putting into spoken or sung words, or even un-languaged dance, some act of affirmation. One sub-component that is generally useful is that of *expressing appreciations*. It's simplistic (and yet okay for young children) to just say "Bless Daddy and Mommy and Aunt Suzie, and Ginger the kitty …" But it's more powerful to thank people for something specific that they have done or given.

A variation is the technique of the "Greek Chorus," in which several people are instructed or coached in what to say together, or sing together, adding mood, reinforcing, reflecting or resonating with affirmations. Indeed, many other dramatic devices may be woven together, depending on the needs of the moment.

Specific imagery is a most important principle, because people tend to generalize, speak in abstractions, which serve as unconscious forms of avoidance of sharper awareness and commitment. Such modes of speaking leave everyone a bit vague about what is being said. In some contexts this is probably adaptive since it performs the social function of "small talk." However, in ceremonies, it detracts from the effectiveness of the activity. Instead, paint pictures with words: We want to thank Uncle Joe for his presence at this and so many other family occasions—it takes a lot of effort to come through and show up. He had to plan, pack, and fly in from Florida—not an easy trip in this day and age.

The architecture or staging of the event is important. Are there natural areas of trees, edges or sections of the room, stones or other elements that can be made part of the ceremony? One common technique is to note the four directions, each with a different symbol, a large rock, perhaps a few items on that rock or standing beside it. (This acknowledging of the four directions comes mainly from the Native American Indian tradition. If the people are sympathetic with this rich tradition, sometimes the spirits and/or qualities of the four directions are named and called in invocation.)

In that spirit, another technique is to have a circle of small rocks, each participant having been asked to bring one from home that seems special. A ball of yarn, or several balls of different colors, can be laid down around the circle of participants and creating a "mandala," a circular diagram that suggests the way the soul is whole by integrating and balancing diverse elements.

Designing or conducting a ceremony may benefit from the inclusion of a degree of playfulness. It is often helpful to include some room for improvisation. Consider the potentials of new developments in media, communications, electronic amplification, and the like. Ceremonies might vary in tone from solemn to lighthearted, and some might even combine bits of both, with more serious moments being followed by a bit of satire or foolishness. This implicitly acknowledges the complexity and many-faceted nature of the event and the key participants, and the inclusion of different emotional elements even makes the ritual more authentic. If an event is too purely silly, it is a bit demeaning; if it is all too solemn and stiff, it becomes stifling.

Some people have created wakes and memorials that include, along with the expressions of sadness, some reminders that the person who died would be would be affirming life and the importance of enjoying being together.

Other Elements

Many celebrations include some acknowledgment of the season or time of the year, and address the symbolism of the occasion in relationship to the calendar. Similarly, if some symbolic meaning, however simple, can be attached to the choice of location, the set-up, any props or lighting effects, the clothes chosen, and other factors, this meaning should be explained to those attending so they can notice, appreciate, and share in the significance.

If food, costume, special clothes, types of music, artistic decorations, or other elements are chosen, or if any kind of altar or other equivalent focus of attention is chosen, these, too, may be woven in and commented on by the master of ceremonies. It's not always necessary to have some outside person conduct the event, although that has certain advantages in many situations. The key point is that the main people participate in planning it and think about its component elements rather than just letting events unfold naturally or spontaneously. While there may be certain moments or sub-events in which spontaneity is great, on the whole, planning and structuring an event makes spontaneity even more effective. Too much non-planning actually inhibits everyone because genuine spontaneity doesn't come forth if folks are even a bit disoriented and confused.

Training & Conclusion

For those considering becoming masters of ceremony, it is worthwhile to surf the net, read at least ten books, apprentice to some others doing this work, and deepening one's own commitment by talking with others, and weaving together the psychological, artistic (dramatic), spiritual, and playful elements. Programs for training celebrants have been operating in Australia for over twenty-five years, and more recently a related program, "Celebrant-USA" has begun a program for learning this role.

Dramatists who have an appreciation for psychology and spirituality may be able to help ordinary people heighten their experiences of major role transitions, rituals, celebrations, and ceremonies. The key is taking the time to plan events, thinking ahead of the people attending, and considering ways of balancing involvement and low demand for performance.

References (with Notations by Elizabeth Clontz)

Note: Many other references may be found on the webpage that supplements this chapter: <www.interactiveimprov.com/ritualswb.html> as well as further anecdotes, ideas.

Beck, Renée, & Metrick, Sydney Barbara. (1990). *The art of ritual: A guide to creating and performing your own cermonies for growth and change.* Berkeley, CA: Celestial Arts. (This offers a good description of types, elements, and applications of rituals, suggestions for the ritual process, and sections also on altars, ritual guidelines, symbols, and crafting and consecrating tools for rituals.)

Biziou, Barbara. (1999). *The joy of ritual: Spiritual recipes to celebrate milestones, ease transitions, and make every day sacred.* New York: Golden Books. (Paperback version: (2001): *The joys of everyday ritual.* New York: St Martin's-Griffin. (Here is a collection of sample rituals for life transitions and occasions. Each ritual design includes intention, timing of ritual, ingredients, plan and a related story. Why our society needs rituals. Elements of rituals. Tools for creating rituals—colors, scents, food and drink, music, crystals and gemstones, objects and artifacts, physical acts, elements of nature, conscious breathing, meditation, and visualization/ guided imagery. Creating an altar.)

Biziou, Barbara. (2000). *The joy of family rituals.* New York: St. Martin's Press.

Blatner, Adam. (2000). A new role for psychodramatists: Master of Ceremonies. *International Journal of Action Methods, 53* (2), 86–93.

Imber-Black, E., & Roberts, Janine. (1992). *Rituals for our times: Celebrating, healing, and changing our lives and our relationships.* New York: HarperCollins. (Extensive selections on rituals in society today, purposes of ritual, understanding rituals in family heritage, planning a ritual, ritual meaning through symbols and symbolic action. Exploration and examples of rituals for daily life, birthdays, anniversaries, holidays, life-cycle transitions. Engaging others in rituals, revitalizing rituals, ritual stories, transforming rituals with painful memories.)

Roberts, Janine. (1999). Beyond words: the power of rituals. In Daniel J. Wiener (Ed.), *Beyond talk therapy.* Washington, DC: American Psychological Association. (Good practical tools. Although oriented to applying in therapy, easily adapted to the broader issues. Many good references.)

Suggs Patricia K. & Suggs Douglas L. (2000). Rituals and celebrations for older adults: marking passages, demonstrating support. *Aging & Spirituality, 12* (2), Summer, 2000

Websites

Nina Strongylou is an example of a person who designs and conducts rituals for individuals: <www.home.earthlink.net/~planaritual/mysteria.htm>

<www.joyofritual.com> Barbara Biziou not only conducts rituals, but also has many writings on her website (under the link to articles).

<www.celebrantusa.com> describes one training program for people who design and conduct rituals.

Chapter 6

REFLECTIONS:
A TEEN ISSUES IMPROV TROUPE

Staci Block

"Reflections" is the name of an ongoing troupe of high school students that has been a continuing program for over sixteen years in New Jersey. The troupe offers interactive, improvised presentations on topics relevant to youngsters, as well as functioning as a wholesome and skill-building activity for the teen troupe members. It uses methods derived from Playback Theatre, Theatre in Education, sociodrama, and Theatre of the Oppressed (Chapters 1, 10, 15, and 21), as well as various warm-ups and theatre games (Appendix B). The presentations are offered about once a week to some school or agency in the region. Most audiences are middle school or high school students, though the troupe occasionally presents to older primary school or adult groups associated with a variety of other agencies. Scenes generally address various common social and health issues of early and mid-adolescence.

The troupe is composed of approximately eighteen young people ranging in age from fourteen to eighteen, who volunteer to participate and make a fair commitment of time and energy. A full cast consists of six seniors, six juniors and six sophomores, with three boys and three girls in each age group. The youngsters in the troupe are ethnically diverse, and are drawn from many different high schools in the county. The cast members have a range of experience, and stay in the troupe for an average of two years. The activity involves weekly rehearsals and acting in the performances. The improvised nature of much of the performances frees the actors from having to spend a lot of time on memorization and rehearsal, so the rehearsals are devoted instead to the development of team spirit, trust, improvisational skills and planning.

The presentations themselves generally require about three hours for travel, performance, interactive discussion, and occur usually after school, evenings or weekends.

Reflections has done over eight hundred performances and to date has had over one hundred cast members. The program held its first auditions in 1990 and has been going strong ever since. It has earned a wonderful reputation, educating the community and has provided a place for teens to come together and be creative and supportive of each other. It is a youth activity group that performs a community service—creating forums for talking about sensitive issues.

The traditional school year program starts up in September and ends in June. The group continues to perform during the summer, and since there are not as many cast members around, the time is used to integrate new members and get them ready for the Fall as well as to perform for places that the group normally does not get a chance to go to during the school year.

Funding for the program is mainly from the Bergen County Division of Family Guidance, Department of Human Services in Hackensack, New Jersey. They provide the director's salary, a place to hold the rehearsals, and the use of one of the county vans. The schools and agencies who book the program also make donations. The group also has occasionally held fund-raising events.

Rehearsal

The cast members attend a three-hour rehearsal once a week. (Further details of the rehearsal process are noted on the webpage supplement for this chapter.) Group rehearsals parallel what needs to happen on stage. Because the cast members improvise and do not use scripts, they need to trust each other and support each other while on stage. They need to be open to hearing each other's offers, bounce ideas off each other and integrate them into the scenes, giving and taking focus. An atmosphere is created in the rehearsal space for all of this to happen. The director empowers the entire group to work together and be there for each other. This process is evident in performances when the cast members support each other and help "save" the scene in the event that it needs saving (without the audience ever knowing the difference!). To illustrate the way rehearsals offer a skills-building and wholesome experience, consider a typical session:

"Focus!" shouts Darnell, age 15; the group star of the evening's rehearsal, reminding the entire cast that one person needs to speak at a time. "According to the commitment sheet, we only have three people signed up for the juvenile detention center show next Saturday; it would be great if we could get a few more!" Bonnie, age 16 says, "I really want to do that show but my mom has a dentist appointment. She could drive me there but I am going to need a ride home." Lauren, age 17, excited about having recently received her driver's license, offers, "I can drive you home, no problem!" The group applauds Lauren for stepping in to help. Darnell moves ahead to talk about the "missed cues" of the week.

Samantha, age 18, had signed up for last Wednesday's performance for the juniors and seniors at one of the local high schools—about emotional abuse in dating relationships. The county van was waiting at the meeting spot at the call time, and Samantha did not show up, nor did we hear from her that she was not coming. Samantha apologizes to the group, "I take responsibility for that and I am sorry. I guess I have a lot of stuff on my mind right now, college applications, my parents getting on my case, pressures at school and my so called 'friends' being real jerks. I know that this is no excuse for missing the show but I hope you understand." Justin, age 14, says, "We understand and if there is anything you want to talk about, we are here for you."

Staci, the director of Reflections adds, "it sounds like things are pretty overwhelming, what might you be able to do differently? How do the rest of you deal with situations that are similar in your own lives?" A discussion with the group ensues about responsibility and making commitments. Cast members share how they handle stress in their own lives.

"Let's create a scene" Staci says, "let's take a high school student who is overextended and involved with a lot of activities. What other characters do we need in this scene? What is the conflict in this scene? Where does this scene take place?" Cast members make their suggestions and volunteers run up to the performance space to improvise the scenario. Cast members are invited to "tag" into the different roles and keep the scene moving. When the spontaneity around this particular issue starts to dwindle, the scene is brought to a close. Staci invites the group members to share anything that they would like about this experience, either from one of the roles that they played or from their own observations. The group is now better prepared with material from their own lives in the event that they are asked to do a performance about teen stress. Perhaps it also helps those individual cast members deal with stress in their own lives more effectively.

Performance

Through improvisational theatre techniques, cast members educate and raise issues for the audiences on a wide range of topics. Topics for performances include peer pressure, dating, parent/teen conflicts, substance abuse, conflict resolution, prejudice, and much more. Any topic requested that is related to teens in some way is considered for performance.

Reflections reaches out to a variety of audiences, including middle schools, high schools, community groups, client groups, conferences, training programs, parent groups and combined parent/teen audiences. Considering the actual schedules of the students, eighteen has been found to be the optimum number of students for maintaining coverage for performances. The group performs during the school day, the evening, or on a weekend on an average of four times a month. Cast members perform on a rotating basis and are expected to work out their own arrangements with their schools if there is any time that is missed. It usually means that a cast member is absent for part of a school day every four to six weeks. Committing to this group means that there is an expectation that one will attend weekly rehearsals and attend one performance per cycle (which is made up of four shows). There is a daytime cycle running simultaneously with a night/weekend cycle. Schedules of performances are distributed a month in advance and the cast members sign up for the ones that they can make. They also need to commit to the rehearsal before the show. School letters are provided to the cast members when they join Reflections encouraging the schools to support their students in this community service by counting their time missed from school as an excused absence.

Performances often get booked a year in advance but the cast members themselves commit to these shows two weeks ahead of time, choosing the shows that are most conducive to their busy lives. Shows will work no matter how many people sign up for the show and all cast members who show up for a show are utilized. Cast members need to get to the meeting place and then the director transports them to the performance location and back to the meeting place following the end of the show. In the van ride to the show, cast members discuss who is playing what role, where the scene will take place, what the conflict is going to be and the learning points that need to be brought out in the dramatization.

Beginning the performance, the director tells the audience about the goals of the program in general and today's theme in particular, and a bit about dramatic improvisation. Meanwhile, the cast members form an opening tableau, a sort of living statue, representing some dynamic situation. Following this, typically both audience and cast members are led through an interactive warm-up with each other. This helps the audience and cast members to connect with each other and also serves to show how improvisation works.

For example, in the warmup called "gripes," each of the group members shares something that he or she dislikes. Simona shouts, "I really don't like it when my money gets stuck in the vending machine!" Norman yells, "I really don't like it when people judge me without even getting to know me." Kristopher shares, "I really don't like it when people think that I only eat rice and beans just because I am Hispanic!" They are conducted as if part of an orchestra. Whoever is conducting these gripes points to each cast member when wanting him/her to speak, and the volume can be raised or lowered and can be stopped at any point. This technique warms the audience up to wanting to express their own gripes, and the conductor gets the interactivity going by inviting audience members to participate in the griping. One audience member is called on at a time to offer this or that "pet peeve." Following this, cast members huddle on stage and each chooses one of the audience's gripes that he/she feels most connected with. The audience's gripes are restated expressively by the actors and this heightens the sense of interactive rapport. Even if audience members don't get their own gripe chosen, they still get to say it out loud and be heard.

The next segment of the performance consists of cast members improvising a scene relevant to the topic that has been requested. The facilitator, who might be the director, a student intern, or a long time cast member, tells the audience that the performers know "who" they are in the upcoming scene and "what" needs to happen but that the dialogue is not rehearsed. The scene is enacted and at a high point of conflict the facilitator shouts, "freeze" and the cast members begin to engage the audience in dialogue while remaining in character. They talk about what they are perceiving, what they are thinking about, and how they are feeling. Audience members ask questions, make comments and suggestions to the cast members who are trained to stay in role no matter what happens. No matter what the issue is, the characters need to be real and the cast is encouraged to "play for truth."

For example, after a bullying scene for 6th graders the facilitator says, "So tell us, Nick, what is it like to have done absolutely nothing while you watched your friend get picked on by the kids in the cafeteria?" Nick says to the audience, "I was afraid that they would start picking on me. I wanted them to stop but I just didn't know what to do. Do you have any suggestions?" A discussion then takes place with all of the characters. In this case, the students in role as the bully, the victim, and Nick, the innocent bystander, as well as the audience, all become part of the process. The issues in the scene are raised through discussion so that learning takes place for the audience as well as the cast members.

Audience members often suggest alternative ways for a character to behave. At times cast members will enact these ideas and other times, depending on how warmed up the audience members might be, they are invited on the stage with the cast to play one of the roles, dramatizing an alternative behavior. Through this process, audience members get educated and entertained at the same time. One or two more scenes will be improvised depending on the amount of time booked.

At the very end of the performance, the cast members come out of character, introducing themselves by sharing their name, age, school they attend, the length of time that they have been in Reflections and anything that they would like to say about the topics or themes that have come up during the performance. The audience is reminded that the cast members were acting and that the roles they played may or may not reflect their own attitudes, thoughts or feelings about the material. After the show, audience members often come up to greet the cast members and share how they were able to identify with the issues in the scene.

A variety of psychodramatic techniques are used to make the underlying psychological and social dynamics more explicit. For example, the *double*, in which one person acts as the living "voice over," shows what a character might be thinking and feeling, even if he or she isn't admitting it to the others in the scene.

Another technique acts as a kind of projective test for the audience. The actors may set up some players in a pose—the roles are established, but the nature of the conflict is not. The facilitator who speaks to the audience says, "Here we have a parent and teen. What conflict do you see going on here?" Audience members make suggestions, often projecting their own personal issues onto the characters. The cast members listen to what is being suggested and then begin to enact the scene. The process which follows, with the cast members staying in character, is the same as previously discussed.

A third approach involves Playback Theatre, as described in Chapter 1. Our group uses this format and its component techniques in rehearsal as well as performance, because it serves to bring group members closer to one another and provides a sense of deeper understanding into each other's lives. From this, they also develop a greater empathy for the roles they create on stage.

Selection, Joining, Integrating New Members

Reflections is a youth activity for those who are fairly healthy and mature enough to fulfill their commitments. It's not meant to offer therapy or help for troubled youngsters. As seniors graduate, they go off to college and leave the group, so there is an ongoing turnover of an average of four to six young people every year. Recruiting is informal, by word of mouth. One way involves current cast members recommending acquaintances who they think will be a good fit for the program. Another way comes from the performances. Teens come up afterwards, inspired by this approach to drama, and express their eagerness to join. Preference is given to freshmen who are at the end of their first year of high school, so as to ensure a longer period of involvement.

Sometimes Reflections will offer to do a workshop for a theatre class in a high school. The director has her antenna up for recruiting future members and will invite the participants to contact her if interested. "Improv Jams" have served to be a valuable recruiting technique. Every other month, on a weekend night, Reflections hosts a county wide event at which the cast members and teens in the community get together and interact in an evening of improvisational fun. The event is advertised in the local newspapers and cast members may invite personal friends. Teens mix, mingle and socialize, refreshments are served and the director and cast members teach improv skills, theatre games and exercises for everyone to try. Not only does this provide teens with a fun way to meet new people who share a common interest, but it stimulates interest in the future membership of Reflections. Finally, other than their intrinsic vitality, being a teenager in high school, and a readiness to make a commitment to the program, there are no prerequisites to be part of the group.

Program Rituals

In the Fall, the group goes on a wilderness trip led by an adventure-based counselor. Group members go through initiative, problem solving activities. Not only is it a fun and bonding experience for the cast, but the elements about teamwork provide metaphors that give the group a lot of mileage in the upcoming year. Other rituals include a holiday party, an end of the year party, an open show for family and friends, a reunion for which all of the alumni from the past and the current members of the group are invited to share with each other, play, improvise, do playback theatre and reminisce. It has been extremely beneficial to do some kind of an overnight trip in September or October so that connections amongst the group members form rather quickly. Upon leaving the group, rituals include such things as a Last Will and Testament, a Senior Spotlight and an individualized, interactive good-bye. Group members are encouraged to make entries in the legacy book, signed by former members of Reflections.

Mistakes and Learning

Mistakes have been made along the way and as a result, a lot of growth and learning has occurred. When this program first started, there were no specific performance requirements. There were some cast members who would perform at most shows and other cast members who only wanted to attend rehearsals, but did not want to make the commitment to doing many performances. Over time, this built up resentment amongst the cast members who were putting more time into the program. Out of this came the whole idea of having the performances occur in cycles, with each cast member doing an equal share. Those who could not make the commitment as outlined would not be allowed to be part of the program.

Through experience, the director of this program learned to empower the cast members to take on more and more responsibility for themselves as a group. This included such things as deciding who was going to bring in snack for the next week, calling cast members to do shows if no one had signed up, and conducting orientations for every new member who came into the program. The more responsibility that the director "let go" the more the cast members grew, and so did the program! Granted, in doing it this way, things don't always go as perfectly, but that is just considered part of the learning process.

Two cast members serve as snack coordinators, four cast members on the communication team assure that there are cast members to perform at the shows, and orientation assistant volunteers explain the guidelines of the program to each new cast member. There are other roles in the group, too, such as group secretary and festivities coordinator.

At the end of one particular school year over half of the group members graduated. That fall, with half of the group being brand new, it was like starting all over again. A lesson learned was to make an effort to have an equal number of cast members per grade so that a fewer number of new cast members would need to be integrated each year. This way, new cast members rise very quickly to the level of the rest of the group in skill, commitment, and enthusiasm.

Every cast member returning to Reflections for the next school year schedules an individual session with the program director over the summer. During this session, goals are reviewed, commitment is assessed, and changes in the upcoming year are discussed. Cast members are encouraged to make suggestions to the program. Strengths and things to work on are discussed with the cast member so as to actively involve him/her in the learning process.

Because the cast is usually comprised of teens who are very busy and actively involved in many extra-curricular activities, there needs to be a balance between being flexible enough with their attendance to rehearsals and performances and consistent enough so that they are making a substantial commitment to this program to ensure the program's success. This is a tricky thing to figure out. Group members have a certain amount of absences that they can use over the year. However, in order for them to perform in a show and have it count for them as part of the cycle requirement, they need to attend the rehearsal prior to that particular show. This helps the group members who are performing in a particular show feel more connected and warmed up to each other as having just recently worked together at the last rehearsal.

Variations

There are other kinds of groups who do similar work. Some employ improvisational techniques while others use scripted material, often coming out of an improvisational process. Some might use a technique where at a planned moment in the script, the audience is asked to vote on a particular ending that they would like to see and then the actors will enact that ending (already rehearsed ahead of time). Some use volunteer teens or adults and others use professional adult actors. Some groups focus only on one topic, such as AIDS education, while Reflections' performances address many different kinds of issues. Reflections keeps its performers in "character" as they dialogue with the audience following the enactment; in contrast, some other groups have the actors introduce themselves afterwards, and then they dialogue with the audience as themselves. Therapy groups can use these techniques in performances for audiences. There are some troupes whose actors, as part of their own healing process, will share their own stories for audiences, opening themselves up to questions and feedback.

Summary

Reflections is a program that empowers youth to educate others through the use of improvisational theatre. Working together as a team, the group members can deliver the best possible performances. To make this work soar as well as to have the teens feel comfortable taking risks with each other, it is essential to create a safe space for them to explore the issues for presentation. Empowering the teens to take responsibility as members of this program facilitates their developing their leadership potential and sense of self. The director needs to trust the process of this work. For the director, training in groupwork, action methods, and improvisation is strongly recommended.

References

See webpage supplement, <www.interactiveimprov.com/reflectionswb.html>, and references in related Chapters 10, 25, and Appendices A & B.

Chapter 7

CULTIVATING A PRESENCE IN A COMMUNITY THROUGH APPLIED THEATRE

Mecca Burns

As this book attests, theatre can be applied in many ways in a community. In this chapter I will show how a single organization, the Presence Center for Applied Theatre Arts, addresses a broad range of needs in Charlottesville, Virginia. *Presence* is a collective of theatre artists whose varied backgrounds combine to produce an abundance of projects and programs. In our approach, applied theatre is meant to encourage a conscious link between social change and personal change.

The name, "Presence," derives from our experience that drama can foster a sense of wonder and willingness to feel deeply, be moved, and still remain compassionately available. This applies whether the dramatic process allows a single child's fantasy drama to unfold or assists an entire neighborhood's untold history to emerge. Instead of a specific agenda on what should happen, we draw on a wide array of methods with which to respond to each unique situation, allowing for modification and innovation by the participants.

Background

Presence was incorporated in 2002, when the four founders were members of a local Playback Theatre troupe (see Chapter 1). Over many years each of us had integrated theatre arts with education, therapy, social activism and other endeavors. Two of us, Mecca Burns and Brad Stoller, especially valued our training with Augusto Boal and other teachers of the Theatre of the Oppressed (see Chapter 21). We decided to pool our backgrounds and expertise to reach a wider range of groups in our community and use approaches that seemed outside the domain of Playback Theatre.

Rather than signing people up to become members of Presence, we more often link with individuals and groups around certain projects. This creates a flexibility that encourages people to be involved to the degree that fits for them. In the process, we have crossed paths with many people and groups that we might not have otherwise.

Funding

Although we feel rewarded by the fun, artistic fulfillment, personal growth, and the satisfaction in contributing to the community, some of us do make a living through this work. Our funding generally comes from a variety of sources, including honoraria, grants, tickets for events, and class fees.

When we offer workshops and performances to schools, universities, libraries, social agencies, or other organizations, we generally negotiate an honorarium or stipend to compensate the time spent planning and implementing the program. These have ranged from $50 to $7500. If the need is great and the project is interesting, we may work on a pro bono basis. We seek grants for long-term projects (e.g., the Charlottesville Living History Initiative) which benefit the community as a whole. A state humanities foundation, a local community foundation, and a foundation set up by our local superstar band have all provided funding. Some grants require tax-exempt status, and for those we have been sponsored by The Little Red Cap, a nonprofit organization directed by a Presence member.

Tickets are sold for public performances, and a fee is charged for adult classes such as *Contact Improvisation* and *The Embodied Voice*. We have been known to barter for home-grown vegetables and other goods and services. Once we co-led drama therapy groups with a psychotherapist who accepts Medicaid payments for group therapy. For those who would benefit from our classes but can't afford them, we created a Drama Scholarship Fund community grant. We endeavor to work things out.

In general, we are sustained financially by our willingness to apply theatre to whatever needs arise in our community. Unquestionably, our best marketing strategy is building relationships over the years, cultivating a steadfast, long-term presence in the community. Our main publicity is through word of mouth.

Programs

When theatre is applied to social issues, each situation warrants a unique approach. Some groups are eager to jump up and join in; others prefer to sit back and witness the event. Some audiences are too large or unruly to be interactive on their feet; the space is too small; or there are disabilities to consider. Sometimes the location is outdoors where it may be hard to hear, so the troupe makes use of mimed actions, signs, and even giant puppets. There are always ways to make it work, and planning can be an incredibly fun, creative part of the whole process.

Over the years, we have led interactive theatre workshops for numerous groups, including social studies teachers, secretaries, college students, foster parents, and peace activists. We work with each organization to vividly define the purpose of the workshop. Whether it is to bring history alive through drama, to develop leadership, to decrease burn-out in the social services, to delve into issues of race and identity, or to explore conflict within an organization, we enjoy rummaging through our wide array of tools to design a workshop that fits the specific needs. These workshops typically run from one to three hours and involve 5–25 participants.

Long before we incorporated as Presence, we had found ways to translate people's feelings and life experiences into drama. During the 1980s we worked in psychiatric hospitals, creative drama classes, and a residential setting for the mentally handicapped. In the 1990s we began to focus more on social justice issues, devoting attention to indigenous cultures, environmental education, gender equity, and leadership development. Please see the webpage supplement to this chapter for descriptions of these.

Recent Projects and Productions

Since 2004, we have rented a studio in an artists' cooperative in downtown Charlottesville. At any given time, we may have several projects going on, led by different people. Some examples include workshops and performances on foster care; teacher training workshops; or adventures in street theatre. These will be described briefly, as well as the ongoing drama therapy groups for children with special needs which provide consistent revenue. Then I will go into more detail about the Charlottesville Living History Initiative, a larger project.

"Just Before the Dawn"/Foster Forum. In 2003 we were commissioned to write and produce a play for a faith-based foster/adoptive care agency in Memphis, Tennessee. The executive director contacted us through the National

Association for Drama Therapy because they wanted something that was entertaining but also dealt sensitively with issues of child abuse. We performed for an audience of over 800 people in lieu of a traditional keynote speaker at a fund-raiser.

Here at home we had led several Playback/Forum Theatre workshops on the foster care system, and some of us had personal experiences to draw on. To develop the piece, we consulted with foster parents and social workers who shared their stories and suggestions. The cast met several times to improvise with this material, using drama therapy techniques to help the characters come to life.

We ultimately created a 45-minute multi-media theatre piece in which "a father who has lost touch with his young son confronts his own past and finds his soul." The dialogue was supported by live singing, an original music and sound effects score, and shadow-action dance, through which we witness the main character's inner struggles. The characters included a deadbeat dad protagonist, a dedicated foster mother who is also a gospel singer, a shady music promoter-friend who shares secrets of the past, a social worker who is a "survivor" herself, and—presented through a recorded voice and lighting effects—, the spiritual presence of the protagonist's grandmother.

While the audience in Memphis was too large to be interactive, we have performed the play several times closer to home for foster parents and caseworkers. We conduct a brief *talk-back* in which the actors stay in role while the audience asks them questions—a technique also called *hot seating*—, or we add Playback Theatre so that audience members can share their own experiences.

Applied theatre productions are often brought to wherever the audience is, and therefore require ingenuity and resourcefulness in lighting and staging. Often we can't even get into the space until just before the show. Yet even if we experience a tech nightm>are, these audiences seldom notice. They are captivated by watching their lives reflected on the stage.

"The Dramatic Moment"—Teacher Training. In Charlottesville we have been asked to train teachers of all age levels to use drama to ignite students' interest in academic subjects. In 2002 we developed a teacher-training workshop called *The Dramatic Moment* to help middle and high school teachers vitalize a social studies curriculum. We adapted our usual repertoire of theatre games and improvisational techniques toward the goal of bringing historical events to life. We used Process Drama methods (as discussed in Chapter 9), with the teacher guiding the class to invent an imaginary world in which they are reporters, health workers, or scientists, investigating a real life problem.

We have been inspired by the Living Newspaper productions which originated in Europe in the 1920s and similar efforts in the USA in the 1930s with the WPA's Federal Theatre Project. These programs addressed topics such as housing, labor unions, racism and public utilities, and were staffed by WPA-sponsored reporters, writers, actors, designers, and crew members. Today, the live dramatic action in this documentary theatre form can be supported by digital technology, weaving in historical, images, songs, speeches, and sound effects.

We have worked in college classrooms on issues of race and identity, using Playback Theatre and Image Theatre (from the Theatre of The Oppressed). For example, participants in a Latin-American History class constructed living sculptures (i.e., "tableaux), using their own bodies to first depict the actual situation of race relations in North American society, then how race relations might someday be. The professor's goal was to supplement the class readings with the power of nonverbal expression to enhance the students' lived experience of race relations.

Street Theatre: On several occasions, Presence has joined with our local Peace and Justice Center to engage the public on a larger scale, addressing issues of militarism and global economic exploitation. We may raise a little money for supplies, but these events are volunteer-driven, for the expression of political sentiments.

We spent time in the Lab exploring our own relationship to these issues, and planning non-violent action through theatre. One of our original members, James Yates, PhD, has been the creative force behind most of these enactments. At a demonstration protesting the 2003 invasion of Iraq, some of us became characters at a macabre "cocktail party," wearing ghoulish masks and filling glasses with blood-red liquid poured from oil cans, under speech-bubble signs that read "No Blood for Oil" and other slogans.

On "Buy Nothing Day" we marched down a major highway, in role as part of a madcap parade, a horde of hypnotized "shoppers" wielding shopping carts, wearing bar-code-emblazoned T-shirts and pinwheel sunglasses. This followed a morning of Invisible Theatre—another Theatre of the Oppressed technique—at a newly-sprouted merchandise outlet where we posed as compulsive shoppers.

On Earth Day we became myopic scientists who capture and measure a twelve-foot long fish puppet while giant animal puppets sang a song of mourning. And one year, Charlottesville's annual Dogwood Parade featured a new contingent: Americans for Peace and Justice. This included characters playing "Mom" proffering apple pie, a marching band, Uncle Sam and Lady Liberty on stilts, and signs with quotes advocating peace by famous Americans.

Children with Special Needs. I personally make my living mostly as a drama therapist, providing weekly drama groups for children with developmental and emotional issues. The program is called "The Art of Friendship," and focuses on strengthening interpersonal skills. Through the vehicle of improvisational fantasy play, kids play characters and stories that they love. Strongly influenced by David Read Johnson's *Developmental Transformations* and Stanley Greenspan's *Floortime*, we follow the children's own creative impulses to shape dramatic vignettes that metaphorically express the realities of their lives while they interact with others in the room. The drama groups are very small and individualized, generally 2–4 children.

We offer weeklong programs in July for children both with and without disabilities. The ambience of summer infuses the groups with a spirit of pleasure and relaxation. We transform our studio into a setting for magic with a network of cords to suspend fabric and structures for climbing, swinging and crawling. Children can conjure an ocean, a forest, a cave or a castle to delve into. A physical therapist assisted the first summer, and we have also imported a sculptor, a dance therapist, a music therapist and an African drummer. In addition, we have been blessed with a wealth of teen volunteers who bring the ratio of helper to child down to 2:1 or even 1:1.

This year we have been hired by special education programs to provide drama therapy for high school students with emotional and behavior issues and learning disabilities. We utilize theatre games, Image Theatre, Process Drama, or Developmental Transformations.

The Charlottesville Living History Initiative: Housing, Education and Racism

The goals of the Living History Initiative are to utilize theatre and the arts to increase public awareness of the history of our small southern city, to give citizens a role in the process of interpreting this history, and to encourage involvement in our community's decision-making process. When we began the project, we expected to devote ourselves to it for about a year. However, once we began excavating the psychosocial infrastructure of our city, we realized it was a long-term commitment.

As a group of mostly white theatre artists, we wished to reach across the racial barriers that seem so intractable in our city. It is a conundrum for us because we feel a need to address these issues that affect us all, yet there is a climate of wariness around white involvement. From the start we sought guidance from black colleagues and citizens on the best course of action, but we constantly found ourselves thrust back into a leadership role. After all, we were the ones who had initiated the process, and people expected us to be specific about what we were trying to do before they decided whether to get involved. At least one thing seemed clear: Vinegar Hill was a natural place to begin.

In the aftermath of the "urban renewal" that took place in many cities in the 1960s, vital stories were buried along with the trauma of displacement. Charlottesville's lost neighborhood was known as Vinegar Hill, and its full-scale demolition inflicted a wound that has never healed. In January, 2004, we staged a reading of a play titled *Vinegar Hill*, written several years earlier by Teresa Dowell-Vest. We mailed invitations to former residents, pastors, and community workers, which we followed up with phone calls. The event consisted of the play, a slide show of photographs of the neighborhood in the 1950s, a supper buffet, and Playback Theatre. The emotions stirred by the play and the slides found expression as our troupe improvised enactments of the stories that were unearthed. Heroic deeds were recounted that had never received full recognition. The rapt attention of the audience was like a healing balm that let the tellers of the stories feel heard in a deeper way.

The abovementioned event was the culmination of several months of planning. We conducted extensive research on the history of Vinegar Hill and made contact with dozens of individuals and organizations. We created a backdrop for the performance which doubled as an installation at the art center, containing vintage photographs, news articles, interactive maps, audio recordings of oral history interviews, and a tape recorder to allow visitors to record their own memories and reactions.

In this theatrical means of documenting local history, it helps if all audience members feel represented in the cast. When we first performed Playback after *Vinegar Hill*, I remember the chilly atmosphere that presided in the room. The ice was broken after the first *moving fluid*, when the actress in the front of the cluster gestured and spoke the word "NO!" with quiet passion. Gradually, I felt the suspiciousness dissolve, especially in later humorous scenes when the racially-mixed crowd laughed together.

We performed *Vinegar Hill* again for Juneteenth, a national annual celebration of the end of slavery. Next we were invited to participate in The Charlottesville African-American Cultural Arts Festival. The Festival's promoter had seen a play online called *Now Let Me Fly* by Marcia Cebulska, being staged nationwide to commemorate the fiftieth anniversary of the Supreme Court "Brown vs. Board" decision that launched the process of racial integration. We performed in a historically black school where we had once created a Living Newspaper on black history. *Now Let Me Fly* reminded me of a Living Newspaper, with evocative images from the Civil Rights Movement projected as a backdrop.

Producing this play proved to be an amazing catalyst for community involvement. The mostly black cast was composed of people of all ages and from all walks of life. Since it was a staged reading, the time commitment was much less demanding. Several hundred people attended the event.

We originally planned to follow the play with Playback Theatre, to allow us to reference Charlottesville's own history of "Massive Resistance" (i.e., a state mandated attempt to block desegregation). During the rehearsal process, though, we realized this was premature. The actors were accustomed to scripts, and we hesitated to impose our improv values. We made a mental note to begin workshops on improvisation, and began offering them that fall.

At one of these workshops we met Caruso Brown, a marvelous collaborator with whom we have now written and directed three original plays. He is the drama director and playwright for a large, socially-active black Baptist church attended by several of the actors. Our first presentation, *The Living Classroom*, was produced that winter to commemorate schools and schoolteachers in the segregation era. We performed in the original black high school for a distinguished audience—the alumni who had attended the school in the 1940s and 1950s before it closed.

In 2005 and 2006, we produced original plays for the African American Festival. Both plays reflected community issues that had generated endless debate and ongoing animosity. The 2005 play, *The Project*, was a multimedia theatre piece on the current school achievement gap and its historical underpinnings. Two high school girls, one African-American and one Caucasian, are assigned to a history project, "School Desegregation and its Legacy." Working together becomes a struggle for them until elders in the community teach them about the historical forces that shape all of our lives. This play was indeed a metaphor for our experience in the Living History Initiative. Just like in the play, many of our assumptions have been challenged—including ones we didn't even know we held.

The 2006 sequel focused on the lack of affordable housing in Charlottesville. A housing crisis threatens to destroy the tenuous friendship built by our two young heroines, and the white girl's family tries to "help" in a way that is perceived as intrusive and patronizing. After the 30-minute play, we held a Forum Theatre process (described in Chapter 21), "jokered" by two black community leaders, newly trained in the method. Neither had witnessed Forum Theatre, but they had moral passion, fearlessness, understanding of the issues, and, in a word, "presence." Finally we were using interaction *and* improvisation, and really sharing the leadership. (More about the Living History Initiative may be found on the webpage supplement.)

As with the foster care work, and the children's drama group, we look to the participants to provide the content. We don't have to know all the facts ahead of time. Rather, we provide a process, a means of translating their ideas and emotions into artistic expression.

Training and Staff Development: Presence Lab

What helps to integrate all this, and provide stability, is a process that's invisible to the public eye. For several years we have conducted a weekly Presence Lab, where we transform the raw materials of voice, movement and story into creative experimentation. If presence was a tree, the roots would be our influences, the fruits would be our projects, but the trunk would be the Presence Lab.

A weekly lab is a chance to experiment, to explore innovative ideas and play with new forms. Sometimes a member will want to try out a structure they've dreamed up before using it with another group. Sometimes we use the lab to "workshop" a theatre piece or script. More than simply rehearsing, we use techniques derived from drama therapy and other approaches to flesh out the characters' motivations. Often we spend time on interpersonal concerns, applying the same techniques to ourselves that we might offer to another organization. For example, when planning a workshop on conflict for our local Peace and Justice Center, we first explored the conflict within our own group and how it could be channeled more fruitfully.

In the Lab, we used drama techniques in our early visioning sessions, when faced with the task of writing a mission statement. We turned it into a kind of game. Each person took a turn moving in response to another person's stream-of-consciousness rant about what our mission should be, while a third person witnessed and took notes. Another day we enacted a timeline in the room to envision where we hoped our organization would be in five years. Yet another time, we constructed Presence as a living organism, with each of us playing a vital function: skin, arms, digestive system, brain, blood.

Once we amused ourselves by applying theatre to the infamous defense mechanism of *projection*, noting that it might be fun to treat this troublesome tendency in a playful manner. In real life, when someone asks, provocatively, "Why are you so controlling?" the one accused usually denies it. In this game, he or she takes on the projection, accepting the "offer" (a term used in improv), and playfully exaggerates it: "How *dare* you speak to me that way! Guards, seize him!!"

One of the most useful forms we have developed in our Presence Lab is something we call Personal Myth. The protagonist begins to narrate her story, while the other players instantly portray each person, object and feeling she describes. As the protagonist delves deeper, she begins to really taste the promise of drama. It is a bit like lucid dreaming. There is a moment when she realizes, "Wait a minute! This is theatre—I can make whatever I want happen!" She discovers that she can use the other players to enact her worst fear or her most fervent wish, and to notice her own response.

We spent the last year of the Lab focusing on Developmental Transformations. We sponsored a workshop led by a teacher from New York City which helped people who hadn't trained in the form.

Today, Playback Charlottesville has evolved to fill many of the functions the Presence Lab originally served. We are constantly discovering ways to bridge Playback with other approaches, especially Theatre of the Oppressed, and, currently, Marshall Rosenberg's *Nonviolent Communication* approach and Ruth Zaporah's *Action Theatre*. These innovations bear fruit in our ongoing relationships with a women's prison and a group of homeless men, as well as occasional public performances.

What transpires in the Lab and our rehearsals is emotionally, physically and intellectually invigorating. Through this exploratory play, we discover what it is that binds all our work together.

Summary

A theatre company can function as a collective whose members share resources and assist each others' endeavors. Over the years we have tenderly cultivated relationships with many local organizations—social agencies, churches, schools, and other groups. When there are cultural barriers, it takes a particularly long time for trust to build; in fact, it is a lifelong process. We believe the arts can play a vital role in reaching people on a deeper emotional and aesthetic level.

Further References and Associated Methods on the webpage supplement to this chapter: <www.interactiveimprov.com/presencewb.html>

SECTION II

APPLICATIONS IN EDUCATION

Adam Blatner

There continues to be an expectation that young children will perform for audiences, memorize lines, and rehearse plays. The *Peanuts* cartoon children illustrate this on their now-classic Christmas television special as they suffer through the preparations and anticipations of their Christmas pageant. Winifred Ward, the pioneer of creative drama in the United States, specifically warned against pushing children to perform for outside audiences as early as the 1920s, and more, offered a more wholesome alternative: Have the children enjoy drama just for themselves as a process rather than as a product.

Alas, as youngsters grow older, there are general expectations again that the dramatic impulse be channeled into traditional theatre forms. For those who enjoy this as a special activity, that may be fine, but what about the great majority of children who used to enjoy make-believe and feel they have to give it up unless they commit themselves to specialize? It's like asking people to give up singing unless they take on ever-more-complex and demanding forms of musical performance! The arts should be developed so that in addition to those who want to specialize to a high degree, able to perform and even compete, there are many more who deserve to enjoy the rich heritage of drama and the other arts at a simpler and more participatory level.

In Chapter 8, the field of creative drama is presented, along with the use of role playing to explore problems and develop social and emotional skills. In Chapter 9, the idea that drama can be a tool for learning about other subjects, for exploring them as a kind of simulated situation. The advantage in this Process Drama approach is that this experiential mode of education also integrates a range of interests and abilities, critical analysis and creative problem-solving, social skills, imagination, and often an interdisciplinary mixture of science, arithmetic, reading, history, political science, and so forth.

Another way of challenging youngsters is to have a troupe of actor-teachers present a problem situation and then interact with the class in exploring creative solutions. This Theatre-in-Education method is especially important in a culture that is recognizing the need for the development of social and emotional skills. The challenges of countering cultural pressures for premature involvement with sexuality, drugs, bullying, racism and other forms of prejudice, violence or intimidation in dating relationships, all these are also tied up with health issues as well, and people are becoming increasingly aware of the need for these kinds of programs in the schools.

John Dewey and others almost a century ago were noting that the best learning is experiential, learning by doing. Drama offers the natural vehicle for this kind of learning, especially as learning is recognized as encompassing more than the mere acquisition of dry facts. In an era of information overload, the skills of how to interact with information so that one can manage oneself in this complex world requires a balancing of both sides of the brain. Again, drama is the pedagogic method of choice, involving youngsters while offering the intrinsic motivation of challenge mixed with fun.

Chapter 8

CREATIVE DRAMA AND ROLE PLAYING IN EDUCATION

Adam Blatner

This chapter introduces readers to two ways of using drama in education—creative drama and role playing. Creative drama is used widely in schools and other areas to develop the basic skills involved in theatre arts with emphasis more on improvisation and less on the production of plays for audiences. Role playing is used in classrooms and other educational contexts (such as in the training of physicians, managers, and various other professionals), for purposes of promoting empathy and developing and practicing skills in communications and problem-solving.

Creative Drama

In schools, creative drama is used to help youngsters to explore, develop, express, and communicate ideas, concepts, and feelings through dramatic enactment. Creative drama involves, among other things, those activities in which people are helped to expand the repertoire of roles they can play and develop skills in playing creatively and expressing those roles. While it has been used mainly for children between the ages of four and twelve, there are also many ways of adapting creative drama for teenagers, adults, and the elderly.

Some creative drama remains focused on working improvisationally, but many teachers also consider the process to include the use of stories. At first the children just use the general plots and are encouraged to improvise on the rough plot line. Later, they may engage in playmaking in which the youngsters are helped to devise their own plot and script, perhaps as a way of dramatizing themes in their own lives. Finally, creative drama, in its broadest sense, has expanded to include many of the activities mentioned in this anthology which is why one of the foremost writers in the field, the late Prof. Nellie McCaslin, expanded the title of her classic textbook so that her last edition, finished just before she passed away, is "Creative Drama in the Classroom *and Beyond.*" (The first edition was published in 1968, and went through a total of eight editions; this last, in 2005, has many useful references. Professor McCaslin's thoughts about this chapter may be found on the webpage supplement: <www.interactiveimprov.com/mccaslinwb.html>)

History

Creative drama has two general foundations, one in the USA, the other in England. Those in England, mainly beginning with the pioneering work of Peter Slade in the 1940s and 1950s, generally formed the foundation for the work described in Chapter 9 on Process Drama. Beginning in the 1980s, though, increasing areas of cross-fertilization began to blend elements from both traditions. In the United States, after there being a few precursors including those influenced by the educational philosophy of John Dewey, the main early pioneer was the educator, Winifred Ward. Her major publications about creative dramatics were in the late 1920s through the 1930s. Ward's books and direct influence inspired many followers who have added their own modifications, such as Ruth Beall Heinig, Geraldine Brain Siks and the aforementioned Nellie McCaslin. These pioneers developed Ward's basic ideas, added more improvisational elements, and also published textbooks that found widespread use.

Beginning as a teacher of creative drama with children in the 1930s, Viola Spolin began to develop improvisational exercises, "theatre games." She was influenced by Neva Boyd's writings about children's games and adapted these as opportunities for improvisation. These began to become popular in the 1960s and spread more widely in the 1970s and thereafter. In part this was because her son, Paul Sills, was active in developing improvisational comedy as a drama form in Chicago, as described in the Foreword to this book, and improvisation has continued to develop as a growing element in contemporary theatre.

Increasingly, not only creative drama teachers but also middle school and high school drama teachers began to incorporate theatre games as a component in actor training. These activities helped actors young and old to become far more mentally, physically, and emotionally flexible. (This was also a major goal of Moreno, beyond his interest in the therapeutic applications of psychodrama!)

The field continued to evolve. In the 1970s, the term "creative dramatics" was renamed "creative drama" because the term "dramatic" tended to suggest the goal of expressing what would today be considered overly-dramatized emotions. The emphasis was more on recognizing the theatrical dynamic of living as-if and heightening imaginativeness. The activities could also express rather subtle nuances of feelings or more thoughtful role-taking experiences.

(A similar tension has emerged in the realm of improvisational comedy: While many troupes go for what's called the "gagg," emphasizing the broader and sometimes more ribald elements of comedy, other groups are more intrigued with the process of exploring a situation, seeing how the creativity can keep evolving interesting possibilities.)

The intellectual foundation for using drama in education in general is more fully discussed by Richard Courtney's more recent books, as noted in the general bibliography in Appendix A.

Methods

Some school programs prescribe a certain amount of drama development, especially in the elementary years, because there is a recognition of the values of creative involvement. It is often mixed with other arts activities, including movement, music, mime, puppetry, artfully designing costume elements, flags, and so forth.

A program might begin with simple imagination exercises that help participants to attend to stimuli arising from within rather than without. There are many adults, products of traditional education and the barrage of major media, who have become somewhat numb to this source. They might find it life-enhancing to reclaim their imaginations. (A further discussion of the cultural inhibitions to drama may be found on the webpage supplement: <www.interactiveimprov.com/inhibitions2drama.html>

There are thousands of games, warm-ups, and other exercises that have been developed for different age levels and degrees of experience. Appendix B has an annotated bibliography of various resources, books and CD-Roms with exercises that help promote self-expression, broaden communications beyond just talking, and open participants to becoming more conscious of their potential range of nonverbal communications.

Creative drama attends to identifying the elements of story, analyzing the problems involved, and considering alternative solutions. In this way, it contributes to the infrastructure of critical thinking skills. There is also a playful way of addressing a variety of behavioral problems, helping children to re-focus themselves in more constructive ways.

Gradually, more complex skills are developed, integrating play, pantomime, puppetry, mask making, and creating a plot or story line. At this point, some drama teachers move towards creating the kinds of scripted and rehearsed drama that can be presented to others. Others stay more with improvisation, exploring further variations with process. Adding the dimension of poetry, and dramatizing these elements, becomes a way of teaching literature and helping youngsters to be sensitized to the richness inherent in language.

Expressive drama skills should be recognized not just as a foundation for doing theatre, but for many challenges of adult life—from giving toasts at weddings to engaging in political debates. It is shameful and unnecessary that the prospect of having to speak in public should be considered by many as one of the most feared predicaments. While the contents of the talk may be addressed in social studies or management classes, it is useful to develop the skills of managing one's voice, gaze, and other performance elements. As it stands, increasing numbers of young people seem to have lapsed into a remarkable degree of inarticulateness and lack of clarity in speech. Furthermore, popular music subtly implies that a strong, unintelligible dialect is cool.

In addition to helping lay the foundation for greater success in many adult vocational and avocational roles, the development of dramatic skills also fosters success in extensions, other types of performance, story-telling, and theatre.

The Need for Drama in Education

Finally, we must note that in increasing numbers of school systems, arts and drama classes are being squeezed out in order to "teach to the tests" imposed by national standards programs. This trend should be resisted. It is important to advocate for the practicality of arts education in our own age. In global competition, what we need most is the capacity for creativity. This requires the integration of right and left cerebral hemispheric functions, intuition and imagination as well as straight reason, emotional sensitivity and material practicality (Pink, 2006). This more balanced capacity must be cultivated through a more balanced curriculum.

Role Playing in Education

Although role playing has a little overlap with creative drama, its method derives more from Moreno's psychodrama and is then integrated with other drama in education approaches. It can also be used itself in addressing the more relevant social issues young people face nowadays, and in the service of developing social and emotional learning. More specific goals include those of helping students develop greater understandings of situations and the feelings of the people involved. Role playing also offers an experiential vehicle for developing skills in communicating, problem-solving, and self-awareness (Blatner, 1995).

Role playing may be used to explore the real problems in young people's lives—not so much the problems of the individuals so much as the problems of general groups or types of people. In that sense, it is like sociodrama (discussed in Chapter 15), and in its interest in general issues, it also has similarities in scope with Theatre in Education and the Theatre of the Oppressed. The point being made is that enactments can tend to slide into being more like personal psychodramas and this tendency should be resisted. When role playing brings out the cultural and social assumptions and attitudes involved in a situation, the method is closer in spirit to sociodrama. However, in general, role playing is concerned with finding more effective solutions, while sociodrama would give less attention to the problem-solving—especially regarding how an individual might best respond.

I envision a reality television show that includes a measure of role playing in which participants can be helped to step back from their situation and reflect on the way they're playing their part. With this opportunity, plus feedback from others, participants consider other ways of more effectively responding and set up opportunities to try out these new responses. As it stands, so many situation comedies, soap operas, and reality shows seem to depend on the subtle and slightly sadistic enjoyment of watching people compound their mistakes and make their predicament worse. What if the goal were to explore ways of responding to a situation in the most uplifting fashion, aspiring to the noblest values?

Role playing is even more effective when used with older students, in high school and college. It has already begun to be an established training method for professionals and people in business and organizations.

History

Role playing was used in schools in the 1940s and 1950s by J. L. Moreno (see the chapter on psychodrama) as well as a few students (Haas, 1955). In the 1960s, Shaftel wrote a book on its applications in education. Other associates grasped the idea and developed applications in business (Shaw, Corsini, Blake & Mouton, 1980). This is further discussed in Chapter 13.

The idea of teaching psycho-social skills as well as other subjects has been around for a while. In the 1970s, it was called "Affective Education," or teaching "values." The problem was that more traditional parents saw this as overlapping with religious education and serving a secularist agenda. Therefore, there were political resistances to such programs. More recently, however, a few factors have been tipping the balance. There has been an increasing amount of research on social and emotional learning, and businesses are also recognizing the importance of more refined levels of maturity in the domains of interpersonal effectiveness. This, in turn, creates a greater demand from the business community for the inclusion of more psychological skill-building procedures in the curriculum. However, this trend is still needing more support to gain headway.

Another support for including the teaching of social and emotional skills is that interpersonal competence and personal maturation is needed to deal with increased media and peer pressures for the use of alcohol, drugs, sex, problems with bullying, prejudice, as well as coping with other problems of adolescence. While conventional approaches of instruction offer some information, the skills involved cannot be learned by sitting and listening passively to a teacher or reading a book. Rather, students learning a skill need to learn to feel their own bodies and minds in action—in standing up to another person, in practicing negotiations, in tolerating slight waves of shame that accompany making a mistake, not freezing, carrying on, improvising. Like learning to swim or ride a bicycle, interpersonal skills must be learned experientially. Role playing is the natural laboratory for this type of learning (Blatner, 1995; Shaftel, 1982). More recently, many people with backgrounds in psychodrama are applying these role playing methods in education internationally. In role playing, social, interpersonal, historical, and other kinds of situations are explored by setting up a situation and having students take the role of the people involved.

Alas, some teachers don't use the role playing method properly, and as a result, students can come to hate this approach. The most common error is the failure to warm the students up. Some teachers, naively thinking the process is simpler than it actually is, proceed with assigning roles and plunging students into an imagined situation. The students feel on the spot, anxious, confused and ashamed. They need the teacher to develop the situation and gradually warm them up to their roles. There is a real art to warming people up. The teacher and other classmates might interviewing them in role for a while, making the procedure playful and emotionally safer. (A simple exercise for warming people up is described on my website: <www.blatner.com/adam/pdntbk/talksho. htm>)

The key to role playing is to keep the tone easy so the players don't feel too much that they're on the spot. Improvisation is vulnerable to anxiety; beyond a small-but-tolerable level, and the creative juices just dry up. So the teacher has to have enough time and offer enough different kinds of warm-up exercises that are carefully designed to lead into the current problem to be examined.

In other words, those who object to role playing almost always report that what they witnessed or experienced, on further questioning, suffered from the director making this or similar mistakes. The teacher needs to be able to maintain a cheerful, positive, friendly, and gentle context. You can't scold people into opening to the subtle currents of spontaneity's dynamics.

Enact: A Program Using Role Playing in Education

In New York City, one of the more extensive programs is *Enact*. The program was founded and directed by Diana Feldman and staffed by over 50 actor-teachers working with thousands of students, teachers and parents in public schools every year in some of the city's most underserved communities. Ms. Feldman is a drama therapist, educator, and performer herself, and in her early experiences in theatre in the 1980s, she was impressed with the power of drama as a way to promote personal and social awareness. She began to work with some of the more difficult children, the "special populations" in the schools— i.e., developmentally delayed and autistic children who did not respond to traditional methods of teaching. Using nonverbal techniques, music, and role play, she found that these in modified form were relatively effective in reaching these kids. From this, Feldman began to work with children who had been labeled "at risk," youngsters with severe behavioral problems, who, without help, tended to drop out, become violent, or turn to substance abuse.

Enact hires professional actors from many ethnic backgrounds, picking talented people who have a good deal of spontaneity. After a good deal of training in the program's methods, they are matched with a community, a school in which the students can experience role models regarding ethnicity, race, religion, and so forth. These actor/teachers go directly into classrooms to conduct the role playing sessions, weave in theatre games, and then work with the teacher and students for weeks and sometimes even years. There is ongoing training for these teachers, coaching, and consultation. The program works from elementary through high school.

The method, developed by Feldman around 1987, involves a style of role play facilitation that meets resistance head on and bypasses it as a way to identify core issues for a group. A significant goal is that of helping the students identify unspoken feelings that are being expressed in inappropriate behavior. In doing so, the actor-teachers do a fair amount of ground work in both interviewing the teachers and counselors and doing a kind of role-playing-as-assessment. Feldman and her staff have been impressed with the pervasiveness of post-traumatic psychological dynamics that lead to a high level of both guardedness and a general distancing or flooding from emotion—and that distancing then makes it difficult for them to reconnect clearly with the core issues and respond more effectively. Feldman's specialized version of dramatic distancing and variations of what in psychodrama is called the "double technique" enables Enact's actor/teachers to help traumatized students identify their own feelings. This approach also offers a corrective emotional experience, letting the children know that there are adults who care about vulnerability and don't judge them for it; rather, they help everyone share in the reality that humans can be both tough and vulnerable.

For most schools, the arrangement has two actor/teachers going into the school and working with about three classes with about 30 kids in each class (thus dealing with around 90 kids a day. Sometimes there are two or three teams in a large school. Occasionally, twenty or more teams may be at different schools around the city. The program in 2005 had *Enact* working in fifty schools in the greater New York City area. Five of these had long-term contracts because of the needs of the children, and often required two or three teams each day plus an on-site social worker. There are also teams going to after-school programs.

Enact also offers a program closer to Theatre-in-Education with the actors performing a scripted and rehearsed small play, as a stimulus to discussion, for larger groups of 250–500 youngsters in an auditorium. The follow-up is in the larger group or, better, the actors go into classrooms to work with smaller groups. Sometimes the play is scripted according to material gathered from working with the kids as a dynamic focus group, and sometimes the play includes some of the youngsters themselves. The longer-term projects involve creative drama processes, starting with spontaneity training exercises. These then move more toward playmaking, generating an informal production with the kids as actors.

For example, after the tragedy of 9/11/01, the attack on the twin towers, *Enact* toured the schools with a play called "Finding the Words," a docudrama about six kids who had to evacuate their school. Because the themes were so powerful, it was decided to have adult actors playing the parts of the children; if the youngsters themselves had to play it, we thought the feelings would be too overwhelming. This technique provided more _role distance._ To refine their roles, the actors listened to tape recordings of the younger kids in order to capture their current slang and voice tone. They also had some of the children in their programs serve as consultants to the playwright and director, which was good for the kids involved and made the play more authentic. This performance was well received by the teachers and other school aides as well as the children in the schools where it was presented. Discussions were used to follow-up.

Another play named "Cooked" grew out of the violence around sneakers at one of the schools in the Bronx. It toured the schools and will now be played off-Broadway for two nights.

Recognizing that many, if not most, of these kids are emotionally quite brittle, Feldman and her colleagues are cautious and meticulous in the way they do role playing, building in distancing techniques so the kids don't feel unduly exposed. For example, in a classroom, the actors might be the ones who play out the initial conflict—in a way reminiscent of both Theatre-in-Education and Boal's Forum Theatre, but in briefer vignettes and using more interactivity according to the size of the group. Naming the unspoken feeling is one of the goals. Often the situation portrayed is developed according to the needs of the group and the kinds of issues that were raised in the previous few days or weeks.

For example, after September 11th tragedy in New York, her teams were called in to work in classrooms to help students cope. Simple role playing is no panacea though. It must be modified, especially in addressing post-traumatic issues, so that the students don't become re-traumatized. For example, in dealing with the World Trade Center collapses, the scenes portrayed dealt with how fear and shock were coped with in other (more distanced) contexts. Consequently, when the actor-teachers set up a simple scene about someone being caught off guard on the street, the students immediately named the feeling and as they warmed up, they spontaneously discussed their feelings about the Sept 11th tragedy. They were allowed to participate at their own readiness level.

Another goal for the scene work is that of coping with the kinds of peer pressures that are commonly experienced by city youngsters. After helping students identify the core feelings, some of them are ready to participate, come up and replace our actors, and in role, practice new solutions.

A recent study commissioned by the Department of Education showed that the *Enact* program was one of the most successful programs in New York in preventing school dropouts. The program is also recognized as offering conflict resolution programs. Over the last x years, the program is estimated to have served over 100,000 students in the greater New York City region, and has been found to be useful in both special and general education classes. Finally, the program has begun to be used in teacher and parent training because it offers new and effective principles and techniques replacing the punishment-oriented habits of previous generations with a more constructive encouragement and problem-solving-orientation.

Summary

Creative drama is widely used in many schools as a way to build a range of skills associated with the artistic and expressive dimensions of enactment. Role playing is more focused on understanding situations and exploring different approaches for effectively coping, allowing for some rehearsal, refinement, and mastery of new skills. These approaches may be adapted for people of any age past early childhood, and in a wide range of situations. In other chapters, role playing techniques are applied in business, prisons, and so forth.

References

Many more references on website supplement: <www.interactiveimprov.com/creativedrama.html>

Blatner, Adam. (1995). Drama in education as mental hygiene: A child psychiatrist's perspective. *Youth Theatre Journal, 9,* 92–96.

Blatner, Adam. (2006). Role playing in education. Retrieved from website: <www.blatner.com/adam/pdntbk/rlplayedu.htm>

Blatner, Adam. & Blatner, Allee. (1997). Applications in education. In *The Art of Play: Helping adults reclaim imagination and spontaneity.* New York: Brunner/Mazel.

Feldman, Diana. (2003). *The Enact manual: A guide to conducting classroom workshops for social and emotional learning.* New York: Author: <www.enact.org>

Feldman, Diana & Sussman-Jones, Fara. (2000). Unwinding resistance and externalizing the unspoken: The 'Enact' method in the schools. In P. Lewis & D. R. Johnson (Eds.), *Current approaches in drama therapy.* Springfield, IL: Charles C. Thomas.

McCaslin, Nellie. (2006). *Creative drama in the classroom and beyond* (8th ed.). New York: Pearson/Allyn & Bacon. (1st edition, 1968.) (Many references, and edges into discussions about applications in working with problem kids. The most current and definitive text!)

Pink, Daniel. (2006). *A whole new mind: Why right-brainers will rule the future.* New York: Riverhead.

Shaftel, Fannie & Shaftel, George. (1982). *Role playing in the curriculum* (2nd ed.). Englewood Cliffs, NJ: Prentice-Hall. A revised edition of the authors' 1967 book, *Role Playing for Social Values.*

Chapter 9

PROCESS DRAMA IN EDUCATION

Gustave J. Weltsek-Medina

Process Drama is a major approach to drama in education, prominent in England and Canada, then spread to Australia and other countries around the world. Beginning in the 1990s, it began to be used more in the United States, integrated with creative drama (which is described in Chapter 8). In the creation of process drama, the teachers become facilitators or catalysts, while the students become co-playwrights, actors, and implicit audience all mixed together. During the unfolding series of enactments, students may exchange roles within a scene (similar to the technique of role reversal in psychodrama) or shift roles as they enter another scene.

In Process Drama, the teacher's involvement as a player in the drama is more prominent, and the goal may be the learning of subject matter—history, social studies, even science—using drama as a vehicle, or the exploration of issues like social justice and equity. The teacher and the students imagine a situation, and in many cases the teacher actually becomes one of the figures within that situation. If, in order to learn about both astronomy, physics, and group problem-solving, they play being on a space ship, while the teacher might not take the role of the pilot, she might "be" one of the engineers. The challenge is to allow the students to find themselves faced with making more decisions, and the teacher then becomes a combination of resource and fellow inquirer.

As another example, imagine a class addressing the historical issues associated with the American Civil War in the mid-19th century. The teacher says that the class members are members of President Lincoln's cabinet—and the teacher is also a cabinet member. They begin to discuss how to decide various predicaments at that time. In process drama, scenes can shift, so that in this example, the class might then segue (a shift of scene) from the President's Cabinet to a southern plantation and the predicament of a slave family facing the plight of one or more of its members being sold and taken away. Then in a following scene the class members might become members of a southern state legislature addressing the problems that might come up if uneducated slaves became free.

All kinds of subjects can be investigated in ways that make the subject matter more relevant, alive, and unforgettable. Situations can be creatively imagined that address the human dimensions of literature, language arts, math, history, science, and other subjects, as well as personal and social issues.

The term, "process drama" was popularized by Dr. Cecily O'Neill (1995), to contrast it with more traditional theatre approaches that are aimed at producing plays for an audience—what O'Neill called "product-oriented" drama. The point O'Neill makes is that the important learning is inherent in the *process of participation in drama itself*. It's not necessary to have any kind of "product" in the sense of a scripted play at the end, or a performance done for outsiders. (More about history and other elements on the webpage supplement: <www.interactiveimprov.com/procdrmwb.html>

This approach to interactive drama arose in England, out of the pioneering work of Peter Slade in the 1950s, Brian Way in the 1960s, and especially, from the work of Dorothy Heathcote and Gavin Bolton in the 1970s and continuing to the present. Other innovators in Australia and Canada, such as John O'Toole, Jonathan Neelands and David Booth, have also shared this general orientation.

Method

These improvisational explorations are based in the idea of creating *fictional worlds* where student/participants can problem-solve. The fictional worlds may involve a few students at a time or an entire class and might last anywhere from one class period to several days, weeks and even months. These improvisations create social interactions between students in role where moments of theatrical tension provide spaces where problems are posed. For example: a drama might be created where the students are part of a committee planning a local political campaign, the crew of an explorer's ship, or survivors on a desert island and are challenged to identify the various problems that arise in such situations and attempt to come up with solutions.

Process drama may be used to address problems in literature, history, social studies, political science, anthropology, and other humanities, and it can also be used to bring to life subject matter in math, science, and language. Also, in light of some postmodernist approaches that seek to promote a more culturally diverse perspective, many progressive educators engage students in drama explorations as a way to engage with issues of gender, race, sexual identity, bullying, drugs and alcohol, shoplifting and daily ethics. (Such themes are also addressed by the Theatre in Education and Social Activist drama programs mentioned in Chapters 6, 10, 21 and 25.)

Some teachers help the students question how power is exercised in groups and society and which groups are "marginalized"—that is, treated as if they weren't worthy of even being included in the discussion. For example, some books that approach drama in this way include Medina's (1999) work with sixth grade children of Mexican descent (see supplement and references), concerning issues associated with crossing the border into the United States; Warner's (2001) work with Native American Indian youth concerning the genocide of their people; and Grady's (2000) work with gender and race through drama.

A key concept in process drama terms is "experiential"—describing what happens during an experience as if it were happening to me and I am also making it happen" (Bolton, 1997). In role, students experience the situations and take responsibility for coping with them. Through explorations in drama, individuals experience problem-solving and through reflection they become aware of their ability to solve problems as they interact with others experiencing a common challenge.

As another example, a class might address a social or historical problem using the setting of an imagined courtroom, in which students take on various roles: prosecutor, defendant, defense attorney, and members of the jury. In a traditional theatrical production, the action would be made to approximate reality in many details, but since the goal of the drama in education is to think and learn, highly polished or rehearsed elements, the right costume, and so forth are only distractions. Courtroom scenes not only help students to appreciate more subtle ethical conundrums as they apply to the real feelings of the people involved, but they also teach about the complex issues that are part of the underlying realities of legal proceedings. Instead of continuing to think in the simplistic terms of good guys and bad guys that they pick up from the popular media, they're plunged into the predicament of dealing with people on both sides of the question who sincerely think they're right and can present plausible reasons for their positions. As a result, students gain more realistic problem-solving skills that can be applied in their actual lives.

In process drama, improvisation is used to create fictional worlds where participants take on roles answering who, what, when, where and why a character exists. Having no script to work from, as in production-centered theatre work, the character's traits, actions and justifications for actions are not predetermined or defined by an outside source. Rather it is the individual's life experiences that define each aspect of the role.

A typical process drama exploration may begin simply by asking the group, "What would you like to do a play about?" This is not mere permissiveness: Students are called to become more explicitly aware of themes that are relevant, and by naming them, compiling a list together, they warm up to their own priorities, become more clear about what is important and why. So, with that simple question, the class begins to compile a list of topics.

In one such discussion, perhaps the issue of bullying is brought up because of a recent incident involving students in the school. The facilitator then constructs the skeleton of the drama, focusing on creating access points for participants who add the vital organs to the fictional world.

Many explorations begin with introductory drama strategies containing basic elements of the topic to be explored—in the above case, bullying. These introductory strategies act as gateways into the creation of a larger fictional world. In this incident the teacher might ask the students to create a tableau or human sculpture depicting a physical representation of their feelings about bullying. The objective here is not to create a visual reproduction of the bullying moment, (pretending to punch someone's lights out, for example) rather the students are asked to create an image of their feelings about the bullying incident. The result of these emotional representations are usually very abstract sculptures with participants in contorted positions of rage and pain with facial features distorted into expression of fear, doubt and confusion. The human sculptures do not immediately force participants into embracing a fictional role. Instead it hits on the deeper personal relationship to the issue of bullying, through a relatively non-threatening exploration of making physical sculptures. The strategy serves dual purposes, introducing the topic of bullying and the concept of communication through play and drama using the body. When the instructor adds the idea of taking on a role the students are already in tune with the idea of pretend, improvisation and the emotional content that can be assessed for authenticity.

Basic Strategies

In the process drama literature, some basic strategies are noted below. (These are explained at greater length on the webpage supplement: <www.interactiveimprov.com/procdrmethodswb.html>, and the specific sections are noted in [ ] brackets.)

1. *Questioning* involves the initial posing of the problem, from which the issues to be addressed become the basis for the creation of a "fictional world," a situation to be dramatically enacted and explored. It also involves subsequent discussions in or out of role. [#quest.]

2. *Working "as if"* or "working in role": Immersing the students in the little details, so they are operating from within the predicament the opposite in a sense from reading a scene and "discussing" it. [#livthro]

3. *Problem-solving* is a way to begin and continue the drama by allowing issues to emerge from within the fictional world that require answers. For example in the drama developed around bullying, the issue of finding alternative responses to violence might come up. The group would necessarily explore scenarios in which non-violent routes are taken to solve the problem. [#probsolv]

4. *Teacher in Role* is an artful way for the teacher to be more of a facilitator, not a source to whom the kids turn for answers, but more of a bystander who asks provocative questions. Morgan and Saxton (1987) have identified nine roles a teacher may take within any one drama. One, for example, is the person who has been away and needs to hear what has happened. Another is playing the "second in command," which enables the teacher to say things or not, depending on what s/he feels the children need. (E.g., "Oh, I'm sorry, I'll have to refer that question to Dr. Rossi." or, "Well, that is what I have been told to tell you.")

5. *Reflection*: Here there is a great power in putting the action on hold for a time, pushing the "pause" button, calling "cut," or "freeze" and teacher and students temporarily step back from their role and take a look at what has been going on inside the fictional world.

These strategies, although containing very distinct elements, are used in conjunction with one another, as complementary parts of a whole. An in-depth explanation of several strategies in terms of their relationship to each theorist follows. (On the webpage supplement to this chapter, <www.interactiveimprov.com/procdrmethodswb.html> there are more detailed descriptions of the aforementioned methods.)

Strategic Considerations

Like any skill, it takes years to perfect the ability to know when to apply a particular strategy. There are some instances when you might reconsider using a process drama to explore an issue. Some issues may be too close to the surface of a particular group and by using this kind of approach, you might drum up such strong emotions that the exploration becomes counter productive. One such moment could be something like exploring an issue of rape immediately after the school has experienced that particular tragedy. Although process drama might be used, you have to remember that as a drama educator you are not a child psychologist or therapist. In these instances it would be wise to use such an approach in conjunction with someone trained in the particular area. There are many fundamental strategies that one may easily master with the proper direction.

Training

Process drama is generally done by teachers who have taken extra training in these strategies. (A lot more training is needed than can be gained from just reading this chapter or even several books.) All over the world there are Universities which have programs dedicated to teaching people how to use Drama in Education strategies in a variety of situations. In England the University of Northampton, and the University of Exeter, both offer graduate degrees specializing in Drama in Education. In Canada the University of Victoria offers in Australia the Charles Stuart University offers intensified training in Drama in Education through their theatre degree program.

In the United States, New York University, Arizona State University, Eastern Michigan University and The Ohio State University, each offer degrees focusing on the use of drama as an educational strategy. And these are only a representation of the many colleges and Universities around the world who offer similar programs and degrees. You may also find several informative hands-on seminars and workshops offered through the various professional drama organizations such at AATE (American Alliance of Theatre Educators), AEA(American Educator of Art), IDEA(International Drama Educators association) and ATHE (Association of Theatre in Higher Education). AATE's webpage (<www.aate.org>) offers links to AEA, IDEA and ATHE and is a fantastic place to begin a primary search for information on process drama.

Summary

Process drama strategies hold many exciting and powerful opportunities for personal growth and self-discovery as well as avenues for interdisciplinary explorations. The creation of the fictional world also brings individuals together as they solve problems inherent within that world whether they be social, mathematical, or philosophical. This interaction creates moments of tension, conflict and realization where issues of ethics, morals and meanings of existence come into play while individuals act and react to the situations they have created using a myriad of education and learning tools in the solving of fundamental problems. Process drama strategies provide avenues for discoveries in all areas where humans must think and act, alone or together, in order to survive in an ever changing world.

References

Webpage supplements with references: <www.interactiveimprov.com/prcdrwbrefs.html>
Further explanation of methods: <www.interactiveimprov.com/procdrmethodswb.html>
Further comments on history, status: <www.interactiveimprov.com/procdrmwb.html>
Some further examples: <www.interactiveimprov.com/procdrexampwb.html>

Bolton, Gavin. (1979). *Toward a theory of drama in education.* London: Longman. (This text is a great source for the theoretical underpinnings behind process drama, connecting learning to developmental stages of play.)

Booth, David. & Gallagher, Cathleen (Eds.). (2003). *How theatre educates: converging viewpoints.* Toronto: University of Toronto Press, 2003. (Edited by two of the for most Canadian authorities on process drama the book brings together several first hand sharing of teacher's experiences with process drama. The reflections cross the gambit form using drama for exploring issues of race, gender and culture to the successes and failures of and new visions for process drama.)

Edmiston, Brian, & Wilhelm, Jeffrey. (1998). *Imagining to learn.* Portsmouth, NH: Heinemann. This is a wonderful text supplying a rich mix of theory and practice focusing around issues of ethics though process drama.

Grady, Sharon. (2000). *Drama and diversity: a pluralistic perspective for educational drama.* Portsmouth, NH: Heinemann. (Several case studies are provided with in depth descriptions of the practice taken to explore issues of diversity through drama.)

Heathcote, Dorothy; (Edited by Liz Johnson and Cecily O'Neill). (1984). *Dorothy Heathcote: collected writings on education and drama.* Essex, UK: D.P. Media Ltd. (The authors have compiled the writings of one of the pioneer minds of process drama. They present several of Heathcote's landmark explorations which she takes apart to examine their fundamental educational value.)

Manley, A and Cecily O'Neill. (1997). *Dreamseekers: creative approaches to the African American Heritage.* Portsmouth, NH: Heinemann. (This text provides several outlines and reflections on lessons using process drama to explore issues of culture. The text does a great job of positioning the authors of the articles within their own cultural identity as a way to understand the complexity of engaging students in discussions of culture.)

O'Neill, C., & Lambert, A. (1982). *Drama structures: a practical handbook for teachers.* Portsmouth, NH: Heinemann; (also: London: Hutchinson, 1983.) (A well-constructed and easy to use how to book on implementing a process drama exploration. The authors provide several in depth explanations of strategies and the logic behind using a particular strategy.)

O'Neill, Cecily. (1995). *Drama worlds: a framework for process drama.* Portsmouth, NH: Heinemann.

Saldana, Johnny. *Drama of color: improvisation with multiethnic folklore.* Portsmouth, NH: Heinemann, 1995. (As the name suggests the text introduces readers to folklore as a way to facilitate a process drama exploration.)

Spolin, Viola. *Improvisation for the theatre: a handbook of teaching and directing techniques.* Evanston, Il: Northwestern University Press, 1970. (This is an essential text for anyone wishing to move further with their interest in process drama and improvisational theatre. This complete glossary of improvisational strategies offers a wide variety of explorations, with detailed explanations of how to facilitate them.)

Useful Web Sites

The American Association for Theatre Educators: <www.AATE.org> (This is a professional organization for teachers of primary and secondary school drama educators and many Universities and Colleges that have training programs for drama educators. This webpage has many links to funding resources, lesson plans, federal, state and local agencies for the arts as well as a wide range of journals and publications.

International Drama Education Association (IDEA): <educ.queensu.ca/~idea/ index.htm> This is a gateway to webpages dealing with drama in education resources from all over the world. This organization is probably the closest in spirit to process drama, though it has many other side approaches also involved.

Drama Victoria: <www.dramavictoria.vic.edu.au/> This website has a good deal of particle information about many opportunities for careers using Drama.

The Council of Drama and Dance Education: <www.code.on.ca/> The webpage for this Canadian-based group has links to activities and resources for the novice as well as the experienced drama practitioner.

The Drama in Education web site, <www.stemnet.nf.ca/~mcoady/not only contains countless lessons plans and integration suggestions it also has a comprehensive links section that connects you to hundreds of other resources from Drama in Education to Creative Drama to Production oriented theatre.

This website: <www.questia.com/popularSearches/drama_in_education.jsp> is truly one of the largest resources for texts on drama in education and features some of the top names as well as many new arrivals. The titles cover the gambit form high theory to practical hands-on lessons. This web site actually allows you to read entire texts on-line for a small fee.

Chapter 10

THEATRE IN EDUCATION

Allison Downey

Theatre in Education (TIE) is a type of interactive drama that uses elements of theatre, including scenes performed by actors, to emotionally engage the audience in addressing a particular social or curricular issue. A facilitator then processes the scenes with the audience through their participation in related activities and discussion. The melding of the theatrical components with the educational activities move the piece from being a "play" to being identified as a "program." TIE programs deal with a particular topic that is relevant to a specific audience. The programs are toured by a cast (or team) of *actor/teachers* to the target audience, and performed in their own environment, be it a school setting, juvenile detention center, or community space.

A primary goal of TIE programs is to motivate the audience to explore the complexities of the issues at hand. It is the scenes in the drama itself that draw the audience into the issues emotionally and give the conflict a sense of urgency and reality in a way that a rhetorical discussion may not. Once the audience is hooked in to the story, they are more likely to invest in the processing activities and techniques and more likely to grapple with the issues raised. TIE programs seek to challenge the audience and the performers; to raise questions rather than offer answers. There is no assumption that the performers have any "right answer" to impart, but rather the goal is that both performers and audience members explore the topic together. The drama serves as the catalyst for discussion and the activities provide structure for the exploration. Significant issues might be pulled from history, literature, science, newspaper headlines, or imaginations.

History

The method now known as Theatre in Education began in England in 1965. (Further history, as well as other techniques and so forth, may be found on the webpage supplement to this chapter: <www.interactiveimprov.com/thtrneduweb.html>) In an effort to democratize theatre, making it accessible to all ages and economic groups, and to revolutionize the school system Theatre in Education companies began creating programs that encouraged student involvement, exercised their critical thinking skills and emphasized their civic responsibilities. Because the programs were developed by professional theatre company members, in conjunction with professional educators and administrators, and also funded by the arts councils, the quality of the production elements was extremely high. By the 1970s TIE teams reached all levels of the school system addressing countless issues and curricular topics (Jackson, 1993:23). The programs activated the curriculum, placing the students at the center of historical conflict and in the position of decision-makers.

In 1975 a team of graduate students in New York University's Educational Theatre Program brought Theatre in Education to the United States and founded the Creative Arts Team (CAT), which remains the premiere TIE company in the United States. The CAT (which has since moved its program to the City University of New York, CUNY) annually works with more than 35,000 young people and associated adults from all five boroughs of New York City, addressing such issues as violence prevention, exclusion, community building, peer pressure, self-esteem, HIV/AIDS prevention, health and sexuality.

In 1997, the author, along with Lynn Hoare and Avis Strong (having been heavily influenced by the work of the CAT in New York) co-founded the Theatre Action Project in Austin, Texas. Examples from the Theater Action Project's program, "It's in Your Hands," will be used to illustrate TIE concepts and approaches.

TIE in Action

At a juvenile detention center in Austin, Texas, 25 youths between the ages of twelve and seventeen arrived stone-faced in orange jumpsuits and slippers, one by one entering the cafeteria with their hands behind their backs, escorted by security officers through the tight security door. Four actor/teachers, including the author, enact a 90-minute TIE program titled "It's in Your Hands," aimed at the cycle of bullying and violence in schools.

One of the actors played a young person provoking another girl: "Not gonna step up?" she taunted. The one teased pulled a knife from her backpack, stood for a moment questioning her next move. "Freeze!," the facilitator announced, stepping into the center of the scene. The actors "froze" in their positions maintaining a *tableau* while the facilitator faced the audience, "We see she's got her hand on her knife. What should she do now?" The audience erupted as if they were five-year-olds shouting to bring Tinkerbelle back to life: "Take her down!" "Show her who's boss!" "Stab her in the back!" "Just walk away."

The facilitator stepped in: "Let's get some hands up so we can hear you all, one at a time." A voice called out, "Can't walk away and be all that!" One of the teachers intervened with what could be considered the "right" answer. The facilitator responded, "That is one option, let's hear some more options." More hands jumped in the air, perhaps because it became apparent we were not looking for "the" answer, but rather were seeking to brainstorm possibilities. And then, "Don't use the knife, man, or you'll end up in juvie like me!" "Yeah," replied another youth. "It ain't worth it." Thirty minutes later the toughness had softened, the masks had dissolved and the young men were offering advice to fictional characters and engaging in discussion, often disagreeing with one another's opinions in a non-threatening manner.

The teacher and director of the juvenile detention center asked us to return because they felt strongly that this approach reached the young men, three of whom were awaiting trial for murder, in ways that few others had. The young men were critiquing the choices and subsequent consequences of the characters in our story, and in essence, projecting their experiences onto the characters and processing them in a safe environment.

This program was also performed for two other populations and designed to appeal to and apply to the needs of young people caught in the cycle of social conflict, such as those with a high recidivism rate at a local elementary alternative school. To ensure that our scenes would reflect the reality of these young people's experiences, we began by interviewing the students in our target classroom. We based the program's central conflict around challenges articulated by the students during their interviews. A comment from a student evaluation of "It's in Your Hands" explains: "My thinking has changed because now I know that the other person is or could be feeling like they're being pressured to fight also."

Defining Theatre in Education

The TIE network of the American Alliance for Theatre in Education (AATE) in its 2000 newsletter suggests that a program might be considered TIE if it includes the following criteria. The work:

- makes use of both scripts and improvisation and is presented in workshop style
- includes full student participation during at least part of the presentation
- makes use of traditional and innovative tools of theatre and drama practice including dramatic conventions and techniques such as teacher in role, whole group role playing, "hotseating" (to be described further on), forum theatre, and so forth
- includes educational goals accessed through theatre
- is narrowly focused with specific goals aimed at a specific age group
- uses theatre and drama to raise questions and issues for student exploration rather than supplying ready made answers given by the performers
- is designed so students take their own responsibility and the work empowers students on an equal basis with the teachers in the exploration of the subject matter.

I would add to this list that in TIE original pieces are created for specific populations and facilitated by actor/teachers who process the scenes and activities by interacting with the audience. While there are exceptions, Theatre in Education is most often performed for around 30–60 students (perhaps a combined classroom) so as to create an environment that encourages dialogue and exploration. Typically, the style of the piece is realistic, though at times the topic may be effectively addressed using melodrama, musicals, science fiction, historical incidents and comedy (Mirrione, 1993, p. 74).

TIE companies embrace a variety of organizational structures to devise programs. The original companies in England worked collaboratively to devise programs in ways that were entirely egalitarian. Members then are referred to as a "TIE Team," rather than a "cast," reflecting the democratic and educational basis of the form. In creating "It's In Your Hands," we, too, chose to be equally involved in all aspects of the decision making process. While this approach enabled us to explore many more options than we might have otherwise, it was also extremely time-consuming and not entirely efficient. Later, we moved to a "directed collaboration," in which actor/teachers "workshop" the script under the leadership of the director. We hired directors who would make the final decisions about the program after significant actor/teacher contributions via the workshop process. There are some companies who commission playwrights to devise scripts in isolation, however. In general the structure of TIE companies offers actors significantly more input on the final program than in most traditional theatre experiences.

Method

In choosing the topic for a TIE program a company may face a variety of considerations. The content can be determined by those providing the funds; what is of interest to the team at the moment; and/or by a community's needs. Organizations or communities may approach the company with an issue they would like addressed and they either commission the program or help seek funding to support it. "It's in Your Hands" was ultimately supported by a social services agency and the arts council. Other pieces have been commissioned by school grants and other community funds. Because the devising process is extremely time consuming, and therefore, expensive, it is advisable to identify "funders" before creating the program.

The length of the TIE programs vary according to the company involved, shaped by the needs of the target population, the schedule and logistics of the hosting party, the goals of the program and funding. Our first program lasted only 90 minutes due to scheduling constraints of the school and funding limitations. We extended the learning experience by providing each child (and teacher) with a resource packet filled with activities to help them make the connection between the program and their own experiences.

Structures of TIE Programs

The structures used by TIE programs vary from company to company and project to project. Typically, though, most programs incorporate the audience in suggesting directions for the plot as it unfolds, and sometimes they are even brought into the action of a scene. Thus, we speak of audience members as *participants*. A specific program is designed to fit the goals and needs of the target group. Often there is a single storyline that serves to engage students in the topic. The scenes of this drama may be processed by a facilitator through discussion and/or activities that explore the dynamics of the situation.

In the case of "It's in Your Hands," we geared the program to prepare students to brainstorm alternatives to violence and to critique the successfulness of the different choices based on the anticipated consequences. We believed that it was imperative for the program to enable students to thoroughly examine the dynamics that led to the conflict and the multiple perspectives of the situation before judging the choices. Without introducing ourselves or getting the students' attention, we started our scene, which captured the students' focus immediately. Our initial scenes were followed with questions that checked their understanding of the "who, what, where, and why" of the scenario.

We emphasized this with an activity entitled, "Role on the Wall" in which the main character is depicted on a piece of butcher paper, or in our case a white board, and information about the character's situation and feeling are added to the picture as the scenes continue (Neelands & Goode, 2000:22). As the conflict was introduced we incorporated activities and techniques that would explore the intentions and experiences of the characters to broaden our perspective of the "causes" of the conflict. The techniques we most frequently employed for this purpose included *hotseating, voices in the head*, and *inner monologue*:

Hotseating. The fourth wall is eliminated as students and the facilitator ask a character questions about their perspective on and role in the conflict and/or offer advice to the character. The facilitator has an integral role in functioning as a moderator.

Inner monologue. Another way to "get inside" the thoughts of a character without breaking the fourth wall is to have a character verbalize their experience in a monologue format. (This would be close to the soliloquy technique in psychodrama.) We often had our actors "break out" at the end of the monologue to address the audience and ask for advice. This approach may or may not require the intervention of a facilitator. We often used inner monologue to reveal the perspective of the antagonist, so that we weren't caricaturizing any characters as simple villains, but placing their choices in the context of the pressures they faced.

Voices in the head. This technique, similar to the psychodramatic *double* technique, dramatizes the pressures on the character in the midst of making a decision. The participants brainstorm the people and events that may influence the character's decisions. The students then either surround the character or from their seats verbalize what these influential people might say to pressure the character. This experience simulates the confusion that character might feel at the moment of decision and can help students to empathize with the situation.

When the scenes progressed to the moment of high conflict, rather than our prescribing a certain ending and risking delivering the message that we were leading students to the "right" answer, we stopped the action of the story at the moment of decision—to fight or not to fight—and had the students brainstorm what might happen next. Yet, given this was a violence prevention program, we did have a bias. We felt strongly that if we fully physically enacted the fight we would be reinforcing violence as an option, and our goal was to explore alternatives to violence without a moralistic approach. The participants were accustomed to seeing violence as entertainment in other forms of media, so we sought structures that would allow students to examine the potential consequences of their suggested solutions. We stopped the scene at the moment of decision, not the moment of highest physical tension.

To spark discussion about possible physical and emotional consequences of choosing to fight, we created realistic and abstract *tableaux* with a facilitator encouraging students share their "reading" of the image.

Tableau. This technique involves a "frozen picture," an event or experience is distilled into a single image. The actor/teachers hold positions in relation to one another that highlight power dynamics, emotions, and pressures.

Using *Image Theatre* techniques borrowed from the Theatre of the Oppressed (see Chapter 21), we could engage the students in visual brainstorming without judgement. I was often surprised to find elementary students offering sophisticated "readings" of the image: that the character must have felt trapped in a box, or pulled between good and evil weighing on their conscience. Faced with such scenes, and as a frequent element in conflict resolution programs, students are encouraged to suggest alternative endings for the conflict and analyze the results or consequences of that choice.

Some companies actually involve the participants in re-enacting the scene, in dramatizing their own suggestions, as Boal practiced in his Forum Theatre. In the final incarnation of "It's In Your Hands," students teamed up with actor/teachers to select an alternative ending and weighed the pro's and con's of that choice before presenting their suggestion to the whole group. At that point the actor/teachers improvised the alternative endings and a facilitator processed the effectiveness of each choice with the students. We felt that this strategy best exercised the students' decision-making skills.

Actor's Requirements

This powerful work requires unique skills and qualities from the performers for the program to be successful. Excellent actors are needed to make the scenes believable. If the actors will also facilitate the processing of the scenes as opposed to having a separate facilitator, they will need to be skilled as teachers as well, thus the term, *actor/teacher*. The term reveals the dual responsibilities of the role. While there has been a movement to return to the term "Actor" to emphasize the central role of theatre in the program, we chose to refer to our casts as actor/teachers to highlight the demands of the position. In auditioning actors for our first Theatre Action Project tour of "It's In Your Hands," we identified the list of qualities and abilities we were seeking and developed activities for the workshop/audition that would exercise and reveal these skills. The *acting skills* include:

Ability to maintain character. An actor/teacher must be able to concentrate and not be distracted. It is a common occurrence for programs in schools to be interrupted by announcements over the intercom, bells ringing, students being pulled out of class. It is crucial to be able to stay in role and continue the scene with the same intensity as before the interruption.

Role flexibility. An actor in TIE must be able to play multiple characters believably and move into and out of role with ease and clarity. In many TIE programs the actors will play multiple characters and even step from within a scene immediately out to facilitate the processing of the scene. This requires a great deal of focus from the actor to maintain distinctions between characters, including their role as facilitator.

Taking direction. As in any theatrical production it is imperative for the actor/teacher to take direction well, to take suggestions from the director and realize them in a scene.

Improvisational skills. Many companies use improvisation as a tool for devising the programs as well as a technique in the production itself. In our programs we would develop the "script" based on the actor/teacher improvisations of scenes and in some cases commit the scenes to scripted dialogue and in others have a basic structure for a scene with scripted opening and closing lines, but the body of the scene performed improvisationally. Strong improvisation skills are integral to being a successful actor/teacher.

Scale. This term refers to the ability to act in close proximity to the audience so that the "fourth wall" can both appear and disappear.

The *facilitation skills* include:

Synthesize information. In processing the scenes, the facilitator can make connections between the students' comments and experiences and the theme and events of the program. The facilitator should be able to identify key components of students' comments that might otherwise seem to meander and thread them back to the focus of the scene.

Flexibility. This involves the ability to respond to unexpected participant needs in the larger contexts. For example, at one point our program was moved outside during a fire drill and the actor/teachers continued the scene in the courtyard.

Listening. Because the goal is for students to critically process and discuss the issues, it is imperative that the facilitator listens and accurately hears what the participants are saying.

Questioning. The facilitator role requires the ability to pose the appropriate form of question needed for processing, i.e. to recognize when to use clarifying questions to confirm information, and when to offer open questions that draw students out rather than lead them to a predetermined conclusion.

A third group of skills involves maintaining oneself as a *team member*, which requires:

Collaboration. Team members need to be able to work together well, as a true ensemble, through the training, devising, and performance process. In TIE programs there is rarely, if ever, an "off-stage" moment. While one actor/teacher is facilitating the others constantly engage in the program.

Passion for the work. A TIE program performance requires a great deal of energy and enthusiasm from the actor/teachers to motivate the participants to invest in processing the conflict. A deep commitment to the audience and/or the issue being addressed is crucial for actor/teachers to continue to flourish in this field.

Especially in the beginning of a company, and when TIE is new to an area, it is challenging to find actor/teachers who are experienced in this form and equally strong in acting and facilitating. During the first couple of years of Theatre Action Project, we essentially trained our teams in the tools, techniques, strategies, and theories of TIE throughout the rehearsal process. As directors we learned to recognize potential in actors whose facilitation skills were not yet honed. We were committed to investing in the development of a community of actor/teachers.

It was also important to us to select a team that the audience could identify with, since the program would only be effective if the participants could relate to the experience of the characters. This challenge extended beyond casting actor/teachers who could believably "play" young. We served a population that was primarily African-American and Hispanic. While the magic of theatre drew students to suspend their disbelief regarding the age of the actors, and to transcend racial and gender lines in connecting with the characters and the storyline, we were committed to hiring people of color who were quality actor/teachers. Because TIE as an art form is usually new to a community, it requires raising the profile of the company, publicizing the work, essentially educating the public and the theatre community about the form and reaching out to diverse populations if a company is to attract passionate and diverse individuals to audition.

The role of the TIE director requires special skills as well. Unlike in traditional theatre, it is the charge of the TIE director to shape the program to maintain a smooth structure infused with storytelling, while incorporating the audience *into* the performance. The continual establishment and dissolution of the fourth wall requires clear distinctions and smooth transitions. In the rehearsal process, directors must include and create activities that exercise many of the skills for the actor/teacher described above.

Whereas in traditional theatre the director's job ends opening night, the director of TIE usually attends performances throughout the run of the program and continues to offer feedback. Because the audience not only contributes applause, but offers "lines" in the script, processes the scenes, and in some cases directs the ending of the programs, the "show" is only half complete when the first performance begins. It is imperative, then, for the director to be able to give feedback about experiences and incidents that presented themselves during the performance and for continued re-working or touch-up rehearsals and re-working throughout.

Training

Given the unique demands on actor/teachers and directors of TIE, how does one get trained to practice TIE? There are excellent undergraduate and graduate programs offering MA degrees or the terminal Master of Fine Arts Degrees that address Theatre in Education. Programs range from Educational Theatre programs like that at New York University and Emerson College in Boston to MFA programs in Child Drama, Applied Theatre, and Theatre for Youth in schools such as The University of Arizona and the University of Texas. While the educational programs offer excellent preparation and training for a career in Theatre in Education, an interested and motivated individual can get "trained on the job."

While TIE has strong roots in England, it is still a relatively new form in the United States. One of the challenges of compiling an official list of domestic TIE companies is that the form is so varied, constantly developing, and therefore difficult to define. Given the fluid nature of the approach, most TIE programs are not published, and therefore not easily accessible. I have included in the web supplement information about a few companies doing TIE as well as additional resources for further exploration. This powerful work is being practiced in the

United States, and the more we share our experiences with TIE the more this successful approach will become a standard and not an alternative form.

References and Resources

Webpage supplement: <www.interactiveimprov.com/thtrneduweb.html> has further resources, and there are other links at <www.tonisant.com/aitg/Theatre_in_Education/>
   Contact Information: <www.theatreactionproject.org>
   Also: <www.cuny.edu/creativeartsteam>

Boal, Augusto (1992). *Games for actors and non-actors*, Trans. Adrian Jackson. London: Routledge.

Jackson, Tony (1993). Introduction. In T. Jackson (Ed.), *Learning through theatre: new perspectives on theatre in education*. London: Routledge.

Jackson, Tony (1993). "Education or theatre? The development of TIE in Britain," In T. Jackson (Ed.), *Learning through theatre: New perspectives on Theatre in Education*. London: Routledge.

Landy, Robert (1982). *Handbook of educational drama and theatre*. West Port, Connecticut: Greenwood Press, Pp. 63–77.

Neelands, Jonothan & Goode, Tony (2000). *Structuring drama work: A handbook of available forms in theatre and drama*. Cambridge: Cambridge University Press.

Oddey, Allison. (1994) *Devising theatre: A practical and theoretical handbook*. London: Routledge.

Chapter 11

PLAYBUILDING WITH PACIFIC ISLAND STUDENTS

Daniel A. Kelin, II

"Playbuilding" is an improvisation-based, exploratory theatre technique that I have used to help Pacific Island students increase group cohesion, build verbal confidence, explore the range of verbal expression and develop problem-solving skills. Engaging students through drama gives purpose and meaning to language. It helps those who are limited in speaking English to develop language skills, which is a significant step toward expanding reading and writing skills as well. A further benefit is that it draws on ESL (English as Second Language) students' interest in deepening their cultural identity. The work builds naturally on the oral and dance traditions and offers students significant and personal ways to achieve success. The process as outlined here generally involves 8 to 25 students from ages 9 and up over a period of at least ten sessions, each lasting between 45 and 90 minutes.

When asked to implement drama programming with ESL students, it seemed appropriate to apply this process; many schools in Hawaii have an ever-increasing concentration of these students, primarily from across the Pacific, the Philippines, Micronesia, Samoa, the Marshall Islands, China and Southeast Asian countries. The most common approach I take is a combination of cultural stories, storytelling, and drama. None of these traditions are used in a completely pure form; instead, we adapt each as fits the situation, students and time frame, building from the students' own understanding and experience, and creating processes that reflect their needs and interests.

In such a residency, the students explore communication through drama, and then, apply the ideas to a story of their own culture, analyzing its structure, developing a verbal outline, and creating a narrative that accompanies a simple playing out of the story. This, finally, leads to developing the story into a brief play with dialog and action that, ideally, involves whole groups of students or even an entire class. The process involves and engages students at every step. They decide how involved they are and how to best shape their involvement. They review and assess their involvement and their creations and alter their work as they choose.

The Process

To begin, the participants build knowledge of and comfort with the techniques. I start with ensemble-building exercises, noting to the students that without group collaboration we will never succeed. From there, we concentrate on physical expression, experimenting with creating frozen images of various characters, actions and ideas. This is an essential first step. For these young people to make the leap into playbuilding requires they have sufficient time to understand the process. This step also establishes an atmosphere of playfulness, taking the pressure off "being right" and encouraging the students to experiment and explore.

I then introduce a cultural story, always from the culture of at least some members of the class, inviting the rest of the students to learn more about that particular culture. I always tell the story, not read it, as the students come to rely on the words in the book as the "correct" version of the story. It is a chance for me to model the improvisational nature of the playbuilding process. However, once a group becomes comfortable with the playbuilding process, the students themselves should become the collectors and tellers. In some cultures, stories are the property of family or community. For this reason, I proceed with caution when it comes to sharing stories. There are unwritten rules and guidelines about particular stories and ways of telling. I seek counsel before taking on an unfamiliar culture.

The class then has a common experience and sense of the story that will guide the next few steps in the process. This common experience is akin to one that brings cultures together, as many cultures have particular ways and times to share stories.

Since playbuilding should reflect how the students hear and understand a chosen story, it is important they take ownership of the story by creating a verbal outline of the story. This outlining serves three functions: (1) noting the main events in such a format increases the sense of the student's control; (2) it anchors the story more deeply in their memories and; (3) it encourages students to see the story as a sequence of events from which they will be able to build. Having the participants discuss and recount the story repeatedly throughout the process helps them not only commit the story to long-term memory but also helps them remember and include the small events, thus becoming active participants in the shaping and preserving of the story.

Once the story has become the common property of the class, it is time for them to put their drama training in action, experimenting with creating the different characters and actions suggested by the story. They should "try on" the characters, discovering the range of ways to express a particular character or action. For example, in a Samoan story, there is an eight-legged, winged, beast chasing a boy and his dog. The students create several different frozen images of the beast physically, first as individuals, then with partners or in small groups. There is little need, at this step in the process, for the students to share their experimentations with each other. This step is analogous to the initial drafts when writing an essay. Those drafts are for the writer, not the reader.

The students then bring some of their "experiments" to life dramatically: They make their beasts breathe, make sounds, or move or fly about the room. Finally, students combine the characters, events and character encounters they have experimented with into a variety of on-the-spot tableaux (physically frozen images). An example might be to show what the boy and dog look like in a variety of moments: seeing the beast, running from the beast, being caught by the beast. This gets them thinking about the little pieces that make up the whole and, for the playbuilding process, offers the students a safe period of exploration and confidence-building. Without thinking about it, they are developing a physical vocabulary they will draw on later when reconstructing the story in play form.

Throughout this process, I always strive for full and active participation on the part of all students in the class. Instead of asking small groups of students to playbuild a whole story, I ask them to each take on a single section of the story. Breaking up the story takes the pressure off any one group and encourages the whole class to support and possibly help each other. It also encourages the students examine closely their particular part of the story. Instead of getting overwhelmed trying to create and stage a whole story, they can apply their energies to enriching a small section of the story. This choice also gives a chance to demonstrate this whole process is accessible and doable. Ideally, once the whole class has worked together through the process with one story, small groups of them should be more ready to take on a whole story by themselves.

Small groups of students each choose a specific scene or series of events from the developed outline so the whole story ends up distributed amongst the groups. Each group divides the characters within their section, assuring that every individual in their group has a character. Often the stories have fewer characters than number of people in a particular group, so groups should be encouraged to be flexible in their planning. They can double characters up, expand characters, and even create new characters (within reason), problem-solving in ways we teachers might not think of (e.g., they may anthropomorphize objects, as Lewis Carroll did with the clocks or flower in his *Alice in Wonderland* stories). As long as the story itself does not alter significantly, the number and type of characters is not a huge factor. If a character is engaged in a battle with a demon, does it matter how many demons there might be or how many heads it might have? I have seen plants made up for four students simultaneously and stories about a girl become a trio of girls without the storyline changing one bit.

Creating Tableaux

The groups then decide on the key events within their chosen scene and create tableaux depicting those events. A tableau (plural: tableaux—pronounced ta-blows) is a physically still image that encapsulates the essence of a scene or character encounter. It is an immediately accessible technique that gives the students a high degree of control and demonstrates their understanding of the scene or story on which they are working. Tableau is also a good technique for encouraging their physical investment in the story. I have found that, when dialog is added into the process too early, the students get caught up in the words and forego action. By creating a series of tableaux, the groups have the chance to focus on the interaction and physical action of the characters. After finishing the tableaux, the students have outlined the physical world and actions of the characters, a step that leads directly to the next couple of steps in the process.

The number of tableaux the groups need to create is flexible depending on how well the students are working together and how easily they are taking to the process. I have the groups work on only one at a time, to insure that the whole class will move forward at a similar pace. Each time they create a new tableau, the groups review the other ones they created. Eventually the groups will be practicing their tableaux with ease and confidence, since they have several times to rehearse. Students are encouraged to add elements that reflect their own understanding of the culture or enrich details of the story or characters. This step is repeated as necessary, being sure to engage the class in discussing and evaluating the tableaux as they share them for each other, commenting how successful groups are at communicating the actions, characters and ideas of the scene and offering ideas for further exploration.

The discussions, used not only here but at subsequent steps in which the students share their developing work, are a key part of the process. The students will learn to evaluate and improve their own work by practicing the evaluation process, both as evaluators and as those evaluated. The instructor should be ready to lead the discussion, posing questions to encourage the students to think about what they see or are doing, and to guide the discussion, making sure the students don't get stuck just complaining or giving pat answers such as "It's good."

The previous is part of a scaffolding philosophy. If students playbuild immediately after hearing the story, they may be too overwhelmed to know where to start. Developing a series of tableaux mirrors the idea of the verbal outline, giving the students a chance to imagine the overall before diving into the intricacies of the story.

Narrative Slide Show

The groups next create narratives to accompany each tableau, developing a kind of "narrative slideshow." Either one student acts as narrator as the others share the tableaux or the group divides the narration amongst various members. The narrators put the narration into his/her own words, not worrying whether it is the "correct" version of the story.

In the same way that the tableaux demonstrate the students understanding of the basic action of the story, having them create a series of narrative statement to accompany the tableaux demonstrates their comprehension of the overall sequence of their part of the story. Creating the narration is a first step in the development of dialog, a way for the students to solidify their understanding of the actions and intentions of the characters.

Each of these preliminary steps can be repeated as necessary, to encourage the student to looker deeper into the story, emphasizing those parts that they believe are most important to the understanding of the story. It also offers the class a chance to discuss the ongoing creations, commenting how successful groups are at clearly communicating the events of the story and possibly what key events may be missing.

Completing each of these previous steps contributes to a sense of accomplishment in the students, preparing them for tackling the more complicated step that follows. With students who have little to no experience with theatre and/or lack confidence with language, I have found that these steps are crucial to later success. As they are encouraged to play with the structure and content of the story (without significantly changing the basic storyline), they begin to feel comfortable contributing ideas, and are introduced to the idea that stories are not concrete, unchanging entities. Stories change in the mouths of each teller, yet still retain integrity and purpose.

Building Scenes

Finally, the groups develop full dramatizations by creating dialog and action. First, I encourage the students to forget about the narration and tableaux, using them simply to inform the choices they will make in recreating the story in play form. I do ask them to incorporate the tableaux as single moments in the playing of their scene. This gives them something to aim for, always knowing that the scene will move through each and every of the tableau they created. This also insures they will continue to be physically active in the scene. This last is an important concept. My experience has been that the students lose a lot of the physicality when they start concentrating on dialog. Subsequently, this last step should be given the most time, giving adequate time for students to evaluate their process an individuals and as a group.

The developing dialog will most benefit from this repetition. When developing the words and dialog, I have found that the students tend to go for the easy and obvious, at first. This makes sense, since they are developing their English language skills. Therefore, it is important to let them explore the obvious. Just as with each of the previous steps, the students need the time to explore, need the time to experiment, and then need the time to evaluate, rethink and implement their new understanding. Throughout, the instructor encourages risk-taking and imaginative solutions to problems through thought-provoking questions and challenges.

Since we are attempting to build verbal confidence in the students, not rushing the playbuilding process creates other possibilities for the students to exercise their language skills. As they work with their partners, they are actively using group discussion skills. When they are sharing their ongoing work, they are practicing their oratory skills. After watching other groups, when they evaluate and offer suggestions, they are engaged in practical language use. I refer to the sharing as "rehearsals" to clarify that the work is not final and the pressure is not on for them to get it "right" or "perfect." I tell them the final "performance" will be when we present the whole story without stopping.

At the end, the groups officially perform their scenes. Having every group perform lessens the pressure on any single individual or group. As the success of the performance is dependant on everyone in the class, then everyone has a vested interest in helping each other do well. Moreover, the informal performance reduces the pressure to be perfect. If problems come up, the class can always start again and can repeat the performance as many times as they wish. In reality, the in-class performance is icing on the cake. The true learning has occurred through the process of reconstructing the story into a play. With the vast amount of discussion, rehearsal and sharing that has occurred, the students have had many opportunities to use and practice their language skills in useful and purposeful ways.

Reflection and Evaluation

For the process to be a rich one, it should be full of supportive questions and encourage the students to explore, takes risks, discover and apply those discoveries. Each time a group shares a developing scene, the whole class should reflect on the choices made and how the group sharing might develop their ideas further. The following *questions for the performers* can be jumping off points for developing scenes:

- Did you stay focused on the story or character? Why or why not?
- Did you build the story together with your partners?
- Which moments were the strongest?
- What could you have done differently?

    Questions for those watching:

- What moments were the strongest?
- Did the performers listen to each other as well as talk?
- What could they have done differently?

    Open-ended statements can also help students reflect on choices. "I thought I did a good job on/with ..." "I think it would be better if I ...," "I think (name) did a good job, because ...," or "I think (group name) need to concentrate on ..."

The kinds of questions that keep the students focused and productive include questions on character and conflicts. When students can identify what their character is pursuing, they will be able to build the dialog and action of their scene as the dialog and action communicate the character's need or goal. The various characters' goals put them in opposition to each other, which fuels the development of dialog and action. Students should identify and clarify the characters' needs, goals, obstacles to those goals, and creative ways to overcome obstacles. The instructor should also pose questions that help the students clarify the central conflicts and how they keep the characters from achieving their goals and what choices the characters make to solve or overcome the conflict.

As the scenes become richer and more detailed, the questions asked should become more focused and specific. Was the story clearly communicated? What was missing or extra?

How might the performers clarify what their character is trying to achieve? Did the words the performers used help communicate the story? What else might the different characters need to say to help clarify their goals or the overall story? Did the physical actions seem in keeping with the story? Was there a nice balance of action and dialog? Which might the group explore more?

Expanding the Process

When stories and other traditions of their culture are added into the mix, students become very connected to a process that reflects who they are and celebrates the unique and fascinating aspects of their ancestry. Students are then prepared to collect, share, read and write more such stories. The ideal residency advances to a new level by encouraging everyone in the class to collect tales from their own family or relatives and bring them to class to share. Not only does this increase their personal connection to the process, but it also gives the students a chance to participate in the play-building process again, but this time small groups of the students play-build from a whole story of their own choice. The students, then, become experts, culturally, as storytellers and as the dramatizers of the stories.

Conclusion

Playbuilding can be a powerful tool when the process weaves students' own cultural elements into it, as demonstrated in this chapter. Readers might be interested in following up with this approach and incorporate other methods, such as the use of videotape playback. The mini-movies thus created could act not only as indicators of their accomplishments, but would also serve to preserve the unique aspects of their cultural literature. The process could benefit from the following: (1) Develop a curriculum for training teachers to use this process, and to become comfortable with these methods; (2) Weave in processes that evaluate this method's effectiveness. Over time, research should examine the way teachers teach, how students from these various cultures learn best, and how effective these methods are, compared with others, not only for teaching English, but also the other less tangible benefits mentioned at the outset.

References

Further references on playbuilding, descriptions of techniques and examples may be found on the webpage supplement to this chapter, <www.interactiveimprov.com/pacificwb.html> As well as at: <www.geocities.com/scbwihawaii/members/kelin-d.html> or some of the author's work at <www.prel.org/eslstrategies/drama.html>—

Brauer, Gerd. (2002). *Body and language: intercultural learning through drama.* Westport, CT: Ablex.

Burke, A. & O'Sullivan, J. *Stage by stage: A handbook book for using drama in the second language classroom.* Portsmouth, NH: Heinemann, 2002.

Dyson, A. H., & Genishi, C. (Eds.). (1994). *The need for story: cultural diversity in classroom and community.* Urbana, IL: National Council of Teachers of English.

Kelin, Daniel A., II. (2003). *Marshall island legends and stories.* Honolulu: Bess Press.

Kelin, Daniel A., II. (2005). *To feel as our ancestors did: collecting and performing oral histories.* Portsmouth, NH: Heinemann, 2005.

Chapter 12

THE FICTIONAL FAMILY IN THE DRAMA CLASS AND ACROSS THE CURRICULUM

Muriel Gold

The Fictional Family is a role playing technique that I have found useful for training in a number of settings: drama or acting classes; drama educators; educators in a variety of disciplines; and mental health professionals (Gold, 2000). I developed this approach over twenty years ago, and found that it helped class members develop the ability to empathize and deepen character development (Gold, 1991). It can also be adapted for use in secondary education and college as well as graduate studies or continuing education programs. The technique involves students creating and "inhabiting" a fictional character— i.e., one different from themselves—, in order to experience situations and a family life different from their own. One need not be a professional actor to learn in this way.

> "... Suddenly she felt a great urge to become someone else, one of those passersby walking through the snow, for example. Her deepest desire was to live in some other place than within herself, for just a minute, one brief minute, to see what it is like inside a head other than her own, another body, to be incarnated anew, to know what it is like in some other place, to know new sorrows, new joys, to try on a different skin from her own, the way one tries on gloves in a store, to stop gnawing on the one bone of her actual life and feed on strange, disorienting substances ... to inhabit profoundly another being with all the knowledge, the compassion, the sense of rootedness, the

efforts to adapt and the strange and fearsome mystery that would entail."—Anne Hébert (1990)

In her brilliantly written novel, "Anansi", Anne Hébert describes the despair of her protagonist, Pierrette Paul, who is overcome by the thought that she will be confined to being herself, with no possibility for change, for the rest of her life. Pierrette's solution is to become a professional actress. However, the use of the Fictional Family technique, as well as many other approaches in this book, also are a response to this hunger for role expansion.

What if you could temporarily belong to a different family, have different parents and siblings, different grandparents, different extended families, and live in an environment different from your own—richer, poorer, rural, urban— or even in a different historical era? How would this experience affect your personality, your attitudes and lifestyle? And, after having experienced your new character in a variety of new situations, how would this ultimately affect your choices in life? "What if" can be a powerful avenue to an experiential approach to understanding others.

Preparation of Fictional Families

The technique involves the class or group dividing into subgroups of roughly five members. Each group is instructed to invent a fictional family; the group decides upon a family name, historical and socioeconomic background, geographical location, religion, and the ages and various relationships of each of these five characters. They even generate a two generation history, inventing a family tree that goes back two generations. The group members at some point during this warming-up process decide who will play which role, and each person who takes a role has a greater voice in deciding other features of his or her role: birthplace, profession, income, religion, likes and dislikes, and other elements of personal history. More importantly, the group members, half in role, partly negotiating with the others as these characters are formed, begin to define their attitudes to and the nature of their relationships with the other family members.

Each writes a sketch of his or her own character's autobiography. To help the group members delve into their characters, they are given a list of character questions to fill out such as: What was my childhood like? What were my parents like? What were my friends like? Do I feel lonely? and so forth.

Organization of The Fictional Family

This character development takes time. If the technique is being used over the period of a number of class sessions, some of the preparation can be done in class, and other parts as homework. Thus, part of the "improvisation" involved is the act of thoughtful creating, or perhaps in dialogue with a friend—but not in the heat of the role playing yet to come. (There is a kind of improvisation that comes with creative writing, too—it's not all in fast-paced enactment.) If this method is applied in a workshop setting, with more limited time allocated to the exploration of the roles, those registered should be sent some instructions about how to prepare themselves in advance. This preparation sets the tone for serious in-depth character work and aims to eliminate a frivolous approach to the technique.

One of the many strengths of the Fictional Family technique is its flexibility. It's been used in a university drama class that extended for two terms; as two-hour sessions once a week for family therapy trainees; or for three-hour sessions once a week for three or six week session, for graduate drama therapy students. These latter workshops sometimes culminated in a performance. On another occasion, Women's Studies students explored these roles in two-week sessions of two hours each. In the workshop situations that lasted six-weeks or less, students were expected to both organize their fictional families and complete the character preparation assignments out of class before the class started and the teacher began working with them.

Through the identification and exploration of their characters' personalities and their interaction within a fictional family, students or group members are at the same time exploring their own attitudes and prejudices while exercising their capacity for empathy. Most of the Fictional Family work is done by improvisation so actors are often surprised by the words that leap out of their characters' mouths. They are also surprised by the similarities and dissimilarities between themselves and their characters.

A Student's Experience

A sophomore university student in a Women's Studies course wrote in her journal:

> "In writing about Hermione I originally thought I would just invent
> a character completely different from myself. She's introverted and
> enjoys spending time alone. I am extremely extroverted, and could
> spend 24 hours a day with people. Although we both grew up in Nova

Scotia, I grew up on the mainland, and only ever visited Cape Breton. She has a twin brother, I had three brothers, none of whom was my twin. At first all I saw were the differences.

It's the internal similarities I found interesting ... externalizing themselves through the body of a 14 year old girl. When I was sitting here creating her character my roommate walked in and I told her how badly I felt for this young woman to whom I was giving a life. She asked why, since she was only my imagination and a class project. I had no answer.

Then I got up and walked around my room.... I was trying to figure out what this girl's life meant to me. I came to see that the character is the complete opposite of me, and at the same time, scarily similar ... The biggest similarity I think is that her mother's girlfriend is the equivalent to my half brother. And now I know I never gave him a chance. This is how Hermione treats her mother's girlfriend, she has never given her a chance for the simple reason she has taken away her mother."

Fictional Family work is in-depth character work in a family unit. Unlike scripted work, the characters and the situations are created by the actors themselves. In contrast to most role playing sessions in education or business, in which a situation is presented and participants take on roles usually for one session, the Fictional Family is a more complex and sustained type of role playing, and the characters are being developed from scenario to scenario. Nor is this merely dramatic improvisation, in which the goal is mainly encouraging spontaneity; Fictional Family work, while also encouraging spontaneity, includes a variety of techniques all focussed on continuity of character exploration and family interaction.

Rationale

One might ask, why a *family*? Why not a motorcycle gang, or a work group, or a therapy group? First, not every student has experienced these types of groups. However, one or more of their fictional family characters may envision being part of a motorcycle group, or be involved in a particular work or school situation. Character is largely formed within the family, therefore placing the character in a family can act as a powerful springboard for spontaneous dramatic scenarios. In cross-family scenes students can interact with their fictional family friends and colleagues who dwell in another fictional family (Gold, 1991).

The family forms a common basis of experience, a unit to which everyone can relate. Even the most sheltered and naive students have been exposed all their lives to the depth and intricacy of family relationships of one sort or other. Their perceptions, their communication styles and their modes of interacting have been shaped within the confines of their own families.

The fictional family structure provides the students with an opportunity to choose a position or age status in the fictional family similar or dissimilar to their position in their real-life families: they can choose to replay experienced family conflicts and sibling rivalry, or invent new or previously-imagined family situations and controversies. They can play out their fantasy character. For example, had they always wished to be the independent older child, or the spoiled baby, they can now delve into this character and discover the advantages and disadvantages each person encounters whatever h/er position in the family, and in life, may be.

Preparation Techniques

In class, the students are warmed up with visualization and physicalization techniques before they begin to interact with each other in their small-group scenes. The point of warming-up is to help actors in their character development process. Visualization techniques involve stimulating actors through sense memory to recall or create mental images Whereas visualization exercises are aimed to assist actors to develop their characters' emotional lives, physicalization techniques are aimed to create characters' physical lives. Also, before students play any scene they are asked to improvise the scene that is imagined to precede the scene to be enacted with the others. To further clarify this process, consider five different types of the creative process:

a) "Spontaneous" Improvisations in which students are given little or no time to prepare presentations; my goal here is to assist actors to let their characters speak without preparation so that unexpected characters' emotions and/or thoughts might spontaneously emerge.

b) "Prepared" Improvisations for which they are given ten or more minutes to prepare and rehearse; here the goal is to foster team collaboration in a limited time frame.

c) "Polished" Improvisations which they prepare and rehearse out of class, but there is no written script or outline; the objective of these types of improvisations is to allow students to obtain additional input about their character development from their peers.

d)   Scenes which are developed out of class from students' original script outlines; this work is designed to start them on collaborative writing, a component considered to be a valid element in the actor's process.

e)   Script development; in addition to developing writing skills, this experience provides students with an additional method of analyzing their characters. They put words into their characters' mouths and then are forced to deliver these particular lines.

Obviously, some of these more prepared approaches should be kept together, rather than flutter about in a loose collection of notes. A journal is required. Journal writing and character diaries form an important component of the Fictional Family experience. The journals include not only what is written in activities (d) and (e) above, but also express participants' personal reflections and insights gained throughout the experience. The character diaries help sustain interest in their character and gain insight into their characters' behavior.

In the drama class university model, the Fictional Family improvisation is not introduced until the sixth session and, throughout its use, creative warm-ups and improvisations are maintained. During these warm-ups and relaxation exercises students are fed visual, tactual and sound images to help foster their imaginations and lead into the family improvisations. A goal-oriented step-by-step approach is described which educators can follow and/or adapt according to the specific learning goals of their particular disciplines. The reader can find a wealth of warm-up exercises in some of the books noted at the end of this chapter.

The Fictional Family Across the Curriculum

The use of the Fictional Family methodology can enhance students' learning across the curriculum in secondary and post-secondary programs. University instructors teaching language arts and/or language across the curriculum as well as teachers across the curriculum who are not drama teachers need not be intimidated by the Fictional Family methodology. They need not feel that they must be trained in drama to apply the methodology to their various disciplines. First, unlike other drama methodologies, the teacher is not "in role" as a teaching strategy. Often teachers who are not drama specialists find the prospect of working in role daunting.

Second, the technique, with its familiar structure, quickly engages students in writing and improvising. And the inherent goals of the methodology—to enhance personal growth to nurture, to stimulate, to validate their efforts—are all compatible goals of the teacher in any subject area. It is the students' efforts and involvement and excitement which will ultimately be key to their successful learning.

The diversity of backgrounds and structures chosen by the fictional families (multicultural, socioeconomic, intergenerational, stepfamilies, alternate lifestyles) create awareness of social issues. Although the technique was designed for drama students, it has also been applied in training of drama educators, educators in a variety of disciplines, and mental health professionals.

David Dillon, Professor of Education, at McGill University, offers his students examples of a number of possible Fictional Family scenarios from various subject areas (e.g., language arts, social studies, moral and religious education, etc.) which can complement and enhance the more usual learning means of talk, reading, and writing. He stresses that the goal of organizing students' learning dramatically through the Fictional Family technique does far more than merely providing an interesting alternative to traditional classroom work. Rather, it can powerfully shape the very way in which learners come to understand the information they encounter in school.

Few teachers have had experience with drama as a learning medium, particularly its approach of evoking from students rather than directing them. Most teachers need a structure or protocol within which to begin using drama for learning. Dr. Dillon states that the Fictional Family methodology offers such structure for teachers while still leaving openness within it for improvisational and creative possibilities.

Judy Kalman, Professor at Concordia University, uses the Fictional Family methodology in a university *composition course* and as well as in her course *Writing Across the Curriculum (WAC)*. After searching for new ways to make writing exciting for her students and to bridge the gap between writing and knowledge in other areas, Kalman was drawn to the idea of the Fictional Family construct. She had no idea what excitement Fictional Family would engender in students from all disciplines, from fine arts to business.

I have said that an important component of the drama class is the development of *writing skills*. This component is true for learning in all disciplines. My Fictional Family classes are structured to encourage and nurture creative writing (i.e., through playwriting, narrative, poetry), journals, free-flow inner monologues and integration of individual work to create performance pieces. I offer examples of my students' writing inspired by the stimuli of the Fictional

Family's use of visualization, physicalization and improvisational exercises (see Gold, 1991)

Inventing autobiographical scenarios to develop character is valuable not only for actors but also for writers of fiction such as novelists, playwrights and screenwriters. Furthermore, it can spark interest in a subject heretofore uninteresting to a student. The moment a character is born, its interior life begins. As the story unfolds, the exterior life of the character develops. The interaction between the character and its environment, the obstacles it encounters, and its behavior and responses to that environment and obstacles, reveal the character's personality. Students who find they can succeed in creating a 'real' character will be motivated to study that character's environment whether that environment be rooted in social studies, history, geography, or political science.

A former student of mine who uses the Fictional Family methodology in her secondary school drama classes sent me her assessment of the work's influence on her students. The following is just one example. (Student's name has been changed.)

"John Doe's work, although a bit twisted, is a great example of how well this project works for students with severe problems. He is sixteen years old, is repeating Section II for the third time and has never, in his high school career, handed in such an extensive piece of work. His character autobiography consists of five neatly typed pages. He is a drug user, has been in juvenile court and comes from a broken home. I am extremely pleased with his progress, self-discipline and control since he has begun the fictional family."

Student needs in the new millennium are forcing the adoption of new academic standards, which are in turn producing the need for new approaches to the teaching of history in the classroom. Dr. Samuel Kalman who teaches history at McMaster University, says he uses Fictional Family because the model combines auditory, written, and visual learning while at the same time provoking students to think critically, rather than merely repeating facts handed out in a textbook or a lecture.

The technique can be used as a learning medium in the classroom in the teaching of literature. It has long been the preserve of the English teacher to help students learn to experience literature, or stories, more fully and deeply, particularly through understanding and identifying with various characters. This step can be difficult when characters in a story represent life experience quite different from those of the students who encounter them. Yet the success or failure of students in "seeing through the eyes" of a character is a key factor affecting the quality of their experience of a story.

In recent years, new expectations have also cut across the curriculum, affecting all teachers regardless of their traditional subject matter expertise. One such new expectation is multicultural education, designed to help us all understand and at least, tolerate, if not appreciate, the cultural and social differences among the North American population, differences which increasingly exist in close contact with each other in our cities and our classrooms. Another goal of multicultural education is to combat ignorance of others who are different from us, thus freeing us from fear of each other.

The two goals of literature teaching and multicultural education can be integrated and achieved together. The Fictional Family methodology offers students the experience of relating to a diversity of cultures at the same time as they explore the understanding of and identification with fictional characters. When teaching in any discipline, diversity and multiculturalism often appear within a wide variety of social issues. In the Fictional Family scenarios, topics such as ageism, sexual assault, mental and physical disabilities, death, divorce, substance abuse, bullying, stepfamilies, gender stereotyping, and teen-age suicide appear. These topics should be inseparable from the work with Fictional Family.

Despite widespread acknowledgement of the importance of dealing with gender issues in education, their treatment in schooling still remains a problematic area. The Fictional Family technique can work as a powerful tool to create awareness in its participants of gender discrimination, sexual stereotyping, and traditional perspectives of women as lesser contributors to a variety of cultures and fields. Through dramatic enactment of their fictional family characters' lives, societal attitudes and behaviors are clearly reflected, giving teachers an ideal opportunity to underline the connections between these attitudes and behaviors. By seizing this opportunity, they can facilitate the group's sensitivity to, and awareness of, the possibility of effecting change. Numerous examples from the scenarios enacted in classes range from such topics as lesbianism, family violence, eating disorders and other more subtle manifestations of sex differentiation. A student playing a 65-year old Muslim woman wrote in her character diary:

> "Sometimes I wonder at the irony of my life. I have always advocated for a woman to know her place. I scoffed at the liberties my husband granted me, and am often disgusted by the behavior of my daughter-in-law. But at the same time ... I am completely at my son, Gulran's, mercy. Gulran could strive for an education, for a glorious career and no one blinks an eye. Yet if I, as a young person, pursued something

other than to be a good wife and mother, I would have been scorned, even disowned from my family. I harbour some resentment from this situation … this "trap".

I have said that the Fictional Family technique can be used as part of one's own subject matter. The scenarios can be used to teach not only such subjects as English literature, composition, creative writing, and history as mentioned above, but also principles of ecology in the fields of science and technology, and economics in the social studies.

Drama always deals in very specific and particular examples. Thus, basing drama activities on *ecological issues* usually means looking at very specific and localized examples of these larger issues, that is, the causes and effects of one family's activity on the planet's ecology, as well as local social issues on environmental concerns. Fictional Family character and context development which center on conflict over environmental issues enlighten students to the applicability of ecological principles and their responsibilities around them— both within the family and the home—to a broader social arena.

Summary

The Fictional Family dramatic technique has been offered here as a powerful tool both in the drama class and across the curriculum A variety of other uses of the technique are outside the scope of this paper but have been dealt with in a variety of texts which are listed below.

References

For more about the author's books, papers: <pages.infinit.net/murielgp>

Bandler, Richard, Grinder, John, & Satir, Virginia. (1976). *Changing with families*. Palo Alto, CA: Science and Behavior Books Inc. (Patterns of effective communication with families can be applied to working with fictional families. A variety of warm-up exercises in this and other books in this section can be used to help in the Fictional Family process.

Benedetti, Robert: (1970).*The actor at work*. Englewood Cliffs, NJ: Prentice-Hall. (A comprehensive approach to self-discovery in the development of basic acting skills with numerous examples.)

Field, S. (1982). *Screenplay: The foundations of screenwriting.* New York: Dell. (A guide to create multi-dimensional characters for the purposes of screenwriting, noting how to build character and create dialogue.)

Gold, Muriel. (1991). *The Fictional Family in drama, education and groupwork,* Springfield, IL: Charles C. Thomas. (A step-by-step approach to the Fictional Family technique in an introductory university acting class and suggesting individual professionals in a variety of disciplines adapt it for their own use. The book relates the technique to the Stanislavski System, Brecht's Epic Theatre, Theatre of the Absurd, and to other actor training techniques.)

Gold, Muriel. (1998). The Fictional Family and family therapy: Dramatic techniques with family therapy trainees. In J. MacDougall, & S. Yoder (Eds.), *Contaminating Theatre.* Evanston, IL: Northwestern University Press. (This chapter presents a variety of Fictional Family techniques useful to family therapists in their role of promoting communication and healing within families.)

Gold, Muriel. (2000). *Therapy through drama. The Fictional Family.* Springfield, IL: Charles C. Thomas. (Therapeutic applications of the Fictional Family with specific populations (family therapy trainees, drama therapists, graduate drama therapy students, and drama students) are described. The book addresses ways to work with particular problems such as rape survival, and themes such as improvisational scenework training and transformative learning. Four of the seven chapters are contributions by a number of other authors who have worked with the technique.)

Hodgson, John & Richards, E. (1966). *Improvisation.* London, UK: Methuen. (Based in the concept that the same skills need for the actor are the same as those required for productive living.)

Landy, Robert (1985). *Drama Therapy: concepts and practices.* Springfield, IL: Charles C Thomas. (Chapter on "Extended Dramatization" inspired the application of Gold's Fictional Family technique in the drama class.)

Moore, Sonia: (1985). *Training an Actor.* New York, NY: Penguin. (Grounded in Stanislavski theory, with numerous examples of improvising for the theatre.)

Shurtleff, M. *(1978) Audition.* New York, NY: Walker & Co. (Centered on "getting the part", offering a clear-cut approach to creating dynamic characters.)

Chapter 13

APPLIED DRAMA IN BUSINESS

Joel Gluck & Ted Rubenstein

Drama is used in organizations worldwide to develop a wide range of skills, including leadership and management, communication and presentation, diversity and ethical awareness, coaching and facilitation, organizational development, and other areas of human relations essential to the needs of business, non-profit, and governmental institutions.

A natural vehicle for the experiential learning of social and emotional skills, drama has become increasingly popular in corporate training as the need for a heightened degree of "emotional intelligence" at all levels in the organization has grown (Goleman, 1998).

The use of techniques derived from improvisational theatre, in particular, is a match for the rapid changes that the business world must face. Unscripted improvisational drama is a metaphor for what corporations now recognize is needed: spontaneity, quick thinking, alternative solutions to old problems, acceptance of difference, flexibility and listening. Indeed, there are now hundreds of theatre artists applying these methods in business, and conferences have been held about "applied improvisation." (See references below, as well as the website supplement to this chapter: <www.interactiveimprov.com/businesswb. html>.)

Although it is not known who first used drama in a business setting, the use of improvisation and simulated situations to assess performance was applied in military officer and intelligence personnel training as early as the 1940s (Bronfenbrenner & Newcomb, 1948). In recent years, throughout the world, theatre companies, drama therapists, and organizational psychologists have built training programs, either as new businesses or within their existing organizations. This growth has been met with enthusiasm by corporate human resource and training departments.

In this chapter we will highlight two examples of organizations that use drama techniques in business. The first, The Ariel Group, Inc., based in Arlington, Massachusetts, offers theatre-based training in leadership presence and communication skills to organizations throughout the world. The second, Dramatic Diversity, located in Chicago, is a theatre-based company that helps organizations create a more inclusive working environment, valuing diversity.

The Ariel Group, Inc.

Founded in 1992, the Ariel Group (<www.arielgroup.com) specializes in training organizational leaders in communication skills and relationship building. At the heart of the Ariel Group's work is the concept of "leadership presence," defined as "the ability to connect authentically with the thoughts and feelings of others, in order to motivate them to a desired outcome" (Halpern & Lubar, 2003).

The skills of an accomplished actor are very similar to the skills of a respected leader. Great actors demonstrate passion, empathy, authenticity, creativity, confidence, self-control—talents that are equally present in great leaders. They possess, in a word, presence. In Ariel Group programs and one-to-one coaching, facilitators draw upon a wide range of interactive drama, improvisation, and role-play techniques, stretching participants to access the potential of their body, their voice, and their creative imagination, all informed by an understanding of what actors focus on when doing their best work.

The Ariel Group offers practical, theatre-based exercises for improving one's presence as a leader, developing skills in all four areas described by the company's "PRES" Model—four areas that experienced actors often excel in:

*P*resent: being in the moment, flexible; handling fear, distraction, pressure, and the unexpected

*R*eaching Out: strengthening relationships through the ability to empathize and make connections

*E*xpressive: aligning the use of voice, body, energy, and emotion to convey clear, compelling messages with passion

*S*elf-Knowing: acting from one's deepest values and beliefs, building trust and credibility through authenticity

Program Snapshot

Depending on client need, an Ariel Group program can range from a one-time event to an integrated curriculum unfolding over one to two years, incorporating participant self-assessment, group trainings, learning assignments, and individual coaching. A typical training is one to two days, with an average class size of six to eight participants per facilitator. (For special events, other approaches have been developed to make working with larger groups possible.)

Frequently, the participants in a class know one other or even work on the same team within their company; in other programs, such as The Ariel Group's public programs, or their collaborations with universities offering executive education, participants can come from a variety of different organizations—and, sometimes, a number of different continents. The best location for an Ariel Group program is a retreat center, hotel conference room, or other off-site location, although on occasion workshops (and one-to-one coaching) are delivered right in the workplace.

Instead of the kinds of activities found in standard corporate training—PowerPoint presentations, business case simulations, or, in some instances, competitive challenges or trust exercises—in Ariel Group workshops, participants are invited to join in what might best be described as a very condensed theatre conservatory training. Since "acting" (or its business equivalent, public speaking) is very high on the list of popular fears—outranking the fear of death in some surveys!—gaining participants' trust can take some cajoling from the facilitator at the outset. But, before long, the entire group is participating in warm-ups, breathing and voice work, and improvisational theatre activities. Often, even the staunchest cynic in the group begins to relax and have fun.

Throughout the program, links are made to the business rationale for each activity. The facilitator often refers back to the PRES model, as well as to a brainstormed chart comparing the skills of actors to those of leaders. As the program proceeds, the activities become progressively more challenging—incorporating improvisation, dynamic use of the voice, and the use of personal stories—stretching participants' ability to let go of their inhibitions and communicate in creative and dynamic ways with the group. At the same time, the work begins to deepen, inviting participants to share aspects of their own lives, telling the stories that helped shaped their values and make them into the leaders they are today.

By lunchtime on the second day, the group has come through an experience together that has been practical in its application to business and leadership, while also a great deal of fun, in moments deeply moving, and memorable throughout. Significantly, over the course of about 12 hours, participants have seen one another take risks, become more expressive, and change their communication behaviors in ways that they had previously not imagined.

Applied Drama in Presence Coaching

In the final afternoon, a standard Ariel Group program ends by offering each participant an opportunity to practice the skills they have learned, by working on a challenging one-to-one interaction, a business presentation to a group, or some other difficult communication situation. The Ariel Group facilitator actively coaches these role-plays; the whole group participates and gives supportive and constructive feedback along the way.

Coaching an Interaction. A typical example involves a challenging one-to-one situation. The participant, whom we shall call Phyllis, is a leader whose feedback has been that she does not give people the time of day; she is a results-oriented pacesetter, who would love to be seen as more of a visionary. In this role-play, another participant plays Jake, a young member of her team who seems to do the bare minimum, lacking enthusiasm. Phyllis's goal in the role-play is to see how she can motivate and influence Jake. She starts off:

Phyllis: So, Jake, I wanted to talk with you today about why you're not getting your work done. Every time I walk past your desk you seem to be surfing the web.

Jake: Well, I … I was researching that assignment you gave me.

Quickly the role-play devolves into accusations and defensiveness. The facilitator checks in with Phyllis to find out if she is making headway on motivating Jake. Instead, Phyllis feels the conversation, although typical for her, is not working at all. The facilitator asks for a volunteer to step in to play Phyllis's role (a technique borrowed from Augusto Boal's Forum Theatre, to let multiple people play the protagonist) and try an alternative opening:

"New" Phyllis: Hi, Jake! Thanks for meeting with me today. How are you doing?

Jake: Uh, fine, I guess.

"New" Phyllis: You know, Jake, I've gotten the sense over time that you do not seem as happy or excited about the work as you were before. I just wanted to check in with you about it. How are you feeling these days?

As the role-play continues, the participant playing Phyllis really listens to Jake, connecting with him on a human level. The facilitator checks-in with Phyllis and the group about the effectiveness of this new version, and Phyllis expresses excitement about the difference she is seeing.

The facilitator suggests Phyllis step back in and try again, incorporating what she learned from watching the second role-play. By the end of the 25-minute coaching session, Phyllis declares: "This is something I really want to remember: I have to connect with the other person as a person, *before* I can make them see my vision for what needs to change."

Coaching a Presentation. Another common example is a presenter who, when delivering business content to a group, tends to get dry, serious, and unexpressive. One approach the coach can take uses an imaginary scenario:

Facilitator: So, Bill, I'd like you to try your presentation again, but this time, I'd like you to imagine that you've been asked to come speak to a first-grade classroom. The rest of us are all going to pretend to be first graders. I'd like you to do whatever you need to do to grab our attention—change your voice and body language to get us involved. OK, everyone, let's pretend we're all in first grade.

(The group immediately becomes a talking, laughing, crying, and distracted bunch of playful kids.)

Bill (in a serious adult voice): Umm ... oh ... this is hard! Uh, hello kids, I'm here to talk with you today about the challenges we face in migrating three incompatible organization-wide legacy database systems into the modern world. As many of you already know from seeing Rita's report, we are proposing data warehousing as the option of choice....

Facilitator (side coaching): OK, let's pause for a second. What do you notice is happening?

Bill: Well, they're not really paying attention to me.

Facilitator: That's right. It's not easy to talk to first graders! You might have to really change what you're doing to get their attention. Give it a shot.

Bill: OK.

Facilitator: And, action!

(Group resumes their noisy play.)

Bill (with a more dynamic voice, making a big gesture with his arms): Hi kids! How are you today?

Audience: Fine! ... My band-aid is loose.... Are you Tommy's daddy? ... Hey! She took my cookie!

Bill (moving right up to the audience, bending down, in a suspenseful voice, with big eyes): So, kids, do you want to hear a story?

Audience: Yay! ... A story! ... Yes! ... Does it have dinosaurs in it?

Bill (making big gestures, and using his full vocal range): Once upon a time, a loooooooonnnnngggg time ago, there was a big, ugly, Mean, Old, THREE-Headed MON-Ssster!! (He hisses like a snake and makes a scary face.) You know what it was called? The Legacy Databasssse!!!

Audience: Ooooooooo!!!

After another minute or so, the facilitator stops the action, and invites the audience to applaud for Bill and comment on what he has done. The feedback is powerful: Bill is acknowledged for stretching his body and voice much farther than the group has seen him do before. He seems to be connecting with his audience, rather than talking over them. And, most important, his passion feels real.

Before Bill is through, the facilitator invites him to try his speech once again for a business audience, but this time incorporating what he discovered in the first-grade version. The result: Bill is much more expressive than in his first run-through, and begins to improvise, sneaking in metaphors and humor to get his point across. The entire group comments on his transformation.

Rationale

Leaders are responsible for the authentic excitement of their teams and organizations—but first they must learn to access their own passion. Whereas emotion is often left out of the workplace, the Ariel Group's programs encourage participants to bring their emotions with them.

The vehicle of theatre proves to be ideal for getting that message across, allowing participants to explore greater expressiveness and authenticity in an environment that feels simultaneously safe, fun, and challenging—where it is OK to make mistakes. Through acting, improvisation, and role-play, the Ariel Group's programs stretch corporate leaders out of their comfort zones, helping them experience tangible improvements in their communication and leadership while developing each person's own unique presence.

Dramatic Diversity

Dramatic Diversity (<www.dramaticdiversity.com), based in Chicago, has been using action-oriented, unscripted theatre since 2001 in corporate settings, in a management consultancy process that begins with assessment, followed by program design, service delivery and outcome evaluation. Dramatic Diversity has formed partnerships with experts in diversity, industrial and organizational psychology and drama therapists to provide companies with a thorough analysis, training, and implementation of diversity initiatives.

Assessment

Once a company recognizes the need for specialized training in diversity, a team of industrial-organizational psychologists conducts a thorough assessment— lasting days or weeks—to clarify the company's challenges, needs, and goals. Top executives are interviewed first, to identify the core problem and who in the company has the necessary influence to create change. Next, employees at all levels are interviewed, to elicit root metaphors and narratives.

A root metaphor is a set of words or phrases that capture how individuals within the organization talk about the company, its product or service, and the ways diversity is/is not embraced by employees. The team listens for specific language used to describe groups, work teams, cliques, and specific employees. Words such as "those people", "suits", "them" or "you know those 'fill-in-the-blank' people from the 'fill-in-the-blank' department" indicate negativity or territoriality—obstacles to embracing diversity.

For example, when employees were asked how one gets promoted inside their company, several said, "You mean the good ol' boy network?" This kind of language not only suggests an informal, unwritten process for promotion—it also conjures up images of sexism and racism.

The assessment team also elicits specific incidents in which preferential treatment, discrimination, or prejudice was an issue in the workplace. These stories can range from brief occurrences—such as an ethnic joke told during lunch—to long, ongoing events such as a promotion process tainted by political agendas or interdepartmental warfare.

Program Design

The assessment team compiles the metaphors and narratives into a brief report that is then shared with a program design team, comprised of theatre directors, actors, drama therapists, playwrights, diversity experts, and psychologists. The team begins to craft activities and scenarios that will be used in training the employees on diversity initiatives and practices. Consistent with theories in drama therapy, these scenarios are similar to the narratives discussed during the assessment—however, the details are significantly changed so as to create a sense of distance and preserve confidentiality.

For example, in one company, a financial services firm, the assessment team unearthed a narrative concerning the recent hiring patterns of new employees. According to many observers within the company, during the course of a year only Caucasian men, over 35, with a similar height and weight seemed to be hired. While this was not accurate according to personnel records it was the perception of many of the employees. This narrative was crafted into a short scenario about a restaurant owner who had decided to offer only one menu item. This scenario was enacted with managers becoming customers at this imaginary restaurant. After a few "visits" to this restaurant the entire group started talking about the perceptions that employees had about the "one item menu" hiring practices.

The final program design typically includes five to six scene-starters that initiate an unscripted role-play. These starters offer a brief character description and a description of the given circumstances, i.e., the who, what and where of each scene—participants then make up the plot, outcome, and lines for the scene. The scene starters are designed to provoke conversation, ideally providing the seed for an entire story comprised of several scenes told through improvised dialogue. As the story is created, ample time is given for the group to discuss the issues that have been raised during the scenes. As this unfolds, the group is not encouraged to connect the scenes to "real" events within the company. That is saved for the final phase of the program when action items are created.

Once the program is designed, it is converted into a set of concrete outcomes or goals—focusing on measurable results such as customer satisfaction, increased sales, and employee retention. The design team must draw clear connections, to clarify how opening up discussion through role-play and improvisational storytelling can deliver improvements to the bottom line for the corporation. This might mean pre- and post-tests of employee attitudes and values, comparing ledger sheets before and after training, or conducting customer satisfaction surveys. The specific measurement tools are recommended by an industrial-organizational psychologist and executed by the client company.

Delivery of Services

Following the design of the program and outcome measures, the client company is ready for training—depending on the size of the company, this might range from a full day to several weeks, spread out over several months. The training team might visit a company six to eight times a year, conducting improvisational storytelling sessions with employees, while at the same time continuing a discussion among the employees about the real issues facing the company.

On the first day of training the scenarios are introduced, as are exercises that encourage spontaneity. The exercises might be physical warm-ups or theatre games that maximize silliness and fun. In subsequent sessions the scenarios are played out and the story begins to be told. The plot and setting of the story can be quite fantastical or realistic, but the facilitator encourages the group to keep the story metaphorical and away from the specific incidents that might have occurred. Distancing the material in this way is deliberate: encouraging the use of metaphors helps prevent employees from becoming entrenched in office politics. This is in contrast to a typical psychotherapeutic setting in which the therapist encourages clients to use role-play to reflect on specific situations.

For example, in one company, a promotion was the subject of some controversy, and was ultimately cast as an issue of discrimination. The two employees involved were barely capable of sitting in a room together. Whenever the subject of the promotion came up their interchange quickly escalated. As both employees were high-ranking managers, subordinates would rally behind their respective leader. To make matters worse, with potential for a lawsuit, executives were quick to contain any discussion about the issue. Clearly, a direct role-play was not indicated.

The scene that was provided involved two "students" vying for a top spot with a valued professor. Employees took turns playing out not only how they would relate to the imagined professor but also how the two competitors might interact with each other. As each employee took his or her turn playing out the scene, the group discussed the various endings and plot twists. No conclusions were drawn, instead, the group was asked to talk about which scenes resonated, reflected, or were in opposition to the values of the group.

The role of the facilitator is to clarify and amplify the issues drawn from the discussions. Once the issues are clearly articulated, the group is asked to generate a to-do list of actions based on what has been learned during the sessions—a set of concrete items that include what needs to be changed, who will make the change, who will evaluate the change, by when it will happen, and what financial or human resources are needed to make the change.

After a set period of time, usually within six months, the facilitator returns to the group and some of the same scene starters are presented to the group. To help them examine their progress toward achieving their goals, the group is asked to look at the scenes and stories that were created before and explore the possibility of "rewriting" the script. The improvisational scenes presented in this second round continue to be distanced, metaphorical scenes rather than real-life examples. This helps maintain greater spontaneity, which in turn sparks rich dialogue about the health of the group and the group's efforts.

Evaluation

After the training is complete, the assessment team returns to the key executives, now armed with the results of the concrete measures generated by the group, as well as other outcome measures such as cost savings, profit margins, and customer satisfaction numbers. The key issues that were raised and wrestled with are also discussed. At this point the executives are encouraged to make whatever changes worked into more permanent elements of company policy.

Conclusion

The use of dramatic methods is by no means a new approach to corporate training, and its value is becoming increasingly recognized. One challenge for the practitioner in this work is to balance the oftentimes competing demands of management with the needs of employees. The practitioner must also embrace the ambiguity that unscripted role play encourages, while at the same time focusing the work into concrete outcomes.

Executives often comment afterward how informative the experience was for management. One insight frequently shared is that this form of training challenges tired and entrenched ways of thinking and doing business. Employees and managers alike begin to see each other and their customers as people, human beings with similarities and differences. This outcome is perhaps the most dramatic—helping people value, not just tolerate, different ways of looking, speaking and behaving.

References

Webpage supplement to this chapter: <www.interactiveimprov.com/businesswb.html>

<www.appliedimprov.net>: This community of those applying improvisation in business has conferences and an online discussion group.

<www.tonisant.com/aitg/Training_and_Development: Sant's *Applied & Interactive Theatre Guide* lists books and organizations' websites relevant to the use of theatre in corporate training.

Bronfenbrenner, Uri, & Newcomb, Theodore M. (1948). Improvisations—an application of psychodrama in personality diagnosis. *Sociatry, 4*, 367–382.

Goleman, Daniel. (1998) *Working with emotional intelligence.* New York: Bantam. (Goleman's thesis, that emotional awareness and control is central, not subsidiary, to how we approach life and work, changed forever how we think about intelligence. This, his second book on the subject, applies the EQ concept in business.)

Halpern, Belle & Lubar, Kathy. (2003). *Leadership presence: Dramatic techniques to reach out, motivate, and inspire.* New York: Gotham Books. (A clear and thorough approach for leveraging the knowledge and skills of actors in the business world. Contains practical exercises and inspiring examples of actors and leaders facing and overcoming challenges. The authors are founders of the Ariel Group.)

Koppett, Kat. (2001). *Training to imagine: Practical improvisational theatre techniques to enhance creativity, teamwork, leadership and learning.* Alexandria, VA: Stylus. (The author, a professional trainer, management consultant, and actor, demonstrates how to effectively transfer improv techniques to the day-to-day business environment.)

Shaw, Marvin E., Corsini, Raymond J., Blake, Robert, & Mouton, Jane. (1980). *Role playing: A practical manual for group facilitators.* San Diego, CA: University Associates. (A reworking of Corsini's 1961 edition, *Role playing in Business and Industry,* this book is an introduction to role play in the development of human relation skills, selling, interviewing, teaching, counseling, supervising, etc., in business and other contexts.)

Chapter 14

MUSEUM THEATRE

Catherine Hughes

In addition to using drama in school settings, this modality also can be used to bring alive the learning in museums and related quasi-educational institutions. Museum theatre is a relatively new field that is ripe for the employment of improvising actors, innovative directors and collaborative playwrights. Especially in the last decade, one can happen upon improvised theatrical performances taking place in the most unlikely places. In the past, museums were thought to be reserved for quiet contemplation and appreciation, full of masterpieces, historic artifacts, scientific collections, and cabinets of curiosities, but changes are happening. Exhibition halls and galleries across North America, the United Kingdom and Australia, as well as in other parts of the world, have come alive with the sound of actors communicating with visitors—exchanging ideas, debating questions and sparking discoveries. The staff of museums and similar cultural institutions, such as zoos, aquaria, and historic sites, have ventured into the realm of drama and performance, transforming once static, tradition-bound storehouses of knowledge into vibrant and challenging percolators of ideas.

A visitor at the London Natural History Museum today might engage in discussion with an actress playing Mary Anning as she tells about her 19th century discovery of the Ichthyosaur. Or it becomes possible for visitors to "conduct research" in the wetland habitat of the Central Park Zoo with characters aptly named, "Perfesser" Lily Marsh and "Perfesser" Pete Bog. One can ask questions about the history of white settlement with an actor/tour guide while on a tour through the National Museum of Australia. You can even jump into the action of "SciProv," improvisation about science, at the Lawrence

Hall of Science in Berkeley, California. These experiences represent the fresh new ways museums and dramatists have found they can work together.

Necessarily broad in its definition, the umbrella term "museum theatre" includes any theatrical or dramatic experience visitors to zoos, aquaria, historic sites, and museums of all disciplines may have in the course of their visit. Museum theatre reflects the influence of many theatrical models. At some institutions such as Plimoth (sic) Plantation, the experience situates the visitor in another time, like a time machine, and they can interact with historic role players who inhabit the site. In other museums, there is a suggestion to role play much like a creative drama game, as at the Columbus (Ohio) Art Museum, where visitors are encouraged to try on costumes from the Dutch Golden Age and imagine they are painters of the period. Some museums, such as Boston's Museum of Science, offer visitors adult-targeted plays with improvised discussion, giving people opportunities to debate provocative ethical and social issues surrounding current scientific advances. (Some of the techniques used by here are in part based on Boal's Forum Theatre, as discussed in Chapter 21).

The common ground for such dramatic experiences is that they draw equally from the arts of museum education and interpretation, and theatre. Traditional methods such as little cards or plaques explaining designated artifacts don't really communicate with visitors of all ages and backgrounds, while the collaboration of theatre artists and museum educators leads to multi-modal experiences that make the exhibits more relevant and meaningful. It leads to a kind of interactive theatre that breaks down the 'fourth wall,' that imagined barrier in traditional theatre that separates actors and audience, placing actors amidst their audience with immediate feedback and dynamic potential. It is live without a net and requires talent and *chutzpah* (a yiddish term describing a quality of near-brazen boldness). Anything can happen!

History

Colonial Williamsburg in Virginia has used non-professionals for more than 40 years, playing the roles of blacksmiths, wheelwrights, and so forth. They describe their jobs to visitor as if they are still doing them, living in the early 17th century. The Science Museum of Minnesota in St. Paul first began incorporating theatre into its public programming in 1971 by hiring actors to interpret exhibits while doubling as security guards. The 1990s were challenging years for many institutions in the United States, as funding sources evaporated and a push to sell tickets and boost the take at the door escalated. Museum educators were looking for new and more effective ways to reach and educate visitors, and they found success hiring actors and incorporating theatrical techniques.

Meanwhile, there were a number of historic sites, or open-air museums, in the US, such as Plimoth and Colonial Williamsburg, that had already been using first-person interpreters to add a human dimension to their architecture and furnishings. Early on, such living history programs were limited to first-person representations of another time. As such, no comment on the ramifications of actions taken in that day on the future could be entertained. The situation was exclusively in the present moment of the historic period of the site. This often left the visitor puzzled, and worse, frustrated, as many of their questions could not be answered. Consequently, living history of this type was circumscribed in its power and scope. This situation began to change as more museums began to experiment with theatrical forms in the late 1980s, extending the notion of how living history might be done.

Interpreters working in these sites were often historians, and did not necessarily consider themselves actors, and indeed, to this day many still do not. Rather than following in the traditions of the theatre, they were following in the footsteps of Artur Hazelius, founder of Skansen in Stockholm, the first open-air museum. Hazelius decided to use costumed interpreters and musicians to animate the historic site, believing that otherwise, "Skansen would be nothing but a dead museum, a dry shell of the past" (Anderson, 1984, p. 19). The discussion of who should portray characters in museums has always been an open question. Jackson's (2000) observation about 'first-person' interpretation illustrates some of the issues:

> "'First-person' interpretation, however, unlike other more theatre-based techniques, occupies an in-between territory in which visitors are often quite unconscious of being acted to, let alone being in role themselves. There is no denying that 'First-person' is a form of acting, even though partly disguised by the spontaneous nature of the exchanges between character and visitor. It might be argued that the very 'inter-activeness' of 'First-person' makes it more vital still that it be undertaken by specialist interpreters who are equally adept in interpretation and in performance" (p. 211).

Anyone working in museum theatre, be they actors or interpreters, must develop the necessary subtle qualities of being a very good performer and an equally good communicator, and must be mindful that the *raison d'etre* for existing within the world of a museum is to create memorable, educational experiences for the visitor. There is incredible satisfaction in this type of work, but it is not just in a performance, it is in the interaction as a whole.

The 1980s were a heady decade for museums, which increased their attendance to unprecedented levels. More people were choosing to spend their leisure time in exhibition halls and galleries of all disciplines. Alongside this growth in visitors, public programming of all types proliferated, and many museum theatre programs began at this time. There were numerous individual reasons to turn to theatre. At the Museum of Science, Boston the use of theatre grew out of a desire to approach topics that did not lend themselves to demonstration or lecture, such as women's' roles and achievements in science (Hughes, 1998). It grew out of a need to address ideas left out of exhibitions, or outdated, outmoded galleries. An actor in role can rectify an oversight or update label copy. If we learn, for example, that a fossilized ichthyosaur was first uncovered by a twelve year old girl in 1812, an actress playing her—the aforementioned Mary Anning—can transform that exhibition. Another historic example is to have an actor play Sir Issac Newton, who can, rather than build on existing myths surrounding his life and work, burst the myths. It is an effective surprise to have Newton deny that the notion of gravity came to him from a falling apple.

Aside from the goal of providing educational experiences, there was also a wish to reach visitors emotionally, to move beyond the dry acquisition of facts. The founding director of the U.S. Holocaust Memorial Museum, Jeshajahu Weinberg, a former theatre director, put it succinctly:

> *Theatre is effective if it triggers processes of identification in the audience, when it arouses empathy. I am trying to transpose the same principles of empathy to the museum. Theatre is a place where your emotions get involved. The museum, usually not"* (Strand, 1993, p. 51).

There is also the exciting and challenging prospect of telling an untold story through theatre, which goes to the heart of what museum theatre in all its many forms is so good at—offering the alternative view, a different perspective, questioning science, reexamining history, confronting difficult and complex issues, marrying emotion with the facts, revealing human enterprise, all of which is in essence telling the untold story. And this is what makes museum theatre so necessary, for without it, many stories are left untold.

The International Museum Theatre Alliance (IMTAL) was founded in 1990, and a related organization, IMTAL-Europe, was founded in 1998. Now they have memberships representing more than 200 museums and individuals! In Australia, museum theatre practitioners are poised to form their own national network, IMTAL-Australia in 2004. In the museum of today, then, drama has become a major element, and its application a dynamic opportunity for ingenuity.

Various Techniques and Programs

Museum theatre involves engaging visitors in the willing suspension of disbelief—in pretend, or imagination—to enhance the educational experience that happens within a museum. It ranges from storytelling and living-history interpretation, to musical and dramatic presentations, to creative dramatics, puppetry, mime and much more. There are many ways to use museum theatre, and a variety of techniques and approaches to choose from, depending on the particular educational goals and needs of the institution. Theatre provides a versatile and dynamic form, inspiring constant experimentation with styles and content.

There has been a recognition of the need for a variety of entry points into exhibitions for different learning styles, which theatre and drama can provide. All ages are targeted, from elders to school children. In more process-oriented dramas, museum educators work with groups of school children, who can take on roles in extended workshops to explore the ideas of a museum. For instance, in one historic house program, students are divided into two groups, one of which takes on the roles of the servants and the other become the masters of the house, and half way through the day, the groups switch roles. A program such as this necessitates actors leading the children in role to sustain the action.

Common to many museums are individual characters who interact with visitors, based on training in dramatic techniques and necessary research. The characters at the Palace Stables in Northern Ireland train in history and then improvise freely with visitors. The Natural History Museum in London has a large repertoire of varied characters, including the aforementioned Mary Anning and the History Men, two life size puppets, designed to satirize the stereotypical image of scientists in white coats. The History Men roam the exhibition halls, observing and seeking patterns as they watch visitors. Visitors in turn watch them, as they humorously conduct experiments, such as measuring visitors' heads and marking down their findings. All of this is done without words, for the History Men are mute. Puppets can work on many levels, as Roy Hawkey (2003) states in his article detailing the Natural History Museum's theatre program: "Puppetry offers the advantage of being able to present sensitive issues more easily and more acceptably than with live actors in a role" (p. 47).

At the Central Park Zoo in New York, there are three sets of characters that have been developed to interact with visitors. Jonathan Ellers, director of the theatre program there, describes their practice:

> Performers are trained not only in the science and biology their characters would need to know, they are trained in myriad "points of entry" for every conceivable kind of visitor or visitor group—particularly children. Lots of attention is paid to learning how to approach visitors, allowing visitors to initiate an approach, coaxing visitors to approach, and inviting visitors to participate in their own interpretive experience. Performers are supplied with jokes, anecdotes and—particularly—props and creative dramatics activities, all of which they may use at their discretion, depending on the visitors comfort, receptiveness, and willingness to "play."

One set of characters at New York's Central Park Zoo are "Perfesser Paul R. Bear" & "Perfesser Paula Bear," (the character names are often plays on the subject matter; in this exhibit, they interpret in solo shifts), who introduce themselves to visitors as "The World's Foremost Authority on Polar Bears and Polar Bear Behavior." Costumed in a many-pocketed vest—loaded with props and visual aids, and bright orange in color order so the Perfesser can be seen from the air by the research helicopter—the character boldly dares visitors to attempt to stump him/her with questions about Polar Bears. (There's some merging of the theatre artist and clown here, related to Chapter 30 on clowning.)

At the Zoo's tropic zone, "Jungle Jim and Jungle Jane" enliven "Base Camp Discovery," and Jim and Jane interpret the tropics as a team. Keeping in touch via two-way radios, one character mans the location, the "base camp," where all research is assigned and recorded; the other character serves as the "field researcher." "Base Camp" is set up at the entrance of the exhibit. As visitors particularly young ones) enter, the "base camp" researcher invites them to take "assignments" doing research in the tropics. "Assignments" are age specific everything from "finding the blue frogs" (for the very young) to taking a census and mapping activities for older kids. Once assigned a "research project," the young researchers set off to find the "field researcher" who helps them with their assignment. The kids (and sometimes adults) then report their findings to "base camp" either by radio, or by returning physically to "base camp."

The Zoo's wetland habitats are interpreted by "Perfesser" Lily Marsh and "Perfesser" Pete Bog: Lily and Pete interpret wetland habitats. Unlike the other characters, Lily and Pete are actually doing research in their habitats—each performance "shift" being a period of time during which the performers do very real but very simple research—taking water and air temperatures, tallying frogs & turtles, and doing simple water quality tests etc.—in which visitors (particularly the young ones) are *invited to participate*. Like the other characters, they have myriad props, jokes, anecdotes and creative dramatics activities to facilitate interpretation, but they are also given poetry (written for two readers reading simultaneously) to perform, and are given basic guidelines for improvised "scenes" to help them segue into and out of activities.

The Museum of Science, Boston has been working out an experimental model in collaboration with the Current Science and Technology (CS & T) program. They are testing out Science Improv, in which they take a scientific headline from the news and improvise a comic skit from it before an audience. Then an "Official" CS&T person corrects any "exaggerations" the two actors might have inserted for comic effect. The idea is to get people interested in current events, and then to see how to look critically at what they find in the news. Their structure is COMEDY!COMEDY!COMEDY!—science facts—COMEDY! COMEDY!COMEDY!—science facts.

As a last example of how museum theatre has been used, Bill Singerman from the Field Museum in Chicago took classes with the improvisational actors associated with the famed Second City Theatre Club of Chicago and out of his work with them, created a dynamic collaborative teacher workshop that incorporated improvisation, called *Bringing Dioramas to Life*. He wrote of the project:

Teachers of all grades and disciplines were divided into groups of about 6–8 in the Mammals Halls. Second City educators Anne Libera and Larry Grimm led the activities. I observed as Anne asked one group of teachers to examine a diorama featuring the famous Lions of Tsavo. After a brief discussion of the diorama, she asked the teachers to become the animal as a group. This activity was a modified version of an exercise called Part of a Whole.

One teacher became the body, another, a leg, a third, the tail. Gradually, they worked as a team to become one unit—a human lion mirrored after the male specimen in the diorama. By physically recreating the lion, they became more engaged with the cat and were focused on examining it in greater detail. They captured and orally described the ways in which the paws touch the ground, the way the mane and whiskers flair, the position held by the tail, etc.

Next, teachers were divided into smaller groups. They were instructed to select a diorama featuring a number of animals posed in a naturalistic setting. Their task? To come up with three freeze frames—a before, during and after. In other words, teachers had to create a story—what is happening in the diorama? What happened right before the animals were frozen? What will happen next?

Some teachers came up with scenes in which animals were scouting for food, others were listening for predators, some animals were teaching their young.

In doing so, participants were able to bring the diorama to life; they were able to look beyond the animals frozen in time and think about how the animals' positioning, postures, expressions and environments inform us of their behaviors and environments.

The response was overwhelmingly positive. Teachers discussed how this kind of activity could engage all kinds of learners, how it would help make students enthusiastic about exploring dioramas and how it would focus their students' attention effectively.

In sum, the workshop was wonderful. Using improvisation to bring dioramas to life is certainly a technique I will continue to use in the future.

There are infinite possibilities for the use of theatre in museums, which are inspired rather than limited by a museum's mission and collection.

Effectiveness

Visitors enjoy and engage with museum theatre, and indications are that they learn as well. At The Science Museum in London (Bicknell & Mazda, 1993), 95% of visitors surveyed support the idea of theatre in a museum. 85% of the sample agreed that the characters in the Museum's drama program made people want to get involved with exhibits and 90% felt that the actors made the exhibit more memorable. At the Museum of Science, Boston people were inspired to write supportive comments on cards they left at the end of their visit. One visitor commented, "The performance was informative, stimulating and educational. It sure does challenge and foster discussion." Another said, "This one [show] moved me in so short a time." The results from these museums' studies and others collectively suggest that theatre can be a powerful learning tool in the museum setting.

Research and evaluation can help both museum and theatre folk learn how to do better, more aesthetically pleasing and educationally satisfying museum theatre. There is wonder in trying to discern the currents rippling below the surface as children sit rapt before a musical about sea turtles, as adults debate the merits of cloning, and as teenagers experience a first-person account of slavery. In realizing and articulating that wonder, we fertilize the field of museum theatre.

References

Further anecdotes and references may be found on the webpage supplement:<www.interactiveimprov.com/museumwb.html>

Anderson, J. (1984). *Time Machines.* Nashville, TN: American Association for State and Local History. (This is a very established book on the first-person interpreting and living history by a well respected practitioner and teacher.)

Bicknell, Sandra and Xerxes Mazda, 1993. "Enlightening or Embarrassing? An evaluation of drama in the Science Museum." London: National Museum of Science and Industry, p. 22. (This well done evaluation provides insight into how visitors make sense of interacting with actors during their museum visit.

Hawkey, R. (2003). All the (Natural) World's a Stage: Museum Theater as an Educational Tool. *Curator* 46(1): 42–59. (This article details the successful and highly wide-ranging theatre program at the Natural Hisory Museum in London.)

Hughes, Catherine. (1998). *Museum Theatre: Communicating with Visitors Through Drama.* Portsmouth, NH: Heinemann. (This was the first book devoted to the field of museum theatre. It is a very personal account of an actor's journey into the world of museums, and her subsequent evolution into a hybrid "museum theatre" professional. It covers such issues as copyright, ethics, and philosophy, as well as the nuts and bolts of museum theatre.)

Jackson, A. (2000). Inter-acting with the Past: the use of participatory theatre at museums and heritage sites. *Research in Drama Education* 5 (2): 199–215. (This research study looks at interactive theatre in two sites: Plimoth Plantation and a Drama-in-Education program at an historic house in the UK.)

Strand, J. (1993). The Storyteller. *Museum News,* March/April: 40–43, 51.

SECTION III

APPLICATIONS IN PSYCHOTHERAPY

Adam Blatner

For years, psychotherapy was thought of mainly as talking, but J.L. Moreno developed ways of adding action methods. Subsequently, a number of approaches to therapy and counseling emerged that involve different kinds of physical involvement. While drama as a component of total milieu therapy was reported to have some effectiveness in the treatment of major mental illnesses, this approach has generally been replaced by the use of medications. More commonly, drama has been found to be useful in dealing with milder neuroses, addictions, personality disorders, conditions in which some re-evaluation of attitudes and patterns of response is needed, whatever the state of the patient's neurophysiological state.

In addition, there is a kind of "therapeutic" benefit that comes with using the techniques and concepts that were first used to treat the more disturbed and applying them to help relatively normal people become even more resilient and healthy. To this end, new fields of endeavor have emerged or become more popular, such as life coaching, spiritual direction, group facilitation, organizational development, and others. Good tools should not be limited just for those in the socially-defined "sick role." Truly therapeutic procedures can often be helpful with healthy people who are seeking to become more healthy. After all, most, if not all, normal people have residual "issues" that can continue to be addressed, released, and cleared. This process can proceed with no implication that the people served are in any way sick.

In this sense, psychodrama and drama therapy should be viewed as root forms that have applications not only in the social institution of health care delivery, but also in education, religion, business, politics, child rearing, home life, conflict resolution in the home, and so forth. Indeed, all the categories in this book really overlap significantly, so there's a certain amount of arbitrariness in our classification which has been done more for organizing the book in accessible groupings than having these sections reflect absolutely separate fields of endeavor.

As part of the evolution of psychotherapy, there has been a growing recognition of the need for patients to be helped to have emotionally re-educative experiences. This involves the inclusion of physical action, imagery, emotions, reason, and other dimensions. A more holistic approach is needed especially for people who are suffering from a variety of types of addictions and the residues of acute or chronic trauma. Drama offers a range of techniques that includes "right brain" as well as "left brain" abilities, and helps to integrate and balance these functions. Drama should not be thought of as a single approach, but rather a vehicle that can be adapted to simpler or more complex modes of work. The techniques constitute a range of tools and the context is a psycho-social "laboratory" or context within which the different therapeutic approaches may be creatively applied according to the individual needs of each patient.

Chapter 15

PSYCHODRAMA, SOCIODRAMA, ROLE PLAYING, AND ACTION METHODS

Adam Blatner

Psychodrama is a method in which people are helped to explore a problem by improvising an enactment as if it were a series of scenes in an unfolding play. This process is facilitated by a trained director, and others in the group often take supporting roles of other people or elements in the drama. Sociodrama, role playing, and the use of action methods are derivatives of this core approach. Historically, psychodrama has been a root form for many of the other methods discussed in this book.

Although psychodrama has been most widely known as a form of psychotherapy, mainly in group settings, it should really be viewed as a complex of techniques and concepts that also can be applied in many non-clinical settings, in education, business, community relations, and so forth. The context of psychodrama might be thought of as a kind of psycho-social laboratory, and the various techniques the different tools that can be used to investigate interpersonal and group relations. These techniques can also help people develop skills in communications, self-awareness, and problem-solving.

The classical form of psychodrama is a group procedure that generally lasts around two hours and can evoke deep emotions. Sociodrama, role playing and action methods are more widely adapted for use in the aforementioned non-clinical applications and also serve as adjuncts to individual or group therapy.

Psychodrama was invented by Jacob L. Moreno, M.D. (1889–1974), a prolifically creative character who also was one of the pioneers of role theory, improvisational theatre, social psychology, and group psychotherapy, as well as writing about the role of creativity in philosophy, theology, and culture. (<www.interactiveimprov.com/morenowb.html>)

One of Moreno's main insights is that the most useful way to cultivate creativity is through promoting spontaneity. Another important related idea is that in general the setting needs to be experienced as safe for spontaneity and improvisation to emerge, because it is a subtle operation of the nervous system that is inhibited in states of anxiety. Therefore, activities that lower anxiety, such as the context of play and the development of trust in a group supports improvisation, which then increases the likelihood of the discovery of more creative solutions to problems (Blatner, 2000).

Another of Moreno's important insights ran a bit counter to the dominant trend in his time towards just talking in therapy. A few educators and others have noted for years that the best learning happens through experiencing and doing. Yet there people are afraid of exposing themselves in drama, and this resistance is discussed more on the webpage supplement: <www.interactiveimprov. com/inhibitionswb.html>. That's why warming-up is needed. Still, for those who are less inhibited, such as children, doing and drama are natural ways to explore and learn. The challenge of psychodrama, then, is in part to establish a procedure that warms people up to becoming comfortable in improvising and acting, in playing with the activity of role playing in the service of insight, rehearsal, and explorations.

The Method

The basic idea of role playing is simple, deriving from the make-believe play we all engaged in as children: Set up a scene and play it out as an improvised drama. The refinements of this basic idea are extensive however, especially as the challenge involves working with a range of problems and contexts. Conducting classical psychodramas can be complex and demanding, so when working with more difficult situations or emotionally disturbed people, only well-trained professionals should lead the group.

The method involves a client or main role player, whose problem is to be explored, and since the method derives from the theatre, he or she is called "the protagonist." A "director" is often the group's main therapist, and in non-therapeutic groups, the key facilitator. The director's role includes producing a dramatic enactment, analyzing psychological and group dynamics, offering support, and other therapeutic functions. Those group members who are asked to help in play roles of other people in the enactment are called "auxiliary egos" or "auxiliaries." These auxiliary roles may also include the protagonist's inner self or part of himself (i.e., the "double" technique), and sometimes even an inanimate object or spirit. Those group members witnessing but not participating directly in the enactment constitute the "audience," though they at times are invited to shift roles, become auxiliaries, or be helpful in other ways. The action takes place in a specially designated area, the "stage." Some classical psychodramatists actually have built a low stage—one that is only one or two steps high—on one side of their group therapy room, as this offers certain advantages. However, it's possible to conduct psychodramas on the floor to the side of the group in a conference room, on a playground, or almost anywhere.

Since creativity is a prime value—and psychodrama is almost unique among the therapies in its clearly explicit goal of helping people to be more creative in their lives.The method itself, as well as its theory, is open to continuous revision, development, and creative adaptation. New techniques and new integrations with other therapeutic approaches continue and make this approach anything but orthodox or dogmatic. Psychodramatic methods can be woven into the course of almost any other type of therapy, and this may be its main value in the long run.

Sociodrama

While psychodrama focuses on the particulars of the individual, who is a complex of *specific* roles and relationships, sociodrama, in contrast, focuses on a general social role or role relationship. A protagonist expresses the dynamics resulting from the competing influences of a number of roles being played, mixed with that individual's unique blend of temperament, interests, abilities, and background; these are in turn embedded in relationships with other people who are similarly unique in their makeup, and thus each relationship is unique. Yet the general roles they play have their own characteristics, and these social role characteristics, apart from the individual elements, are the focus of sociodrama. Thus, in sociodrama, a group might explore the more general predicament of, for example, a parent of a medically chronically sick child; or a couple dealing with the visits with either partner's parents. The focus is on what many different people in such situations might have in common, those factors provided by the culture, the system, the predicament, separated from the unique particulars of each individual's life. In spite of lacking the focus of psychodrama, there is nevertheless a surprising amount of depth, variation, and insight that can be gained simply from exploring the dimensions inherent in a given role! (Sternberg & Garcia, 2000). Other examples of issues addressed in sociodrama might include those arising out of the interactions of teenaged boys and girls, parents and children, police and minorities, professors and college students, etc. One of the advantages of sociodrama is that it highlights the cultural factors impinging on the personal issues in our lives, bringing into shared awareness the ways different people define the relevant social roles.

Sociodrama is an especially meaningful method because our culture is in a state of change more intense than ever in history. It seems that every role is being challenged: what is a good parent or student? What makes for being personally attractive? What is the measure of success? Psychodramatic methods can be adapted for addressing these without having to get into the particular problems of the individual, and this makes it more applicable for schools and community settings in which too much personal self-disclosure would leave the individual feeling too vulnerable.

If we were to bring a truly humanistic approach to social studies, including not only just the thinking faculties, but also empathy regarding emotional issues, sociodrama would probably be recognized as a core teaching method (Blatner, 2006). I imagine a classroom, whether it be within the departments of history, political science, philosophy, or literature: As the topic is considered by the group, roles of those most clearly involved are identified, proponents, opponents, the ones caught in the middle, their relatives, those who have to pay the dues in the long run, the grandchildren who have to grow up in the world based on the decisions being made now. Using psychodramatic techniques such as "the double"—one person offering a kind of "voice over," speaking what generally doesn't get expressed in ordinary discussions—the deeper feelings and hidden assumptions involved in such discussions are brought to light.

One of the more interesting techniques in such a sociodramatic process is that of changing roles. For ten minutes, one might play the role of a woman considering an abortion, and then the director might have everyone shift roles. The next role might be that of a protestor, for or against, or of the unborn child. Using the principle of surplus reality (i.e., including fantasized possibilities), drama can grant an imagined voice, as if those who cannot think or speak could, for this time out of time in the dramatic setting. And then a bit later, the roles are changed again. The purpose is to learn the skills of empathy, of really imagining what it's like to be in another's predicament, looking out on the world with a different set of priorities or assumptions.

Frankly, I envision sociodrama becoming a major method not only in college education, but also in many other settings, perhaps even including international politics. The chapter on Healing the Wounds of History gives a hint of this potential. Sociodrama offers a way to balance objectivity and subjectivity, reason and emotion, the mind and heart. The range of subjects that can be addressed with this approach is rather wide, at least as a partial or adjunctive experience to deepen the learning of many subjects within the humanities, arts, and even sciences.

Role Playing

In some settings, the term role playing is synonymous with psychodrama, but in most settings, it tends to refer to an approach that is aimed *not* at going "deep" into the subconscious, seeking to foster insight, but rather, at working out how better to actually deal with a problem. In this sense, it is closer to the process of simulation used in military or business training programs. (In psychodrama, this approach is called "role training.") (See webpage supplement to note some of these more interesting types of simulations.) Also, role playing is discussed further in Chapter 8 as part of general education.

Role playing ignores—appropriately—the issues of *why* someone reacts the way they do, especially in terms of personal background. A tendency to whine, for example, would *not* lead to an exploration of earlier childhood experiences and complexes related to victimization. Instead, the process would focus on helping the protagonist notice whining behaviors and replacing them with more effective self-assertive tactics. The focus of role playing, instead of being on self-understanding, tends to be more task-oriented, such as how to develop the skills of interviewing, or how best to be interviewed for a job. Politicians role play their debates. In a more technological sense, astronauts in their flight simulators and large armies in training doing war games are also role playing, recognizing that in highly complex systems all the glitches can't be anticipated and the best way to find out what can go wrong is to do a practice run.

The warm up is still needed, but the themes and explorations address alternative responses and better ways to handle them. Sometimes a role reversal is needed in order to understand the other person, or some doubling or other techniques can bring out the unexpressed thoughts or feelings, but not so as to make them problematic or neurotic. The point is that human relations are subtle and learning the right way to assert oneself, modulate one's emotions, present a request, and the like varies with each individual's temperament. It's a knack one must obtain by doing, to get a deep feel of the skill involved—it's not something that can be learned from a book or even a demonstration, because each person's individual blend of abilities and weaknesses make for slight differences in response.

Instead of sharing, what often happens in role playing is others are able to get up and show how they would try to deal with the problem. Sometimes these alternatives are helpful for the first person who played the role in question; at other times, what becomes apparent is that there may be no glib or smooth or guaranteed successful way to cope, and this validates and supports the person who first expressed his frustrating predicament. (This technique has also been adopted, perhaps unconsciously or coincidentally, in the Forum Theatre technique of the Theatre of the Oppressed, as described in Chapter 21).

Applications of role playing include the teaching of human relations skills to managers, doctors, other kinds of people helpers (Shaw, M. E., Corsini, R., Blake, R., & Mouton, J., 1980). Sociodrama is more for teaching the deeper understanding of other people or cultural attitudes, and the two approaches may be artfuly integrated. In general, though, it's important for the group leader to counter tendencies to make the sessions "therapeutic," psychodramatic, focusing on the individual as if the problems were due to deeper neurotic patterns. To allow that to happen generally leaves the rest of the group feeling as if a subtle contract has been broken, because this isn't the kind of exploration they bargained for. (Of course, if the group is expressly there for deeper personal explorations, either for therapy or re-structuring in the service of deeper personal growth, then psychodrama is more appropriate.)

Applications

Psychodramatic methods first had their primary use in psychotherapy, and action-oriented treatment was a refreshing alternative to approaches that were confined to verbal dialog. Of course there continues to be an important part of therapy that can only be addressed through simple discussion, but at certain times the experiential and action modality breaks past habits of verbal defensiveness. Psychodramatic techniques came to be integrated in Gestalt therapy, family therapy, and many other modalities, often without these roots being clearly acknowledged. The point here is that is worth knowing about the source because there is yet much richness of concept and technique that has not yet been fully utilized.

Applications of role playing in education are discussed in Chapter 8. More recently there's been a movement towards promoting the learning of social and emotional skills, and role playing and similar action approaches are natural vehicles for really learning its component lessons. Emotional intelligence in the workplace has become an equally important area of application, and many psychodramatists and those with similar training have gone on to add this modality and its associated ideas to the challenge of helping managers, teams, executives, and workers more psychologically sophisticated and effective.

Psychodramatic Techniques

In the following section, a variety of techniques are described so you can get an idea of what goes on in psychodrama. For example, imagine that a man—let's call him Joe—has a problem with his boss, Mike, and doesn't know how to deal with it. Let's say this is happening in a therapy group, but it could equally as well be happening in some management support groups. Psychodramas may be imagined as having three general phases: warming up, the action, and sharing. Each phase is important, and neglecting them can cause problems.

Warming-Up: The first step is to warm up the group, which the director as group leader does by helping the group members get to know each other. There are many examples of warm-up exercises in the other chapters in this book, on the supplemental webpage, and in Appendix B at the end of the book.

It's more than mere technique, though. A group leader who wants to use role playing must learn to be comfortable in presenting the situation in an easy fashion. There is far more to the process than just setting up a situation and telling people to take certain parts and start acting. Alas, this is the way some untrained group leaders use the method, and as a result, a lot of people get turned off to role playing. Yet this should not be blamed on the method itself. It was the leader's not knowing how to warm up the group and the people in role! Done properly, role playing is an easy and enjoyable procedure. Adequate warming up eliminates performance anxiety.

Enactment: The next step is to set up the scene and play it out—what would be an example of what goes on with Joe, the protagonist, and his boss, showing some specific places—such as Mike's office, or perhaps Joe's workplace, where the two men have some contact. Perhaps a specific interaction would be portrayed.

The Auxiliary: Someone from the group, say, Bill, is picked by Joe to play Mike. The director has the protagonist tell and show how his boss, Mike, acts and commuicates. Then Joe shifts back into his own position and shows what he said. Mike responds in the style that was shown, and also begins to warm up to what it's like to be Joe's boss.

The Encounter: There is a peculiar intensity that is quickly generated when two people talk directly to each other in the here-and-now. Psychodrama seeks to promote this more honest and open encounter.

The Double: Another person is picked to play the role of Joe's inner self, what he might think but not say out loud. In addition, the auxiliary—the other person—say express a few statements that might be occurring to him but these ideas or emotions are uncomfortable. This is the "voice-over" dimension that helps people to dig a little deeper, and to recognize a bit more distinctly thoughts or feelings that otherwise remain buried. This is one of the important intermediate goal.

Role Reversal: In addition to having Joe show how he imagines his boss, Mike, would act, so that the auxiliary can play him, later on in the enactment, the director might have Joe again shift roles and imagine himself in the predicament of his boss. The fellow playing Mike now reverses roles also, and portrays how Joe was acting during the encounter. For a time, the actual Joe gets to be in his bosses situation. When people are properly warmed up to a situation, there is often some empathic insight that comes out of really imagining what it's like to be in the other fellow's position. The predicament of being in role evokes a mixture of imagination and intuition that doesn't happen so readily in mere talking about a problem. Just asking someone, "Well, how do you think the other person feels?" doesn't generally do the job, but playing for a time the other person's role results in more frequent breakthroughs.

Cutting the Scene: In the course of the action, the director might have the participants pause, almost like a director making a movie might call "Cut." This suggests that there can be a dramatic time out of time in which people can re-consider what's going on in this scene. Some less-informed journalists have misused the term psychodrama when talking about a psychologically-rich drama, but unless the process has this breaking out of role and reviewing the situation from a more reflective frame of mind, there is no real possibility of transformation, and that's what makes it therapeutic psychodrama.

Replay: Another element in psychodrama makes it more like rehearsal: The technique of replay gives the protagonist the opportunity to take a part of a scene and do it over, to clarify what might be going wrong, to explore other alternatives, and to practice or refine responses that might be more effective. In this sense, some psychodrama can be like rehearsal in music, or an astronaut using a flight simulator to develop skills and confidence in coping with unexpected situations.

Further Action: As the director shapes and works with the protagonists, moving the people involved through different scenes, there is room for pauses, reconsideration of the situation from different viewpoints, and opportunities to try do clarify a point, dig a little deeper, or explore a different possible response. So, although there may be pauses, moments of awkwardness, on the whole, there's a flow. To be able to confidently direct without being pushy requires a good deal of on-the-spot supervised practice, learning-by-doing, and can't be learned from a book or adequately expressed just in words.

Sharing: After a protagonist has explored a problem and has come to a point of closure, instead of the group "analyzing" his situation, in psychodrama the practice is to promote sharing. That is, people are encouraged to talk about what there was in their own lives that might resonate with what they witnessed happening in the protagonist's situation. This reduces the vulnerability of the protagonist to people's judgments, no matter how much they might be disguised as sincere efforts to be helpful.

Other Techniques: Some other techniques and examples are noted in Chapter 26 (The Art of Play), and elsewhere. There are literally hundreds of other psychodramatic techniques and variations, a goodly number listed in Blatner (2000). Many more have been developed as warm-ups, some by psychodramatists, some by other dramatists, and these sources are noted in Appendix B.

Derivations

A number of chapters in this book are direct or partial derivatives of psychodrama, such as bibliodrama or Playback Theatre. Role playing has been applied in scores of forms of psychotherapy, such as in the shuttling technique (using the "empty chair") of Gestalt Therapy, adopted by Fritz Perls in the 1950s; or in the technique of "family sculpture," adopted in the late 1960s. It was also applied in the early T-Groups in the late 1940s, and these evolved into the sensitivity training and encounter groups of the 1950s through the 1970s. Action methods in general were used as warm-ups in all kinds of group processes, in business and management training as much as community building.

Summary

Some of the readers of this book may be interested in applying drama in the practice of psychotherapy. Psychodrama offers a wealth of ways you can enhance your abilities to diagnose and treat the various types of problems you may come across. Psychodramatic methods can further be integrated with other applications noted in this book.

References & Resources

For further references and information, go to the webpage supplement to this chapter: <www.interactiveimprov.com/psychodramawb.html>

The American Society for Group Psychotherapy & Psychodrama (ASGPP) has a website with many informative sections, links to the psychodrama associations in other countries, and more: <www.asgpp.org>

Blatner, Adam. (1996). *Acting-in: Practical applications of psychodramatic methods.* (3rd Ed.). Springer Publishing Co. (This is the best introduction to the method, spelling out the how-to in some detail, though, of course, learning to be a psychodramatist mainly requires a process of experiential learning.)

Blatner, Adam. (2000). *Foundations of psychodrama: History, theory, and practice.* (4th Ed.). New York: Springer. (Presents the rationale for the method's use in greater depth, and also has many references.)

Blatner, Adam. (2005). Psychodrama (Chapter 13). In R. J. Corsini & D. Wedding (Eds.), *Current Psychotherapies*, 7th ed. Belmont, CA: Thomson—Brooks/Cole. (This has some of the more updated references and also notes how the method can be integrated with a more eclectic style of clinical work.)

Blatner, Adam. (2007). Papers on Psychodrama. <www.blatner.com/adam/papers.html> (Many papers, lists of books, photographs of Moreno, other early historical pioneers of the method, current trainers, papers on various aspects of psychodrama, links to some related websites, and other resources may be found on this website.

Blatner, Adam. (2006). Enacting the new academy: sociodrama as a powerful tool in higher education. *ReVision: A Journal of Consciousness & Transformation, 28* (3), 30–35.

Corey, Gerald. (2008). Psychodrama in groups (Chapter 8, pp. 185–215). In: *Theory and practice of group counseling* (7th Ed.). Belmont, CA: Thomson Brooks/Cole.

Dayton, Tian. (2005). *The living stage: A step-by-step guide to psychodrama, sociometry and group psychotherapy.* Deerfield Beach, FL: Health Communications, Inc.

Gershoni, Jacob. (Ed.) (2003). *Psychodrama in the 21st Century.* New York: Springer. (An anthology of recent work being done in the field.)

Karp, Marsha, Holmes, Paul, & Bradshaw-Tauvon, Kate. (Eds.) (1998). *Handbook of psychodrama.* London & New York: Routledge-Taylor & Francis. (Another good anthology, mainly of the good work being done in the U.K.)

Moreno, Jacob L. (1946–1969). *Psychodrama, Vol. 1, 2 & 3* (last two with Z. T. Moreno). Beacon, NY: Beacon House. (These are the classic texts written by the inventor of the method.)

Moreno, Zerka T. (2006). *The quintessential Zerka: Writings by Zerka Toeman Moreno on psychodrama, sociometry, and group psychotherapy.* Compiled and edited by Toni Horvatin and Edward Schreiber. New York: Routledge.

Sacks, James M., Bilaniuk, Marie, & Gendron, Jeanine M. (2003). *Bibliography of psychodrama: Inception to date.* <tomtreadwell.com/02ref/index.htm>. (Over 5000 entries, including hundreds of books, in many languages.)

Shaw, M. E., Corsini, R., Blake, R., & Mouton, J. (1980). *Role playing: A practical manual for group facilitators.* San Diego, CA: University Associates. (Excellent bibliography, oriented mainly to business and organizational audiences.)

Sternberg, Pat, & Garcia, Antonina. (2000). *Sociodrama: Who's in your shoes?* (2nd ed.) Westport, CT: Greenwood Publishers.

The Journal of Group Psychotherapy, Psychodrama, & Sociometry. Published by HELDREF, 1318 18th St, Washington, DC 20006. <www.heldref.org> (From 1997–2003 this journal was named *The International Journal of Action Methods,* but is returned to its old name.)

Requirements for Certification and a Directory of Certified Trainers and Practitioners of Psychodrama may be obtained from the American Board of Examiners in Psychodrama, Sociometry, & Group Psychotherapy, PO Box 15572, Washington, DC 20003-0572.

Chapter 16

DRAMA THERAPY

Sally Bailey

Drama therapy applies techniques from the theatre to the process of psychotherapeutic healing. Beginning in the early 20th century with helping patients in hospitals and community programs to put on plays, the field began to increasingly integrate improvisational and process drama methods and emerged as a separate profession in the 1970s. The focus in drama therapy is on helping individuals grow and heal by taking on and practicing new roles.

While most forms of psychotherapy use talking as the major mode of treatment, drama therapy uses role playing, storytelling, theatre games, psychodrama, and other drama processes, as well as puppets, masks, and the preparing of performances for the group or close others. The goal is not the entertainment of the audience, but rather to help the clients understand their thoughts and emotions better or improve their behavior. The element of action added to giving voice to feelings offers clients a more holistic experience for healing.

Most drama therapists come from the world of theatre. They are individuals who realize the healing power of drama through therapeutic experiences they've had in their education or career and want to facilitate change and growth in others. A smaller percentage of drama therapists come from the field of therapy. They have a Masters or Ph.D. in social work, psychology, or counseling and realize that talk therapy isn't enough; they want to use hands-on, creative ways of exploring problems and practicing behavior changes with clients.

The drama therapist is trained in four general areas: drama/theatre, general and abnormal psychology, psychotherapy, and drama therapy. Each of these categories involves a number of required classes, many of them experiential, where one learns by doing, practicing, getting supervisory feedback, and refining skills. In the end, the drama therapist is able to facilitate the client's experience in a way that keeps the client emotionally and physically safe while the client benefits from the dramatic process.

Two Continuums

Drama therapy is a broad field because in the search to find the right emotional distance for participants, a drama therapist can intentionally shift methods along two different continuums: *The first continuum* ranges from enactments that are fictional to others that are more true-to-life. In fictional work, clients pretend to be characters different than themselves. This can expand clients' role repertoires (the number of types of roles that can be accessed for use in real life), or it allows clients to explore a similar role to those they play under the guise of "not-me-but-someone-like-me." Non-fictional work allows the client to explore his or her life directly. Clients need to have good ego strength to be able to do non-fiction work.

The second continuum ranges from enactments that are performed for an audience to enactment used as a process by and for the group's own experience. In performance approaches, also known as "presentational" or product-oriented methods, actors prepare to perform for an audience; in contrast, in process-oriented methods, everyone gets involved in the moment and creates the drama as they go. The only "audience" are the other group members and while there might be a replay of a scene to look at other alternative choices, there is no rehearsal for formal presentation.

Traditional theatre uses mainly a fictional, presentational approach. Some drama therapy approaches involves clients putting on a play designed to express common themes in their lives. In addition, the process of preparing the performance is itself therapeutic. Approaches that are performed for an audience and deal with more non-fictional, true-to-life issues include Forum Theatre (as part of the Theatre of the Oppressed), Self-Revelatory Performance, and Playback Theatre. Though these are presented in this book in other chapters, it should be noted that all these are considered to be part of the scope of drama therapy. Masks, puppets, and rituals might involve both fictional and non-fictional elements, and usually are presentational, but sometimes can be part of a process-oriented approach.

Considering more process-oriented approaches to drama, on the more fictional side, this includes many theatre games, improvisational exercises, and the process drama-in-education approaches, as well as some forms of role playing—especially those that involve more role-distance. Psychodrama is non-fictional and typically done in a process-oriented workshop, but sometimes it done in a way that is more presentational (such as when Moreno held open sessions in New York City). Sociodrama would be a good example of a processes-oriented method which falls between the two poles, weaving fiction and nonfiction together as does David Read Johnson's Developmental Transformations.

The two continuums intersect, and depending on how the drama therapist uses a particular method, will change where the method falls so that how an approach is used could be identified on a two-dimensional graph.

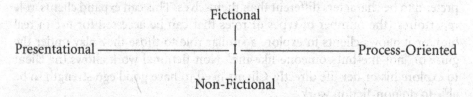

Key Principles

A typical drama therapy session begins with a "Check-in" in which clients share how they are feeling. This provides important information to the drama therapist about how to lead the group that day and what issues are ready to be worked on. Next, the "Warm-up" gets everyone focused on each other and on being in the "here and now." A warm-up also loosens muscles and prepares imaginations so everyone is ready to work together creatively and safely. Each session usually has at least one major activity that is participated in and then discussed by the group. Those who have taken on a role need to "de-role" afterwards in order to reconnect with themselves. The group ends with a closure activity: a game, a ritual, a review of the session, or a song.

Renée Emunah (1993) has identified five stages through which most drama therapy groups progress. Her five stage theory parallels established wisdom from group dynamics on how successful groups form and grow. The first stage is *Dramatic Play* where the group gets to know each other and the therapist through playing together to develop trust, group cohesion, and basic relationship skills. In the *Scenework Stage* they continue playing and begin focusing on developing the dramatic skills they will need as they continue in treatment. All humans develop basic dramatic skills at the ages of 3–5, a time when they naturally begin learning about the world through imitation and dramatic play. Once we enter school, we are encouraged to develop abstract reasoning skills and use them to the exclusion of hands-on forms of learning. However, drama is like riding a bike. You never forget how to do it. The Dramatic Play and Scenework Stages allow clients to get back in touch with those forgotten skills and feel confident using them again.

Stage Three focuses on *Role Play*, exploring issues through fictional means: perhaps acting out a generic family conflict or a familiar character from a fairy tale that goes through a crisis shared by group members. When the group is ready, they can move on to Stage Four: *Culminating Enactments*, where personal issues are acted out directly through psychodrama or autobiographical performance.

The ending stage is *Dramatic Ritual*, which involves closure to the work of the group. This might be the sharing of a performance that has been created by the group in public or the private sharing of a ritual or an evaluation session where clients can review what they've learned and how they've changed.

Not every drama therapy group works its way through all five stages. Some groups aren't together long enough to develop the skills and trust to reach the Culminating Enactment Stage. This is especially true in this day of limited reimbursement by health insurance for mental health services. Age and developmental level makes a difference, too. Children often get the full benefit of emotional healing through play and fictional work alone and there's no need to move on to some of the later stages.

Basic Concepts

While drama therapy techniques may differ from therapist to therapist or from session to session, there are concepts which are common to all forms. The first is using *metaphor through action*. Behaviors, problems, and emotions can be represented metaphorically, allowing for symbolic understanding. A set of behaviors can be looked at as a "role," such as the role of mother, victim, or hero. These roles can be played out in a dramatic situation, leading to a greater understanding of the role as helpful or harmful. An emotion can be represented with a metaphorical image: anger displayed as a volcano, an exploding bomb, or a smoldering fire. These images can be dramatized, allowing the client more insight into the qualities of the emotion and how it functions positively or negatively in his/her life.

Concrete embodiment allows the abstract to become concrete through the client's body. We all experience life first through our senses and our bodies, and only later through language and abstract thoughts. Acting out an idea or an experience allows it to become "more real" so it can be dealt with through feeling rather than just through thought, in the moment rather than through past or future projection. Embodiment allows clients to "experience" or "re-experience" in order to learn, to practice new behaviors, or to experiment with change. This is particularly important for clients who are kinesthetic or visual learners (estimated to be at least two thirds of the population).

Distancing allows the therapist to change the degree to which the role being played is *like you symbolically* or *like you actually*. Children intuitively use distancing to protect themselves from shame in play by acting out characters *similar to them*, but *not them*. Pretending to be Gretel, abandoned in the forest by her parents, allows a child to explore her feelings of being punished or emotionally abandoned by her caregivers. Playing a role quite different from oneself often feels more comfortable than playing oneself directly. In some cases an experience is too "close" to us for us to see our part in it. We need to take a step back (metaphorically speaking) and see the experience in a wider context: to see the forest in order to see the tree.

Sometimes a situation is too emotional or intense for a client to encounter in therapy without becoming overwhelmed emotionally. More distance, through fictionalizing a situation, using a metaphor to represent the problem, or using a technique like puppets, removes the situation a step from reality. On the other hand, some clients will create so much intellectual distance from an issue that they can't get in touch with their feelings (see the story of Henry later). They need *less* fiction and *more* emotional involvement to be able to face the issue honestly and directly.

Certain drama therapy techniques tend to create more distance and others less distance. For example, psychodrama, which deals directly with the personal, nonfiction history of the client, is less distanced. Puppets, theatre games, and improvised fictional characters are more distanced. Some techniques can go either way, depending on how they are used. The performance of an autobiographical play is less distanced than performance of a fictional play. Role play can be close to oneself or distanced, depending on the role being portrayed. (A note here: as every actor knows, the emotions in *any* role can feel very real while the role is being portrayed!)

Dramatic Projection is akin to concrete embodiment and employs metaphor. It is the ability to take an idea or an emotion that is *within* the client and project it *outside* to be shown or acted out in the drama therapy session. A client's difficulty asking for help (an internal problem) can be dramatized in a scene with puppets or through masks, so the problem can be seen, played with, and shared by the therapist and the group.

The creation of *Transitional Space* is an important component in many therapeutic and learning environments, but it is essential in drama therapy.

Transitional space is the imaginary world that is created when we play or imagine together in a safe, trusting situation. It is a timeless space in which anything we can imagine can exist, a place where change and healing can happen, created jointly by the therapist and the clients playing together.

Incorporating the other Arts. Drama therapists use music, movement, song, dance, poetry, drawing, sculpture, mask-making, puppetry, too. Just as the theatre is a crossroads where all the arts come together, drama therapy allows all the arts to come together, too. Starting with writing and then enacting the story or poem or beginning with drawing and then embodying it through drama is a natural way to progress.

Applications

Drama therapy is primarily conducted in groups, although it can be used in individual, couples, or family counseling. It can be found in a wide variety of settings, used with many different kinds of clients. Any therapy group that uses talk therapy could use drama therapy.

For some groups the action methods of drama therapy are more effective. Recovering substance abusers are notorious for being disconnected from their feelings, for making up endless excuses (rationalizations), and for "being in denial" about their addiction. Drama therapy bypasses the excuses and denial, getting right to the addictive or dishonest behavior. Nonverbal clients or children, who may not be good candidates for verbal therapy, can often participate in drama because they can show, rather than say, how they feel.

Drama therapy is practiced in clinical settings, residential settings, correctional facilities, educational situations, corporations and businesses, community action settings and social and recreational centers. The same techniques might be employed; what changes is the contract (or agreement) between the clients and therapist to work on a specific goal for particular problems that the clients want to change.

Clinical Settings. The art therapies began to be included as treatment modalities in psychiatric hospitals in the U.S. after World War I when talk therapy and medical interventions were not successful in helping veterans recover from "shell-shock" (now called Post Traumatic Stress Disorder). The arts brought unresponsive patients back to life. In the early 20s and 30s, inclusion of the arts in hospital programming was expanded. (Phillips, 1994). Today drama therapists in psychiatric hospitals or outpatient mental health settings work with a wide variety of clinical diagnoses including eating disorders, depression, schizophrenia, bi-polar disorder, addictions, or Alzheimer's disease. In the past, hospital drama therapy groups could work together over long periods and do in-depth work. Today, with shorter hospital stays, groups tend to be short term or one-time sessions.

Medical settings can use drama therapy, too. Anne Curtis and Paula Patterson, two drama therapists in Florida, work with acutely and chronically ill patients of all ages in medical hospitals. Puppets, music, movement, clowning, fairy tales, and guided fantasies to safe healing places help stimulate patients' immune systems and create hope. Even staff members ask for drama therapy sessions to help them deal with their stresses, frustrations, and disappointments.

Residential Settings. Years ago, recovering substance abusers stayed in treatment for one to three years in order to learn how to live without drugs and/or alcohol. Today, three months is considered long-term and 28 day programs are the norm. A drama therapist is lucky to get one session per week with clients over four to twelve weeks.

I worked thirteen years in a long-term residential treatment program for recovering addicts in Washington, DC. A drama group of 12–14 residents, lasting three to six months, focused first on drama games and improvisation to build group trust, social skills, drama skills, communication and understanding, and the idea that we can learn life lessons through metaphor and action. Later, we would work on deeper issues through psychodrama and gestalt therapy.

One of my favorite success stories involves Henry, an older recovering alcoholic, who revealed one day that he was going to be kicked out of the program for "lack of motivation." He always participated fully in drama, but he never talked in other groups and wouldn't work on issues in individual therapy. When I asked why, he said, "Well, I hardly know what my feelings are! How can I talk about them?"

"Maybe you can't talk about them," I offered, "because you've ignored them for so many years that they feel like strangers to you. How would you like to meet them?"

"Sure!" He said.

He picked group members to represent four of his feelings and sculpted them in chairs. The auxiliary playing "Fear" hunched over looking at the floor, his arms across his chest, protecting himself. "Pain" looked away, afraid to make eye contact. "Sadness" bent over into her lap and covered her face with her hands. "Rejection" sat defiantly with his back to Henry.

Henry introduced himself to each Emotion and each, in turn, came alive to speak to him about how much they missed being part of his life. They expressed how deeply they cared for him and that they wanted to help him complete treatment.

It was a turning point. Henry began to talk in his other groups and in his individual therapy. He started to acknowledge his feelings, to identify and understand how they related to his behavior. He also began to take more risks in revealing the secrets and shames he was carrying inside. And because he was able to reveal them, he could let them go.

The exercise worked for him on three different levels. On a metaphoric level, he was able to reconnect with emotions he had "cut off" during his addiction; on a practical level, he was able to practice talking "with feeling" to another person; on a relational level, he made a deep connection with the group members he chose to play parts in his psychodrama. The group members learned about their own relationships to the emotions they portrayed as they gave voice and body to them. They felt more connected to Henry, to themselves, and to each other. Six months later Henry successfully graduated from the program.

Social and Recreational Settings. One of my first drama therapy jobs was to create an arts access program for children with special needs at a non-profit community arts center in suburban Maryland. I integrated students with disabilities into regular drama classes and productions by helping teachers identify ways to make adaptations that "leveled the playing field." I created programming in special education classrooms for teaching social skills, self-expression, or an aspect of the curriculum. Theatre companies comprised of adolescent actors with and without disabilities created original plays dramatizing their own ideas. Some of this work could be categorized as educational drama, some as therapeutic drama, some as drama therapy, some mixed them all together.

The performing troupes were originally designed to be venues for disabled actors to explore issues of difference and to provide awareness education to non-disabled audiences. However, my actors had different ideas. They told me right off that they were sick of dealing with their disabilities "24-7." They wanted to explore rebellion, responsibility, growing up, falling in love, being rejected, friendship and family: in short, being an adolescent. We created many plays together: about pirates, the wild West, time travel, shopping at the mall, soap operas, a video dating service, modernized fairy tales, even a murder mystery entitled *Death by Grammar.* Each play became a metaphor for their issues, concerns, hopes and dreams. Each rehearsal process became a laboratory for the development of better social skills, flexibility, responsibility, self-discipline, communication abilities, and the development of higher self-esteem.

Parents reported that the dramatic experiences their young people had in our program helped them develop a greater level of independence, responsibility, and self-discipline. Most of my former actors are now young adults holding down full time jobs and living independently in apartments. One job coach at a school-to-work transition program confided he could always tell which of his clients had been actors of mine: they had more self-confidence, better communication skills, and the self-discipline necessary for succeeding in the world of work.

Other Applications. In other chapters in this book, theatre artists and drama therapists work in a variety of contexts—in prisons, psycho-education (as in theatre for health), schools, working with the elderly, and promoting community action. Some anecdotes about each of these areas are noted on the web-page supplement to this chapter: <www.interactiveimprov.com/dramatherwb.html>

Becoming a Drama Therapist

Most drama therapists begin their training in theatre at the BA, MA, MFA or Ph.D. level and often work in professional or educational theatre before training in psychology and drama therapy at the MA level.

In North America there are three graduate programs in drama therapy approved by the National Association for Drama Therapy: New York University (NYU) in New York City, California Institute of Integral Studies (CIIS) in San Francisco, California, and Concordia University in Montreal, Canada. Students in these programs study for two years full time, taking courses in drama therapy, psychology, psychotherapy, ethics, and research, and complete 800 hours of internship using drama therapy with at least two different populations of clients and a thesis project.

People who already have or are working on Masters or Ph.D.s in theatre or mental health, (i.e., counseling, social work, or special education) can pursue Alternative Training in drama therapy. Alternative training allows students to create individualized programs around a specialty. Alternative Training must be overseen by a Board Certified Trainer (BCT), who is approved to mentor, guide, and train drama therapy students. The BCT helps the student plan an annual learning contract and serves as an academic advisor.

Registry: The Professional Credential.

RDT (Registered Drama Therapist) is the credential nationally recognized in the United States as the professional designation for drama therapists. Registry is a peer review of education, training, and experience qualifications. This is different from certification which is earned through testing or licensure (set state by state by law). Currently, registry is the only recognized professional credential for drama therapists; there is no licensure for the title "Drama Therapist." New York State and Wisconsin have recently passed licensure laws that *include* creative arts therapists, among them drama therapists. Beyond the education and training requirements set by MA approved programs and alternative training, a candidate for registry must document at least 500 hours of professional or educational work in theatre, 1,500 hours of work as a professional drama therapist, and have three letters of recommendation which attest to his/her clinical skills, professionalism and ethics. Once one becomes an RDT, one must keep up with training via continuing education hours.

For more information about drama therapy, contact the National Association for Drama Therapy at 15 Post Side Lane; Pittsford, NY 14535 or check out the NADT website at <www.nadt.org>.

Bibliography

(Further notations on website supplement: <www.interactiveimprov.com/dramatherwb.html>

Emunah, Renée. (1994). *Acting for real: Drama therapy process, technique, and performance.* New York: Brunner-Mazel.

Jones, Phil. (1996*). Drama as therapy: Theatre as living.* London: Routledge.

Landy, Robert. (1997). Drama therapy: The state of the art. *The Arts in Psychotherapy, 24* (1), 5–15.

Lewis Penny, & Johnson, David Read. (Eds.) (2000). *Current approaches in drama therapy.* Springfield, IL: Charles C. Thomas.

Philips, M.E. (1996). The use of drama and puppetry in occupational therapy during the 1920s and 1930s. *American Journal of Occupational Therapy, 50* (3), 229–233.

Chapter 17

REHEARSALS FOR GROWTH

Daniel J. Wiener

Rehearsals for Growth (abbreviated as RfG) is a method that involves having participants learn and engage in improvisational drama, variations of theatre games, in order to expand their role repertoires and break free from habitual reaction patterns. RfG is used as an aid in psychotherapy, as an aid in the training of therapists and other people helpers, and just for the pleasures and benefits of personal development. (In that respect, it also partakes of the category of empowerment and a bit of entertainment, education, and community-building, too.)

RfG was developed in 1985, a synthesis of my vocation as a psychotherapist and an avocational involvement in team comedy improvisation. I had also had some exposure to psychodrama and drama therapy so was sensitive to the power of spontaneity and creativity in helping people become more mentally flexible and vital. Theatre games arose from a different tradition than psychodrama warm-ups, yet they shared a similar sensibility, and I found they too could be usefully applied in doing therapy. Even more than in working with individuals, I found RfG was helpful also in helping couples and families to work out problems.

After using RfG in therapy for a few years, I also found these methods helpful in the training and continuing education of both student and experienced therapists. The skills of spontaneity, imagination, intuition and empathy were even more relevant to their work. In 2000, I also extended this application as a form of personal development, in the service of helping healthy people to become even more mentally flexible and vital.

As a therapist, I had noticed that both successfully improvising players and people in healthy relationships showed the same three key attitudes and practices: (1) validating other's ideas and impulses (called "offers"); (2) taking turns in leading and following; and (3) playfully challenging habits and routines. When clients and their relationship partners enacted brief improvised scenes during therapy sessions, I found that I could readily spot important relationship problems that had not been mentioned in talk-only therapy. Moreover, clients were also able to experience their difficulties in a new way. Later, I began to offer improvised tasks as a way of "stretching" clients to try out new roles and responses with their relationship partners, finding that from these "rehearsals" they learned to apply some of these changes to their real-life "performances."

Since 1991, my colleagues and I have been using RfG for social skills training, education and recreation as well as continuing to apply it to therapy. The educational uses are similar to those of "Kidprov," a program developed by Brad Newton (1998) while the recreational uses overlap considerably with The Art of Play and TheaterSports (methods described in Chapters 26 and 27 in this book). The forms, principles and techniques of all these applications are interchangeable; what differs is the contract with participants and the focus on off-stage post-enactment processing (elaborated upon below). This chapter focuses on RfG personal development groups (Groups), which resemble in process the Women's Empowerment workshops described by Leeder and Raybin elsewhere in this volume and can be run in a manner similar to RfG applications for these other purposes.

Rationale and Description

The basis of RfG is the discovery and playful exploration of alternatives to the social choices we typically make. The advantages of improvisational play include: accessing playfulness; expanding interpersonal trust; opening to creativity; experiencing spontaneity; broadening sensory, emotive, and movement expressiveness; and co-creating new realities with others.

It is the application of this last advantage, co-creating new realities with others, that is of most practical benefit in enhancing relationship functioning. In life generally, and especially in relationships, we develop predictable roles and habitual responses, forgetting that we can make other choices. Established relationships (most obviously dyadic ones) have a collusive quality to them, wherein each partner responds to the other's offers in predictable ways, setting in motion a predictable sequence (or "script"). The resulting relationship dynamics then cement the tradeoff of safety for novelty, often resulting in boredom and over-familiarity ("Harry? I've been married to Harry for eighteen years and know just who he is. What could possibly be new about him?"). By staging improvised enactments, the Director undoes the predictability, setting loose an adventure in spontaneity and provoking a challenge to the relationship's status quo).

In order to experiment and explore other choices we all need safety, meaning immunity from such real-life consequences as being judged or punished. RfG always begins by inviting, never pressuring people to participate, and establishes a framework of safety by providing clear physical and social boundaries around play activities. At the start of a session, an area of the room where play activities take place is specified as "the stage." People mark their entrances and exits from their dramatic (make-believe) roles by moving in and out of the stage area. The rule is, "Anything goes on stage," short of actual, violent physical contact. The extent of nonviolent physical contact between on-stage players is negotiated off-stage before enactments. All on-stage activities are treated as playful fictions; off-stage, people are held accountable, as themselves, for their words and deeds to the same extent as in ordinary social life.

This is not to say that the experience of improvising a character in a game or scene is stress-free. As noted above, adults are comfortable with the predictability of their lives and typically experience apprehension at not knowing what they will be called on to do next. This "adventuring" into the unfamiliar promotes growth via heightened involvement and constitutes both the thrill and the terror of participation in RfG enactments.

RfG activities are drawn or adapted from improvisational theatre games developed originally by Viola Spolin (1963), Keith Johnstone (1981), and many others. The core techniques I have adapted are described in my 1994 book, *Rehearsals for Growth: Theater Improvisation for Psychotherapists*, and in other materials noted at the end of this chapter. Literally hundreds of distinct RfG activities have been developed and utilized in therapy and new forms and variations are devised continually. The improvisation skills that these activities both draw upon and develop further include: accepting offers; freeing imagination; storymaking; expanding expressiveness; and using status (power). I classify RfG activities as either exercises, which feature unusual performance rules and conditions for enactment by people as their familiar social selves (non-dramatic enactment), or as games, which add the dimension of pretense through people playing characters other than themselves (dramatic enactment).

Personal Development Group Features and Process

My Groups participants are typically well-functioning adults between early 20s and mid-50s; there are two-thirds men and one-third women, unlike therapy, where this ratio is reversed. Most have been in, or are concurrently in some form of psychotherapy. Many come into the Group with what psychodramatists term "role hunger," the desire to take on or experiencing more fully some role which is insufficiently available in real life. RfG enactments often serve as "appetizers" for this role hunger. In the eleven Groups I have led in the past 15 years, I have noticed that members form social friendships outside of the group more frequently than do members of RfG therapy groups, and have led to one marriage and two business partnerships thus far!

It is the character and depth of such processing that further distinguishes Groups from those devoted to recreation, education, social skills training, or therapy. In recreation, processing is limited largely to sharing of player and spectator experience, with some non-critical feedback on what made the exercise/game/scene work or not. In education, the goal is to enhance learning (particularly in the area of language skills); processing focuses on both overcoming any self-blocking which occurred during on-stage enactments and giving feedback regarding on-stage competitiveness. Scenes are often repeated in order to give participants the opportunity to practice what they have just learned. In social skills training, processing connects players' on-stage experience with their real-life social difficulties (e.g., getting a date, dealing with an obnoxious co-worker). And in therapy, processing is woven into the dynamics of verbal group therapy, with the important added advantage of putting sentiments, attitudes and perceptions to the "laboratory test" of on-stage experience. Unlike forms primarily intended to produce performances for an external audience, RfG Groups value exploration and discovery over competence, at the pace and to the extent that each group member sets for him/herself.

RfG Groups are run as playful and supportive experiences for from 6 to 12 people, typically meeting weekly for 2 to 4 hours at a time from 10 to 25 times. The contract with participants is for mutual personal discovery through voluntary participation. Group sessions are started with members socializing and warming up by reporting in a circle on their present mood and energy, what differences they've noticed about themselves during the prior week, and what elements of previously-developed stage characters have surfaced. Groups close with members summarizing what they've learned or experienced during the group, also offering each other feedback regarding others' performances. In Groups, neither the entertainment value of scenes nor the cleverness of the performances is particularly prized, distinguishing this application from that of recreational performance improv groups. Further, unlike therapy, members in Groups are not asked to uphold the confidentiality of other members and extensive verbal processing of personal feelings is not encouraged. There are also no common educational or social skill objectives of group activity. Group members, who are called 'players' when they volunteer to go on-stage, first warm up with verbal and movement exercises, then play RfG games before going on to improvise brief, loosely structured single or thematically-linked scenes. In the first 3 or 4 group meetings improvisational skills are built, so that players are capable of performing more advanced games and more complex scenes later on.

A RfG Growth Group Example

The following example refers to RfG games and exercises described in *Rehearsals for Growth: Theater Improvisation for Psychotherapists* (1994); page numbers on which these descriptions are found appear in brackets ([]).

Warm-ups. The group, seated in a circle, tells a story in a made-up-language-sounding gibberish, accompanied by gestures. [p. 129]. At the end, group members pair up (i.e., break into dyads), discussing what they thought the story was and sharing their conclusions with the whole group.

Next, working with a different partner, they play *Body Offers* [p. 68] in pairs. First, Ted stands with his legs wide apart, hands on his head and mouth open wide. His partner Lucy cups her ear close to Ted's mouth for two seconds and Ted says, "thank you" to acknowledge Lucy's response to his offer. Moving back to neutral, Lucy now goes first, standing erect, one hand on her hip, the other pointing straight ahead. Ted stands slumped in defeat, one hand covering his eyes, and Lucy says "thank you," ending that round.

The Director now instructs the pairs to continue the movement-response process with the second player adding a line of dialog. Lucy, responding to Ted on his hands and knees with his head thrown back, stands along side him, putting her hand on his head and saying, "Good dog!" When the Director adds the instruction for both to move and speak twice following the first body offer, Lucy sits on a chair with her hands folded on her stomach, head forward and eyes closed. Ted runs over to her, saying excitedly, "Gran'ma, look what's happened!" while tugging at her sleeve. Lucy slowly pulls away, opening one eye and mumbling in a sleepy, cross tone, "Willy, leave me be. Grandma needs her rest." Ted as Willy jumps up and down in front of her, practically shouting, "But the cow got into the garden and is eating the cabbages!" Lucy as Grandma jumps up, and begins stumbling forward, holding Willie's arm and shouting, "Bessie,! Out of there, now!!" The scene ends.

Supportive coaching by the Director establishes a relaxed, permissive atmosphere where the spirit is, "try it out," rather than "get it right." Scenes are sometimes suggested by the Director, sometimes by the entire group and at still other times by those individuals who wish to play the main characters. Such scenes are unscripted; players improvise most of the dialog, mime props, and are free to invent plot changes along the way, so long as there is a thread of continuity from what had previously been established within the scene.

Enactment. In the example that follows I have added brief remarks in brackets to note how the Director's choices in RfG personal development groups might be different from the choices made for clients in RfG therapy groups.

Ricardo, in the Group for 2 months, was a slender, well-dressed man in his early 30s who had been a participating though passive member. Well-liked by the group, he had been a helpful partner to others staging their scenes, improvising capably. Now, at the urging of others, Ricardo shyly stated he wanted to explore a character who was socially confident with women [In a therapy group, any enactment would have been preceded by considerable discussion of his personal history and feelings]. I immediately invited Ricardo to play the first scene as "Pete," the male friend of a woman ("Becky") who was having trouble with her overly-aggressive boyfriend, "Mike." [This initial choice of scene allowed Ricardo to "warm up" to the character he wanted to assume in a social encounter with a woman]. Valerie and Kevin offered to play the characters Becky and Mike.

The scene was set in Pete's living room. Becky came to Pete's door; once inside, she started crying. Pete invited her to sit next to him and tell him what upset her. As Becky, sobbing, came out with the story of being dumped by Mike, Pete became angry, almost forgetting Becky's presence as he vowed to get "that bastard Mike." I called "Cut!" and switched the scene to a bar where Mike sat drinking with his buddy "Lonny" (played by Ted). Pete entered and confronted Mike, demanding to know how he could hurt Becky so. With a few asides to Lonny, Mike sneeringly told Pete, "If you're so concerned for her, make your move. I'm through with her." I called "Freeze" and asked Pete to do an Inner Monologue, a technique where the character soliloquizes while other on-stage characters remain frozen in position. At first Ricardo had difficulty staying in character as Pete; then Pete declared both his attraction to Becky and how risky it felt to disclose this feeling to her (In therapy, I might have brought up another person to serve as either an *auxiliary ego* with whom Pete could role reverse or a psychodramatic double to express and work through Pete/Ricardo's conflicted feelings). After ending this scene, I asked the group-as-audience what they wanted to see happen next.

While they wanted a scene where Pete would ask Becky for a date, I felt a modification would serve Ricardo better, so I asked Ricardo to coach another member to play Pete in the requested scene. After Ted volunteered to play Pete I took him and Valerie aside, directing them to play Pete initially as nervous and Becky as hesitant. Ricardo, standing alongside me just offstage, was to call "Freeze" whenever he wanted to have Pete behave or speak differently.

After a few pleasantries that established the scene, Pete, visibly nervous, began to propose, rather indirectly, that Becky might join him for dinner Friday night after work. When he made no move, I froze the scene and asked Ricardo if he was satisfied with the way Pete was handling himself. Ricardo shook his head and told Ted to "come right out with it." Ted as Pete now made a more direct proposal but retained the nervous manner and strained tone of his previous delivery. This time, Ricardo froze the action, repeating with lively energy how Ted was to deliver the line. I suggested that he take Ted's place and show us how to play Pete. Without hesitation, Ricardo exchanged places with Ted and asked Becky for a dinner date. The scene continued with Becky stalling cautiously and Pete friendly but persistent, ending with her accepting the date invitation. I froze the scene and asked Pete to deliver another Inner Monologue. He did so in a jubilant manner, saying how pleased he was with himself and looking forward to a wonderful time on the date. To the applause of the group, Ricardo left the stage and joined the off-stage seated group circle.

Post-Enactment Processing. Following each set of on-stage enactments, players return to their seats and their real-life personae to verbally process their work. This processing allows the "observing selves" both of players and spectators to contribute, building group connections over shared experiences, and offering useful feedback that guides the next enactments. Ricardo accepted the compliments of the other group members. Valerie said that Pete's confidence in the last scene made all the difference in inducing Becky to date him. Ricardo reported that he now could really see himself owning his "Pete-side" around women. In the socializing talk preceding the Group action in a subsequent session he reported drawing on "Pete" to get two dates.

Functions of the Director

As leaders of Group experience, Directors function, at once, as teachers, process facilitators, role-models of nonjudgmental playfulness, sideline coaches, theatrical directors, and off-stage authority figures. One challenge for Directors is to maintain respectful curiosity as a group norm that neither supports showing off nor becomes intrusive into the personal dynamics of members' private lives. While they may join the on-stage action they may never entirely immerse themselves in the on-stage action, as they are like "grown-ups" responsible for "kids'" safety on the playground. Directors structure Group activity, reminding members to switch dramatic roles when entering or leaving the stage area.

One critical function of Directors is to coach on-stage enactments, calling out suggestions that maintain the scene in progress if possible and ending it if not. Skillful directing requires a light, sure touch, a capacity to guide discovery without hesitating to intervene to keep the onstage action on track. The following "Signs of Good RfG Improvising," modified slightly from Wiener (1994, pp. xix-xx), are offered here as a Director's guide to running successful group scenes:

Clear boundaries. Players respect the Director's clear boundaries that define the play context and what is permissible in playing. Players are clear with themselves and one another regarding the distinction between group member-as-person and player-as-character, both on- and off-stage.

Balanced contribution. There is frequent contribution from each player and a balanced sense of contribution, an equality of give-and-take. Players are observant and responsive to the offers of one another; they listen and don't talk over one another.

Character acceptance. Players give and fully accept character, making others look good without imposing conditions for how they themselves appear (e.g., clever, heroic, sexy, high-status, central to the scene, etc.). They put developing the scene ahead of showing off or hiding out.

Wide expressive range. Players use movement and gesture in an appropriate way corresponding to their characters and story; they fully use their expressive range, according to the spirit of the situation.

Strong character. Players stay in the present moment when they don't know what is happening or when their imaginations are blank. They do not become defensively self-conscious or utilize protective behavior (e.g., breaking character to apologize to the off-stage audience, panicking, quitting the scene, blaming other players) unless they playfully incorporate such actions into the scene.

Positive outcome. Players are often surprised and pleased by the outcome of the scene; they enjoy having co-created and shared an adventure and like each other at the end of the enactment. They accept and learn from what occurred and quickly let go of judgments of self and of others.

Spontaneous idea development. Players: develop the first idea offered; make specific offers; are willing to allow both the obvious and the irrational or unconventional; and justify these offers, making them work in the scene (i.e., they do not censor or block the offers of their own imagination). Players are not planning ahead, but are making it up as they go; they remember where they have been and reincorporate previously-used story elements.

Training of Directors

RfG has predominantly been applied to therapeutic uses and most of those trained to date have been therapists. Workshops at mental health agencies and professional conferences have introduced RfG to perhaps 1500 therapists since 1987. Starting in New York City in the early 1990s and continuing to the present in the Hartford, CT area, I have offered a 60-hour RfG Certification Training program to 44 mental health professionals. As of 2006, there are eighteen Certified RfG therapists, many of whom have been leading their own RfG groups. One, Charlotte Ramseur, has run RfG groups for substance abusers in recovery; another, John Phelps, runs them under the title, "Playing with Trouble" as social skills training for court-mandated adolescents. I have led Groups in my private practice since 1986 and have been leading an ongoing "Adult Playgroup," intermittently since 2000 in the Hartford, CT area.

References

Further information about this approach may be found at Dr. Wiener's RfG website:<www.rehearsalsforgrowth.com> or by emailing to: <dan@rehearsalsforgrowth.com>

Books in Appendix A, especially by Emunah, Johnstone (1981), and Spolin's books.

Johnson, David R. (2000). Developmental Transformations: Towards the body as presence. In P. Lewis and D. Johnson (Eds.), *Current Approaches in Drama Therapy*, pp. 87–110. Springfield, IL: Charles C. Thomas.

Johnstone, Keith. (1981) *Impro: Improvisation and the theatre*. London: Methuen.

Jones, Phil. (1996). *Drama as therapy: Theatre as living.* London: Routledge.

Newton, B. (1998). *Improvisation: Use what you know—make up what you don't!* Scottsdale, AZ: Gifted Psychology Press. Kidprov website: <www.kidprov. com>

Wiener, Daniel J. (1994). *Rehearsals for growth: Theater improvisation for psychotherapists.* New York: W. W. Norton.

Wiener, Daniel J. (2004). *Rehearsals for growth: Collected Papers, 1991–2004.* (See website.)

Chapter 18

INSIGHT IMPROVISATION

Integrating Meditation, Theatre, and Drama Therapy
Joel Gluck

An application of dramatic methods for personal development, Insight Improvisation was created in 1993 as a way to integrate active, expressive techniques with the skills used in meditation: mindfulness, acceptance, relaxation, and slowing down. Insight Improvisation is best practiced in a workshop or classroom setting, or as a way for two people to work together in a movement studio for two to three hours. A typical session (or portion of a longer workshop) begins with a check-in, a meditation, and a movement/ sound warm-up, and progresses to a culminating activity—a solo, pair, or small-group improvisation or performance. (Further information about Insight Improvisation and related approaches appears on this chapter's webpage supplement, which may be found at: <www.interactiveimprov.com/ insightimprovwb.html>)

Insight Improvisation differs from most forms of theatre in that it replaces the focus on performance—that is, presenting an artistic work for an audience—with a focus on the participant's body-mind experience. The art that results from an Insight Improvisation activity grows out of the practitioner's process of being mindful, moment-by-moment, of her own body, her senses, her thoughts and feelings, as well as her relationship to others onstage or in the audience. Insight Improvisation is a vehicle for self-exploration and self-discovery. It is a combination of drama and contemplative, transpersonal work, an integration of spiritual and theatrical practices for the purpose of personal growth, learning, and transformation.

History and Related Methods

Insight Improvisation derives from two sources: meditation and experimental theatre. Its development was inspired by several teachers whose approach to theatre has been influenced by Eastern philosophy, including Open Theater playwright Jean-Claude van Itallie; Ruth Zaporah, dancer and creator of Action Theater; and director/improvisor Scott Kelman. All three focus on getting out of the head, paying attention to the body, and letting go of preconceptions. In a similar vein, the practice of authentic movement—created by Mary Starks Whitehouse, one of the pioneers of dance-movement therapy (Pallaro, 1999)—is central to Insight Improvisation. Other influences include the wisdom of meditation teachers such as Joseph Goldstein and Jack Kornfield; Gregory Kramer's Insight Dialogue, a form of meditating in relationship; the many forms of drama therapy (see Chapter 16); and many other, creative forms of theatre and psychotherapy.

Core Concepts

Insight Improvisation is based on three concepts—central to the practice of meditation—which are reinforced through each experiential exercise. The first, *mindfulness*, is the discipline of bringing the mind back to focus on an object of attention, remembering to return to the present moment. The second, choiceless awareness (or *choicelessness*) is an orientation of openness to whatever is present, allowing information to enter through all channels: the five senses (including all kinds of bodily sensations), thoughts, and emotions. A third underlying concept is *lovingkindness* (also known as *metta* in the ancient Pali language); this refers to the basic human capacity for caring for oneself and for others. For actors and improvisers—and all human beings—mindfulness, choicelessness, and lovingkindness are essential for being ready and present, open and "in the moment," and connecting with others with a positive attitude, in performance and in life.

Structure

There are three kinds of activities comprising Insight Improvisation:

• Meditation in Action—Ways of meditating as well as making meditation dynamic (e.g., through movement, expressing one's inner experience aloud, and connecting with others).

- Contemplative Theatre—Combining meditation practices with theatrical activities, e.g., exploring mindful improvisation with voice and movement, working with a text, playing roles, and performing stories.

- Contemplative Drama Therapy—Applying a meditative approach to the therapeutic uses of theatre and improvisation, as a path of personal growth and exploration.

This chapter describes two intensive weekend workshops, centered around Contemplative Theatre and Contemplative Drama Therapy; elements of Meditation in Action are also incorporated. Each workshop is comprised of five main sessions, running from Friday afternoon or evening through Sunday afternoon. Note that Insight Improvisation is made up of more than 50 unique activities, of which this chapter only briefly summarizes roughly half; for details, please see the webpage supplement to this chapter.

Weekend Workshop #1—Contemplative Theatre

Session 1: Introduction to Insight Improvisation

Warm-up and Welcome. The workshop begins with an invigorating movement warmup, and an opening circle of facilitator and participant introductions. The facilitator introduces two key concepts: mindfulness and choicelessness.

Introductory Sitting Meditation. The concepts of mindfulness and choicelessness are demonstrated with a guided meditation on a single object (such as the breath); there is then a transition into an open-awareness meditation—also known as *vipassana* (Goldstein & Kornfield, 1987). Objects entering the field of awareness (including all five senses, as well as thoughts and feelings) are to be noticed and accepted. As the workshop proceeds, the practice of *vipassana* becomes a model for a different approach to acting, one that emphasizes being present and letting go of "performing."

Authentic Movement. In this practice of moving spontaneously, the whole body leads the way, rather than just the head. The facilitator plays the important role of nonjudgmental witness, while all of the group moves simultaneously with eyes closed (having been instructed to open their eyes slightly when necessary to avoid collision). Authentic movement is a kind of moving meditation; the practitioner finds that he can be present to the smallest bodily impulses and sensations, and is freed from any expectation of moving a particular way. After a few minutes, the facilitator invites participants to begin to notice other aspects of their movement, how certain bodily positions may evoke particular physical images or childhood memories.

Image-Story-Image. Participants meet in small groups to share a physical image and a brief childhood memory that they discovered in their authentic movement. The facilitator provides coaching on how to "perform" a story mindfully in the large group circle, slowing down and focusing on one's own body and senses rather than on the audience. A key question is posed: How do I stay in contact with myself—my own center—and not give away my center to the audience?

Through meditating, moving mindfully, and sharing their stories and images, participants leave this first session feeling present, open, and more connected to one another.

Session 2: Exploring Mindfulness and Choicelessness

Meditation on Sound. Day Two begins with a meditation that develops mindful and choiceless awareness through focusing on sounds occurring naturally inside and outside the space, plus, optionally, the sparse addition of bells, drums, other musical instruments, or relevant text spoken by the facilitator.

Walk-Stop-Walk. For these next two exercises, created by Scott Kelman, the group gathers in a semi-circle audience to one side of the space. Half the group walks in the space while the rest observe. The instruction is to walk until you stop, then stop and "check it out"—check out the floor, yourself, the audience, others in the space, the clock on the wall, etc. When you're done checking it out, walk. This exercise provides a chance for those moving to experience the tension and interplay between performing and just being. For the audience, the surprise is how fascinating and satisfying such a simple, unplanned performance can be.

One-minute Solo. The participant enters the space and performs an improvised solo for one minute, at some point during the minute acknowledging the audience (i.e., through making eye contact). Kelman's key instruction: "If you have a good idea, don't do it." This exercise explores our habitual ways of being in performance—what happens when we are left without our good ideas to hide behind? Participants often discover that they become acutely aware of their relationship to their own body and movement, to their surroundings, and to the audience.

The Amplification Exercise. Inspired by Ruth Zaporah's Action Theater (Zaporah, 1995), the basic form of this exercise is a solo improvisation. Start with a sound-movement impulse (e.g., gesturing with the arms and making a face while saying "zah!"); then amplify it in some way—make it bigger, stretch it out, make it quicker, focus on a piece of it, slow it down, etc. At any point one can continue to amplify the original impulse, drop it completely (returning to neutral), or have a brand new sound-movement impulse. The Amplification Exercise elicits enormous energy and physical/vocal expressiveness while cultivating awareness of body, senses, and inner imagery—demonstrating that a performance based on principles of meditation need not be slow, silent, or passionless.

Interlude: City Meditation/Nature Meditation

Following lunch, participants go out alone and explore their surroundings, without planning or following "good ideas." Instead, the focus is to follow the gut, discover what is next, moment-by-moment, and pay particular attention to the senses: colors, smells, sounds, etc. Upon return, participants can journal their experience in any form they like—free-verse, story, drawing, haiku, etc.

Session 3: Insight Improvisation with a Monologue

Improvisational Singing Warm-up: Chords, Jams, and One-Liners. This session starts with singing in a circle—not conventionally "beautiful" singing, or even a recognizable song, but group and individual improvisation with the voice:

- *Chords.* Participants simultaneously take a deep, relaxed in-breath, and each sings a single note on one out-breath—each time producing a unique chord. The result is a kind of improvisational group chanting meditation.
- *Jams.* Similar to Chords, but on the out-breath each person can make any sound, using changes in pitch, volume, changing vowel sounds, adding consonants and pauses.
- *One-liners.* One person whispers a short phrase or sentence in another's ear; the recipient then sings the phrase improvisationally, attempting to capture the sound and imagery of the line through movement as well as voice.

These three activities are also practiced as duets and trios using movement and contact in the circle. This warm-up lays the groundwork for speaking/ singing a monologue later in the session.

Spontaneous Writing. After introducing the afternoon's activities—writing, editing, and performing a monologue—the sequence begins with a ten-minute "free write" following Natalie Goldberg's (1990) guidelines: in brief, to not worry about anything (grammar, spelling, the quality of the writing, the content), but instead to keep the hand moving and keep going for the jugular, for what's important. The writing that results from this exercise can vary enormously—including stories, dreams, poetry, random recollections, and outlandish nonsense. Following the writing, participants pair up with a partner, swap text, and "edit" one another's writing by underlining words or phrases that move them. Once edited, the writing becomes more fragmented, less logical, and often more evocative—perfect material for the exercise which follows.

Performing a Monologue. In this culminating activity of the day—based on an exercise by dancer Christie Svane—participants speak, sing, and fully embody their own writing, building on the skills learned in the workshop so far. As in the Amplification exercise, this activity is about letting go of logic and instead going with spontaneous impulse. Pausing and breathing, using maximum vocal and physical range, and repeating words and phrases from the text are all encouraged. With the support of the group, each person finds his or her own approach, creating performances of unexpected beauty, humor, and feeling. The workshop continues with an optional evening of one-to-one coaching with group support.

Session 4: Applying Insight Improvisation in Relationship

Metta Meditation. After a period of free movement and stretching in silence, this session begins with a guided lovingkindness meditation. Next, participants sit in pairs, make relaxed eye contact, and engage in a *metta dialogue*, sharing messages of lovingkindness with one another, and with all beings. As *vipassana* meditation suggests a model for awareness, the practice of *metta* offers a different approach to the actor in approaching the relationship to fellow actors and audience.

The Three States. This exercise is a new, duet variation on authentic movement. Working with a partner, each person can move anytime into one of these three states: moving alone, moving in eye contact, or moving in physical contact (being respectful of the other's physical limitations). This exercise can range from slow and gentle, to raucous and playful, to filled with implied meaning—an exploration of the essence of relationship. Pairs explore together and then are invited to improvise with the group witnessing. Participants are often deeply affected by the Three States: in one workshop, two men moved together with such stillness, silence, and caring, that the audience was brought to tears.

Session 5: Integrating Skills

Storytelling. This activity is an opportunity for participants to draw upon all of the skills developed during the workshop, and receive individual coaching.

Playwright Jean-Claude van Itallie's guidelines for performing stories form a powerful container within which participants can discover emotional depth, humor, and creativity (van Itallie, 1997, pp. 54–55).

The basic guidelines are to begin with vertical (self-relaxation) and horizontal (seeing and being seen by audience) moments; tell the story in the present tense using brief phrases (no "ands" or "ums"); embody and speak as the different roles; and be free to jump in time and setting. Insight Improvisation adds to these elements an emphasis on slowing down and letting go of "performing"— to instead completely enter the story physically, vocally, and emotionally, moment-by-moment. Performances of stories can range from the deeply moving to the delightfully ridiculous, and tend to make very satisfying final performances for the weekend. The weekend ends with a final reflection and closing circle.

Weekend Workshop #2—Contemplative Drama Therapy

Session 1: Introduction—Authentic Movement & Psychodrama

Warm-up and Welcome. The session begins with a guided meditation and movement sequence, incorporating *vipassana* meditation and the Three States exercise (see above). In the opening circle, the facilitator introduces the weekend, and two main goals:

- To learn and practice the *psolodrama* technique (described below).
- To create a confidential, safe space in which participants can share from their depth and witness one another.

Authentic Movement and the Witness Role. The role of the witness in authentic movement is introduced: Instead of the facilitator being the witness for all, now participants are asked to work in pairs, one mover and one witness. An observant, nonjudgmental witness is necessary for authentic movement, psolodrama, and most Insight Improv activities; conversely, these practices also help one to develop a compassionate inner witness.

Psychodrama. In addition to authentic movement, the other main ingredient of the psolodrama form is psychodrama, the system of therapeutic role-play developed by J. L. Moreno (see Chapter 15). Psychodrama is introduced by working with one participant's real-life scenario, and demonstrating the five psychodramatic operational roles—protagonist, auxiliary ego, double, director, and audience—as well as other basic psychodramatic concepts, such as role reversal, surplus reality, the psychodramatic spiral, and role rehearsal. During an optional subsequent session, the remaining participants are invited to be protagonists in their own psychodramas.

By the end of the first afternoon/evening, each participant has had the experience of moving mindfully and witnessing/being witnessed, as well as sharing an aspect of their own personal journey. Feelings of community and common purpose have begun to take root.

Session 2: Building Toward Psolodrama

Warm-ups to Psolodrama. Following brief group meditation and authentic movement, the day begins with a series of dynamic, fun, pair improvisations—*impulse dialogue, role dialogue,* and *yes! improvisation*—designed as warm-ups for practicing psolodrama one-to-one with a partner.

The Empty Chair. In this classic exercise, which originated with Jacob Moreno (and was adapted by Fritz Perls for Gestalt therapy), one participant, as protagonist, sees someone sitting in an empty chair. It could be someone he has unfinished business with, or someone he would really like to talk to, living or dead. Working in pairs, with a partner playing the role of double, each participant plays out the dialogue with the empty chair figure, eventually reversing roles and becoming the other.

The Five Roles. This activity was designed to serve as a bridge between the empty chair and psolodrama. Participants work in pairs, with one acting as witness, and, if needed, as a coach. The active partner begins with authentic movement, out of which emerges a scene between two characters—i.e., the protagonist (herself at some time in her life) and an auxiliary ego (any other character, real or imagined). There is no need to use an empty chair—the participant uses movement in the space to bring the scene to life. As the improvisation continues, the facilitator (or the witness) prompts the role-player to add, one by one, the roles of double, director, and audience to her improvisation, until a multifaceted scene has been played out.

This session's work serves to demonstrate how one can play out a real or imagined scene by oneself, fully embodying each of the roles. For some participants, the empty chair and the five roles can be deeply moving experiences, dynamic ways of working on real life issues. Personal breakthroughs often occur during this session.

Session 3: Introduction to Psolodrama

Psolodrama. This advanced exercise is a melding of authentic movement and psychodrama, and in many ways is the most powerful Insight Improvisation structure, a vehicle for self-discovery. ("Psolodrama" is a term I coined to suggest a mixture of solo, drama, psyche, and a bit of soul.)

As in authentic movement, psolodrama requires two people, the psoloist and the witness. The witness provides a nonjudgmental container for the work: he observes, keeps time—usually 15 minutes or more—and, if the psoloist so desires, shares his observations afterward. The psoloist begins with authentic movement, being aware of body sensations, emotions, and inner imagery that may be leading her towards a character or scene. The psoloist then adds sound, then words, and then finds herself in one of the five psychodramatic roles.

The solo improvisation that develops is a series of monologues and dialogues featuring these roles. At any time, the psoloist can return to stillness, silence, and authentic movement, or can shift roles or scenes. No distinction is made between fact, fantasy, past, present, or future. As in any Insight Improvisation activity, all of this is performed largely intuitively; the psoloist consciously avoids doing her "good ideas" but instead works with internal imagery, sensory awareness, etc.

Psolodrama is not a performance for the benefit of others, but a personal process. The psoloist need not clarify things for the witness, but instead trusts that the witness will get what he gets. The psoloist's goal (as in the spontaneous writing exercise, above) is to go for the heart of the matter—to not avoid, delay, or dance around the issue; but instead to dive in and embody completely the images and feelings that are arising. The results are often moving, scary, hilarious, passionate, beautiful, cathartic, and insightful—all one could ask for in a work of theatre. (Transcripts of sample psolodramas can be found in this chapter's web supplement.)

To introduce psolodrama, the facilitator can use a handout describing the basic principles, as well as a live demonstration. Participants practice psolodrama in pairs (ideally in breakout spaces for privacy) and then gather to discuss their experience and ask questions. The afternoon can end with one or more psolodramas in the whole group—the facilitator provides live coaching, as one psoloist works at a time with the rest of the group as witness. The workshop continues with an optional evening of one-to-one coaching with group support—including psolodramas or work on specific issues thru psychodrama or other means.

Sessions 4&5: Psolodrama Practice and Supporting Exercises
The agenda for the final day of the workshop depends largely on the needs and desires of the group. Activities can include the following:

Shared Vipassana. In this exercise, the "meditator," observed by a witness, begins with authentic movement, and opens up to awareness of the six sense doors (the five senses, plus mind objects—thoughts, images, memories, etc.). As the meditator moves, he can share aloud what he is experiencing: "tingling in right foot," "sound of wind outside," "thinking 'what is my witness seeing right now?'" As he continues, he can add more expression to his sharing, using sound and embodying images that arise: "I'm in a swamp—I sink into the mud—blubblubblub ..." As in authentic movement, the meditator lets go of planning or controlling, and instead follows the body, sensations, and imagination and shares what is unfolding moment by moment.

Role Stream. Similar to shared vipassana, the role stream is practiced in improviser—witness pairs; the improviser begins with authentic movement. In the role stream, the improviser begins to notice what roles or characters are suggested by his movement, and embodies and speaks as them. For example, a certain physical position or movement may remind the mover of a bear hibernating in a cave. He may choose to speak as the bear, in a bear-like voice: "mmmmm ... I don't wanna get up ... leave me alone ... oh, it's been so long since I've eaten!" The mover can drop a role at any time and return to stillness, or to movement, and see what arises next.

Shared vipassana and the role stream together are ideal prologues to psolodrama, helping a psoloist follow her natural organic process of unfolding, rather than relying on the mind to choose particular roles or issues. Participants are taught a four-stage process for practicing psolodrama, in which the witness uses bells or verbal signals to take the psoloist through four stages: authentic movement, shared vipassana, role stream, and then psolodrama itself (the first three stages can be a few minutes each; the psolodrama typically requires at least 15 minutes).

Sung Psolodrama. Singing while improvising can be a powerful channel for connecting with one's own emotions. Sung psolodrama is the same as psolodrama except that everything spoken is sung. As in performing a text (above), the singing is not meant to necessarily be beautiful or have a recognizable melody—if the psoloist aims for singing, what comes out may sometimes be more like rap, or elongated or expressive syllables. What's important is that the psoloist allow herself to be fully present to and touched by her own song, helping inspire and deepen what comes next.

The workshop ends with a final opportunity for each participant to do a psolodrama or psychodrama, and receive coaching/direction from the facilitator and group support.

Applications

Insight Improvisation's concepts and activities make for powerful actor training—new actors must develop a sense of awareness, calm, and connection to themselves and others as a foundation for their craft. Experienced theatre artists have used Insight Improvisation as a way of sourcing performance material; exercises like psolodrama, storytelling, and performing a text can plant seeds for a one-person show.

Insight Improvisation is also a form of drama therapy. It can be used by a therapist as a way to help clients and groups transform dysfunctional patterns, through developing greater awareness in moving, feeling, speaking, and interacting with others. The combination of meditative awareness and connection with body, mind, and emotions can help individuals overcome personal inhibitions, tap into unexpected sources of creativity, and bring mindfulness into day-to-day life, work, and relationships.

Finally, Insight Improvisation is a set of tools for working together one-to-one—designed for actors improvising together, friends wishing to engage in an expressive form of co-counseling, and those on a spiritual path exploring creative approaches together.

References and Related Reading

The Insight Improvisation Homepage: <www.jgluck.org>. An online source for Insight Improvisation practitioners, with articles and program information.

Goldberg, Natalie. (1990). *Wild mind: Living the writer's life.* New York: Bantam. (Goldberg describes an improvisational approach to writing that helps us break free of old patterns, pointing the way to greater authenticity.)

Goldstein, Joseph, & Kornfield, Jack. (1987). *Seeking the heart of wisdom: The path of insight meditation.* Boston: Shambhala. (Two pioneers who brought *vipassana* meditation to the West share their approach.)

Kramer, Gregory. (2001). *Meditating together, speaking from silence: The practice of insight dialogue.* Portland, OR: Metta Foundation. (Kramer explores the idea of meditation as a vehicle for relating to others.)

Pallaro, P. (Ed.). (1999). *Authentic movement: essays by Mary Starks Whitehouse, Janet Adler, and Joan Chodorow.* Philadelphia: Jessica Kingsley. (Essential writings of the creators of authentic movement.)

van Itallie, Jean-Claude. (1997). *The playwright's workbook.* New York: Applause Books. (Van Itallie, author of the groundbreaking plays, *America Hurrah* and *The Serpent,* teaches his approach to storytelling.)

Zaporah, Ruth. (1995). *Action theater: the improvisation of presence.* Berkeley, CA: North Atlantic Books. (The author challenges practitioners to approach movement, sound, and language in radically new ways.)

Chapter 19

LEARNING TO PARENT APART: DRAMA IN PARENT SKILLS TRAINING

Deborah J. Zuver & Mary K. Grigsby

One Saturday morning a month a dozen parents who have been court-ordered to attend a parent education program gather in a museum conference room. These participants have recently failed mediation attempts with a co-parent and their child or children are caught in the middle of their conflict. They may need help in managing their own emotions, learning ways to effectively navigate the world of co-parenting and assisting their children in coping with the transition of the changing family.

The Durham Family Court wants these parents to gain an understanding of how children are affected by such conflict, how parents can reduce the level of conflict, and that they can choose to return to mediation to resolve their differences. This is a tall order for the parent education program, Learning to Parent Apart (L2PA), to accomplish in only four hours. L2PA has been highly successful in utilizing drama to address the often difficult and emotional issues that these dysfunctional, high-conflict families face.

Initially, many participants anticipate being admonished during the class for a shameful lack of parenting skills or enduring a didactic lecture or video telling them how they should parent. Instead, L2PA interactively builds on parents' strengths and resources and treats them as the experts on their families. In spite of any skepticism and resistance, participants are put in role as their "best" parent from the first contact with an L2PA facilitator, thus setting the stage for shifting perspectives. Drawing on their personal expertise as parents can inspire participants to reach toward their higher selves, empowering them to strive toward becoming the best parents they can be during this difficult time.

L2PA uses scenarios and enactments to give parents a gut-level emotional understanding of the issues and help them process new information. L2PA participants explore ways to address the impact of separation and divorce for scenario children at different ages. New options emerge as participants consider various ideas and resources.

Since co-parents attend L2PA on separate days they are afforded the space to step away from their own perspective and consider other points of view. This helps parents maintain focus on the children's needs rather than on their conflict with their ex-spouse. Additionally, co-facilitators model working cooperatively and effectively while sharing responsibilities and sometimes portraying differing viewpoints.

The L2PA Process

L2PA uses realistic fictional scenarios and situations to engage participants. The participants' specific issues are intentionally not included in the crafting of these scenarios, to allow the parents some distance to consider more general problems of parenting apart. Most participants are relieved to focus on the family in a scenario whose issues broadly parallel their own in general rather than in specific ways. Personal experience forms the subliminal backdrop for scenarios and enactments.

From the outset, participants are guided to make a distinction between their roles as ex-spouse and co-parent. This is helpful when a parent is stuck in a competitive need to be the "good" or "correct" parent. The importance of the child having a healthy relationship with both parents is emphasized. Discussion among participants is typically rife with suggestions for reducing conflict as well as reflections on how personal change is possible as participants embody their role as strong, reasonable, and caring parents.

The enactments and activities allow parents to experience the effect of focusing attention and energy on children rather than on parental conflict. Participants are encouraged to think of themselves as "parenting experts" acting as consultants to the scenario parents. This experience as an objective third-party expert encourages parents to maintain their best parent role for the duration of the class.

L2PA is structured on six progressive steps:

- Affirming parenting strengths

- Addressing a fictional scenario
- Speaking with the child, a role-played enactment
- Advising the fictional parents
- Acknowledging the other parent's strengths
- Imagining vividly a positive future

1. Setting the Stage: Affirming Parenting Strengths. As the program begins, participants divide randomly into pairs and take five minutes to share their strengths as a parent. Comments often include: "I give them love." "I listen." "Gotta have a sense of humor." This simple verbal exercise gently kick-starts the class, immediately easing participants into interaction in a nonthreatening manner and setting the stage for stepping up the level of involvement. This activity also helps facilitators with the sometimes difficult task of priming an audience for participation.

To illustrate, we will follow the experience of a typical divorcing father, "Sam" (not his real name), who has been court-ordered to attend L2PA. Sam is angry and resentful for having to give up a Saturday morning for a class when he feels that failure to come up with a viable custody arrangement is all the fault of his ex-wife. From the moment he enters the class, Sam appears agitated and impatient, merely biding his time. He has no intention of participating, and sits down with his arms crossed. Despite himself, Sam began to talk in this first exercise as he is eager to point out that he is always consistent with his kids and that he is proud of his relationship with them. He engages with a partner, chosen at random, for this first exercise, and that partner in turn shares his or her own parenting strengths.

2. Addressing a Fictional Scenario: Meeting the Child. Participants are divided into three groups of about four participants each. Each group is given a card with a different brief scenario about a particular fictional child and his or her parents. Each scenario is designed to highlight a specific stage in child development and demonstrate varying issues that are common with high-conflict, divorcing parents.

Sam's group receives the following:

> "Since Will and Monica separated, four-year-old Tonya has been reluctant to go to sleep at night and has recently begun wetting her bed again. She has been hitting and biting children at her day care. Will and Monica have agreed to shared custody, so Tonya spends one week with each parent. Neither parent sees her on their "off" week. (During the week with one parent, Tonya has no contact with the

other one.) She is noticeably more clingy when dropped off and picked up from either parent's home and she often complains of stomachaches and headaches. Will and Monica think Tonya is too young to understand what is going on so they don't talk with her about the changes in the family."

The five-minute task for each group is to identify behaviors and feelings of the child in the scenario and make any suggestions for what the parents might do to help the child. Groups then reconvene to discuss "their" families with the whole class, and everyone gains some familiarity with the stories of each of the three fictional children. Group discussion is guided to include additional information about normal child development for each age group and how children respond to change and stress. The exercise subtly begins to help parents focus on the distinction between feelings and behaviors, and the importance of addressing the child's emotions and experience. Sam began to make connections about his own children's behavior. He comments that he knows from experience that the parents in the scenario should have talked with Tonya about the separation.

3. A Role-Played Enactment: Speaking With the Child. In this part of the process, participants take a step closer to the scenario child by enacting a role and directly engaging the scenario child, played by one of the facilitators. Each group receives a slip of paper with a strong emotional comment that the child has made to his or her parent.

Tonya's comment on the paper given to Sam's group, reads: Tonya: "I'm scared to go to bed. Is your friend going to be here again, Daddy (Mommy)? I don't want your friend tucking me in. Will you stay with me?"

The group is challenged to create a list of possible responses for the scenario parent that are appropriate for the situation and the child's age. When the groups reconvene, rather than simply *reading* the list of scripted responses, a spokesperson from each group is asked to *say* one of the responses directly to the child.

Sam is the spokesperson for his group. A co-facilitator has quietly slipped into role as Tonya even before the directive was completed. At this point, having slid a chair toward Sam, she speaks, as Tonya, her comment directly to him, putting him in role as Tonya's dad. With this prompt, Sam responds to Tonya directly. A conversation unfolds and an enactment is launched. The room is intent on Tonya and how she will respond.

At a choice point in the scene, the other facilitator pauses the enactment with questions for participants: What is Tonya feeling? What's going on in the scene? What approach did the parent take? How else might a parent react? The group is empathic; they care about this child and they vicariously relate to the immediacy of the situation. They offer ideas and the enactment continues, trying alternative responses perhaps with another participant in the role of Tonya's parent.

Considering differing vantage points enriches the scenes. Responses may range from a parent soothing Tonya with the promise of a good-night story and lights out as usual, to a mother poignantly reminding her child that her daddy will always be her daddy and her friend is just a friend. At one point, Sam mentioned that he wondered whether Tonya was afraid of the friend. He is then encouraged to check that out with Tonya, and the scenario was played out further.

The emotions that parents bring into the room are palpable. These strong feelings are channeled toward caring for each scenario child and discovering ways to respond to a child's needs, resulting in enactments that are heartfelt and moving. Scenes holds the group in rapt attention as would any engaging story. The momentum builds as participants consider a child's plight and the parents' interaction. No one refers to "the role play;" rather, they refer to scenario children by name, "Tonya," as if she had become an actual person they were talking about.

Sam, who started out the class focusing on his frustration with his ex-wife, has shifted his attention to Tonya's needs. In his role-played conversation with her, he infused the scenario with his understanding of what was important to the child emotionally and developmentally by drawing on his own values and experience, making a difference for Tonya, just as he might be empowered to do with his own children.

4. Shaping the Outcome: Advising the Fictional Parents. The next enactment activity takes participants closer to the scenario parents. Each participant receives a card with background information about either the mother ("Monica") or the father ("Will") in one of the scenarios. Participants are asked to take on the role of advisors to these parents in the scene. Two groups are formed, each as advisors for one of the two parents, and they meet separately to strategize about how that parent might reduce conflict on a personal level and for Tonya.

In the scenario that Sam has, the card for the advisors of Monica (Tonya's mother) reads: "Monica: You tend to run late picking Tonya up from Will's home, usually because of responsibilities at work. He uses that as an excuse to yell in front of Tonya. After Tonya has been with her dad, you like to talk about everything—you ask her where they go and who goes with them so that Tonya can share those activities with you, too."

The card for the advisors for Will (Tonya's father) reads: "Will: You always have Tonya ready to be picked up, but Monica seldom has enough consideration to be on time. No matter how loudly you remind her, she acts as though she doesn't hear and, as they leave, starts pumping Tonya for every detail about your time together."

Groups generate ideas for "their" parent and come together to discuss how the scenario parents might reduce conflict between one another. Part "reality TV" and part theatre, the intensity and immediacy of the scenario parent's situation challenge the participants. A range of perspectives and insights emerge. The subtext is that there may not be a single right or wrong response to reduce conflict; there may be several responses and the litmus test is how the child may perceive it. Simply being "right" may not be the best way to take the child out of the middle of the conflict. Sam observes that while it seems easy to come up with ways for Will and Monica to "be adult" about this for the sake of Tonya, he has found that the process is more complicated.

As they reconvene, the groups have a ready list of ideas they came up with, but instead of sharing those, the group is asked to consider something else: what helped them come up with their options? Responses often include that knowing something about the other parent's perspective gave them a different point of view. Some were moved by how Tonya is affected by her parent's conflicts. Speaking in role as "advisor" allows participants to access another role within themselves. Sam said, "I guess you can remember to just be your better parent."

5. *Co-Parenting: Acknowledging the Value of the Other Parent.* This next brief activity takes participants away from the scenario parents and lands them right back in their own conflict situation. On one side of a blank index card, parents list what their child loves/likes/values in their other parent. Some parents do not even pick up a pen; others begin a long list. Parents are asked how difficult or easy the activity is and to reflect on why that may be. The brief discussion that follows focuses on continuing to help the parents see the world from their child's perspective instead of their own. It reinforces the shift from viewing a co-parent as hated ex-spouse to recognizing that person as an important person in the child's life. Having just provided advice to scenario parents, participants are often able to transfer this experience to reflecting on their own need to maintain the conflict level.

On the flip-side of the card, participants list ways to support their child's relationship with his or her other parent. For some this can be difficult. Sam said that his son recently placed a photo of his mom near his bed. It would be tough to have his ex-wife's photo in the house, but Sam saw that it meant a lot to his son and realized that his son had a right to a relationship with his mother.

6. *Imagining a Positive Future*: As these activities conclude, participants are guided to reconnect with their own situation through a visualization exercise. They are asked to sit comfortably and imagine three years in the future when their children are secure have adjusted well to the changes in the family. As they picture their child's appearance, achievements, and adjustment, parents begin to reflect on how their parenting made a difference in their child's life. They consider how applying tools and new perspectives reduced the level of conflict and helped their children cope over the intervening years.

Concluding the Program

L2PA's six-step structure is designed to help participants recognize and access their parenting strengths by engaging in fictionalized enactments, developing new parenting perspectives, and applying them to their own lives. As the four hours draw to a close, parents often comment how quickly the time passed. Many participants mention verbally or on written evaluations that the scenarios and role plays have made a difference in how they view their children's experience of the separation/divorce.

Addressing Challenges

Multiple challenges are inherent to court-mandated educational programs. Many L2PA participants come to class with trepidation and fear of being judged or labeled negatively. These parents are involved in highly contentious legal issues regarding the care of their children. They have generally not worked through the strong emotions that accompanied the demise of the romantic relationship and carry those feelings with them throughout the court process. Like Sam, these parents are typically extremely angry, even bitter, and resentful towards their child's other parent. When friends and family members rally to support each parent, further polarization of emotions can occur, creating an us versus them or good parent versus bad parent mentality.

L2PA begins to address this challenge from the initial phone registration. Facilitators offer respect and convey the assumption of parents' expertise on their own family, so that parents themselves will accept this role. Holding the class at a local children's museum helps to disarm potential resistance as it is a location known by most participants and may hold memories of happy experiences with their children. This neutral environment, in contrast to a court building, therapy office, or school where associations may not be as positive for some participants, reinforces the nonjudgmental, non-punitive mind-set.

Perhaps the greatest challenges for L2PA facilitators are educational and cultural differences of the participants; however, emotional reactions of parents cut across ethnicity and socioeconomic strata. The population served by L2PA ranges in age from parents in their early twenties to grandparents in their sixties. Income ranges from less than $10,000 annually to above $60,000 annually. Education levels include individuals who are illiterate, those who have had some high school, and those with varying levels of schooling all the way to post-graduate. Culturally, the class serves individuals from various racial, ethnic, and religious backgrounds. On some occasions, an interpreter was required to bridge the language barrier for a participant. Providing instructions through multiple modalities circumvents literacy differences. Written materials, whether posters, handouts, or exercise instructions are read aloud as well as presented visually. Because scenes and exercises are interactive, they do not rely on reading ability, but simply require that individuals draw from their own knowledge and wisdom as parents and that they be willing to share those with others.

Another challenge for the program is the limited time frame. By state regulation, the class is four hours in length. To adequately cover the required curriculum content in the short amount of time, each interaction with participants must be optimized to have purpose and meaning. Every L2PA activity has been carefully designed to move the course toward the stated goals, consistent with the course philosophy. L2PA must provide information and at the same time provide participants with the means to take in and internalize that information so they can return to their families and apply it.

Challenges are also met through the group interaction. It is in this way that parents share a tear or a laugh and find solace connecting with others coping with similar issues. Participants often comment that the support and understanding from the group of parents like themselves has made an important difference in how they see their situation.

Discussion

Parents who are court-ordered to L2PA typically leave the class appreciative of the experience. Parting comments often include statements such as, "I didn't want to be here but I am glad I came," or "This has been really helpful; thank you for offering it." Although hurt and angry feelings toward their co-parent persist, participants are often able to acknowledge the importance of that person in their child's life.

Many changes occur during the brief class. Stoic, quiet parents begin to open up and share their experience and strength. Overtly emotional parents step out of their own experiences for a time and are able to rationally access decision-making and problem-solving skills. Like Sam, many fathers who have felt marginalized and forgotten by the court system leave feeling heard and valued. Several participants have reported remembering specific scenes and exercises from the class that have helped them in their parenting. The most common feedback on evaluation forms is a wish that the class had been offered earlier in their separation process.

When educators have a lot of information to "cover," the temptation is to present it dispassionately so that emotions do not get in the way. This generally results in a bland, cognitive exercise with limited practical learning. Instead of sidestepping emotions, L2PA uses enactments to harness these strong feelings directly to the information. L2PA participants spend four hours invested in caring about specific children who are hurting and need both their parents to help them get through a difficult family transition. Parents take away an experience of reaching inside for their "better parent" role. Thus, the drama of real-life experiences takes center stage to stir us to action.

For related programs, further examples and references on webpage supplement to this chapter: <www.interactiveimprov.com/learn2parentapart. html>

References

Kramer, K. M., Arbuthnot, J., Gordon, N. J., & Hoza, J. (1998). Effects of skill-based versus information-based divorce education programs on domestic violence and parental communication. *Family and Conciliation Courts Review* 36(1):9–31. (Describes a study that looked at skill-based divorced education programs. Findings suggest that parents with greater communication skills exposed children to less conflict.)

Neumann, G. (1998). *Helping Your Kids Cope with Divorce the Sandcastles Way.* New York: Random House. (A guide to help readers appreciate how kids perceive divorce; includes scripts and arts-related interactive exercises to use with every age group.)

Chapter 20

DRAMA IN PRISONS

Clark Baim

For many years drama has been used in prisons and probation services, though most of these programs have involved more traditional forms of scripted and rehearsed theatre. However, there are innovative approaches that use more improvisation and interactivity. John Bergman in the United States developed the first Geese Theatre Company in the early 1980s, and, in 1987, after touring with them, I worked with colleagues to establish the Geese Theatre UK (Baim, Brookes and Mountford, 2002), now under the directorship of Andrew Watson.

Geese Theatre UK (abbreviated as GT) was one of the first theatre companies to specialize in work with offenders, and has been at the forefront of advocating a drama-based approach to promoting positive change. GT's drama-based work includes live performances, creative residencies, drama-based workshops, offence-focused workshops and groupwork. GT uses drama and theatre to encourage self-awareness and to assist individuals in exploring the idea of change and the impact that change may have on their lives. While focusing on each person's responsibility for their own offending, GT also takes into account the connections between personal behavior, choice and responsibility and broader social, economic and political factors.

GT functions as a catalyst. They do not 'teach' or provide moral lessons, but rather present theatre and drama-based work that is relevant to the lives of the audience/participants and invites them to make meaning for themselves. In their plays, the GT performers mirror situations and behaviors and model possible alternatives as a prompt for discussion and debate. In addition, by using dynamic, participatory drama techniques, GT facilitates the active exploration of change and helps people to rehearse new skills.

Special Considerations

Offenders require an approach that is somewhat different from facilitating drama in the general population. Whether one has an 'arts focus' or a 'rehabilitation focus', some of the key themes when conducting change-oriented work with this population include the development of:

• motivation to change, and life goals

• self-esteem and self-determination

• skills in taking the perspectives of others

• skills of cooperation and social interaction

• self-management skills, including emotional self-regulation, problem-solving and considering alternatives and consequences

• more responsible attitudes and beliefs about offending, and what it means to live a 'straight' life

• relationship skills and what it means to become a responsible adult

• empathy for victims of crime

• healing of the residues of early life trauma, abuse and neglect

• more socially positive attitudes and beliefs about violence, sexual interests, justifications for stealing, and relapse prevention.

Some of these themes can be addressed directly while others require a more indirect approach. The methods you use will depend on your skills and training. This chapter will provide a taste of what is possible.

A Special Population

Theatre and drama with offenders shares much in common with approaches for any special population. However, practitioners who work with offenders soon become aware of certain realities in this field of work, some of them rather stark:

• Offender participants often pose a serious risk to the community, the staff, themselves or each other. Workers must be realistic about issues of personal safety

• Participants can pose special challenges for theatre/arts workers who may be perceived as weak, naive, gullible or sexually available

- The participants may have committed crimes that you find abhorrent. The challenge is to hold in mind that the person you are working with is more than his or her worst actions

- The participants may become dependent on you or they may try to take advantage of you or manipulate you in ways you can't always anticipate

- It can be difficult to gain credibility with criminal justice staff

- We are accountable to the criminal justice system and the public at large for the work we do with offenders, as their rehabilitation and welfare are the responsibility of the state

- The values and behavioral norms promoted in drama-based work often contradict the values and norms in the rest of the prison. For example, expressiveness, cooperation and consideration for others may be perceived as weakness when he or she is back in the main population and make your participant a target. It is important to address this issue directly. Otherwise, the values inherent in drama-based work can seem dangerous, alien or naive to your participants.

It is a good idea to bear in mind these realities if you are considering working in a prison, probation or related setting. It is also a good idea to gain from the experiences of more seasoned practitioners, in order to avoid 're-inventing the wheel' and making the same mistakes as previous workers.

A number of examples of how work with offenders may differ from work with other special populations are offered on the website that is a supplement to this chapter: <www.interactiveimprov.com/prisonwb.html>

The Method

The rest of this chapter offers a sample of GT's methods in experiential workshops, including the use of experiential exercises, interactive improvisation using drama structures, and role play.

Mask and the concept of 'mask lifting.' In much of their work, GT uses a powerful central metaphor, which is the 'mask'—a metaphor for the front we all may use when dealing with other people. GT actors often perform in half-mask or full mask, in improvised plays designed to directly address issues most crucial to prison and probation audiences. GT works with the notion that we all wear 'masks,' some habitually, some self-consciously. In performances and workshops, audiences can ask characters in half-mask to 'lift their mask' and can question the characters about the thoughts and feelings underlying their outward attitudes and behavior. When a character lifts their mask and speaks to another character onstage or directly to the audience/observers, they are trying to be more open about their inner thoughts and feelings. It is a powerful and memorable technique that allows GT workers to work with participants to explore the distinctions between external behavior and internal experience.

Processing exercises. In Geese Theatre UK's approach to drama-based workshops and offence-focused group work, the Company often uses whole group experiential exercises to create certain group interactions or to address a given theme. Whether the work is aimed at general themes of personal development or is focused specifically on offence-related themes, GT uses a structured form of processing to help the participants to deepen their understanding and draw personal relevance from the exercises. Processing will generally be divided into 'general processing' and 'personal processing' to distinguish between processing for the whole group or processing that focuses on one individual and how the exercise applies to him or her personally.

One of the crucial goals of processing is to help participants to 'think about their thinking'; in other words, to become more conscious of their thoughts and their decision-making powers. For example, in trust exercises where one person must have their eyes closed, blindfolds are *not* used, because blindfolds take away the element of choice. When participants open their eyes, they do this because they need to feel safe. But more importantly, they also have thoughts that allow them to keep their eyes closed, or to close them again if they open them momentarily. It is important to be able to access these thoughts, because they indicate an active process of decision making. Many offenders do not recognize that they have distinct thoughts and that they make decisions; they have not yet 'thought about their thinking.' These exercises provide participants with an opportunity to reflect on their own thinking, feeling and behavior in a safe way and at a level of distance that feels achievable for them.

Experiential and Drama-Based Exercises

A variety of exercises and drama structures typically used by Geese Theatre Company are described in Baim, Brookes and Mountford (2002), in Bergman and Hewish (2003), and also on the website that is a supplement to this chapter. This section describes a representative sample.

Point of View Circle. Have the group members stand in a circle, with one volunteer in the middle. Instruct the volunteer to look at a fixed point on the wall, with his hands by his side and standing neutrally. Ask the people in the circle to go around and say how many of the volunteer's eyes, ears and hands they see. The response will vary as each person has a different angle of vision.

Ask the group members for their thoughts about what is happening. Responses will usually take in ideas such as everyone having their own point of view, and no single person has all of the information at the start. Ask how this can be addressed. Someone will suggest people change places. Ask everyone to do so. Then repeat the procedure, with everyone saying how many of the volunteer's eyes, ears and hands they see—just as before. People will give a different response.

Ask the group members about what the benefits might be in trying to 'see the full picture' when addressing any problem, issue or theme that may arise in the group. Suggest to them that this can be a common understanding of how people in this group will be challenged, i.e. 'When people challenge each other in this group, rather than saying to each other "You are wrong," perhaps it will be more effective if you say "I'm not sure you've seen the full picture." Groups will normally appreciate this as a principle of how they will operate and challenge each other. The exercise also gives people a language with which to challenge each other productively and non-confrontationally.

This is an excellent exercise to do on day one or two of a new group, because it establishes a baseline of respectful challenging in the group.

Bombs and Shields. Ask the group to spread evenly across the room. 'Pick two new people in your mind's eye, but don't let them know who they are. Now, in your mind, silently label those two people person A and person B. Have you done it? Good. Your job is to keep person A between you and person B at all times. Distance is not a factor, but this is a game with no physical contact. Be aware of the space and the people around you, and don't bump into anyone. Go!'

These instructions will lead on to a challenging series of bobbing and weaving movements, as group members try to get into the correct positions. This should normally not last more than about twenty seconds. When you stop them, you might like to check who has stopped in a 'correct' position with a Person 'A' between them and their 'B.'

This is a high energy game, and in very new groups can put some people off as it can seem a bit frantic. After the high energy part of the exercise, you can process in the following way: "This exercise is sometimes called *bombs and shields*. What would be a 'bomb' for you, or something to avoid? Do you have a 'shield?' What is it? How do you protect yourself, or get protection?"

Frozen Pictures. Frozen pictures is another term for tableaux, a technique well-known to practitioners of experiential drama. In this technique, one or more participants create a still image of characters in situations relevant to the theme of the workshop. The participants in the scene and the observers then explore the thoughts, feelings and behavior of the characters in the scene, and the choices they can make. Frozen pictures can be combined into multi-picture scenes that are, in effect, a series of snapshots. Frozen pictures can be done on the fictional level or the personal level.

Some suggestions for titles and themes of frozen pictures are: The offence; The outsider; Regrets; Consequences; In court; Life on the street; What's good/bad about crime/drugs, etc.; The fight; The victim; Before and after the offence; Me in a high risk situation; How I see my victim/How my victim sees me; Missing home; How I want it to be in X years/How I will get there; What's holding me back; Friendship; Peer pressure; Boredom; Rejection; Hope; Starting to change.

Brief Facilitator-Enacted Scenes. The technique of putting the worker in role draws from the innovative ideas of Dorothy Heathcote (Wagner, 1976). Heathcote calls her method teaching in role. In this technique, the worker goes into role as a character with some relevance to the group members, and interacts with the group members in order to provoke their thinking and challenge them in important ways. Sometimes the worker will first perform a scene and then speak with the observers about what he was thinking, feeling and doing in the scene. This technique works on the assumption that participants will be motivated and capable of speaking from various informed perspectives (Heathcote calls this giving the participants 'the mantle of the expert'-Heathcote and Bolton, 1995). Examples of characters that are relevant to work with offenders: An offender 'like them'; A professional with an interest in a (fictional) case; A witness to a crime; A crime victim or family member of a victim; A reporter covering the story.

You can vary the technique. For example, the worker can be in one role and one or more of the group members can be in one or more of the other roles. The tension between the perceptions of the participants and the perceptions of the character played by the worker often result in animated discussion and very useful challenges. For example, the worker may be in role as an offender who blames his victim and takes no responsibility, while the group members are speaking from the perspective of a family member of the victim. In this situation, the group can often become quite agitated with the 'offender' because they are speaking as advocates for the victim. Used appropriately, this kind of strategy can help develop empathy and awareness of consequences among the participants, and help them to become more motivated to change.

Role Play

In addition to a wide array of dramatic structures and techniques such as those discussed above, GT also facilitates role play where it is appropriate and useful. There are many types of role play, and this section describes some that are useful for working with offenders. The website supplement to this chapter describes other types of role play commonly used by GT.

The different types of role play described below have different (although sometimes overlapping) aims. Some of them operate at the level of 'one step removed' (i.e. they are fictional or based on an event not directly related to the participants) and some of them work on the personal level (i.e. directly personal to one participant). Some of the types of role play can be used on both the level of one step removed and the personal level. For example, a fictional scene may be a warm-up to personal level role play—although this demands a high level of skill and training to facilitate well.

General note: While Whole Group Role Plays may last several minutes or more, the other types of role play should be kept short. This is to keep the role play controlled and manageable. If scenes go on longer than two minutes, it is easy to forget the particulars of what happened when you process the scene. Thirty seconds to two minutes is normally sufficient time to achieve the desired aim.

Whole Group Role Play. The aim of this type of role play is primarily to help participants gain an understanding of other peoples' points of view and the impact of one's actions on other people. As the name implies, in whole group role play all of the participants have a role. The facilitators design the role play to address a theme relevant to the group and ensure that it will offer sufficient roles for everyone to have a part. For example, the group may enact the roles of all of the people surrounding a hypothetical burglary: the family who live in the house, the burglars, the police who try to find evidence, the neighbor, the news reporter, the insurance claim adjuster, the victim support volunteer who comes to comfort the family, relatives of the family and the burglars, etc. When all of the roles are cast, interview each person in role to hear their point of view. Encourage the characters to speak to each other and confront the other characters. For example, a family member may challenge the burglar's distorted belief that no one is harmed by his actions. (Note: It would not be appropriate for some characters to confront others, e.g. a perpetrator of violence or rape to confront a victim.) Exchange the roles so that different people get to play different roles. This type of role play shares much in common with sociodrama, discussed elsewhere in this book.

Forum Role Play. In this type of role play, a fictional scene is first portrayed where there is a dilemma, and a number of different approaches are attempted in order to deal with the dilemma. For example, the scene may portray an inmate feeling threatened because his wife is beginning to take night classes and he is worried she may leave him, but he doesn't know how to deal with the situation. Or, as another example, a role play may portray an offender in a high risk situation where he may re-offend. After the initial scene is enacted, different participants can enter the scene, replace the central character (the one whose behavior, thinking and feeling are in focus) and try to reach a different outcome. For example, several different group members in succession may take the role of the threatened man in the first scenario, or the man in the high risk situation in the second scenario. Much will be learned while the various attempts are made to deal with the situation and improve the outcome. Solutions should be as realistic as possible—no waving a magic wand or suddenly winning the lottery. This type of role play draws from the well-known work of Augusto Boal (1979) and others who have developed his ideas, as described in Chapter 21 on the Theatre of the Oppressed.

Skills Practice: This is the type of role play that most people associate with the term role play. As the name implies, this type of role play allows participants the opportunity to practice a new skill in a safe context where it is OK to make mistakes. In most circumstances, it is best to model the skill first. This can be done by the group facilitators and, more importantly, by more able members of the group; social learning theory (Bandura, 1977) tells us that skills modeling is most effective when the model is close in age and social position to the person for whom the skill is being modeled. When the skill is modeled, it should be broken down into 'mini-steps' or 'micro-skills', with each step named in order to make it clear. When it is time for the person who is to practice the skill to begin the role play, he should first be given the opportunity to review all of the 'mini-steps' and to pre-plan how he will negotiate any difficulties. The other role player in the scenario should be given clear instructions about how difficult or cooperative their character should be in the role play. If the skill is done well, the level of difficulty can be incrementally increased in order to 'harden' the skill. As the level of difficulty is increased, the person practicing the skill should again be given an opportunity at each stage to pre-plan how he will handle the increased level of difficulty. The underlying principle is one of 'no surprises'; in skills practice role play, there should be no surprises, because the focus is on providing a controlled and optimal environment to practice specific skills. To introduce uncertainty into the process can make the skill impossible to practice, which undermines the whole point of the activity.

This brings us to a second key principle of skills practice, which is the principle of the success experience. What this means is that we as facilitators must engineer and direct each stage of the skills practice so that the person practicing the skill has the best opportunity to 'succeed' at each run of the skill practice. This might mean we make the skill level very basic—even unrealistically basic—in the first run of the role play. Later, as the participant builds up his skills and confidence, the role play can be repeated with the level of difficulty increased to realistic levels. The danger of setting skills at too high a level is that we can inadvertently reinforce the participant's feeling of incompetence—thus doing exactly the opposite of what we hoped to achieve.

Some examples of skills typically practiced in prison and probation contexts (see also Goldstein, 1999):

- Apologizing
- Cooperating with other people
- Being interviewed for a job
- Asking questions when confused
- Handling a complaint about my actions
- Communicating with my partner
- Saying 'no'/dealing with peer pressure to offend
- Expressing concern for another person
- Negotiating and compromise
- Handling jealous feelings
- Communicating with my children
- Disciplining or setting limits with my children
- Talking to people in authority
- Accepting 'no'
- Telling someone I am angry with them
- Dealing with my own anger
- Responding to someone who is provoking me
- Relaxing when I am stressed
- Dealing with boredom/staying positive

Conclusion

Drama can be an effective way to help prisoners and ex-offenders to develop positive life skills and an improved sense of their own competence. Drama helps participants to explore new, non-offending futures and practice better ways to solve their problems, relate to other people and engage with the world around them. Drama can also be used to address specific aspects of offending behavior. As workers within Geese Theatre UK and similar organizations have demonstrated, a realistic and committed approach to using drama with offenders can promote an environment where positive change is more likely to occur. Many of the methods used are common to all forms of applied drama used with special populations; the difference is mainly in the unique circumstances of working within a criminal justice setting and the inherent demands of safety, accountability and public protection.

Acknowledgments: Thanks to Sally Brookes, Louise Heywood, Alun Mountford and Andrew Watson for assistance with this chapter.

Contacts and Websites of Interest

Geese Theatre UK's website: <www.geese.co.uk>

The Anne Peaker Centre for Arts in Criminal Justice <www.apcentre.org.uk> (A key resource for contacting individual artists and arts organisations working with offenders in the UK. They also sponsor orientation training for artists beginning to work with offenders.)

Further webpage references at <www.interactiveimprov.com/prisonwb.html>

Baim, Clark; Brookes, Sally; & Mountford, Alun. (Eds.). (2002). *The Geese Theatre handbook: Drama with offenders and people at risk*. Winchester: Waterside Press. (Waterside Press: <www.watersidepress.co.uk> also specializes in books about criminal justice.)

Balfour, M. (ed.) (2004) *Theatre in prison: Theory and practice*. Bristol, UK and Portland, OR, USA: Intellect Books.

Bandura, Alfred. (1977) *Social learning theory*. Englewood Cliffs, NJ: Prentice-Hall.

Bergman, John, & Hewish, Saul. (2003). *Challenging experience: An experiential approach to the treatment of serious offenders*. Oklahoma City: Wood N Barnes.

Goldstein, A. P. (1999). *The Prepare curriculum: Teaching prosocial competencies.* Champaign, Il.: Research Press.

Heathcote, Dorothy, & Bolton, Gavin. (1995). *Drama for learning: Dorothy Heathcote's mantle of the expert approach to education.* Portsmouth, NH: Heinemann.

Jefferies, Jinnie. (1991). What we are doing here is defusing bombs. In P. Holmes & M. Karp (Eds), *Psychodrama: Inspiration and technique* (pp. 189–200). London: Tavistock-Routledge.

Thompson, James. (1998). *Prison theatre: Perspectives and practices.* London: Jessica Kingsley.

Wagner, Betty Jane. (1976). *Dorothy Heathcote: Drama as a learning medium.* Washington, D.C.: National Educational Association.

(And other books mentioned in Appendix B and on the website link relevant to this chapter.)

SECTION IV

APPLICATIONS FOR EMPOWERMENT

Adam Blatner

We are surrounded by political and economic forces that seem overwhelming, dwarfing our individual ability to change the world. Organizations and clubs similarly can seem so big that our small voice gets lost. De-voicing can be considered another type of alienation, of oppression, and it is worse if we begin to forget—or never learned in the first place—that there is an alternative. We can give ourselves voice and develop ways of putting our voice together with other voices. We can develop social activities that may help to change things—and, if not change, at least know we tried. These approaches offer ways to explore tactics that might make us even more effective in our efforts.

Empowerment begins in subtle ways, in relationships, in the home, and ultimately, within one's own mind. Drama offers a more vivid way to work with the unfolding spirit of questioning, challenging, offering alternatives, affirming one's "truth," and witnessing to one's personal experience. We can share in your enactment without having to formally agree with all of your assertions; we can help you to feel seen and heard in your human predicament, and give you space to try out some different possible responses. There is power in wondering "what if …?" and playing it out "as if." This perspective makes drama a vehicle for life rehearsal, and from this, more courage emerges.

Chapter 21

THEATRE OF THE OPPRESSED

John Sullivan, Mecca Burns, & Doug Paterson

The Theatre of the Oppressed is perhaps the most well-known form of applied theatre internationally and has been influential for many of the approaches used in this book. Originating in Brazil in the 1960s, the Theatre of the Oppressed was invented, developed, and disseminated throughout the world by Augusto Boal. This form of theatre helps individuals and communities liberate themselves from oppressive situations and beliefs. TO, as it is sometimes abbreviated (and will be in this chapter) addresses any issues a community desires.

One of the strengths of TO lies in its uncompromising commitment to challenging oppression, and its remarkable construction of theatre events—both workshops and performances—which steadfastly ask us to take action, engage in dialogue, and work for liberation. Another strength is that it draws on the artistry of theatre to infuse social activism with vitality and aesthetic pleasure.

The International Center for the Theatre of the Oppressed estimates that close to 20,000 theatre artists around the world identify themselves as TO practitioners. Centers of the Theatre of the Oppressed or CTOs, thrive in Europe, South America, North America, and India. In addition, there are many applied theatre practitioners who incorporate TO elements into their own approaches to theatre, as various chapters of this book will attest.

In the most well-known method, Forum Theatre, a troupe of actors presents a scene and audience members help change the outcome. Boal has spent over thirty years developing a vast "arsenal" of games, exercises and techniques to prepare actors for this collaboration with the audience.

To many of us in North America, the term "oppression" may sound severe, and may not seem to relate to our lives. Thus it is useful to understand the method's origins within the sociopolitical climate of South America in the twentieth century.

History

Born in 1931, Augusto Boal studied theatre in New York City during his college years. In the early 1950s, he returned to Brazil, where he was influenced by practitioners of political theatre, particularly Paolo Freire, who was seeking to bring education to the peasants of Brazil.

Boal served as playwright and Artistic Director of the Arena Theater in Sao Paulo, Brazil from 1956 to 1971. However, because Brazil came under the control of a right-wing military junta in the 1960s, Boal's efforts to aid the *compesinos* in a literacy campaign ran afoul of the authorities. He was jailed and tortured in the early 1970s, and, like Freire, finally expelled from Brazil. In exile in Argentina, Boal wrote the seminal book, *Teatro de Oprimador* (*Theatre of the Oppressed*).

In Argentina Boal developed *Invisible Theatre*—ostensibly unstaged, politically-charged provocations in the streets and public places of Buenos Aires. Another elaboration was *Image Theatre*, which employed frozen scenes (*tableaux*) to demonstrate power dynamics, and generate dialogue between the indigenous peoples and the descendants of European conquerors.

However, as in Brazil a few years earlier, Argentina's military dictatorship in the mid-1970s swung to the right and began its own harsh repression of dissidents. In 1974 Boal left Argentina and moved to Europe.

In Paris, Boal found that Europeans were oppressed in their own way, under the shadow of *internalized oppression* rather than political rights or material entitlements. In the 1980s he created a new form of TO, first called *Cop in the Head*, and then renamed *Rainbow of Desire* (the title of his third book). This new form connects one's personal reality with the unseen hand of a power dynamic that both nurtures and oppresses. Boal attracted many followers in Paris, where he established the first international Center for the Theatre of the Oppressed (CTO).

In the later 1980s, the Brazilian government had returned to civilian rule, so Boal returned home to found another CTO in Rio de Janeiro. In 1992, he was elected to Rio's city council. Boal and his political/theatrical staff used Forum Theatre to assess the needs and ideas of his constituents and propose laws, and *Legislative Theatre* was born.

Boal was not re-elected, in part because of fierce resistance from Rio's ruling circles. He continued his work in schools, poor districts within Rio and Sao

Paulo, and prisons throughout Brazil. Currently, Boal is experimenting with a new TO system he calls *Subjunctive Theatre* and a formal "Aesthetic of the Oppressed" that connects the multiple strands of his life's work within a unifying framework. Today Boal travels throughout the world, lecturing, conducting workshops, and mounting productions.

Boal attracts the attention of intellectuals and socially concerned theatre artists wherever he goes. As mentioned, his techniques have been integrated into other forms of applied theatre and social action. In many parts of the world, TO practitioners work towards intercultural understanding and political consciousness-raising.

Philosophy

The philosophical thrust of Augusto Boal's work is influenced by Paulo Freire, his colleague and compatriot. Freire's work is founded on the bedrock premise that human beings become more human through authentic relationships and meaningful work. Freire's *popular education* model calls for a teacher/learner relationship where knowledge and learning flow in both directions. Through the process of *participatory democracy*, people begin to reclaim their role as active, transformative agents in the world.

Oppression is defined bu Boal as a power dynamic based on monologue rather than dialogue. The goal is not necessarily to overthrow the oppressors, but to begin a dialogue with them. Boal believes that oppression can best be solved by those experiencing it.

In *Theatre of the Oppressed* (his first of several books), Boal critiques Aristotle's "coercive system of tragedy" which he views as a socialization process. In a Greek drama, the spectator tends to identify with the protagonist as the action gradually builds to catharsis. Ultimately, when the protagonist's tragic flaw is climactically revealed, the spectator feels pity as well as fear of experiencing a similar fate. The spectator is thus purged of the tragic flaw (i.e., typically *hubris*, the arrogance of daring to defy the gods), and societal equilibrium is restored. However, in Boal's view, a little hubris may be vital to help marginalized people challenge their oppressors and achieve social justice. Unlike conventional theatre, the goal of Theatre of the Oppressed is not to achieve equilibrium. The conflicts cannot be resolved in the plot—they must be solved in real life.

(Further details about the history and philosophy of TO, as well as descriptions and discussions of techniques may be found on the webpage supplement to this chapter: <www.interactiveimprov.com/thtropprsdwb.html>)

Methods

The evolution of T.O. approaches was mentioned previously, as it reflects Boal's travels through time and space. Image Theatre, Invisible Theatre, Forum Theatre, Rainbow of Desire and Legislative Theatre will be described briefly here and then Forum Theatre in more detail.

Image Theatre. This approach serves to "uncover essential truths about societies" without relying on the spoken word. It often lays the groundwork for other Boal techniques. Iin Image Theatre, actors sculpt themselves and others into frozen images or *tableaux*, drawing on the rich vocabulary of physical theatre. These living, breathing dioramas convey the essence of some predicament, abstract idea, feeling, or situation. To illustrate relationships between the figures, those witnessing may suggest how close or far apart they should be, how high or low in relation to each other, what direction they face, as well as gesture and facial expression.

The whole group thus participates in elaborating the image, perhaps assigning captions—words, phrases, or dialog—to the figures in the tableaux. The characters may engage in ritualized movements, or speak in soliloquy or asides, muttering or stage whispering—but loudly enough for all to hear their *interior monologues*. In a process called *dynamization*, the frozen scene may ultimately come to life as each figure moves simultaneously toward his or her own desire.

Image Theatre sharpens awareness of how we each interpret what we see, and how we all (as individuals or cultures) tend to assume our interpretation is "right" or "objective." Moreover, working with images avoids privileging those who are more verbally adept, or are native speakers of the language being used.

Forum Theatre. As mentioned, a group of actors present a dramatized situation based on an instance of oppression, designed to evoke an emotional response from the audience. An effective Forum Theatre piece kindles a powerful desire in the audience for a more satisfactory outcome, and audience members are encouraged to implement these desires onstage. To emphasize the interactive nature of the process, Boal re-named the audience *spect-actors*.

To enter the enactment of the Forum, spect-actors may shout, "Stop!" The actors will freeze. The spect-actor enters the playing space, replaces the protagonist and says exactly at what point in the scene the action should re-commence. Then the spect-actor shows how she or he would respond in that scene.

Invisible Theatre. Always performed in public spaces, the purpose is to generate spontaneous public dialogue about an issue by literally and figuratively "making a scene." Passersby do not know that the situation they are witnessing has been carefully planned and rehearsed. Actors planted in the crowd as *agents provocateurs* emerge to vehemently take a side, and thus galvanize onlookers to voice their own opinions on social issues like race or gender. There is dissent among TO practitioners on the ethics of Invisible Theatre, which remains one of Boal's most electrifying means of transforming the traditional monologue of theatre into a dialogue between stage and world.

The Rainbow of Desire. In Brazil, Boal saw overwhelming poverty and police everywhere. In Europe, there was more wealth and less of a military presence. Yet people said they felt isolated and depressed, and the drug and suicide rates were alarming. In time, Boal realized, "The cops were not on the street—they were in people's heads!"

Boal's 1995 book, *The Rainbow of Desire: the Boal Method of Theatre and Therapy*, deals with internalized oppression. Techniques include *Cop in the Head*, in which inner censors are made manifest, and *Rainbow of Desire*, which reveals conflicting desires and concerns that paralyze one's freedom to act.

The concept is based on a metaphor: when white light is projected onto a prism, all its constituent colors are revealed in a rainbow pattern. Similarly, the group members can each reflect a different facet of the protagonist's inner state. Members of the group portray the "cops" that live in our heads, or the various "colors" of our desires. Several participants may each share a story, and the group can choose which story resonates for them, beginning and ending with an improvisation on an actual encounter with a real-life antagonist.

Legislative Theatre. When Boal returned to Brazil and was elected to the city council in Rio de Janeiro in 1997, he took his theatre company into office with him, and together they developed a revolutionary experiment in democratic practice called *Legislative Theatre*. In this system, citizens of Rio (from street cleaners to blind people) utilized Forum Theatre to dramatize their concerns, and then suggest legislation to address these concerns. Thirteen laws were passed through this process, which Boal calls "transforming desires into laws."

After thirty years of politicizing theatre, Boal began thatricalizing politics. Instead of people going to the theatre to escape their problems, theatre is coming to them, empowering them to make changes. Boal's book on this form is called *Legislative Theatre*.

Key Role Designations: Joker, Protagonist, Antagonist, Spect-Actor

Several elements serve as the engine for this encounter: the joker, the actors, and emerging from within the audience, the spect-actors.

The facilitator—or rather, "difficultator," as Boal likes to say—who leads workshops and conducts the forum process is called the *joker*. The term is not meant to imply someone who mocks, or to be associated with surprise betrayals or Batman's arch-foe. Rather, it is derived from the wild card in a deck of cards that is not tied to any particular number or suit. The word implies a somewhat playful, exploratory attitude, an invitation to wonder together, "What if …?"

Indeed, the TO joker plays many roles. More than just the public figure of a forum or workshop, many jokers are organizers, motivators, community activists, directors, technicians, and costume and prop advisors. A joker is a multi-skilled person who works both on and far beyond the stage.

The joker's main challenge is, without censoring or dominating, to ensure that a scene's structure invites the audience to intervene. S/he introduces the event and guides the interactions among the players, sometimes through structured games that have been strategically sandwiched in.

A joker improvises constantly within the process: adding, pacing, modifying and transitioning to suit the unique and evolving needs of each group. Following the enactment the joker will ask spect-actors and players how they felt during the scene, and how well the interventions worked. This dialogue is crucial.

The *protagonist* is the person who is the focus of the predicament. During a workshop, several people may each offer a situation that evokes a feeling of unfairness or oppression, and the group will choose one to focus on, or coalesce several stories to represent the group. The story may be fictionalized yet must retain its essential truth. The protagonist is the primary person to be replaced by a spect-actor in a Forum Theatre performance.

The *antagonist* represents the one who consciously or unconsciously perpetuates the oppression. An example might be a disadvantaged farm worker as protagonist trying to get the ear of the wealthy landowner, who, in this scene would be the antagonist. Who is the oppressor, though? Is a mother who wants to liberate her daughter from peer pressure the protagonist or antagonist when the daughter begs to be allowed to wear provocative clothes or shoes that might be bad for growing feet? Or are the antagonists the peers who are pressuring the girl to wear the "in" fashion? Or are they the editors of the fashion magazines?

Boal has observed that in any situation, if looked at from a different angle, the roles could be reversed. However, when the purpose is to motivate people to take action, ambiguity can create confusion and lack of focus. Still, the ultimate purpose of this theatre is always to spur debate and dialogue.

Playing the antagonist well is a genuine act of service to the community, and it is a challenge that is often reserved for experienced T.O. actors. As this character is rarely replaced, the antagonist must field every improvisational offer coming from the audience. The actor must sense when to increase the oppression and when to back off; this way the spect-actor's solution is truly *tested*, and not merely shown. Acting skill may be an asset; however, untrained members of the oppressed group often excel at playing antagonists because they know their language and tactics so well. This advantage may outweigh all other factors.

The Spect-Actor. The audience is not expected to sit there passively. At a certain point when the action heats up, they are urged to get involved! Audience members who are activist by nature are most likely to step through the "fourth wall" and become an active agent in the forum drama. However, sometimes people intervene who nobody imagined would. The forum process can indeed be transformative. Counter to everything they've ever been taught about the rules of theatre etiquette, individual audience members actually do leave their seats and mount the stage, especially if the issues are burning ones for them. Even if they choose not to intervene, audience members hold the power to do so, and thus are transformed from spectators into "spect-actors"—activated spectators.

Ideally, the Forum Theatre audience is of the same oppressed group as the protagonist. Because they are personally impacted by the focal issues, they have a real stake in attending, and active participation makes sense. Forums are often staged in community spaces rather than theaters, and audience members may recognize friends and neighbors on stage. These factors further amplify the sense of community ownership.

Workshops

Workshops are designed to educate people in the basics of TO, and also to confront real-world issues of oppressed groups. Workshops can be expanded to develop performance pieces: forum theatre sessions; forum scenes for legislative theatre; and invisible theatre scenarios.

The "classical" use of the TO workshop is to work with a group of highly motivated non-actors focused on hot-button local issues, preparing their skills and developing a Forum performance that is to be given with a larger audience of spect-actors. This involves a pre-presentation process that benefits from an investment of 20 hours or more. Including experienced actors in the mix may or may not accelerate the process; actor training alone will never substitute for activist passion and commitment.

A workshop can be adjusted in content and time, reflecting the needs of the sponsoring group. It may be a weekend workshop, or a 3-hour event as part of a bigger conference.

Workshop Exercises

Boal's book, *Games for Actors and Non-Actors*, contains literally hundreds of exercises, games, and techniques. Some are named after far-flung places in the world where they were invented by Boal and others over the years. This book seems to be a favorite of many acting teachers, although it definitely works best when augmented by live experience with TO.

Workshops typically begin with sensory exploration in four categories: feeling what you touch; listening to what you hear; seeing what you look at; and dynamizing several senses. The theory holds that to truly address oppression in the world, we need to revolutionize our own bodies which have become mechanized and habituated to the status quo. The exercises and games are designed to acquaint us with new kinesthetic and tactile experiences, open our eyes and ears to sights and sounds that we had unconsciously filtered out. They also let us connect with others in novel ways, lifting us beyond limitations we didn't realize we had. This warm-up may be followed by image work or other games that link with the main focus of the workshop.

Rehearsal Techniques

Often the joker uses special methods to highlight aspects of a character, situation or intervention. These rehearsal techniques are extremely effective for honing forum pieces, and some can be used during performances and workshops:

Playing to a Deaf Audience. The scene must be enacted in silence. This requires the actors to physicalize what's happening through actions, which will clarify the meaning so that everyone will understand. This instantly transforms a "talky" scene and reveals emotional subtleties.

Interrogating or *Hot-seating.* A character is questioned by the group and improvises in response. This technique is used theatrically to "assemble" a character with layers of understandable intentions.

Styles or *Genres.* Spect-actors request the scene be played as a western, melodrama, film noir, reality TV show, sitcom, horror movie, etc.

As-if. Scenes are played as if characters have reversed status or gender, as if a hurricane is raging, as if all the participants are children, whatever the group dreams up.

Forum Performance

While some applications of TO never lead to a performance, it is the public Forum that allows a larger audience to access TO's process. Forum performances create a context for dialogue that addresses issues relevant to their own welfare. The actors will serve as representatives of their community's needs, aspirations and dreams, inciting others to step out of the audience and test their ideas for change as embodied actions on stage.

The origin of Forum Theatre is told in a dramatic story: At one performance of an agit-prop play in northern Brazil, the peasants became so aroused by the action that they wanted Boal and his troupe to immediately lead them to overthrow the landlords. Boal was in the awkward postion of having to explain that he was an actor and the weapons were only props. That day he realized that participants must enact stories of their own oppression, not someone else's.

The forum actors prepare for the performance through hours of games, explorations of images, and the development of scenes based on experiences that are emblematic for their community. During the performance, the actors must strive to maintain the passionate integrity of their characters when spect-actors replace the protagonist or allied characters. If moved by a particular intervention, a character's mindset and actions will change direction. Otherwise, they must stay within the original boundaries of their characters and situations: easy answers and quick fixes are never useful in addressing complex community issues. The joker will ask certain forum actors—particularly the antagonist—whether they felt changed or resistant during spect-actor interventions.

It is very advantageous to devise forum scenes that are full of action, rather than only dialogue. Otherwise, when it's time to "forum" the play, the audience may not feel moved to get out of their seats and they may end up sitting and talking about the situation instead. This is where the aforementioned rehearsal techniques and sense exercises bear fruit.

"*Stop! C'est magicque.*" An important principle involves the avoidance of "magic." Occasionally, a spect-actor proposes an overly simplistic solution, a *deus ex machina.* This Latin term harks from ancient Greek and Roman drama in which problems could be solved by a "god" who is lowered by a crane to magically restore equilibrium. The phrase suggests a highly artificial way of working out the plot line. Applied to real-life problems, magical thinking doesn't work, so the joker encourages the audience to seek truer solutions.

Often things get disrupted; focus shifts; confidence sometimes wanes. While an atmosphere of kindness and sensitivity tends to prevail, there is no assurance of "psychological safety," per se. The priority is to shake up the system, not prop up a false sense of security. Remember: this approach comes from places in the world where often the only hope for psychological—or physical—safety might be to challenge the status quo.

Ensembles often evolve styles that incorporate elements of their cultures: physical theatre; dance (modern or *folklorico* style); folk music; hip-hop; spoken word; *teatro popular* pageant-style or dada images; and zany set pieces. Any of these may prime audiences to intervene and are used in Forums world-wide. Wherever Forum Theater is used, it quickly incorporates the folkways, lingo, rhythms, appearances and local knowledge of the people making it. From South Bronx in New York City to Lagos, Nigeria, the Forum constantly reconfigures its appearance and adapts its style while keeping its essential rules and character intact.

Training

One can learn beginning skills in a workshop, but the training to be in a Forum troupe is ongoing, and much experience is needed to be a joker. At present, there are few "authorized" training programs, nor is there any official certifying body, and this is both a central virtue and a tricky problem for the TO world. CTOs hold regional, national, and international conferences.

The Scope of Theatre of the Oppressed Today

Practitioners worldwide now use Boal's forms to deconstruct issues such as environmental justice; sectarian violence; human rights violations; institutional racism and internalized oppression; economic and cultural globalization; the death penalty; lesbian, gay, bisexual and transgendered (LGBT) issues; and access to adequate health care. TO methods are rarely applied in the corporate environment, although they could be if there were an interest in transforming power dynamics within the organization.

As the United Sates attempts to align itself with global trends, we have an opportunity to participate in the unfolding of grassroots political change, both here and abroad. Methods like T.O. can promote alliance with others who care about exploring situations without pushing answers on people.

Conclusion

Theatre can be used to question political and social norms and transform how they play out in people's lives. This kind of theatre gives participants the message that, in a play—just like in real life—"if they don't change it, who will?"

   Theatre of the Oppressed methods demonstrate Augusto Boal's great contribution to both the craft of theatre and the needs of civil society: a direct, dramatic form of democracy based on dialogue among multiple points of view. As the inventor of the method himself has said, "Theatre can help us build our future, rather than just waiting for it."

References

Webpage supplement to this chapter: <www.interactiveimprov.com/thtropprsdwb. html> (Further references near the bottom of the webpage)

A good website with articles describing Boal's history, Freire's history, many other links:

Applied & Interactive Theatre Guide website: <www.tonisant.com/aitg/Boal_ Techniques/>.

Boal, Augusto. (1979). *Theatre of the Oppressed*. (C.A. & M.O.Leal McBride, Trans.). New York: Urizen Books. Republished by Theatre Communications Group in New York in 1985. (Original work published 1974)

Boal, Augusto. (1995). *The Rainbow of Desire: the Boal method of theatre and therapy*. London: Routledge.

Boal, Augusto. (1998). *Legislative theatre*. (A. Jackson, Trans.). New York: Routledge.

Boal, Augusto. (2003). *Games for Actors and Non-Actors*. (Revised ed.) (A. Jackson, Trans.). New York: Routledge. (This is probably the most accessible of his writings, and includes a collection of physical/spatial games, image and improvisation structures, scene rehearsal techniques and analytic image interventions. These evolved from Boal's actual practice with groups around the world in a wide variety of social and cultural contexts.)

Cohen-Cruz, Jan, & Schutzman, Mady. (Eds.). (2006). *A Boal companion: dialogues on theatre and cultural politics*. London: Routledge. (A new collection that complements the earlier excellent survey by Schutzman & Cohen-Cruz [1994] noted below.)

Schutzman, Mady & Cohen-Cruz, Jan (Eds.). (1994). *Playing Boal: theatre, therapy, activism.* London & New York: Routledge. (Has many chapters on new applications, variations, implications, and a good glossary.)

Chapter 22

ACTING FOR ADVOCACY

Deborah J. Zuver

Drama can empower people with developmental disabilities to become strong self-advocates. Our program, *Acting for Advocacy* (*A4A*) is a part of Project STIR (Steps Toward Independence and Responsibility), which is affiliated with the Center for Development and Learning at the University of North Carolina in Chapel Hill. The A4A program uses enactment to engage individuals with disabilities as they explore decisions about their lives and strive to become active participants in their communities. Our team of trainers with and without developmental disabilities presents scenes and other drama exercises to guide participants as they develop leadership tools.

Many, if not most, people with disabilities are accustomed to having decisions made for them. A prevalent, well-meaning assumption is that people with developmental disabilities do not really have opinions and preferences and that they certainly do not have the ability to make choices about their lives. In the interest of protecting these individuals, professionals and family members commonly make decisions on their behalf. The self-advocacy movement is an all-out civil rights effort to transform that notion. In recent years, this movement has spawned self-advocacy groups across the country made up of people with developmental and other disabilities.

Project STIR was formed to train these self-advocates in leadership tools so that they can be more effective in lobbying for policy change, speaking up for themselves, and training other self-advocates. A4A applies this approach to youths with disabilities, using enactment, sociodrama, and related theatre techniques to make the learning more effective and interesting.

Enactment

A4A grew from a concept that enactment is an effective way for self-advocates to explore real-life issues and emotions and try out options for dealing with them. Role-plays were previously included in STIR presentations as part of a didactic exercise, but facilitators had intentionally minimized the dramatic power of the role-play. Eliciting an emotional response was thought to distract participants from the 'lesson.' From time to time, however, these generic role-plays hinted at real, gut-level emotion and evoked a stronger audience response, suggesting the potential of using more dramatic scenes to take the process to a more affecting level. When self-advocate trainer Lee McCraven began using the phrase, *Acting for Advocacy*; she wanted to continue depicting realistic situations that are compelling to actor and audience alike.

A defining component of the *A4A* process is that it moves role-play away from being a how-to demonstration of addressing a particular conflict or dilemma, and toward a portrayal of realistic characters who deal with their emotional reactions while problem-solving an issue. Scenes involve audience members on an emotional level and elicit a personal response from them; their input is applied to the problem-solving steps and enacted (Sternberg 1998). Thus, A4A is role-play as process, not product. The principle here is in line with the ancient Chinese proverb: *"Tell me, I'll forget. Show me, I may remember. But involve me and I'll understand."*

A particularly poignant scene took place during a training presentation for twelve group home residents and two staff members in a rural North Carolina community. The scene concerns Amber, a young woman with a developmental disability who is berated by her mother for coming home late after spending the evening with a friend. Mom is worried that this friend poses a danger to Amber and she wants to protect her daughter. Amber contends that, as an adult, she has the right to make her own decisions about friendships. At this point, the scene was paused and resumed several times as the group explored rights and responsibilities from the viewpoints of both mom and daughter. We discussed what each was feeling, what information might be helpful for each to understand, and what might happen next as mom and daughter deal with their conflict. Then we played out the ideas.

Had we attempted to present this balanced perspective through only demonstration or discussion, it would have been difficult to convey so many abstract thoughts and feelings for this audience. One of the actor/trainers exclaimed about the scene, "It makes the audience *feel* what you're doing." Perhaps this response prompts participants to eagerly try on a role themselves.

They shift from passive audience members to active participants, allowing the entire group to practice a range of skills in the process. Feelings and issues are "present," so the discussion is based in the here-and-now.

Even when enactments are brief, characters are drawn and feelings are depicted along with plot development. In the *A4A* approach, a facilitator prompts visual cues (a costume piece or prop) and spoken cues ("action" and "pause") to indicate when the trainers are acting the scene and when the group can offer feedback and suggestions. Trainers plan the character and situation that they will present, but, as in real life, they make up the specific words as they enact the scene, much like a planned improvisation.

The Need for the Program

Many self-advocate leaders in the forefront of the disability rights movement are creating inclusive communities that do not segregate people with disabilities into institutions or group homes. These leaders promote a vision where people live in a setting of their choosing, control their own funds with support as needed, and participate meaningfully in their communities through part-time work and/or volunteer activities. They may make some mistakes and poor choices, but this consequence is not much different from a non-disabled community member. In the past, "disabled" people were generally pitied, seen as needing help with almost everything, or made "special" and placed on a pedestal. They were also "marginalized," meaning that you rarely heard about them or from them in the media. The climate is changing, though, and language is evolving to reflect this shift. "People First" language, used throughout this chapter, puts the person in front of the disability. For example, "a student with a disability" conveys a very different concept as compared with "a disabled student."

As self-advocates take on new challenges, learning and using basic leadership tools is an urgent need if they are to collaborate effectively among themselves and in the greater community. For many individuals, both formal education and experience in the community are limited. Their thought processes may be concrete so they benefit best from hands-on practice. This is where the *A4A* approach can make a difference.

Along with addressing community advocacy issues, many individuals with a developmental disability find dealing with everyday life issues to be overwhelming. A single task may be fraught with abstract ideas and complexities; concrete tools are needed to grasp a range of perspectives and to cope with the emotional component of an issue. For example, one *A4A* scene depicted two adults with a developmental disability who realize that they have the right to date; one is afraid to take the step—the other is ready to shout with joy. Where do they go from here? The scene had the universal immediacy of any compelling drama.

Enacting such scenes can form a bridge from simply learning *about* leadership tools to successfully *applying* them. Groups have been very responsive to this rehearsal for life, eagerly offering ideas and volunteering to try out a role in the enactment. Examples of issues addressed through enactments include:

- Communicating assertively—An individual wants a job in the community, but does not know how to get the necessary support.
- Problem solving—Roommates are frustrated when dealing with the household budget.
- Rights and responsibilities—A group of self-advocates speak with the town council about developing more affordable housing.

Related Methods

The *A4A* approach to enactment as a leadership training tool has roots in drama therapy activities, theatre games, and some elements from Augusto Boal's Theatre of the Oppressed. These approaches emphasize the ways drama can help a community educate one another and share leadership for social change. Because the process begins with the participants' experience, the community can analyze issues and make a plan together to carry out actions. This process can enhance communication and reflection among adults with a strong oral tradition, without the need for formal education and academic accomplishments. Thus, this approach meets the needs of adults with developmental disabilities whose formal education is generally limited. Other approaches are noted on the webpage supplement: <www.act4advocwb.html>

Training the Project STIR Team in *Acting for Advocacy*

Project STIR trainers include self-advocates with several years experience presenting training workshops to other self-advocates, family members, professionals, and other allies. As someone living successfully with a developmental disability, each trainer is a strong role model; audience members readily relate to them. When working with a new audience, trainers introduce themselves and mention something about their lives in the community and any support services they receive for such needs as budgeting, shopping, and transportation.

In developing a project similar to A4A, it is important for facilitators to identify potential trainers who can be effective as both presenters and performers. Project STIR trainers initially participated in an intensive four-session workshop series that I created to sharpen their performing skills. We began the workshop series with theatre games and drama therapy exercises for the four trainers and worked on creating characters and developing original scenes. This process also strengthens and deepens the trainers' interaction with one another, helping to solidify the team.

Facilitators should begin trainer workshop sessions with playful, non-threatening activities that use movement, props, and costumes. Start each session with physical warm-ups to energize and focus each participant, then progress to activities that are sequenced to allow sufficient pacing for each trainer (Spolin 1984). All exercises should be structured and include visual and tactile prompts (e.g., props), which are essential to concrete thinkers. Some open, improvised scene work is possible, but selected, structured activities should precede these in preparation for scene work (Emunah 1994).

Another benefit of trainer workshop sessions is that they provide facilitators with an assessment opportunity, offering a sense of each trainer's strengths and particular style so that activities can be adjusted accordingly. Sessions can prepare a facilitator to know how best to guide enactments when presenting A4A sessions training sessions. For example, by observing how our group worked together, I reflected on a number of considerations including how to set up a scene, who might play the role, and how to pace the scenes (Emunah 1994). Each trainer's particular style of involvement gave me insight as to how to successfully work with and around issues, sensitivities, strengths, and deficits. Participants are learning how to apply some rudimentary critical thinking skills in the moment. The process is very different, then, from just role training and shaping behavior. Self-advocate trainers must first be well-practiced in these skills themselves. The following profiles offer examples of the range of issues that can come up in workshop sessions with self-advocate training staff for the A4A team and how we addressed them.

"Ben" (names disguised) was particularly skilled at mime. His precise movements in pantomiming a lunchtime scene held all eyes, intent on his every move as he tasted and enjoyed his "meal." This talent was helpful in keeping other trainers focused during enactments. When improvising lines, however, Ben tended to repeat and exaggerate what he had already said. We worked with this during a paused scene by identifying what he had repeated and we reinforced that we had heard his first comment. Each participant, in turn, verified what he or she had heard him say. This approach helped decrease the repetition, though he continues to need reminders from time to time; prompting before beginning a scene has been helpful.

"Joyce" was particularly emotive. She could just as easily produce tears as laughter. The intensity of her involvement in a scene prompted my concern that she over-identified with a role. She sometimes felt sad and upset after a scene concluded. Along with the other trainers, we found ways to de-role together. Joyce would tell us a personal memory that the role triggered ("I was remembering my grandpa who died and I miss him.") and we offered her support. Sometimes she needed a few minutes of transition time, but she was able to increasingly modulate herself as the workshop progressed. To ensure that she understood that our scene was pretend, I encouraged the group to become more emphatic about "shaking off" a character at the end of an enactment.

"Lily," with a strong voice and commanding presence, wanted to be the center of attention in any scene and go for the laughs, regardless of the theme of the scene. Her playfulness was contagious and energizing to the group, but she could monopolize a scene so that other characters were diminished. We used concrete visual cues and encouraged Lily to use questions in her improvised scenes and then listen to the responses. Role reversal was also helpful as it required her to shift places both physically and emotionally, which also helped her to shift perspective.

"Diane" had difficulty feeling comfortable portraying someone who was different from herself, particularly if the character's actions were unflattering. We consistently reassured her that others knew she was playing a character and she became more freed up in the enactments. We worked on creating characters that were intentionally opposite to her personality. Such an extreme distinction was easier than subtle ones, and gave her permission to be playful. As the series progressed, Diane also got a better sense of what it felt like to de-role completely. We would often have the group identify ways that a given character was not like Diane's "real" self. Taking off the hat or scarf that represented the character's "costume" with an exaggerated flourish was another concrete way to delineate the actor from the role.

Making Enactments Effective

A4A's style of enacting a scene can be adapted for a variety of groups and a range of purposes. Facilitators can gear the process toward a group's particular needs and abilities, creating an effective and affecting use of theatre in several ways.

Be realistic. A realistically acted role-play, as compared with either a more theatrical scene or a bland recitation, prompts the audience to participate. As a story unfolds and comes to life, the audience becomes invested in the characters and the situation; they are motivated to think about new possibilities to suggest and try out. The process becomes an inspiration for reflecting on personal situations and offers an opportunity to apply problem-solving steps as you provide this "rehearsal" for life. When the scene is "paused," check in with participants to assess how information and emotions are perceived, as you might with any group. Do not be protective by trying for "happy" scenes only. Sometimes actors need permission to be truly in role and expressive; prompts to exaggerate can be helpful. If a conflict situation is portrayed politely, the facilitator can "pause" the scene and ask the group to provide input on how each character might actually be feeling. When the scene resumes, actors are more likely to express genuine emotions. Above all, maintain the safety of the group. It may take only a few seconds of a strong emotion for the audience to "get it" and the scene can be paused (Emunah 1994).

Be clear. Clarity is vitally important for this population. Use specific and broad signals to indicate when actors/trainers are in role and out of role. You might select roles that are further from typical life roles in early activities (police officer, rock star, astronaut) so that participants can clearly and easily distinguish "self" from role. Establish character and setting clearly especially when dealing with evocative subject matter. Choose scenes where each character's emotion and intention is distinct from the other and there is a clear conflict. You can define the space and characters using visual and auditory means. For example, as the session gets underway, use tape on the floor to section off the playing space. Placing the tape can become a ritualized way of getting everyone's attention and focusing the group. Use props to label a place and costumes to label a character; items should be visible, but not so many as to distract from the characters and the action.

Be concrete. It seems that many people who think concretely are able to understand somewhat complex situations when they are depicted in a scene. Perhaps this is because enactment offers a three-dimensional, multisensory way to explore interactions, issues, and feelings (Bailey 1993). You may find that most participants can gain at least some understanding of different perspectives, emotions, and outcomes. Avoid subtleties when working with self-advocates who are new to enactment. Some participants who are unable to track all the information may be able to grasp the gist of the scene and still benefit from it up to their ability level.

Be repetitive. Self-advocates enjoy practicing their new leadership roles and trying to negotiate problem situations more than once. Enactments can be "paused" so that different participants can take a turn replaying one of the characters. Some repetition may also be helpful for the audience to better follow the action, particularly for those individuals who need more time to process information. Use selected phrases repetitively as a cue to help maintain focus and character; participants will become familiar with these and say them to one another. Some of the phrases that we use are:

- "The story is pretend, but the feelings are real." Making the distinction between what is "really" happening and what is happening in the story is reassuring for some participants who need these reminders. Feelings should be portrayed as authentic, though, so that audience members can relate to the scene.

- "Take a moment...." Cuing actors before beginning a scene lets them focus on the character they are about to portray, what that character is feeling, and that they are ready to listen to other actors in the scene. After the facilitator has "set" the scene, another actor/trainer may want to cue with this phrase, pause, and then call "action" to rejoin the scene.

- "Shake off the character." De-roling is an important part of the process after ending a scene. Everyone can join in a vigorous full-body shake, which usually brings smiles as the group switches gears and re-energizes (Sternberg & Garcia 1989). You can develop your own pattern of acknowledging transitions and ways of focusing.

Be Empathic. Identifying the emotions that are involved in a scene will be helpful for participants to learn to distinguish between behaviors and feelings. Such an understanding can be a crucial aspect of problem solving. All too often, the salient issue of an individual's "problem" behavior is that the behavior is an expression of how the individual is feeling. If the group can offer some other less troublesome ways to express or discharge the particular feeling, the "problem" behavior may diminish. As this possibility is explored in the context of the scene, participants can vicariously experience the options presented. Dealing with feelings becomes less abstract and can be very empowering to the individuals. Giving time and attention to feelings validates the importance of them and can give the group "permission" to experience them.

Be collaborative. Facilitate the process of the enactment so that participants and actors can collaboratively create the scene after the initial action is introduced. You can "pause" a scene if it is moving too fast or too slow or if an actor cannot be heard or gets stuck. Periodically review with the group what is happening in the scene and what each character is feeling. You can ask suggestions for what might happen next in the scene, referring to problem-solving steps that you can review (Sternberg & Garcia 1989). Perhaps you want to ask for a first line for a character as the enactment comes to life again. When returning to the scene, summarize the gathered ideas and impressions, then mention the opening line (e.g., Let's begin where we hear the mom say ...) before calling "action."

Applying the *Acting for Advocacy* Approach

A4A's format of enacting scenes can serve as a structured process to rehearse specific problem-solving steps for issues that a group wants to address. A4A can also serve as a tool for strengthening the advisor's role in working with a self-advocacy group. This role involves a delicate balance. An effective advisor is hands-off so as not to impose ideas and decisions on the group, yet hands-on to coach for effective meetings and planning. Opportunities to provide workshops with A4A activities may include supervision meetings with advisors or presentations at conferences or retreat settings. Enactment can allow advisors to try out different styles of interacting with the group and dealing with specific challenges.

Many advocacy and self-advocacy groups are active throughout the broad disability community. Increasing effective collaboration among disability and cross-disability groups is a common challenge and could be explored through an A4A workshop at meetings and conferences. In some instances, groups have a very different focus and may even be at odds with one another. Enactment could provide opportunities for role reversal and offer a means to explore common goals and understand and accept those that are different.

Finally, there are wonderful possibilities for taking the process into the arts realm and shaping stories that emerge through A4A workshops. Some arts organizations are pioneering inclusive performance opportunities and may want to team up to realize such a project. For example, Raleigh Ensemble Players (2004) in North Carolina regularly schedules workshops, classes, and performances where people with disabilities participate, and a disability access director is on staff. Consider the powerful performance piece that could be created to depict the struggle of individuals and groups as they create an inclusive community. Such a production would validate and honor the lives of remarkable self-advocates as it showcases powerful theatre and speaks to the larger community. The piece could be presented for self-advocacy groups as well as for the general public in such venues as libraries, schools, museums, and other community settings.

Conclusion

Acting for Advocacy is an innovative process with a potential to contribute significantly to the self-advocacy and self-determination movement. A more fundamental impact, however, may extend far beyond its obvious training goals. The potential for contributing an application of drama and theatre toward exploring the human condition may be just as important. People with disabilities generally have limited access to drama and theatre and that access is commonly relegated to participation as audience member. *A4A* enactments offer meaningful participation in creating drama. Expanding possibilities to open the world of theatre to individuals with disabilities will, in turn, enrich and inspire the fabric of our larger communities

References

Other groups doing related work are noted on the webpage supplement to this chapter, at: <www.interactiveimprov.com/act4advocacywb.html>

In addition to general bibliography references at the end of the book, especially Boal, 1995; Freire, 1970; Spolin, 1985; Sternberg, 1998; and Sternberg & Garcia, 1989, the following are more relevant specifically to this chapter's topic:

Bailey, Sally D. (1993). *Wings to Fly: Bringing Theatre Arts to Students with Special Needs*. Rockville, MD: Woodbine House. (Offers specific ideas and suggestions for using theatre games and activities with students of all ages.)

Raleigh Ensemble Players. (2004). Available at: <www.gorep.org> (Provides current information about a professional theatre that received funding support from the North Carolina Council on Developmental Disabilities to offer an inclusive approach to productions and workshops.)

Chapter 23

WOMEN'S EMPOWERMENT THROUGH DRAMA

Abigail Leeder & Jade Raybin

We have used drama as an essential element in personal development workshops for women who want to experience a sense of empowerment and a refreshing new sense of identity. Two examples of applied theatre for self-discovery will be described: One, a nine-week theatre class for women, is called *Stories Gone Wild*; the other is a weekend workshop exploring women's sexuality through theatre, called *Pandora's Treasures*. These programs are a mixture of original techniques and those gleaned from various improvisationally-based, non-scripted forms of theatre and personal development practices, crafted to suit the group and our particular goals.

The Groups

Our programs attract women from various backgrounds and ages in the San Francisco Bay area. Class size averages about 12 students per workshop and ages range from 19 to 70, with most in their late twenties to mid-forties. Most participants are low and middle-income professionals or students. On a number of occasions we have had family members participate together, adding extra dimension to the group. Some of the women who join us are new to theatre; others have been professional actors. Our only requirement is that everyone is willing to join us on an adventure of self-discovery, honesty, and personal exploration.

Most participants find out about our programs from word of mouth, on internet networks, or from one of the many flyers we post throughout the larger community. We offer a sliding fee scale and invite participants to pay anywhere along the scale that feels comfortable to them.

The "women only" space and the interactive nature of dramatic play lend to a feeling of safety that is palpable very early on in our work together. As we deepen with one another over the course of our time together, lasting friendships are often formed. It is not uncommon that groups will continue to get together for potluck diners or other events. In an attempt to continue fostering relationships formed in our classes, we make a point to invite past participants to the culminating performance of each *Stories Gone Wild* class.

Stories Gone Wild: A Weekly Class

Stories Gone Wild is a two-hour class held once a week over the course of nine weeks. We meet Sunday evenings in a local community arts space. Class size ranges from ten to sixteen women. During this mainly experiential learning process, we introduce class participants to many modes of drama and experiment with role playing, spontaneity, and revealing hidden parts of ourselves to one another. Drama serves as a venue for women to experiment with unexplored aspects of themselves and to connect more deeply with other women in a supportive atmosphere. The class culminates in a community theatre performance of original and improvised scenes for the participants' friends and family.

The first hour of each class involves exercises designed to remind the group members of their innate capacity for spontaneity, build group trust, and inspire playfulness. The second hour consists of personal responses expressed as solo or small group dramatic skits or performances. We end each class with a check-out circle, which gives participants an opportunity to share feelings that may have arisen and discoveries from the evening.

Warming-Up and Checking-In: Warm-Up games are an essential part of the group process. They help us become present in the moment, get our blood flowing and be unabashedly silly and playful. We begin each class with one or two warm-ups. We draw from a large repertoire of theatre games (see Appendix B).

One example of a warm-up game we may begin with is called *greet, argue and make-up*. (Clifford, 1999, p. 47). In this game we form three different partnerships. With our first partner we act as if we have just been reunited with our best friends. Next, we find another partner and have an argument, and finally we find a new partner and, imagining they were the one we had been fighting with, beg for forgiveness and make up.

After a quick warm-up we check in. We sit in a circle and share with one another about how we are. The check-in is not the focus of the evening nor is it very lengthy. We share about our current life circumstances in a creative manner. We may check in by sharing our feelings and experiences in the form of a weather report, or we may frame our experiences as a news bulletin, such as, "Woman Goes Berserk When New Governor Elected;" "Lost Lover, Found Self;" or "Single White Female Seeks Job and Bike." Alternatively, we may speak gibberish during our check-in, communicating our feelings with gestures and tone of voice. Or perhaps we will check in from the future, speaking about our feelings and experiences from the perspective of ourselves 50 years from now.

Building Trust and Intimacy: Throughout our time together, sharing with one another takes place in the context of performing for each other, doing check-ins and through exercises adapted from Naka-Ima, a practice devoted to honesty, stillness, and being present with ourselves and others. Often we do a milling exercise: Two people walk up to one another, hold hands, make eye contact, and take a moment to slow down and breathe without speaking to one another. Participants are invited to pay attention to their thoughts, judgements and fears as they stand facing the other person. Then they are invited to see if they can let go of all thoughts and ideas and simply feel the other person's essence. We invite participants to stay with one another until they feel a connection has formed before moving on to another person.

In a different milling exercise one person speaks and shares something about how they are feeling in the moment. The intention is to say something that allows the other person to see them more deeply. When the speaker is complete the listener says, "Thank you." The one-way structure alleviates pressure to think of an appropriate response and allows participants receive the full presence of another human being.

Playfulness and Skill Building: Prior to asking group members to get up on stage and take risks, we encourage making fools of ourselves. The "circus bow", a tool from Bay Area TheatreSports, consists of throwing our arms up in the air and celebrating our mistakes. We say with glee to one another, "I messed up!" "I made a mistake!" or "I totally screwed up!" Another way that we create an environment free of pressure is through our motto: "You can't get it wrong!" This phrase often turns into a song of encouragement sung when someone gets nervous about trying something new in front of the group.

In a "gibberish poet" game that we play, one actor translates another actor's unintelligible blathering into an eloquent poem. We also play games that involve creating characters and exaggerating them until they get so big they explode, or getting on busses full of fellow passengers with contagious attitudes.

Methods

There are a variety of techniques we use to explore issues of a political and personal nature. We draw from Playback Theatre and Theater of the Oppressed (see Chapters 1 and 21), and other techniques that explore social issues and personal stories. Two such techniques are *boasting circle* and *machines into monologues*.

In a *boasting circle*, one person steps into the center of the circle and makes a positive declaration about themselves and then strikes a pose that embodies this declaration. Statements have included, "I am a fabulous lover," "I am a loyal friend," and "I love my body." Anyone who identifies with statement or aspires to, steps into the center of the circle and takes a complimentary pose, embodying it for herself.

Machines into monologues opens up dialogue about socio-political issues that may be affecting the group. We choose a topic such as "children," "the upcoming election," or "body image." Participants create an interlocking machine composed of repetitive phrases and movements that express diverse aspects of the topic. For example, if the topic of the machine is "menstruation," phrases may range from "I dread the day" or "It's the holiest of holy" to "Tampons or pads? I just can't decide." The intention of this exercise is to give voice to as many diverse perspectives as possible. After the machine has been established, the facilitator calls, "freeze," and points at one of the actors. The actor begins speaking in character, delivering a monologue about their character's 'take' on the topic. The exercise continues until all perspectives have been heard.

Piece Creation: We introduce participants to a variety of exercises designed to help them develop skits—loosely formed, unscripted "works in progress." Developing scenes and skits in a short period of time affirms that we are all talented performers and in any given moment we can create beautiful and entertaining theatre. Creating quickly allows us to bypass our inner critic and surprise ourselves with the ease with which we can create and perform brilliant material. Through such exercises as free writing and shadow skits, women parody and listen to themselves in pieces that range from farce to tear-jerking testimony.

Free Writing: We often use spontaneous writing exercises as a way to generate material for performance pieces. We provide writing prompts such as writing a letter to the president, an ancestor, a lover, an unborn child, or a part of your body. Women have written outraged letters to the government, comedic monologues proclaiming the benefits of denial, and sincere praises to the strengths of Grandmothers passed on.

Shadow Skits: The 'shadow' is a term developed by psychiatrist Carl Jung to describe the parts of one's psyche that have either been denied, disliked, or kept hidden. One of our favorite exercises is *shadow skits*, a game that involves getting into pairs and spending a few moments talking about and identifying aspects of our shadow. Once each woman has defined the aspect of her shadow she wishes to work with, the task is to make a skit that parodies and/or exaggerates this trait or pattern. One particularly memorable skit, created by Sherise (all names have been changed to protect confidentiality), depicted her lying on the beach when her lover arrives. The lover, eager to please, begins asking Sherise what she would like. She replies, "Oh, just tell me how much you love me and how beautiful I am." Her lover begins professing her elegance and grace, wit and brilliance. After each compliment Sherise grows more and more unhappy, realizing that the sweet words are doing nothing for her. Finally she balks and states, "You know this really isn't working. I know I am supposed to love myself, but all I really wanted was for you to just do it for me. Why can't it be that easy? Why can't *you* just do it *for* me?" Despite her lover's repeated kind words and actions, the praise was never enough. Such skits often lead to insight in a lighthearted fashion.

The Final Performance: The most notable format for sharing during "Stories Gone Wild" is the informal performance that takes place at the end of the nine-week series. During the show we play theatre games, do playback theatre exercises, explore political topics through *machines into monologues*, and perform structured pieces. Although it is optional, most women elect to take part in the performance. Each participant is encouraged to create solo or group pieces. (This is somewhat related to Self-Revelatory Performance, described in Chapter 24.)

Throughout the series we encourage women to begin paying attention to the material that they generate in class and invite them to expand upon it at home for the final performance. By the fifth class we spend some group time talking about the performance and encourage small groups to form outside of class to rehearse.

We also come up with at least one whole group piece that we spend some time developing in class during the sixth or seventh session. In addition to the solo pieces we decide as a group which improv games they would like to perform. Each participant chooses how she wants to participate in the performance.

Many profound shifts have resulted from women taking risks and performing for their community.

Pandora's Treasures: A Weekend Workshop

Improvisational drama can also be used as a powerful tool when exploring the many dimensions of female sexuality. The purpose of the *Pandora's Treasures* workshop is self-discovery, sharing with one another in play and in seriousness, and unraveling shame around sexuality. The work is done with respect for differences and for the diversity of our experience as women. We emphasize laughing at ourselves and letting go of painful experiences from our past.

A *Pandora's Treasures* workshop consists of eight to twelve women, not including the two facilitators. The workshop takes place over a three-day period: Friday evening from 7–10 p.m. and Saturday and Sunday from 10 a.m.–4 p.m. The sessions are held in a local dance studio that we rent, giving us lots of room to move freely and play loudly.

The first night of the workshop is spent getting to know one another, building trust and setting the stage for the coming work. At the beginning of the workshop each participant sets a personal intention for herself related to sexuality. We envision what we want to move toward, whether it is a new feeling in our body, a state of acceptance, or a healed relationship. We declare this intention out loud to the group.

We explore sexuality by making a list of topics that are "up" in people's lives. Without hesitation, lists of over 80 topics are generated. Themes include topics such as "sexually transmitted diseases," "mothers and grandmothers," "intimacy," and "phone sex." We work with this list of topics directly and indirectly throughout the weekend.

The first exercise we do is called *hystericus* and is similar to a "rant" from playback theatre. Four people stand on stage with their backs to the audience. When one of the themes from the list is called out, one person turns around and begins to rant about whatever the word sparked in them. This continues until someone else turns around and cuts them off. Often humorous, *hystericus* gives people the chance to share stories in a somewhat distanced way, and is a great segue into sharing candidly about sexuality.

Another exercise that we use on the first night is called *secret pooling* (Blatner, 1996, p. 39). Each participant writes down a secret, memory, or fantasy regarding her own sexuality. Then we mix the slips of paper up and each person selects one and reads it out loud as if it were her own. This empathy-building technique gives participants the opportunity to share secret or shameful experiences anonymously while also deepening the level of intimacy within the group.

Exploring the Terrain: On the second day of the workshop we explore sexuality through the lens of Action Theater, a form of physical theatre developed by Ruth Zaporah (and mentioned in Chapter 33). Action Theater exercises explore different sounds, gestures, expressions, and words—in this case, associated with sexuality—in an attempt to lessen cultural taboos. Such techniques allow us to get rowdy, loud, and silly, bringing humor and honesty to the physicality of the sexual experience.

One exercise, adapted from Action Theater, involves asking all participants to find a facial expression related to sexuality. Next, each woman finds a sound to accompany her gesture. We then ask five women to volunteer to demonstrate their gesture and sound on stage. A volunteer conductor is found and soon we have a chorus of sounds and gestures, being conducted like a symphony on stage. Gestures can be "looped" (i.e., continuously repeated), heard sporadically at a very high or low volume, or the entire chorus can echo one sound and expression in unison. The possibilities are endless! Throughout the workshop the playful nonchalance of Action Theater and improv games is balanced by the practical empowerment tactics of Theater of the Oppressed, and the compassionate listening of playback theatre and psychodramatic techniques.

Enacting Our Fears and Our Visions: Another notable exercise is a variation of fluid sculptures from playback theatre called *fear/vision fluids*. Four actors create a sculpture based on a fear that an audience member is experiencing. Then the audience member is asked about her vision of how she would *like* to feel in relation to the circumstances. This vision is enacted in a second fluid sculpture.

In a recent workshop, one woman shared that her fears of inadequacy would keep her from developing intimate relationships. As is typical in playback theatre, the focus of the sculpture is on the felt sense of the teller, more than the details of the story. The actors created a moving tableau with sounds and brief phrases that captured the feelings of isolation, of holding back, of feeling frozen, and of being imprisoned by her powerful inner critic. After watching the enactment, we checked in with the teller about what it felt like to watch her fears enacted. We then asked her to share with us her vision for herself, how she would like to feel in the same situation, if anything were possible. She spoke of her desire to feel free, confident and willing to take bold steps toward connecting with others. The actors recreated the sculpture capturing the essence of these feelings. The moving image was one of expansiveness and risk taking. As the group watched, we breathed deeply as we connected to our own sense of personal empowerment and bravery.

Revealing Ourselves: On Saturday afternoon we begin to create material for the closing ritual performance. During the ritual performance, we each share a short self-revelatory theatre piece. In order to help participants generate ideas, we offer writing prompts and discussion time to brainstorm and hone in on a distinct creative impulse. Writing prompts include writing a monologue to "your inner slut" or to "the innocent girl" inside. We work individually to help participants develop their piece and think about how they can be supported by the group. In a recent workshop one woman danced, another woman stripped, another woman asked each of us in the group to take on a quality that she wanted to invoke in her life and called us into the circle one by one to dance with her.

Ritual performance pieces may release past pain, declare a new way of being, or playfully express how we feel in the moment. They are not meant to be polished, but are powerfully motivated by personal intention. In one workshop, perhaps the most moving enactment was the reading of a letter by one of the participants to a man who had sexually abused her. Calling on the strength and courage that she had been invoking all weekend, Joanne spent all of Saturday night composing this letter. Before reading, she announced she was ready to take back her life and her sexuality from this man. This was the first time she had shared this story with a group and acknowledged she had come very far in the last few years on her journey of self-acceptance. Her letter was angry, vulnerable, honest, and full of raw power. Joanne cried while reading most of it, and many of us cried with her. Collectively, we witnessed as Joanne shed painful parts of her past and reclaimed aspects of herself that she had lost.

The closing ritual is a powerful coming together and honoring of the individual and collective experiences shared over the course of three days together. It provides us with the chance to open up and be supported in a circle of women, while also giving us a memory of being seen in our strength and accepted unconditionally.

The Healing Environment

There is a difference between personal development as thera*peutic* rather than as therapy per se. The former recognizes that sharing, opening, and learning is a mixture of growing and celebrating, while traditional therapy is a social contract to address an identified symptom or problem. We assume the participants are basically healthy and resilient, but recognize that healthy people almost always have some unfinished business around personal themes.

We acknowledge that tenderness, vulnerability, and compassion are necessary in order to hold each other through our exploration. We also realize that there are potential dangers of working with intense emotional issues in short-term environments. A woman might open up something that she is not prepared for or that she cannot cope with alone after the workshop. We ask the participants to know their own limits and boundaries and to take personal responsibility for themselves. In addition, we encourage all participants pay close attention to what arises, and if needed, to seek outside support accordingly. At the same time, the short-term nature of this work, the freshness of strangers and the alternative reality of a workshop environment can—and often does—provide a perfect container for profound insights and lasting change.

Due to the nature of this type of work, it is critical that the facilitators are adept at creating emotionally safe contexts. Neither of us are currently licensed therapists, nor do we believe that it is necessary to create a safe space for healing. However, we do recommend that prospective facilitators have a strong understanding of themselves and familiarity with group process. Facilitators of such groups are comfortable with the expression of strong emotions and able to stay calm during such expressions without feeling the need to "fix" participants and make them feel better. Of course, theatre training in the modalities that you are teaching is also extremely important.

The importance of doing such work in a women-only space cannot be understated. The safety that women in a group provide for each other has been, and continues to be, a vital part of the healing that participants experience through the workshops. There is a long legacy of women gathering in circle to witness and foster one another's healing. From the Jewish tradition of Rosh Hodesh, where women gather to tell stories to one another at the new moon, to modern day all-girl poetry slams and sister circles, women gather all over the world to heal and renew themselves.

Conclusion

On a grand scale, we hold a vision where live art and performance take place in the bodies, hearts, and living rooms of the nation. As people rely increasingly on mass media for entertainment, there is a danger of losing the vibrancy of interpersonal connectedness. Programs such as "Stories Gone Wild" and "Pandora's Treasures" offer positive, more participatory alternatives to the popular media. In an era of increasing art consumerism, and diminishing community, it is a relief to have a place to express oneself in an immediate way. It is also delightful to be entertained by the hilarity of our ups and downs, and to let oneself be touched by the commonality of our lives. We strive to inspire the women we work with to believe in the fabulous performer who lives within them, and to take her out of the closet to play more often. The accessibility of heartbreaking laughter, healing, and raucous entertainment with a group of so-called amateurs has many implications for our current culture. This work redefines the notion of amateur, asking only for performers with open hearts and devoted souls to come to the stage. These classes remind us of the beauty of our friends and families, and of what a compassionate audience can do for the blossoming of a performer.

Resources

In addition to our work, there are others also offering workshops and classes that integrate drama methods in the empowerment of women, and these are noted on the webpage supplement to this chapter: <www.interactiveimprov. com/womenpowrwb.html>

Clifford, S. & A. Herrmann. (1999). *Making the leap: Theatre of empowerment.* London: Jessica Kingsley Publishers.

Chapter 24

SELF-REVELATORY PERFORMANCE

Sheila Rubin

Drama may be used to help people discover and share their life stories. While there have been many books and workshops about deepening the sense of meaning in life, drama offers the added advantages of a more embodied and interpersonal process. It can add extra dimensions to the processes of re-discovering and sharing life stories, oral histories, writing memoirs, diaries, journals, and becoming more aware of one's personal mythology. Drama can also be used to help individuals become more aware of their present experience, feel more alive in their bodies, as they re-discover who they are and connect deeply with the powerful creative process within.

Self-revelatory performance (also called simply "self-rev") is a theatre method that helps individuals take the time to craft some series of stories or a life theme into a drama that is then played to an audience of selected friends and families. Self-rev helps people discover that their experiences can be dramatized, that they can be found to be touching, funny, or sympathy-evoking, partaking of mythic resonance, and in other ways, partaking in the aesthetics possible in theatre. A self-rev can be improvised or written through improvisational exercises. One becomes the playwright, creating a story, and working with facilitators to shape experiences so that they can be presented with a higher degree of aesthetic coherence and effect.

Self-rev is a process in which a person is helped to create a brief performance or play that reflects aspects of his or her own life, to be performed for an invited audience. As a class or workshop, each participant works on a self-rev performance, and the teacher acts as facilitator, along with the insights, suggestions, modeling and support by the other group members. While the performance at the end is the culmination, really it is the preparation that is the primary source of psychological benefits for the performer. The optimal time for preparation of a ten-minute piece, which includes a fair amount of homework, is about ten sessions spread over ten weeks. The optimal time for preparation of a 35–50 minute full length performance is of course much longer and can take between 4 months to a year.

Self-revelatory performance is personal material transformed into theatrical creation (Emunah, 1994, p. 224). Some of my Life Stories class members have called it, "suffering turned into art," "pain turned into performance," and "the finally-my-life-makes-sense show." The performance can take many forms: solo or group performance, dance, storytelling, mask-work, puppetry, and mixtures of these or other modalities. While it is a relatively new genre of theatre (that also has been used for selected clients as a type of therapy), its roots go back to the beginning of civilization when life stories were enacted in a tribe or for the community. Emunah (1994, p. 291), who coined the term, "self-revelatory performance," writes that it builds upon the works of Grotowski and Artaud, "... and other experimental theatre directors and companies who explored boundaries, the actor's own process, and the relationship between actor and audience."

The self-revelatory performance process answers needs for the performer/ actor/person to express deep parts of themselves and be witnessed and perhaps healed on a variety of levels. The first need being answered is the act hunger that human beings have, the need to tell their stories as a way to define ourselves. Daniel McAdams, author of *Myths We Live By* writes, "If you want to know me, then you must know my story, for my story defines who I am. And if I want to know myself, to gain insight into the meaning of my own life, then I too, must come to know my own story. I must come to see it in all its particulars the narrative of the self (i.e., the personal myth) that I have tacitly—even unconsciously—composed over the course of my years. It is a story I continue to revise, and tell to myself (and sometimes others) as I go on living." (McAdams, 1993, p. 11)

The self-rev process also serves as an impetus for the actor to gather information about themselves and their life. Sometimes memories of seemingly disparate life events that up to this point had little significance individually but when put together in this new way can form a thread that provides significant insight and meaning. Seniors who participated in my self-revelatory storytelling groups in the outpatient psychiatric hospital benefitted greatly from this. One man in his seventies was able to recall and realize that the act of listening that was so painfully learned in childhood was what probably saved his life when he was a foot soldier on the battlefield during World War II.

"Life Stories": A Ten Week Self-Revelatory Performance Workshop

Since 1997, four times a year, I've been offering ten week classes that teach participants how to make a story out of their own life events. This class, titled "Life Stories: A Form of Self-Revelatory Performance," offers techniques and exercises and a safe container for exploring the creative process and expressing personal material. We meet for two and a half hours once a week in the evening in my office studio, community center, or healing center. Class members are female and male, range in age from 20 to 68, and include races and ethnic backgrounds reflecting the diversity of the San Francisco Bay Area.

The learning involves a growing process of self-discovery, exploring a variety of elements of imagery, personal preferences, and integrating one's own aesthetic style into the process. Some of the facilitating elements that are used to weave together a sort of dramatized personal story telling include theatrical improvisation, writing exercises, spontaneous movement, and various techniques taken from drama therapy.

First we check in. Then I might mention a theme for the evening, followed by individual warm ups, then group warm ups. The group then breaks into dyads. The class might then engage in free writing or more group exercises as we gradually develop stories for the one- to five-minute improvised performance for the group each night, and aiming in general to producing a 10–15 minute final performance at the end of the ten week series.

To begin I ask the class to breathe and take a few moments to reconnect with his or her body: "With your eyes closed or open, do whatever you need to do to transition from your 'driving body' or 'working-all-day body' into an 'aware body.'" I suggest they imagine doing a mental 'body scan' regarding their physical state and their creative process. "Get in touch with what you want from the group tonight." As they share in the checking-in process that follows, one might say, "I notice my stomach hurts." Another: "I spent all week at the computer and I can't even feel my body." Participants often report how the creativity accessed in this class is positively affecting other areas of their lives. They might speak up, requesting a specific exercise or theme, such as: "I really want to work on anger tonight."

The creative process is fascinating. I have great faith in it after working with so many life stories process in workshops, through directing numerous full length self-revelatory performances and also having directed and presented four of my own. The creative process needs containment *and* freedom, structure *and* non-structure. I deal with the inevitable differences in temperament, interests, and cognitive style by offering numerous techniques, a variety of pathways into the creative process. A useful technique is "freewriting," created by Natalie Goldberg (1986), that involves writing without judgment or editing within a fixed period of time. Other techniques I offer include journaling (i.e., keeping a journal of impressions, images that come to the surface of awareness, ideas, associations); theatre games; movement improvisation; guided visualizations; and a variety of drama therapy techniques that may elicit roles, life stories and somatic movement processes.

It's also important to set up a group climate of safety and support. Confidentiality is vital to the process. Participants agree to not share others' personal stories beyond the group. I developed the Life Stories process of creating self-revelatory performance to assist people in verbally articulating what emerges from the body during improvisational processes and to physically embody what emerges from the mind. This interweaving between cognitive and physical process helps to combine mind and body, leading to greater presence and authenticity in people's performances, and also leading to greater aesthetic distance, which creates good theatre. I weave them back and forth among the various facilitating methods, depending on what a particular group needs at the time. Here are some of the types of techniques that I've found to be especially useful.

Creating a Context of Non-Judgmental Support When improvisation is the norm, any seeming "mistakes" are re-framed as "creative experiments. Thus, the workshop uses the context of a group and its potential for support as the container for the unfolding of each participant's solo work. Group cohesion builds as participants work in dyads mirroring each other's movements and sounds, and later using words to mirror back the healing elements of a stories. I invite group to "Listen with a soft heart" and become a "witnessing audience," which is very different from traditional theatre where the audience expects to be entertained. I often ask the group, "How were you affected by this person's story?"

Embodiment Through Movement and Breath I've created a series of somatic exercises which are described on the webpage supplement to this chapter, and also I integrate a wide range of warm-up techniques from various dance therapy, psychotherapy, play, drama therapy, and other sources. I mix stretches, vocal warm-ups, and the aforementioned freewriting, and from these, images or movements occur, which then become the basis of further on-the-feet improvisations.

Somatic Focusing I often begin each evening with a 5–20 minute somatic focusing process and guided visualization to assist students to begin to sense from the inside of their bodies. This leads participants to open their many gates of imagination. I invite them to lie on the floor, close their eyes and direct their attention to attend to more subtle sensations and movements. Some re-experience the movements they made as infants.

This can lead to what I call "embodied stories," stories in which the impulse comes from a "felt sense" in the body. This process is a way to explore and give voice to some of the stories held in the body's various regions of heightened muscular tension. Rather than coming from the cognitive mind, which might tend to say, "I want to tell the story about the time …," the body is allowed to take the lead, as the student attends to an impulse that might arise in the belly, leg, or hand. For example, one student was drawn during this somatic process to the tip of her finger that she had lost in a motorcycle accident when she was a child. She had hid her hand from view for most of her life. As I led her through a series of further exercises to allow her finger to begin to tell its story an amazing thing happened: Her inner storyteller appeared and began to tell her story from a perspective she'd never even considered previously.

Vocal Sentence Play, Sentence Repetition: This exercise uses the sounds within a sentence as a structure for improvisation. One student identified a sentence in his writing: "You are not my boss." I directed him to say it faster and slower, allowing his body to move with the sounds. Eventually he slowed it down beyond any vocal recognition of the words. A deep commanding voice emerged with movements to match. During this process he recalled feeling this way as a child and being unable to have a sense of his own voice in his family. This piece was powerful to watch and transformative for the actor.

Writing and Scene Work

Group members are invited to journal between classes as a way to contain creative material that emerges between sessions-dreams, memories, stories, realizations. During class, we do the aforementioned freewriting for five minutes on a topic that might evoke their creative processes, and the material thus generated can be taken into improvised action. For example, one woman's freewriting generated a striking image: herself as a child sitting inside and beneath the coats in the store while her parents were shopping. I directed her to begin her improvisation with this image, feeling all the sensations in her child body while seeing the tall heavy coats and hearing the disembodied voices of her parents. AS she allowed her body to move with this image, the scene became surprisingly vivid. She then improvised a scene in which she experienced a moment of freedom from the power of her father, "his heavy voice" and the fact that her parents didn't even notice her missing. But in the enactment, as this child heard the sound of her parents' voices become anxious as they realized she was gone and began to search for her, she was able to notice a tinge of victory in her game of hide-and-seek.

Storytelling

Storytelling is such a basic human means of communication. It is ancient and it can be healing both for the teller and the listener. Members are asked to explore themes and identify childhood memories or current adult memories. Stories are windows that we step through. Portals into our stories can include words, images, other people's stories, sounds smells, and movement cues. Stories work in circles, not straight lines. Improvisational drama processes and freewriting allow us to work with everyone's unique way of unfolding story. Finding the threads by listening to other people's stories in the group can evoke memories of even more stories.

Sometimes the "inner storyteller" can provide guidance for the audience and distance from the feelings for the actor. One student I directed used the role of storyteller to take the audience back to her childhood home and provide structure and a through line for several stories she told about her mentally ill mother.

Making or Using Masks

These theatrical props can be powerful adjuncts, offering personal art-sculpture symbols of self-representation. I may direct a student to choose or create a mask that represents a person or element that they need on stage. One student had who had been struggling for years to complete her masters degree was able to realize through the freewriting exercises that she was afraid to graduate because she would be surpassing her mother. I directed her to choose a mask to represent her mother. She choose a mask of a person in pain. I directed her to improvise a scene in which she held and talked to the mask, explaining her challenge to be the first person in this Hispanic family to get her masters degree. She talked to the mask (her mother) and spoke about how hard she had worked and that she was not going to let her mother's pain get in her way of finally graduating.

Authenticity and Presence On Stage

Self-rev is about allowing the self to be seen. One of the elements of this method that allows the pieces to be riveting is the *presence* of the person on stage, the artistic expression of "really being there," in contrast to the way people often dilute themselves with narrative, such as saying, "one might feel," or digressing into explaining the circumstances or offering excuses. Part of the art is helping the performer to not only show their personal experience, but also to be present in the moment, authentic, and in some cases talking to or with the audience. In one sense, it is the best of acting, but in this context, this immediacy communicates the heightened awareness of the performer that "this really is my existence!"

Many participants have some initial anxiety about being in front of a group. We move slowly week to week increasing comfort levels; each member gets a sense of being witnessed rather than judged by the group/audience. We begin improvising for 1–5 minutes in front of the whole group, beginning first in a circle format and eventually moving into the structure of a performer in front of an audience. As workshop members become more comfortable with this, they prepare for the last night, when the challenge is to be authentic in offering a ten minute performance for a small audience of invited guests. Some performers say that they feel a sense of feeling naked. Some say that they feel deeply connected to a deeper part of themselves. Many say they feel deeply heard and witnessed for the first time in their lives.

Bringing Out the Different Parts of the Self

Each individual is a dynamic nexus of a number of roles, not only social roles, but also different and often conflicting parts of the self, "intra-psychic roles." In other words, there are many voices inside, each having its own stories to tell. I like to offer exercises that support each part to speak. We explore parts of the self, such as the inner 'judge,' the 'inner director,' parts of the self that is in some ways the opposite of what one considers oneself to be, the "shadow," as well as roles from different ages. It's helpful to have access to an inner director or "center of the self," to be able to coordinate and sort through the stories. In learning this, the teacher may temporarily model this part of the person that is aware of the larger process, so that this inner director "meta-role," as Adam Blatner (2006) calls it, may become more developed resource for deciding which stories to use.

One common role is the "inner judge," the source of inhibiting self-consciousness. Initially we banish everyone's inner judge from the group the first night so members can access their creativity. Then, in a week or two, we may address this role directly, invite the role of the judge to be exaggerated, explored, and played with through improvisation exercises.

For example, a very polite group member took on the posture of her "inner judge," with an angry facial expression, one hand on hip and the other hand pointing. When I asked her to bring this inner judge into movement, she started pointing with judgment at everything in the room, every crack in the wall, every shoe that was out of line, even other people. Asked to expand the movement, her gestures became larger, and invited to explore the movement, the pointing became huge and unwieldy. As she struggled to control the venom in the pointing from one person to the next, with increasing intensity, her face filled with rage and judgment. Eventually, the finger pointed directly at herself and, hardly able to bear the power of judgment, she sank to the ground. Group members gave her supportive feedback on the power of her improvisation, and the theme of judgment became this woman's focus for subsequent weeks in the workshop.

I suggested other techniques for exploring this dynamic: She might freewrite a story about where this judge complex came from and how it helped her? Other questions she might consider included how she had been judged in her family of origin? How does she judge her family now? How does she protect her family and herself? Her improvisations with this theme each week developed into her final performance, to which she invited her husband. He sat in the audience and watched her riveting performance about the power of her inner judge, and saw his wife explore dramatically the emerging possibility of reducing tendencies to judge the people she loves and instead comforting her scared little girl inside. There was not a dry eye in the crowd.

Carl Jung used the term "shadow" to refer to the part of an individual that seems to the person as "not me." Some of these qualities are denied completely, others a grudgingly admitted as uncomfortable elements. During the life-stories process, we do exercises that invite participants to identify and explore what some of these parts or roles might be. One woman, a dedicated office worker, decided to explore a part of her that hated office work. Two twin brothers taking the workshop each decided to explore a part of themselves that had unspoken feelings about being a twin, being abandoned as a toddler while nursing, and always being compared to his brother at school. A woman who was a waitress for seventeen years explored the part of her that always wanted to break into song in the middle of serving people their dinner. A graduate student who was tired of writing papers played with the part of her that just wanted to be still and silent and refused to move or speak. (Other examples and techniques may be found on the website supplement to this chapter.)

The Deeper Story in Performance

I feel called in my teaching and directing to ask the actor/student to begin to look for a deeper story. This deeper story, the "life story," is found when a person digs deep enough in their own personal process that they come upon an underground river, a human theme, and an archetypal theme. Sometimes the story is in the exquisite details that touch the deeper truth.

Finally, in the tenth week of the class, the group members present their ten to fifteen minute performances, the distillation of their efforts, to an invited audience, people they want to share this with, those who they believe will not be judgmental. Many of the self-rev performances in my class are improvisational, using monologue and other theatrical forms, based on stories and improvisations during the last ten weeks. Some performances are more structured and planned including props and music. The performances are solo. What is deeply revealed by working deeply with self-rev stories is that in addition to revealing our similarities, there is also a shared enjoyment in the sheer uniqueness of each person and presentation. I invite people who've taken the class before, and participants invite friends and family to the performance and reception.

Conclusion

What makes self-revelatory performance distinctly different from other kinds of performance and personal sharing (e.g., poetry reading; solo autobiographical storytelling or performance) is that something psychologically profound happens right there on stage, a sacred event, rite of passage, or a wound healing that the audience is invited to witness. One student, reflecting on her weekend workshop/class experience that resulted in a 10-minute self-revelatory performance, said, "Those extraordinary moments, which can never be reenacted, gave the audience an inside look at individuals finding their way through pain, fear, loss, disappointment, confusion, hopes, and dreams." Something happens while the actor is standing vulnerably in front of the audience, or as they are revealing what has not been shared before, an occasion of transformation emerges through the ritual of being witnessed by a supportive audience; both the audience members and the performer are touched by the depth of strength and hope in the human heart. I do this work because I believe that the work of telling personal stories is the work of the soul, the work of the deepest self coming through to be witnessed. And it is my hope that there will be more places of community where people can do just that.

References:

The webpage supplement to this chapter: <www.interactiveimprov.com/selfrevwb.html>

Blatner, Adam. (2006). *The choosing self: developing the meta-role function.* Website <www.blatner.com/adam/psyntbk/choosingself.html>

Emunah, Renée. (1994). *Acting for Real: Drama therapy process, technique and performance.* New York: Brunner/Mazel.

Goldberg, Natalie. (1986). *Writing down the bones: Freeing the writer within.* Boston, Mass. Shambhala.

McAdams, Dan P. (1993). *The stories we live by: Personal myths and the making of the self.*

New York: William Morrow and Co. (Other books on personal mythology on the webpage supplement.)

Chapter 25

ACTINGOUT: AN INTERACTIVE YOUTH DRAMA GROUP

Kim Burden and Mario Cossa

ActingOut (to be abbreviated as AO) is a youth theatre program in southwestern New Hampshire, in operation since 1989, that involves weekly theatre groups performed by and for youth ages 12–18. It has evolved through a number of stages; at present it is being managed by different group leaders and in some ways that will not be discussed in this chapter. Rather, we are reporting on the general sense of what our program was around the later 1990s.

AO involved two kinds of groups: The main part of the program involved students who prepared and delivered interactive performances on socially relevant topics, thus operating as a kind of Theatre-in-Education (see Chapter 10). A less prominent but still valuable aspect of the program offered workshops for young people who benefitted from learning elements of drama for general socialization, interpersonal skill-building, and spontaneity training—akin to what is described in the chapter on Creative Drama. These workshop participants weren't expected to perform. The AO theatre groups met weekly for one-and-a-half to two hours. Once the programs began, groups formed in two separate towns, each group having both elements of the program, the performance team and the workshop.

The performance group activities included a number of components: developing basic and then intermediate-level improvisational skills; working out outlines for improvisational pieces on a wide range of topics; and learning "basic facts" about issues pertinent to contemporary youth. The workshop (non-performance) groups also involved the kids in drama activities, but there was no push to bring these to the point of performance in the community.

The main focus of this chapter, though, will be on the performance-oriented program, which offered audience-interactive, issue-oriented, improvisational presentations to various groups in the community. AO had about 20 teen actors in each program year. Most stayed in the group for at least one school year, and some remained for several years. Thus, over about 15 years of operation, about 300 teenagers were involved.

We offered an average of 100 performances each program year to groups ranging from schools to service organizations, usually to groups of anywhere from 20 to 200 students, teachers, or community members. Our presentations usually took one of two forms: a class period or assembly, usually lasting about an hour; or a workshop for a small group—usually a maximum of 35 students—that lasted for two to four hours. The subject matter might be pre-planned, at the request of the sponsoring agency—a topic such as HIV/AIDS Prevention. In other settings, the troupe would more actively improvise, addressing a number of topics suggested by the audience. Either way, the audience was also invited to participate in suggesting the way the scenes should be developed, coaching the characters, or by getting out of their seats and entering the enactment, taking on one of the roles during the performance.

Mario Cossa, who formed the first group, integrated long-time involvement with theatre, years of teaching and directing youth, and a special interest in psychology and psychodrama. The program was designed to provide area youth with prevention programming and support groups that were interesting, action-based, and fun. Over the years, the program grew and shifted to include up to two full-time and one part-time staff member and from one to three graduate and/or undergraduate counseling interns. In the later years of the program, there were both performing and support groups in two different towns (Keene, NH and Peterborough, NH—small towns within a 40 minute drive of one another). On occasion, performers from both towns performed together.

Regarding the support groups: for several years there were just two groups, a Premiere group (entry-level members) and an Encore Group (continuing members.) Both groups spent time checking in and using group support, including drama therapy and expressive arts therapy techniques for dealing with personal issues. The second half of the group session was spent working on performances and theatre skills. Over the years, the program evolved so that some groups were "pure" theatre groups while others were for the sole purpose of support and personal growth. In many cases, individuals were members of more than one group, i.e. a theatre group and a support group. Thus, for most of the period of our work, there were both theatre and support groups in each of the two towns.

Over the years we have become aware of and collaborated with similar youth theatre troupes, such as Reflections (described in Chapter 6), and some of these are mentioned in the webpage supplement to this chapter: <www.interactiveimprov.com/actingoutwb.html>

Although AO occasionally used improvisation to develop finished products or set theatre pieces, some of which will be described later in this chapter, the majority of its performances were improvised. Each presentation began with conversations with the sponsor (school, organization, etc.) to establish parameters for the performance. We discussed the size and age of the audience, length of the performance, setting (easy access to the playing space is essential), topic areas to be covered, and if there is anything we should know about the social climate of the audience.

The content of ActingOut performances ran the gamut of contemporary issues including AIDS prevention, substance use and abuse, sexual harassment, conflict resolution, and teen pregnancy. Some sponsors contract for a topic area and leave the specifics up to the troupe; others have particular areas they would like to have covered. Some leave the choice of topics up to the audience on the day of the performance. The details about topic areas were provided to the actors at a rehearsal prior to the presentation so information could be reviewed if needed, possible scenarios explored, an introductory approach developed, and areas of audience interaction anticipated.

The social climate of the audience might be the very reason AO was invited to begin with and is a testament to the power of social theatre in supporting the exploration of real issues. For example, on a number of occasions our actors were asked to help a school community look at the issue of harassment. In one particular instance, there had been an incident in which a student had been suspended for sexual harassment and a good portion of the student body was angry with the other student who had been the one to bring charges that led to the suspension. Our presentation helped the community develop a practical definition of harassment as well as explore the feelings of the perpetrator and victim, and clarify school norms and consequences for harassing behavior.

The following example, although exceptional, is typical of the type of social theatre that AO has presented over the course of its existence. Mario Cossa and a group of four actors were doing a performance at a local, regional high school for an audience of about 400. They had completed the portion of the program focusing on substance abuse issues and, as agreed upon with the school sponsors, were opening up selection of topics to the student audience.

"How 'bout a scene on faggots!" came the challenge from a young man sitting about a third of the way back in the center section of the auditorium. His voice filled the room. "I'm not sure that a scene about bundles of sticks tied together and used to start fires would be particularly interesting," Mario replied, playing for a moment of time and looking to engage this youth and his peers. The young man made eye contact across the room and continued his challenge but in a more direct manner, "a scene about gay people." "All right," Mario said calmly, "would you be willing to play a high school guy who has fallen in love with a girl in his class?" It became clear that the young man was engaged and wouldn't back down. He agreed and joined Mario on stage along with a young woman from the audience elicited to play his "girlfriend."

Once they were on stage, wondering what these characters had to do with a scene about gay people Mario told them, "All right, the two of you have met in school and have developed a relationship, have fallen in love. The only thing is that you live in an alternative universe in which 90% of the people are gay. Don't get too confused by the biology of it, let's just assume that in this universe the union of two men creates male offspring and the union of two women creates female offspring. Males and females can be sexually involved with each other, but of course, being an unnatural union, they can produce no children. The two of you have fallen in love, even though it is against the norm and have decided to come out to your parents."

Because he wanted the parents to play the scene in a non-stereotypical manner, Mario asked the AO actors to be the boy's fathers and the girl's mothers and gave them a brief bit of coaching. They began a side-by-side scene, switching back and forth between the boy's coming out to dads and the girl's coming out to moms. The audience was completely engaged. There was appropriate laughter from time to time, but everyone was watching and focused. Some other students were brought up to play friends in another scene and, because of the modeling by the AO members, they moved into their roles as gay youth with just a bit of joking, but mostly really focused on the scene. At one point the friends, both male and female, were attacking and mocking the straight couple and the young man whose challenge had begun the process looked at them and said strongly, "How dare you make fun of me just because I'm different from you. I have a right to my own sexuality."

The performance had a significant effect on that particular school population. The principal later reported to AO staff, that in the few months following the performance eight students in the school came out as gay, lesbian, or bisexual and were supported in doing so by friends and staff alike. The alternative universe format for working with issues around homophobia was subsequently often used in AO performances in schools, for Diversity Assemblies, and at a conference on Gay, Lesbian, Bisexual, and Transgendered (GLBT) issues called: Affirming Every Person. It was at this conference that the format (still improvised but around a basic structure) was given the name, "If Superman was Gay, Wonder Woman was Lesbian, and Tarzan Swung Both Ways!"

Training the Troupe

We taught these teenagers basic improvisational drama in a systematic fashion, with basic principles which were then elaborated into more complex forms. Students didn't have to be experienced in acting when they first came into our program; they would learn the skills as part of the process. All that was required was an interest in theatre and commitment to attendance and improvement.

AO developed this simple approach for four basic reasons. First, young people came to AO with a variety of interests and skill levels ranging from having been in plays since very young to a simple desire to try something new. Such diversity required a flexible approach to training. Second, the issue-oriented nature of AO theatre required its members to be versed in the basics of various issues of importance to youth and to society at large. Third, given that AO performances were improvisational, its actors need to be trained in thinking on their feet, learning the basics of "who, what and where" (i.e., character, content, and scene setting). Finally, the element of interaction with the audience required great flexibility from both director and actors. Actors needed to be trained to be flexible, open, and available to support audience members who try taking on roles. Once actors were proficient in the basic skills and facts, preparing for performances could take place in the car on the way to a performance, thus minimizing rehearsal time. The following paragraphs document the evolution of the AO training and performance approach.

When ActingOut was first formed its members met for three afternoons a week for two hours a session. They also met for an additional expressive arts therapy group for 2 hours on Wednesday nights. Although the commitment was intense, the openings for fourteen youth were quickly filled, with others going on a waiting list. Attrition for various reasons during the first half of the year allowed additional members to join the group in January. This intensive schedule was important to the initial formation of the peer culture of AO, and was appropriate at the time given that there were no other programs similar to AO in the area at that time. This may or may not be possible for those wishing to begin a similar program, depending upon funding, interest, and youth culture.

The first four months were focused on training in general theatre skills as well as issue-oriented improvisation. Many of the warm-up activities used were based on Viola Spolin's theatre games. (See Bibliography of warm-ups in Appendix B). The actors generated a list of topics that they felt were most important for the various grade levels for which they would be performing and various approaches to the topics were explored. Topics were also generated through non-directed improvisation. An activity variously know as *chain improv*, or *freeze*, was utilized in which two actors would begin a scene about any topic, and another actor could freeze the scene at any point. This actor would then replace one of the actors on stage and initiate a new scene about a new topic, with the remaining actor having to accept what was presented and work with it. Besides providing good training for the actors, it helped the group discover which topics were most important to them.

Once we started thinking about performance, half the group would serve as the selected "audience" (e.g., a third grade class) and the other half as actors, to try on the material as well as the process for integrating audience members into the action. The group members playing the "audience" would provide peer feedback on appropriateness of content, level of sophistication of language, and the degree to which they felt supported in being integrated into the scene. It was also at this time that we began setting appropriate performance norms. We developed a rating scale for language that included: *general audiences* (no swearing or street language at all), *evening tv standard* (the occasional hell or damn for emphasis), and *anything goes* (street language natural to the situation accepted). When we first worked with *anything goes*, it became a contest on how many times and how creatively actors could work certain four-letter words into the scene, but the actors soon developed a sense of what was gratuitous and what served the scene. Presentation sponsors were asked which of the levels they wanted for the performance and the actors adhered to it.

The group's first actual performance was a community presentation for family and friends called *Christmas Eve at Terminal Three*. This piece combined improvised scenes about strangers stranded at a bus terminal on Christmas Eve with an enactment of *How the Grinch Stole the Holidays*, a cross-cultural winter holiday performance that embraced Christmas, Chanukah, and Solstice. For many of our actors, this was their first time on stage and the focus was on performance skills.

The Method

ActingOut's first issue-oriented performance was presented to the 12–14 year old youngsters at the Marlborough (New Hampshire) Middle School in 1990. The first warming-up scene portrayed kids on an imagined school bus, with music playing and lots of noise. Each time the music stopped the overall action froze and two actors would do a short bit introducing a particular topic (tobacco, alcohol, bullying, a friend with an undefined problem, etc.) At the conclusion of this introductory piece the audience was asked to identify the issues presented and vote for the scenes they most wanted to see.

In the early years of AO we would often take six or eight actors to a given performance. As the program has evolved it became more customary to take four actors and one facilitator. This is the number that fit in a car and, given the high degree of audience involvement, provided each actor with a substantial role. Each performance began with some kind of introductory piece after the facilitator provided the framework for audience participation and given the disclaimer: "Although our actors use their own names while in role, the ideas they express and the experiences they represent are not necessarily their own."

In addition to aforementioned "school bus" warm-up scene, another took place at a party. Or we might use what we call "chain intros," which began with two actors in the playing space who have to use each other's name, and introduce one of the possible topics for the day. One actor leaves and another enters, bringing in another topic. After all actors have been seen, the facilitator brings them back out and asks the audience to recall the actors' names and identify the topics or issues they have presented. This provided a warm up to participation for audience members by engaging them verbally.

Audiences were then generally given the opportunity to vote on which topic or aspect of a topic they would like to see enacted first. We generally had time to explore two issues in some detail, so often gave each person two votes. Once the topics were selected we were ready to begin. Since the performance was improvisational, the facilitator worked with the audience to flesh out the details of the topic as it was explored. A scene about substance abuse could involve confronting a friend about their using, or about someone finding out their best friend had been killed by a drunk driver. There was a "dance" between the audience and facilitator to define the scene in a manner that will make for good theatre as well as for rich exploration of the topic.

Sometimes, in place of or in addition to the chain introductions, we did an activity called *issue/words*. This structure emerged out of early audience responses to the material AO presented: the work was great, said some viewers, but the topics are *so* heavy! So structures were developed to help approach difficult topics with some degree of levity. After all, when people are laughing they are paying attention. In *issue/words*, the audience is first asked to develop a list of possible topics that is written on the left column of a chalkboard or whiteboard. The audience is then asked to come up with a list of adjective-noun phrases such as "burlap underwear" or "salacious monkey"—two actual phrases that were suggested—equal in length to the issue list. This list is written on the right side of the board. The actors proceed to enter into short scenes similar to "chain introductions"; the twist is that each short scene must include one of the adjective-noun phrases (the phrase need not be the one written next to the issue.) As the actors use the issues and words, the issues are crossed out and the words erased. After this, the audience is asked to vote for the issues they would like to see put into action.

In the initial stages of the first scene we used our actors and brought a few audience members in to work with them. There was seldom a problem with volunteers but if there were, we used only our actors. When we worked with audience volunteers our actors supported their full participation by asking a question to someone who is holding back, and by not "hogging" the scene themselves.

Just as the action of the scene was getting hot or a point of decision had been reached, the facilitator froze the scene and got the audience involved in interpreting what is going on, evaluating motivations of the various characters, or making decisions about where things should go next. This could be somewhat frustrating for actors (especially if the topic is a seriously heavy one (e.g., a girl's telling her boyfriend she is pregnant only to have him tell her he is HIV Positive), and also sacrifices a bit of the artistic integrity of the scene. However, there is a tremendous dividend in terms of engagement of audience members who saw their ideas enacted on stage. It also took the pressure off audience actors to generate their own ideas about what to do or say next and provided an opportunity for the facilitator to discuss the accuracy of information the characters may have relayed.

Scene Frameworks and Scripted Pieces:

Even though the performances were improvisational, AO developed a number of scene frameworks over the years that were used repeatedly with certain topics. "If Superman were Gay ..." (related in detail previously) was one example. In working with choices between healthy and unhealthy behavior (e.g., alcohol or drug use) we often employed an *angel/devil scenario* in which audience members are invited to play the inner voices urging the character to do or not do a particular thing. (This is similar to the multiple double technique in psychodrama.) In working with issues around nicotine addiction the "Joe Smoker" scenario was often put into action, in which a person trying to quit smoking is confronted by his/her brain suffering from withdrawal, lungs begging for clean air, heart, etc. Although these scenarios were used time and again, they were always new in that the way in which the characters interacted, and outcomes sometimes changed if there were a high level of audience participation.

AO developed some pieces that arose in a process of group improvisation, but ended up being scripted—one being *What the Dragon Stole*, an original musical oriented around the mythic theme of the heroic quest to reclaim a treasure from a dragon (Cossa, 2002); another, *Gray Matter*, being about the nervous system of teenagers on drugs. Even though scripted, the two plays also involved a degree of interactivity with the audience. (See webpage supplement: <www.interactiveimprov.com/actingoutwb.html>.)

Longer Formats

In some contexts, it was felt that a workshop-style approach for events would work best, such as for peer education training days or youth conferences. In those instances we tended to work with smaller groups and for longer periods of time (anywhere from two hours to full days). We included various theatre games as part of the warm up and generally worked toward some sort of performance or sharing in which participants could try out scenes they have developed. As an example, a regional middle school contracted with AO for a full-day workshop with peer mediators in-training. In this workshop, AO did a preliminary introduction that included *issue/words*, and the students divided into small groups, each taking one of the issues from the introduction. Each small group discussed and developed an improvised piece that was shared with the full group.

Over the years, our group structure and some aspects of training evolved and changed. Because we offered support groups in addition to theatre groups, there have at times been discrepancies between the needs of youth who need a support network and those who wish to work theatrically. In the mid-1990s, based on such shifting needs, we began dividing our theatre groups and support groups so that youth who really wanted to perform could focus on performance, leaving support groups free to use drama and other expressive forms to support social and personal growth needs. This change was initiated in light of messages we were hearing from youth as well as requests we were receiving from referral sources.

The initial AO groups were very popular in the region and were populated by a mix of youth from intact, high-functioning families and youth who had been identified as "troubled." Over the years, we began to see a decrease in involvement by higher functioning youth; when we asked members who had dropped out about this many of them said they wanted to do theatre, but didn't want to be clumped in with kids who "needed help." Concurrently, we were hearing from counselors and other referral sources that they wanted to refer youth, but their potential members were highly averse to performing. Given that we had the staffing to meet both support and theatre needs, we experimented with separating the theatre and support groups. This allowed for a wider range of needs to be met, and included youth that wanted to experiment with theatre or expressive arts without having to get up and perform.

Near the end of our work with this program, we offered theatre performance groups in two towns at two levels. The introductory level includes a good deal of comedy improvisation and "nuts and bolts" skills of theatre. The performance group deepened its knowledge of the issues they would perform and took more ownership in creating and preparing for performances. Actors continued to learn AO's basic approach to performance theatre, and travel to schools and community events similar to those described earlier in the chapter.

Conclusion

ActingOut entered the 21st Century as an example of what can be done. It remains to be seen what changes will need to occur to meet the needs of the changing youth culture. We were fortunate over the years to be consistently funded by several federal, state and local agencies, including the Division of Alcohol and Drug Abuse Prevention and Recovery, the Department of Education, the United Way, and several local foundations. Monadnock Family Services, the local community mental health agency, was our "umbrella" agency, which gave AO and several other prevention programs within the agency some financial cushioning. Performances and workshops brought in some revenue. Consistent record-keeping, including pre- and post-tests for effectiveness of basic prevention risk and resiliency factors helped us report accurately and justify our purpose to funding agencies. A number of challenges to such programs continue: the huge impact of the internet on communication, the fast pace of media to which youth are exposed, the increased pressure on schools to "teach to the test", economic influences that prompt youth to need to work more (rendering them less available for after-school activities) and the continual quickening pace of life in general.

To keep up with some of these changes, it may be necessary to create more product-type theatre like *Gray Matter*, include media other than theatre, and move increasingly toward in-school programming. The spirit of ActingOut, however, will continue to be dedicated to promoting social change and providing youth with choices, skill building tools, and peer education through audience interactive, issue oriented, improvisational theatre. We hope this program will stimulate others to apply their efforts in their own communities.

References:

Cossa, M. (2005). *Rebels with a cause: working with adolescents using action techniques.* London: Jessica Kingsley.

Cossa, M. (2006). How rude!: using sociodrama in the investigation of bullying and harassing behavior and in teaching civility in educational communities. *Journal of Group Psychotherapy, Psychodrama & Sociometry,* 58 (4), 183–194.

Cossa, M., Ember, S., Glass, L., and Hazelwood, J. (1996). *ActingOut: The workbook—a guide to the development and presentation of issue-oriented, audience-interactive, improvisational theatre.* Bristol, PA: Taylor & Francis.

Cossa, Mario. (2002). Drago-drama™: Archetypal sociodrama with adolescents. In A. Bannister & A. Huntington (Eds.), *Communicating with children and adolescents: Action for change.* London: Jessica Kingsley Publishers. (A book offering a wide range of practical applications of using action methods in working with children and adolescents.)

SECTION V

APPLICATIONS FOR LIFE EXPANSION AND ENTERTAINMENT

Adam Blatner

So much in our culture partakes of a type of entertainment that is commercialized and performed by professionals for the enjoyment of a relatively passive audience. The types of activities described in the next section reflect a counter-trend towards increasing involvement and participation, resulting in an enhanced sense of vitality as well as interpersonal and group connectedness. Many weave in the dimension of fantasy as a way of countering trends that over-value task and mere fact, objectivity and seriousness. We need both domains to live an abundant life, to flourish. We need the fundamental nutrients of food but appreciate the spices that give it flavor. Drama is the spice and flavoring of life, the "wow!" "aha!" and other devices that amplify the emotional meanings of the events we live.

Meeting at the level of imagination offers a paradox. Instead of thinking I know you based on my learning of your real-life demographic status, I discover that you are mysterious, a little odd in a non-threatening way. I begin to know you in ways that I may never be able to fully understand, and that makes you even more fun, interesting. You can't be categorized neatly. You become more vividly someone who I can be surprised by, and yet you are enjoyable.

Drama as a type of play allows your individuality to be expressed in a relatively fail-safe context. What a nice way to make friends!

Chapter 26

THE ART OF PLAY

Adam Blatner and Allee Blatner

The Art of Play is an improvisational dramatic approach we created in order to help adults reclaim their imagination and spontaneity. Around 1979, Adam (a psychiatrist and trainer of psychodrama) recognized that psychodramatic methods could and should be applied beyond the clinical context—that these techniques could help healthy people learn to enjoy themselves and life more fully. Allee (a creative arts professional) had a lifelong interest in promoting the fun of role playing characters. She had enjoyed role taking during her high school drama activities. Both of us became motivated to explore ways drama could enhance a greater sense of vitality for adults.

We decided that a supportive workshop structure using good group process procedures and offering people ample time and activities for warming-up would form the foundation for more challenging role playing. The central theme for the focus of our method was the concept of "play"—that natural and easy realm children continually pursue. Playing monsters, kittens, warriors and princesses is so easy and refreshing in childhood. As we explored many techniques from psychodrama, creative drama, sociodrama and the creative arts, we met other professionals who were interested in imaginativeness and spontaneity.

The Art of Play is a recreational form performed not for therapy but for fun and socializing. The method may be conducted in larger or smaller groups. A large group would be broken down into sub-groups of 3–4 people. The method can also be conducted in a group of up to 9 people without breaking into sub-groups if there is more than 2 hours—i.e. in a half or all day "play-shop" that allows time for most participants to play their own character. The method begins with various warm-ups, and then in small groups, one participant at a time is helped to play a character from his or her imagination. Another group member acts as a director and the other(s) take supporting roles. The goal is for the main player to explore what it is like to "be" the character "in role," experience the role's environment, state of mind, feelings, and relationships. No personal problems are brought to be solved, and the roles chosen are not to be viewed as expressions of a player's personality. The Art of Play is a social and recreational activity and its success rests in the leader's ability to establish and maintain an emotionally safe, relaxed group space. (An extensive treatment of this method, with related chapters on theory, sample sessions, applications etc., is described in our book *The Art of Play*. See references below.)

Background

By 1981, Adam Blatner had been working for fifteen years in the roles of child and adult psychiatrist as well as a psychodramatist. Adam recognized that the role playing process in psychodrama promised a greater potential than its application in clinical settings, where it was used to work on patients' problems. After a period of talking with Allee, his wife, and contemplating what was most dynamic about this method, he realized that the most energizing element in the process was the activity of role-taking itself—the essential component of children's natural, make-believe play. This insight was substantiated by the fact that both Adam and Allee retained a strong sense of the childlike, enjoying not only playing with their kids, but also with the toys the kids used—hand puppets, masks, make-up devices.

The idea for the Art of Play was stimulated at a Halloween party for adults, when Adam met a fellow costumed as an extra-terrestrial alien. Instead of just saying, "cool costume," and otherwise relating to the person behind the role, Adam related to the role: "Wow, this is an opportunity to learn something about life on your planet." Adam and the guy shifted into a kind of interview with an extra-terrestrial: "What do you folks eat? If I may be so bold, how do you have sex? What is your religious belief?" The fellow played right to the questions and improvised answers that were clever and amusing. Later, he said how much he enjoyed the interchange, and Adam, in turn, not only enjoyed the play, but the "aha!" clicked: Let's have people just enjoy the creation of imaginary roles!

Not long after the party, Adam and Allee experimented. They gathered about nine of their friends in a group room and warmed them up to characters that popped into their imaginations. Then they brought these characters forward and, using modified psychodramatic techniques, helped them to experience the dramatic potentials inherent in these character roles. There was no interest in the group members' actual lives, but only what is was like to be the character and what might happen next if these scenes were to be carried forward.

For example, on being asked to open their imaginations to whatever character "wanted to come through," John (all names are fictional) announced, "I am a steam roller." Adam, as director, facilitated the action by asking, "Can you show us your parts." "What is around you?" At some point, it was fitting for someone to be in the scene—a driver of an automobile in the steam roller's path. Another of the group was chosen and agreed to play that role. The director needs to balance the way the main player wants the scene to happen and the way the supporting player is inspired to spontaneously respond. The result is often an amusing interaction.

Several more workshops ensued. The ideas and techniques were refined and it was tried with different groups such as the staff of an alcohol rehabilitation program or a group of adults in a church community. It became clear that The Art of Play evoked a rich mixture of simple enjoyment and self-discovery. Group members reported that they didn't know they could be that spontaneous.

In 1985, the Blatners wrote this approach up in a privately produced monograph. A few years later, The Art of Play was published and marketed as a psychology book. Since then, it has been used by professionals in a variety of related fields, and this in turn inspired Adam to consider the broader reaches of drama, aside from its obvious benefits as a therapeutic modality. (In 1995, Gary Izzo also used the primary title "The Art of Play" for his book about theatre games and improv—he hadn't heard of our book.)

Benefits

Blatners' The Art of Play method offers associated benefits as participants discover the depth and pleasure that accompanies improvisation and the companionship that comes with sharing one's imagination with friends. Other benefits include the following:

- promotes role flexibility, spontaneity, imaginativeness, and recreation
- offers a pleasant form of "role relief" for people who use role playing for serious purposes, such as in education, therapy, social action, etc. Here's a way to enjoy the richness of character development for its own sake
- provides a wholesome participatory activity that can be enjoyed without needing expensive equipment, travel, and other special elements
- creates a method for personal development, cultivating the human potential, and redeeming qualities that may have been neglected

- makes it possible to recapture the magic of childhood, the child-like (not the child-ish) ability to be young at heart
- allows access to the joyful essence of drama without the hassles of scenery, rehearsals, the politics and economics of a production for an audience
- sets up a way to interact physically, in a friendly way, at the level of imagination, which makes for a kind of encounter that cannot be replicated by the realm of internet chat rooms, video games, and other media with a thicker technological interface
- builds group cohesion, warms people up for other drama activities, emphasizes the power of the here-and-now as an occasion for enjoyment
- sensitizes the mind to the more subtle cues of the creative subconscious by the practice of opening to imagination and inspiration
- develops the skill for playing with children, your own kids and grandkids

Method

It was felt that a group of about nine was optimal at first, but that was for group sessions that might last three or four hours. Later, while working with groups of between 30–150 people, and with time constraints at conference workshops so that the activity was confined to a 90–120 minute session, we found that it worked to have the participants work in small groups of three to five. This allowed people to take turns and enjoy the benefits of playing one of the three main roles in the method—protagonist, director, and supporting player.

The protagonist is the main player whose imagined character is explored. The director's role is to facilitate the optimal experience of the main player. The supporting player (equivalent to the auxiliary ego in psychodrama) takes any role that will help the main player enjoy his or her own character most fully. There may be one, two, or a few supporting players.

When children play, they tend to improvise from the viewpoint of themselves and their chosen role or character. It requires a bit of adult thinking to relinquish one's tendencies to be egocentric and instead to offer one's own imagination mixed with mature judgment in the service of either acting as a directive facilitator or as a true supporting actor who, for the duration of the enactment, strives to become what is most needed by the protagonist or main player.

Children at play cannot achieve this level of focus. They unconsciously compete even as they cooperate. The understanding that people will take turns in the various roles demands a capacity for mature time-binding and a temporary relinquishment of egocentricity. In this sense, the Art of Play offers adults an opportunity to enjoy many of the benefits of child-like play without some of the disadvantages of the subtle intrusion of competing desires.

After the group leader explains and demonstrates the Art of Play, people take to it relatively easily. The skills involved can be developed, so the more one enjoys using the method, the more one practices. The more skilled the participants become, the richer will be the ensuing enactment. Generally, each enactment requires about five to ten minutes. There are skill building and imagination-enhancing opportunities in being any of the three role positions, so it is best to allot enough time—at least 45 minutes for a small group, so that each member of a small group can experience the process from every position. Learning how to direct, facilitate, and draw out could be as much fun as being a main player who learns how to be led into his or her imagination.

The essential process involves a warming-up of the group, a moving into the beginning of the enactment in the small group, a further warming up of the main character, and then having that person play through the role, discovering its intrinsic potential for humor, poignant depth, and interesting variation. In general, there isn't much sharing or processing until after all the group participants have done their own enactments. (Remember, this isn't supposed to be therapy.)

The Warm-Up

It's best if a somewhat experienced person leads the group so as to be able to explain the techniques and engage in some activities that promote a sense of trust and playfulness. A variety of warm-up techniques may be used, such as those mentioned in the many different books in Appendix B at the end of this book. The choice of warm-up depends on the size and nature of the group, the past experience of the group members with drama or theatre games, and so forth. Some groups have already been exposed to improvisation, but for many, the process is brand new. This latter group needs a more gentle and prolonged warming-up as they have layers of inhibition about "showing off," "getting attention," "making a fool of themselves," and other cultural residues that accompany the general social role of behaving as if "grown up."

We often begin the overall process by singing some simple songs together. We use song sheets so that folks don't have to remember the words. The songs are fairly familiar, often popular tunes from Broadway musical shows. Depending on time, we might also introduce a simple dyadic exercise, "draw-a-mandala."

Two people draw together, beginning with one making a circle on a piece of paper with a crayon, the other, using another crayon, adds a design element. They then take turns adding elaborations until it becomes an interesting little picture. The technique shows what simple improvisation can do in the realm of art.

Next we warm people up to the activity of role taking with an exercise called "the talk show host game." Working in pairs, the group members interview each other. One person plays the role of a television talk show host whose job it is to draw out the guest while the other person plays a surprise character. The roles chosen might draw from a variety of categories:

- someone with an unusual occupation

- a person from history—either a famous one, or one who lived out a recognizable role

  (This could also be a person participating in current events, or someone in the future)

- a mythical figure, or someone from the comics, literature, television, or other fictional source

- an animal (and beings that can not in ordinary reality speak English or even speak at all can, in pretend play, speak clearly and express themselves articulately, and often with great insight)

- a plant, something in nature, an inanimate object, even a spirit of some abstract principle

- a family member (but not of the player's actual real life family)

People need not play characters of their own actual age or gender—they can easily be the opposite gender and a very different age. The interviews go on for about five minutes. The group leader calls "one minute to commercial break," then a minute later, winds up the exercise. "De-role and change parts." The one who had previously been the interviewer now becomes the guest, allowing a character to come through his or her imagination. The previous guest now becomes the talk show host and begins to interview and draw out the new guest. After another five to seven minutes, the group leader winds up the exercise and invites everyone to share who they were. "A very clumsy juggler." "A very, very stingy millionaire." "An angel trying to help a nerd," and so forth. The characters mentioned are often amusing in themselves and stimulate others to imagine variations of their own. The more people say who their imagined roles were, the more they warm the others up to the essential fun of imaginative play.

(The talk show host game is further described on my website: <www.blatner. com/adam/pdntbk/talksho.htm>, noted also as a good exercise for developing a basic skill in spontaneity development and learning how to be empathic.)

We then break up into small groups to do the Art of Play method. One person at a time becomes the main player and his or her role or character is helped by one in the small group playing the director to expand that role into a scene and from that, making it a small story. The others in the small group play supporting parts. After about 5–10 minutes, the director helps draw the scene to a close, they de-role, and begin again. Now another person in the group becomes the main player, another person the director, and the remaining others the supporting players. Adults can take turns this way better than children can!

The director's artistic challenge is to help the main character discover and experience a culminating event for his or her role. The director should get the players up and moving, redirect tendencies to talk *about* the scene to action and dialogue *in* the scene—"Don't tell us, show us!"—, keep the improvisation unfolding, and, within the time given, bring it to a close. group members can then finish, de-role, and change parts. No analysis is needed, and generally, no processing. Occasionally, near the end of the session, some people feel they want to talk about ideas or insights they've picked up in the process.

The basic skills involved in The Art of Play are also the most basic theatre arts skills, and these are mainly learned by doing—more like learning to swim than learning by memorizing from a book. There's a knack to it that develops with practice, so the more one uses this method, the better one becomes. (This is true for most spontaneity-training exercises, theatre games, improv methods, and so forth.)

Accessing a Character

The imagination is rich. We all have thousands of potentially available roles derived from all of the images of our culture. These role elements can be mixed up in funny and often incongruent ways. We should recognize that the imagination is very subtly available as a fountain of these roles as ideas. This dynamic is more obvious in the dramas of our night dreams, but if we were to quiet our business-like focusing mind, these more playful possibilities can emerge while awake, also.

After breaking up into the small groups, the group leader has everyone become quiet to "get in touch with their character."

"Imagine you have a kind of dark room or empty dark stage, and slowly bring the light up. Just see who is sitting or standing there. Allow it to surprise you. *Become whatever it is.*"

Some folks will get their ideas immediately even before the group leader suggests these processes of natural unfolding of the creative subconscious mind. Others will get their character only later, after seeing who else in their group has come up with someone. Everyone proceeds at their own pace. The more you do the process, the more open is the flow of images. The process is spontaneous and informal. Sometimes the director needs to remind people, "The character you become need have nothing whatever to do with your actual life." This is to remind people that this is a recreational activity for the imagination, not therapy.

People are encouraged to imagine themselves more vividly in role. "What shape do you have? What kind of garment are you wearing? What object might you be holding? It might be a staff, a pipe, a harp, something else, or nothing." Then, to move the character toward a story, "What or who else is in the scene?" As the main players warm up to their characters, the director assigns supporting roles to the others in the group. The characters may similarly be either animate or inanimate, such as a chair, the wind, a clock, or the surrounding water.

Further Techniques

Part of the novelty of this approach is that it can be extended and deepened using the general range of techniques used in psychodrama, as described in Chapter 15.

Replay: A main character (i.e., protagonist) is free to say, "I want to do this over," just to feel the enjoyment of the activity, or to vary the enactment in some way—a little or a lot. Some people might suggest a replay of a movement of scene element to deepen the main player's warm-up. For example, if a character would, in the course of a given scene, be expected to yell wholeheartedly, many people have not brought their voice skills up to a degree that over-rides their habits of inhibition and soft-spoken-ness. It's liberating to be coached and encouraged by the group to find their voice and learn to express a yelp, roar, cry of anguish, shriek of fear, and other full-throated expostulations.

Role Reversal: This technique is used in two ways: First, a character may take the part of the co-character for short time just to illustrate to the person playing that supporting role how to behave. This generally involves not only what the other character says or does, but also how that role is performed, with what degree of vigor, emotionality, pace, or other variables. The other way role reversal is used is to offer the main character an opportunity to also experience the role of the other person or being in the scene either for understanding or just for a more complete satisfaction of the event. Children do this intuitively. You might have heard kids playing house and saying, "Now you be the mommy and I'll be the baby." In the Art of Play, grown-ups can also transcend the belief that just because they start a scene in one role, they are supposed to finish it that way, also.

Asides: This is the theatrical equivalent of the "voice over." The character turns his head to an imagined audience outside the circle of enactment and shares thoughts or side comments that the others in role in the scene pretend not to hear. Using this device, role playing can be deepened a level, including expressing mixed feelings, secrets, manipulations, and so forth.

Cut or *Freeze*. Just as movie directors can suddenly interrupt the play of a scene, so can the players. Derived from the movies about making movies in the 1940s, "cut" stops the action and prepares for a replay. "Freeze" in this era of video and DVD might also be called "pause." In the interim, some change, or comment is made, but then, when "action" is called, everyone continues as if nothing happened. Little kids call "time out" or, in my neighborhood, "Kings X." The point here is also that the enactment need not be smooth, polished, and finished. There can be a kind of rehearsal, a groping, as the main player is helped to find what responses, counter-actions, shift in situation, might best bring forth the deeper sense and purpose of the character being played.

Other psychodramatic and sociodramatic techniques are noted in Chapters 2 (Bibliodrama), 15 (Psychodrama), and elsewehere. Such techniques can be adapted for use in this recreational context, also.

Integrating Other Dimensions

In addition to drama, some elements from art, poetry, singing, making music, drumming, dance and movement, using props like hats, puppets, masks, and various costuming devices, all can add depth to the overall process. As mentioned in the description of the warm-up above, we also use singing and improvisational drawing as aids.

Sometimes we warm up a group that is somewhat wary about this procedure just by talking about toys we loved as kids, or the kind of clubhouse, fort, or other protected special place we might have enjoyed alone or with others. There seems to be a real hunger for and delight in reclaiming these dimensions of imaginativeness.

Applications

The Art of Play method may be integrated as a warm-up or "cool-down" in workshops that also use other approaches mentioned in this book. It is a good technique for helping actors learn to improvise. Further, it can help them develop the characters they are to play by exploring aspects of those roles that may not be overtly expressed in the script. Many drama therapists use this method as a part of their training, as do some people involved in drama in education. It's a gentle introduction into some sociodrama or role playing, and may be used also as a kind of closure: The larger group breaks into groups of three to five, and they then take turns enacting a scene that would be the most satisfying, wonderful event, something imagined as happening five to ten years in the future. This event need not be something that has any real probability of happening. It might or might not. The point is to exercise the faculty of envisioning positive future events by offering an opportunity to enact them with the help of a few others.

Summary

Many more techniques and methodological subtleties can be elaborated that can deepen and extend the play. Like any good game, the more it's played, the wider the scope and more complex becomes the technique.

There are interesting benefits to this process, if one wants to utilize the component skills. In everyday life, many of these techniques are applicable. The authors in their own life at home occasionally weave in a variety of imagined "alter ego" roles. We may act like parent and child, commander and recruit, two kids playing, or letting our "shadow" complexes be expressed by acting like monsters or villains or pouty babies. The capacity for role flexibility increases, and we learn the phrases that communicate explicitly that we're playing and how we are shifting roles.

Another purpose for this method is that it offers "role relief." This concept recognizes that people can get subtly fatigued or bored or restless in playing the same outward roles in life, such as always being the considerate parent, the service-oriented salesperson, the obedient student. Why wait for Halloween or Mardi Gras to cut loose and let the other inner roles out, giving vent to the opposite qualities? We all need a general balancing process, relief from playing one role all the time. (See the webpage supplement: <www.interactiveimprov. com/morewecanbe.html>)

Our vision is that if more settings would include the Art of Play as a lubricating process, it could help retreats, workshops, and programs lighten up a bit. It is a method that brings many of the benefits of creative drama to adults, integrating sociodramatic methods so that grown-ups can reclaim their natural heritage of imagination and spontaneity.

References

Further quotes, observations, and references may be noted on the webpage supplement:<www.interactiveimprov.com/artplaywb.html>

Blatner, Adam & Blatner, Allee. (1991). Imaginative interviews: a psychodramatic warm-up for developing role playing skills. *Journal of Group Psychotherapy, Psychodrama & Sociometry (JGPPS)*, 44(3), 115–120, Fall, 1991. Available on website: <www.blatner.com/adam/pdntbk/talksho.htm>

Blatner, Adam & Blatner, Allee. (1997). *The Art of Play: Helping adults reclaim imagination and spontaneity*. (2nd ed.). New York: Brunner-Routledge. This book has extensive further references. (It is now available from Amazon. com or directly from author through <www.blatner.com/adam/This book was first published privately in 1985 in a spiral-bound edition, then by Human Sciences Press in 1987. The present edition has been further updated.)

Blatner, A. (2002a). Psychodrama. In C. E. Schaefer (Ed.), *Play therapy with adults*. Hoboken, NJ: John Wiley & Sons.

Blatner, A. (2003).Singing for the Fun of It. On website: <www.blatner.com/adam/level2/sing4fun.htm>

Noxon, Christopher. (2006). *Rejuvenile: Kickball, cartoons, cupcakes, and the reinvention of the American grownup*. New York: Crown/Random House.

Pink, Daniel. (2006). *A whole new mind: Why right-brainers will rule the future*. New York: Riverhead.

Chapter 27

THEATRESPORTS AND COMPETITIVE DRAMATIC IMPROVISATION

David L. Young

Both improvisational drama and improvisational comedy have become recognized forms of theatre since the 1960s. There are hundreds of professional and amateur "improv" theatre performing groups who perform in church basements and comedy clubs across North America. More recently, Drew Carey's television series, *Whose Line Is It, Anyway?*, has brought this approach into prime time television. In schools and college classes, since the 1970s, dramatic improvisation has evolved from being used merely as warm-ups to acting training to an activity that beginners and intermediate players can enjoy as if it were a competitive game. Such programs have been established in parts of Canada and the United States, sometimes within academic programs, and sometimes as an extramural activity.

Now, drama teachers and theatre artists are teaching improvisation in schools and communities, with some involved in informal networks and others part of the actual school curriculum in a number of states. In the early 1980s, regional and national competitions began. Today there are hundreds of teams and tens of thousands of people involved, mainly in Canada, the United States, and also in a number of other countries. A fair number of drama teachers are being supported by their schools not so much for the scripted, rehearsed productions that dominated theatre for most of the last century, but for their involvement in this other type of competition.

History

Improvisational drama was an extension of story telling and enacting and is part of many tribal cultures. As writing entered civilization, the reading and then memorization of lines began, but many theatrical forms continued to include varying degrees of improvisation—including Shakespeare's productions (Hartnoll, 1968)! The renaissance commedia dell'arte also was mainly improvised. In the early twentieth century, most theatre was scripted, but gradually, improvisation has returned, with roots in creative drama and the theatre games of Spolin, and then improvisational comedy emerging as an entertainment format through the Second City troupe in Chicago and others. Meanwhile, improvisation had been making progress as a form of drama, as discussed in the chapters on drama in education. As for competitive improvisation, two pioneers deserve to be noted: David Shepherd—who wrote the foreword to this present anthology—, and Keith Johnstone.

David Shepherd, along with Viola Spolin's son, Paul Sills, was a co-founder of the first improvisational theatre group in America. In the early 1950s, he founded Compass Theatre, in Chicago. This led to related troupes, most notably Second City—also in Chicago—, and other Compass theatre groups in various cities. A number of celebrities today got their start in those groups, such as Alan Alda, Edward Asner, Mike Nichols, and Elaine May.

In 1972, in New York City, Shepherd thought of the idea of competitive team-based improvisational theatre. While viewing a televised football game, he became convinced that too many people had become "watchers" and not "players." In 1974, Shepherd created the prototype competitive format called the Improv Olympics, which incorporated a mixture of professional actors and high school students to produce a high-energy improvisational festival. A couple of graduating high school students who had been participants took this format to the Ottawa-Carlton School District and began an Improv Olympics solely for the schools within their district (Denny, 1996). Because of this, David Shepherd has been called "the architect of the Canadian Improv Games." (Since the 1990s, ImprovOlympics has evolved into "I.O." and has many programs, mainly involving people who mix acting and comedy).

The other major figure in the history of improv was Keith Johnstone. He began as an actor, and in the 1960s at London's Royal Court Theatre, he created an improvisational company called The Theatre Machine. Johnstone was also inspired by the antics of professional wrestling which he viewed as "working-class theatre," and came up with the idea of replacing the wrestlers with improvisers. By the mid-1970s, Johnstone had joined the faculty of the University of Calgary (Canada), where he had his students develop a competitive improv program. They played for audience reaction as much as they competed for a score from selected audience judges. Scores were based on the judges' responses to the humour and inherent risks of the scenes played out before them. Using both students and alumni from the University of Calgary as his actors, Johnstone used a game called "No Blocking" and had the actors literally compete for time on stage.

The actors were not the only raucous participants in the early days of TheatreSports, as the audience was incorporated into the games not only as the providers of suggestions, but also to throw pies filled with whipped cream at the losing actors and their team. Johnstone's intention was that the competition would be just for fun (Foreman & Martini, 1995). This type of off-the-wall entertainment was an immediate success, and with success came the evolution of increased organization, newly developed games, and a more formalized format utilizing more recognizable theatre structures like props, costumes, sound and lighting effects, and a master of ceremonies to facilitate the show. He began the Loose Moose Theatre Company, around that time, and from this, "TheatreSports" had its inaugural public performance at the Pumphouse Theatre in Calgary, Alberta, Canada (Johnstone, 1978). (Further details and related information is available on the webpage supplement to this chapter.)

While most high school drama programs and teachers continue to be recognized only if they win competitions of full scripted plays, increasingly there are also inter-scholastic competitions being held for non-scripted theatre arts activities. Now teachers are being validated if they can develop and enter an improv team into such competitions. Nevertheless, leaders in TheatreSports (abbreviated in this chapter as TS) have encouraged students to play and not worry too much whether they win or not. In some schools, TS team members have higher status and draw more kids into drama programs.

Starting in the 1960s, a measure of improvisation has become an increasingly regular part of drama classes in North America, although it still isn't required. Improvisation is built in to the drama guidelines more in the school districts of Canada, the United Kingdom, Australia and New Zealand. Beginning the later 1970s, improvisational drama has become more of a competitive sport, enjoyed by teenagers and adults in Canada, the United States, and elsewhere. Teams have been sponsored by schools and student organizations.

Improv before the 1970s was mainly a form of comedy, popularized in clubs such as Second City, but then also became a trend within the field of creative drama education, involving activities such as Viola Spolin's theatre games. These warm-up activities were used for acting students in secondary schools and colleges in developing skills that were to be channeled into traditional modes of scripted and rehearsed plays. The spontaneity exercises later transformed into a competitive activity in itself. Groups may develop and be trained in their capacity to improvise well at the beginning, intermediate, or advanced levels. This organization's oath affirms the ideal of "loving competition between teams of students trained to perform spontaneous, improvised scenes" (Denny, 1996).

By the early 1980s, other groups began to form. Now there are professional TheatreSports and improvisational theatre companies performing and competing within this structure of spontaneous theatre to audiences all over the world. There are different classes, as in a variety of other competitions, such as beginners, amateurs, professionals. University, colleges, and local community groups have begun to include improvisational theatre as an active entry-level participatory way of inviting students and new actors into the theatre community.

For students who are less familiar with acting or for that matter who are daunted at the prospect of memorizing scripted scenes, competitive improvisation can be introduced in a fairly gentle way, thus introducing them to some semblance of theatre tradition.

About the Programs

TheatreSports is a general category of improvisational drama that includes a number of sub-organizations. (This paper will describe activities that are part of the Canadian Improv Games). TS encourages students to play, be creative, explore situations, take on different roles, and accept risks. This kind of drama is a potent and integral part of a modern and progressive curriculum, which is an exciting format for young people because it accurately represents the quick shifting, spontaneous momentum of their youth. TS has a fast-paced quality that resonates with the lifestyle quality of young people involved with modern media and technology. Improv's quick scenic mode of delivery, using audience suggestions with scenes lasting little longer than a few minutes, is in many ways a more readily accessible theatrical medium for young people than straight scripted theatre.

Competitive improvisation and TS is a theatrical form of "channel surfing," because for young people, the need to be constantly stimulated is paramount. Improv offers a parallel type of stimulation because when they are engaged in TS activities it provides them with stimulation both as actor/participants within the improvisation, and as viewer/audience members reacting to and giving suggestions to the scene work on stage. Improvised games are so popular because there are scenes and characters that are typically universally understood, and are never overly complex, as would occur if an actor were representing a real person from straight, scripted theatre. Although straight scripted theatre is called 'a play,' one might question whether the rigorous activities of memorizing have much playfulness involved. Improvisation can be a much more liberating form of artistic expression for young people, as they get to use their own words, and characters (mostly themselves) bouncing in and out of actual 'games' (Stanislavski, 1948, 1949; Spolin, 1963; Hagen, 1973; Johnstone, 1979). (Moreno—mentioned in Chapter 15 on psychodrama—around 1921 also wrote about the need for spontaneity to re-invigorate the theatre arts.)

The playing of games has a universal appeal and typically a well understood structure of conduct; it doesn't take much work to convince a group of 13 year olds in a grade eight drama class or a university or college class of adults to engage in the playing of improvisational activities. Also, there are now hundreds of professional and amateur improve theatre performing groups who present their improvisational work from church basements to comedy clubs across North America. The continuing popularization of improv theatre has made both young and old students, ranging in skill from novice to expert, more aware and obviously more willing to take the risks to explore improvisational drama in a classroom or workshop setting.

Improvisation and the games that accompany this format of drama is typically the realm of the high school and the college/university drama or theatre program, because it has the potential to be a strong entry point into a community of learners through trust and playful engagement. Where Viola Spolin's theatre games are more centrally focused on expanding the realm of rehearsal and character development for actors, Johnstone's TheatreSports games and many of the offshoots have developed into the staple activities of the drama classroom.

There are some pitfalls: The leader of a group needs to learn to deal with the psychological problems associated with competition. Some students can begin to ignore the artistic intent of a dramatic scene or production, and focus solely on finding faults. I have witnessed this kind of behavior first hand at district drama festivals. When students from other schools make mistakes on stage, a buzz will go up in the audience amongst the competing students from the other schools, as they consider the detrimental effects this will have on the adjudication. I have seen students fight, cry, and throw temper tantrums while playing improvisational games and TheatreSports competitively, to the point where friendships are placed in jeopardy, and student learning suffers. A wise teacher can modify such tendencies.

A significant advantage of a TheatreSports-like program is that it is more accessible: Many students are not willing or able to memorize scripted scenes, so competitive improvisation can be a way to include and introduce students to the richness of theatre arts. The structure of many of the games makes sense, and offers basic technical strategies that can be mastered and implemented in future theatrical projects.

The Canadian Improv Games

These programs, struggling with school and local politics, gradually grew from a regional festival to a national tournament, and in 1990 organized as the Canadian Improv Games at a national tournament (Denny, 1996). They incorporated the structured nature of the original Improv Olympics and the unstructured nature of TheatreSports and merged them to create a simple set of five improvisational "events" for each team to work with:

(1) Story—demonstrate its ability to show, tell, or recreate a story

(2) Character—portray a character or characters

(3) Style—recreate a style or genre of media, film, or television

(4) Theme—explore a specific theme which is provided for by the Referee/ Facilitator

(5) Life—improvise a scene in a sincere and honest manner, using a life-related scenario that is approved by the Referee/Facilitator (Cook & Young, 1998).

Consider that, in a sense, even scripted and rehearsed, highly produced theatre only exists in an evanescent moment in time; it is thus not necessarily a more valuable or important form of art than the spontaneous creations of the improviser. Admittedly, Keith Johnstone's touring company, The Theatre Machine, was, in his words, a "throw-away form; it is disposable theatre: ideas and memories get re-cycled and the best is really best because it comes out of the moment." However, this description of art as "disposable" does not diminish its value or make it less worthwhile, but rather is a conscious reconciliation and appreciation as to the ephemeral nature of improvisation and its relationship between the improvisers and the audience (Frost & Yarrow, 1990). (Indeed, the emerging genre of performance art reflects this perspective.)

One of the pitfalls in competitive improvisation is that some drama teachers fill their classes with nothing but a various theatre games and avoid the challenges of really organizing their lessons. This gives drama a bad name, cheapens it, aids in drama becoming thought of as a mere frill. Or these classes become the "dumping" ground for the hard-to-work-with youngsters. (Interestingly, some of those problem kids "catch fire" in drama and do quite well.) When done well, though, Johnstone's work is an important a contribution to both the theatre and drama education.

One of the fundamentals is to move the scene forward by accepting the offers and ideas of the other people on stage (or for that matter the audience). Stopping a scene from progressing is called 'blocking', and takes all the energy out of improvisation, and therefore is an attribute that is quickly done away with. Similarly, we do away with all sexism, racism, swearing, and homophobic content when we work on any improv scene; students and their teams are penalized (by deducting points or by losing their stage time) if they indulge in any of these areas. I might add that this is a departure from how I teach the majority of my drama and acting curriculum, where I try to allow the students to self-censor their work without penalty.

Being Just a Kid Again

Another exercise for role taking and role shifting involves the students pretending they are five years old, and then at a moment's notice, they have to be able to pretend that they are eighty years old. It is exciting to see what kind of little bits come out, how many students really find themselves in role play pretending to be a five year old, and what kind of things they draw on to create that character. They play with toys, they have little childish fights, they create puerile male/female relationships, but the authenticity is striking The reality is that every single one of these kids has actually lived through and experienced the reality of being five, so they have an unbelievable ability to pull this type of character together.

When they are asked to play eighty year olds, you end up with a very interesting interpretation. You go from the authenticity of being five, to the fantasy world of being eighty, because eighty is so far beyond their realm of experience and expertise. They have to make up and use their imagination concerning what it is like to be eighty. Essentially the students have to go from the physicality of being five (which they all have experienced first hand) to the physicality of being an old person. How do old people move? How does an old person breathe? How slow does an eighty year old person walk or talk? It was notable how many of the kids reverted back to stereotype mimicry, creating images and ideas from what they have sponged from the media. When asked about the older people that they experienced in their own lives, none of them had grandparents or people that they knew who were that old. This experience provides an excellent example of the dichotomy between mimicry and authenticity in a junior Drama students use of role play.

The Grade Ten's have been working on something called "Cross Hidden Objectives," where I provide the students with a relationship, a scenario, and give each character in the scenario a contrary objective. An example might be a mother and a daughter relationship, where the mother wants the daughter to go to college because she has some money put aside for her, but the daughter wants to drop out of high school to join a rock band. Each one approaches the other with their primary objectives and attempts to get the other one to validate or agree with it.

Many times, I give the characters a stock relationship, like mother/daughter, sister/brother, best friends. Many times the reactions to these scenarios are quite exciting, and you get a lot of the reactions that they themselves would possibly give in these situations, or that they might have heard from siblings or their own parents. The students really let loose during this project, and you can see some real opening up when the students get involved within the role of the objective. In many cases, like in real life, the objectives are never fulfilled to their fullest because in many cases, like in real life, people have to find compromises, and sometimes you actually see that occur in the scene, and those are quite unique moments.

The Grade Eleven and Twelve's are creating an assignment where they create the opposite of their own character. So they create a character that has all the attributes that they feel is their distinct opposite. This has appeal, because they're at the stage of wondering what they are going to do with their lives. This exercise tends to evoke a lot of intellectualized discussions, so the teacher needs to be nimble in turning these into something more sociodramatic. Exposing their imagined opposite qualities is quite revealing. So instead of saying be yourself in this particular scene, being your opposite provides the perfect opportunity to camouflage being yourself. Then the students expose awful relationships with their parents because their opposite character in the scene talks about how much they 'love and respect their parents'. Characters who are positive creative people become very unconfident, very scared, shy people. It is quite an insightful project for the student's to create and reflect on.

"Our Own Little World"

A senior high school student wrote in a term paper, "Drama has given me lots of confidence. Our drama room is our own little world, where we don't have to impress anybody. And I always cherished that, because as soon as you leave the room, you're back in the 'rat race' of comparing, ridiculing, and status."

It is the job of the Drama educator to make sure that our students learn by doing, that no matter what the issues of the day are, we can be assured that our students gain a depth and breadth of knowledge and experience through the collective experience. The Drama classroom is a special and unique place which should provide a climate that welcomes exploration and risk-taking, where the Drama student can creatively solve any problem, where there is no right or wrong, just a multitude of choices. Choices which enable that student to journey into a world of learning and exploration. The Drama student can live a thousand different lives and be exposed to an inordinate number of possibilities; simultaneously that same student can be revealing the most precious and personal moments of inner truth.

In the spring, I spend a good portion of time working on improvisation, TheatreSports, and The Canadian Improv Games, which culminates in a publicly performed tournament. On the last day before Spring Break, we have the entire day dedicated to improvisation, TheatreSports, and The Canadian Improv Games, and students from all over the school come down to watch twelve to fifteen teams of up to eight Drama students perform against each other in the 'dramnasium'. Throughout the day, we will have up to 600 people viewing our tournament. Again, this is one of the best days of the year to 'sell' the Drama program to basically half of our student population, not to mention the staff members who also come to watch. The performances during the day are free admission (as are all in-school activities), and it all culminates with a special evening performance for the championship trophy called "The Golden Horn." For the evening performance we charge admission, and the evening consists of the student championship round which is judged by professional actors, comedians and improvisers, who also perform later in the evening.

In the right doses for the kids who want to do it, the risk taking, public performance, and competitiveness of these activities seems to be invigorating. They work in the classroom together, anticipating the times when they will be in front of peers, friends and family. Actual performance raises the stakes and increases the teenagers' focus.

I teach beginning TheatreSports to young adolescents, and they have an internal league that is highly competitive. Still, it is a relatively safe public forum for immediate evaluation. In contrast to many student projects, in which the grade comes later, in Improv work the feedback comes immediately, by the teacher/judge, which makes the learning address the "teachable moment."

Conclusion

It doesn't take more than a simple web search now to find thousands of links to improve comedy being performed, "workshopped," and experienced regionally throughout North America, Europe, and Australia. One of the greatest resources is Johnstone's own improv summer institute that takes place yearly in Banff, Alberta—a picturesque town in the Rocky Mountains a few hours drive from Calgary, Alberta, for participants from all over the world. Dozens of similar institutes and workshop experiences are offered throughout the Pacific Northwest in both Canada and the United States (see references).

References

See webpage supplements to this chapter for more:

- history and references: <www.interactiveimprov.com/tspwb1hist.html>
- examples of techniques <www.interactiveimprov.com/tspwb2methods. html>
- about the underlying theory <www.interactiveimprov.com/tspwb3theory. html>

Also, further references both in Appendix B on warm-ups and: the supplement to Appendix B: <www.interactiveimprov.com/apxbwarmups.html>

References to Spolin, Johnstone, Stanislavski, are cited sufficiently often elsewhere in the book so as to merit being in the general bibliography, Appendix A, at the end of this book.

Cook, A. and Young, D. (1998). *The Western Canadian Improv Games information guide*. Vancouver: The Western Canadian Games British Columbia Society.

Denny P. (1996). "Our Story—The History of the Canadian Improv Games" and "Quotes FromTeachers and Students" Available: <www.improv.ca>

Foreman, K. & Martini, C. (1995). *Something like a drug—An Unauthorized Oral History of TheatreSports*. Red Deer, Alberta: Red Deer College Press.

Frost, A., & Yarrow, R. (1990). *Improvisation in drama*. London: MacMillan Education.

Hagen, U. (1973) *Respect for acting*. New York: Macmillian Publishing Co., Inc.

Hartnoll, P. (1968). *The theatre: A concise history*. London: Thames & Hudson.

Johnstone, Keith. (1994). *Theatresports for teachers: A resource tool for teaching improvisation and Theatresports*. Calgary, Alberta, Canada: Loose Moose Theatre Co.

Chapter 28

INTERACTIVE MYSTERY THEATRE

Anne M. Curtis & Gordon Hensley

Actors improvise and interact with people for entertainment in the genre known as "murder mystery theatre" and some variant forms. These events are organized so that a troupe of actors follow a loose plot, usually about a murder, that happens in the course of a restaurant meal. Audience members participate by interacting with the actors throughout improvised segments of the show including "interrogation," where guests question "suspects" and participate in solving the "who-done-it."

This form of entertainment emerged in two phases: First, in the 1920s, dinner theatres began with the audience eating dinner while watching a show on stage. Then, in the mid-1950s in London, a mystery play was staged: Agatha Christie's *The Mousetrap*. This play was traditional theatre, with a "fourth wall," (also known as the "proscenium arch") creating an imaginary barrier between audience and actors. In the 1960s, mystery and dinner theatre combined, and in the 1970s, interactivity, humor and improvisation were added. Creative experiments led to the variety of interactive mystery forms available to audiences today, giving them an opportunity to imagine that they are guests at an event where a crime occurs. Guests are drawn into the scene by the players and encouraged to ask questions, observe clues or engage in a specific action.

Interactive mystery events can be divided into three categories: (a) actor-staged; (b) fully participatory; and (c) game style. This chapter will describe all three categories, beginning with the first category, actor-staged shows.

Actor-Staged Programs

The actor-staged murder mystery is the oldest and most commonly known form. Staged usually as a dinner theatre, it combines improvisation and audience participation with a comedic scripted show that leads to a "murder." The audience members then question the "suspects" in an interactive format led by a detective. This interaction is the trademark of the form, giving audience members an opportunity to enjoy being a part of the dramatic action. This participatory style develops a place for audience and actor to merge. This merger creates a playful fictional social environment perfect for cocktails or dinner.

For example, at Sleuths Mystery Dinner Show, in Orlando, Florida, audience members are greeted by characters as though they are fellow guests at an event. Themes include a wedding, reunion, movie premiere, audition and a birthday party. Sets and costumes are appropriate for the occasion. From the moment the audience members enter the facility, the actor is performing, improvising dialogue in character while greeting, mingling and seating the guests at round dinner tables. A forty-minute, tightly scripted "whodunit" is presented on stage, incorporating comedic moments of improvisation involving the audience. After a dramatic murder and dinner service, during which each table decides on questions for the suspects, a detective conducts an interrogation with the help of spokespersons from each table. This segment relies completely on the actors' comedic improvisational skills as they answer the questions and interact with fellow actors and the audience. After dessert the guests individually solve the crime and successful sleuths receive a prize. The entire evening lasts about two-and-one-half hours.

Sleuths' recipe for a successful interactive group experience includes much humor that involves the audience. Professional, well-rehearsed actors assign several roles to the more outgoing attendees. The latter then become minor players in a carefully plotted mystery. With no 'fourth wall' inhibiting participation, every audience member becomes a part of the event as well. This formula has worked well in immersing all who attend in a live theatre experience with a twist (Redmond, 2005).

One of the reasons this form of entertainment is so enjoyable is because it creates a relaxed environment that gives attendees the opportunity to play, to enter a fictional world and forget their own reality for a while. This can often have very positive effects on audience members. One man shared that he had been unable to communicate with his son since a divorce. Discussing clues and coming up with questions over dinner broke the ice and became the catalyst for a new, closer relationship. In another example, a group of severely non-communicative children from a mental health facility entered the theatre and cringed when the actors first spoke to them. As the show progressed they became enthralled by the mystery and playful humor of the characters. At interrogation they completely surprised their counselors by excitedly asking questions! As they left for the bus, these children were still communicating and expanding on the theme! Family groups consisting of several generations enjoy interactive mysteries because it frees them from their normal dialogue patterns (such as "Aunt Edna's latest operation") and gives them the opportunity to discuss clues and interact in a new, creative way.

Mystery dinner shows thrive when they present several different shows so that audiences will return. Some people come annually to celebrate a special milestone such as a wedding anniversary or recovery from a serious illness. Audiences can enjoy interactive mystery shows in many venues beyond the dinner theatre setting. Productions are found at resorts, bed-and-breakfast inns, swimming pools, on train rides or cruise ships. The actors stay in character, interacting with the audience throughout the resort weekend or journey. For example, *The Murder Mystery American Orient Express Train* of Portland, Oregon, supplements its scenic views with an interactive theatre experience. Sixteen passenger cars travel on eight separate itineraries throughout the year, offering transcontinental murder in several states and seasons. Hermetically sealed in the cars, the cast of the mystery interact with guests, a crime is committed, and as the scenic journey continues, clues unfold and the murderer is found. *Seminole Gulf Railway* in Fort Myers, Florida offers a single evening ride on their murder mystery *Dinner Train Theatre*.

Some of shows have historical themes and encourage actors and audience to dress in the style of that historical time-period. Others offer themed mysteries to corporations as team-building events. Guests are assigned roles, divided into "super sleuth teams" and given time frames for finding clues or performing an activity such as photographing something suspicious. The "super sleuth teams" then elect a team captain and work together to guess "whodunit" (Austin & Austin, 2006).

Full Participation Format

Another variation is the fully participatory interactive theatre format, in which there is no pre-determined murder or set solution to the mystery. The host may work from a "playbook," generating a moderate degree of structure. Playbooks are available from sources such as *Palladian Interactive Theatre* (Andersen, 2006).

Such programs are designed for from 20–75 people, and any participant may live or die. No drama ever ends the same twice because the audience members play all the parts, improvise their lines, and sometimes "kill" each other while attempting to achieve the goals outlined in their Playbooks. Members of the audience receive instructional materials concerning background preparation, character descriptions, historical framework and a slang dictionary for the period. Much of the fun is in planning and plotting in the days ahead of the event. There can be up to ten plots, with appropriate props, unfolding simultaneously. Each participant may be involved in one or more of these plots taking place in various rooms in the hosting venue. Roles are arranged in order of difficulty, with simple ones for beginners and challenging parts for die-hard mystery buffs. At the end of the event, a cast party is held in which the Master of Ceremonies (MC) explains all the plots, the participants tell what they were up to, and everyone gets to find out what was really going on. Prizes are awarded for best costume and favorite character.

An experienced, professional MC, with the assistance of one or two Referees, oversees the 20–75 participants. The MC helps the guests adapt to any problems that may arise during the development of the improvised scenes. One participant recalls: "I was in a participatory mystery over a weekend at an old inn. I had notes on my character and instructions such as, '*9:30 pm: Interact in the bar with guests then stage an argument with Bob concerning the money he owes you.*' However, some guests had not followed the directions and had been rushing through their scenes, ending up far ahead of schedule. Just before entering the hotel bar to do the scene, I discovered *Bob* was already dead! So I pretended to be 'psychic' and created a scene with the MC playing *Bob's spirit from beyond.* The show must go on!"

These entertaining interactive events are not exclusively for mysteries, some include romance, history, comedy, and drama. Customized scripts may be adapted to the venue's history. Interactive drama events vary the denouements (the endings), ensuring some repeat business from attendees who want to try playing a different character or using an alternate strategy for playing the same character. This format differs from the actor-staged dinner show type in that all attendees are fully immersed in the action. Actor-stage dinner shows offer varying levels of involvement, from audience members who take on a role in the scene to people who prefer to sit and watch.

Enacting Games

Game-style murder mysteries can be purchased as boxed sets or obtained as information packets from web sites. Games include complete instructions on how to host this activity, including menus, ways to create the setting, and ways to keep the mystery unfolding. Guests receive invitations before the party assigning roles and suggesting costumes. The host plants clues such as props, game-cards, or audio-tapes with additional information. Guests step out of their ordinary lives, into someone else's shoes, role-playing under the guidance of the host. The game-style murder format is especially suited for home parties or modest bed-and-breakfast facilities with smaller audiences. This format is essentially a live-action equivalent of a board game like "Clue."

These games can make a successful social event for groups of family or friends. Students interested in interactive mystery theatre could gain experience by hosting these improvisational games. It is interesting to see non-actors enjoying the opportunity to escape into a fictional role. Recently an economist was preparing for a mystery at a neighbor's party. He spent an entire week researching W.C. Fields, planning the costume and practicing classic quotations in that character's unique voice for all who were willing to listen, including his broker!

Logistics

Planning and implementing a murder mystery is an extensive process. In addition to the regular tasks associated with producing a theatrical production such as costuming, makeup, rehearsing, lighting and sound, the producer-directors need to train the staff to assist with catering and guest services.

A primary decision is how to make the audience members part of the production. The audience needs to feel included in the fictional world right from the start. Greeting the guests with high energy, clear characterization is critical for setting the tone. Amusing, playful interaction helps distance the guests from their "workaday" world and prepare them for the mystery scenes to follow. For example, in one show a comic nurse gets audience members to help decorate with balloons and streamer for her patient's birthday party. Producing directors plan transitions between improvised and scripted segments. The actors help by preparing jokes or dialogues to control a two or three hour production that might include rowdy adventurous participants or audience member's trips to the restroom. For example, when an audience member blocks the action on the stage as he walks by, an actor exclaims, "It's just a *stage* he's going through"!

Wait staff and actors need to be trained to cope with inappropriate behavior or medical emergencies.

Directing the Rehearsal

Rehearsal for this style of work is less time-consuming than rehearsals for traditional three act plays because the scripted segment is under an hour. Script analysis, character development, memorizing dialogue and blocking can be mastered quickly by professional actors. Actors are expected to attend their first rehearsal already off-book and well immersed in the character. This allows the director and actors time to brainstorm creative ideas for improvisational segments. One can speculate what might happen during the event, but the audience must be present for the production energy to be complete. One of the main challenges in directing this type of theatre is helping actors to keep their roles fresh and updated. Improvised humor and references need to be current (Clark, 2005). The director has to strike a balance between giving actors a clear outline of the character, often an easily recognized stereotype, while at the same time giving the actor freedom to develop that character from his own standpoint. At Sleuths, 45 actors are trained to play multiple roles in a wide range of shows. Each actor brings a unique personal interpretation to the role including different accents and personality traits. This promotes creative energy and fresh dynamics between characters. Staying in character in the present moment is the key to succeeding as an improvisational actor. For example recently one of the authors created a new action for a character called "Charlotte", who has just been released from "the institu ... I mean the happy place". During interrogation, Charlotte did "art therapy," comically coloring with crayons whenever she felt overcome with *post dramatic dress disorder*. Audience members picked up on this and a whole new form of interaction involving her "art" ensued!

To keep actors in top form, and to avoid complacency, periodic brush-up rehearsals are needed. The director watches performances periodically and gives notes. These feedback sessions create a tightly-knit ensemble which is an important ingredient for successful improvisation. Successful interactive mystery actors are clear communicators, sociable, comfortable with improvisation and good ensemble players. These latter skills are enhanced by mandatory attendance at special improvisational training workshops to keep skills sharp.

Actor Training for this Work

Actors in this field should be well trained in traditional theatre skills, comedy technique and improvisation. Characters in interactive mystery shows are often stereotypes or comedic caricatures, requiring control of the voice, body, and imagination. In order to improvise, the actors need to know the geography and history behind events that are "current" in the world of the play. Murder mystery actors also need training in staging technique. This work is often in the round, and requires that the actor be seen and heard by everyone. Wait staff skills are important when the actor doubles as a server during the production. Balancing a tray of drinks is something you should practice before you are in character! Mystery dinner show actors multi-task: acting, waiting tables, improvising, attending to the audience, changing costumes, setting props, answering clues, and following the script simultaneously.

Most murder mystery actors also work in other professions. Salaries in this field are mediocre because their improvisational nature exempts these theatres from Actor's Equity rules. Many performers in this work do it for fun or to keep current with their actor skills. Anne Curtis, co-author of this chapter, is a Registered Drama Therapist who performs 8 different roles in 7 different mysteries at *Sleuths* in order to keep up the theatre and improvisational skills that are the cornerstones of her therapy work. "My drama therapy work focuses on helping clients with traumatic stress caused by illness, crisis or loss. Acting in these comic mystery shows, concentrating on creating laughter, promotes the processing of pain absorbed in therapeutic work. Acting in interactive murder mystery shows keeps professional acting skills honed and sharp. Director Laurel Clark (2005) states, "Performing in our interactive comedy mystery shows definitely gives our actors a leg up when they audition for film or commercials because they have already developed a wide repertoire of stock roles."

Initial Steps For Actors and Producers

The first step to take if you have an interest in this alternative form of theatre as a producer or performer is to find it, and see it. There are numerous producing organizations across America, but since most murder mysteries are dinner theatres, they are found via the National Dinner Theatre Association (NDTA), or the American Dinner Theater Institute (ADTI).

Producing a murder mystery requires detailed planning. The producing organization must make the entire event successful and pay attention to every detail. Producers must choose the topic, genre and script that is most appropriate for their needs and location. They must consider what other dinner theatres in their area might be performing, competitive ticket prices, food options, and target audiences. Planning considerations include theatrical production, marketing and box office procedures, as well as meal planning, execution, and clean up.

The murder mystery production is a profit-based entertainment business. The business considerations and financial planning are elaborate. Scripts are often written in-house to circumvent repeated royalties. Many performances are portable to increase show sales. Since maximizing dining table space is a priority, this work is often done in the round or on an unusually small stage. Set design, props, sound and lighting all follow the "less is more" economy.

If you are interested in acting in this line of work take classes in improvisation, directing and acting. Develop your interpersonal skills and confidence by gaining experience and building your acting resume especially in comedies and improvisational troupes. The service industry provides a chance to rehearse your waiter and conversational skills before you add the character and script. Once you sharpen your skills, you are ready to audition. Auditions in this line of work can seem odd, ranging from reading a script, to singing, to improvising multiple characters on the spot. It is perfectly acceptable to ask what the directors are looking for before you audition. Remember that they are looking for actors who can confidently lead a paying audience on an adventure.

Good stage actors do not necessarily make good interactive theatre actors. However, directors are looking for actors who are well trained and experienced. Some directors look for a resume that includes theatre work, improvisational work, comedy theatre and even children's theatre experience (which is often interactive and involves many skills that transfer well to the interactive mystery show). "The key elements I look for during the audition are a natural sense of comedic timing and a clear loud voice" (Clark, 2005). The NDTA holds auditions yearly at theatre conferences across America, and individual theatres will hold scheduled auditions from time to time depending on their needs. Research local theatres, attend their productions, speak with their staff and then call to ask about auditions.

Conclusion

Interactive mystery theatre, in all its varied forms, has a firm footing in the entertainment business because it creates an engaging, playful ambience, an escape from reality that is enjoyed by audience and actors alike. Some professional actors may be uncomfortable with this non-traditional genre because they do not enjoy improvisation or they are seeking a full-time Equity income. However, many professional performers, including an author of this chapter, highly recommend this creative, challenging, yet more relaxed, form of theatre.

Murder mystery dinner theatres are great entertainment and a successful part of American interactive theatre. Constructed from many segments including theatrical production, restaurant management, business skills, and marketing, this complex form requires detailed planning and the development of specific actor skills. Today, murder mysteries are deep-rooted internationally and take on a wide range of forms and genres, revolving around the actor-audience bond and the good clean fun of solving a "whodunit".

References

Further information and references on the webpage supplement to this chapter: <www.interactiveimprov.com/mysterywb.html>

Andersen, A. (President & Director) (2006) *Palladian Interactive Theatre LLC.* <www.interdrama.com>

Austin, A. & Austin, M. (2006) owners *Arizona Performing Arts Theatre, Murder Ink Productions and Team Builders Ink.* (602) 952-8447, Phoenix, Az. <www.murderinkproductions.com>

Ax, Barbara, & Tumielewicz, P.J. (Eds.) (2003). *Regional theatre directory: a national guide to employment in regional & dinner theatres for performers (equity & non-equity), designers, technicians & management with internship.* Theatre Directories Press. Amazon.com

Lynk, William M. (1993). *Dinner theatre.* Greenwood Press, Westport CT.

Miller, Paul M. (1998) *Dinner theatre.* Lillenas Publishing Company, MO.

Web Sites

The National Dinner Theatre Association: <www.ndta.com/>.

The Mousetrap <www.coronadoplayhouse.com/mousetrap/mousetrap_history.html>

The Barn Theatre. <www.barntheatre.org>

Sleuths Mystery Dinner Show in Orlando Florida: <www.sleuths.com>

Chapter 29

MEDIEVAL RE-ENACTMENTS

Thomas M. Stallone

An interesting type of improvisational and interactive drama involves one type of live-action role playing for fun and recreation, as people and actors take on the roles of characters in history, such as at Renaissance Fairs or at events sponsored by medieval re-creation groups such as the Society for Creative Anachronism (often known as the SCA and referred to as such later). Many groups are re-enacting a wide range of historical events, from the ancient world to relatively modern times. This chapter, though, focuses on groups whose members role-play the life and times of medieval Europe.

All around the world, thousands of people eagerly wait for the weekend to come so they can drop their humdrum "real" life roles, and figuratively answer the question "who else can I be?" by stepping through an invisible portal and journeying back into an age where knights fight for the honor of their ladies, and where kings and their nobles hold court at sumptuous banquets. They enter a realm where one can find a minstrel sitting under a tree singing sweetly and playing a lute while lords and ladies listen to his tunes. You enter a pavilion where a seamstress busily ties a sleeve on a new jerkin she just designed as an impatient swashbuckler waits to try it on. You may see a huge bear of a man teaching an apprentice how to use an anvil and forge to make armor. Within the walls of the "castle" you may find a herald busily designing a coat-of-arms for a newly created lord while cooks prepare the evening's feast. The allure of the medieval world inspires many to enter this magical world of re-enactment where modern people create roles for themselves and live out their fantasies.

This "modern" medieval world doesn't pretend to recreate the middle ages as they were—a life often laced with elements of squalor—but rather, these groups strive to create an idealized version of medieval life emulating chivalry, honor, courtesy, beauty, and grace without such inconveniences as the black plague, inquisitions, and intercultural strife. Participation allows people to enjoy an alternative world, experienced fully (in contrast to living semi-vicariously through video games).

There are several modern medieval re-creation and/or re-enactment groups in the United States besides the SCA, some of which are listed on the webpage that will supplement this chapter. There are also groups in other countries. Each group has a particular focus (e.g., swordplay, medieval arts, public performance) or time period (e.g., eleventh century Saxon England, the thirteenth century "Crusaders" region of activity around Lebanon and Palestine—i.e., the "Levant", the War of the Roses) to help concentrate their creative energies.

There are two general types of groups: the re-creation groups, which tend to be a bit more free-wheeling and casual, and the re-enactment groups, which tend to more stringently seek verisimilitude. These latter may hold to very strict standards regulating how costumes are made, what material can be used, what accessories can be worn, how their participants must speak and behave in public, and so forth. Still, there are many overlaps between groups with members from each group attending each others' events and participating in each others' activities. You can find one of these medieval groups located in just about every major college campus and city. The SCA is the largest of the modern medieval groups, by far, so it will be used as the prototype for all the others in describing how the alternate reality is created.

The SCA provides an individual with the easiest access to the modern medieval world. It is not a performing troupe, though on occasions members will put on demonstrations for schools and municipalities. They perform for themselves to enhance the quality of, as they put it, "The Dream"—i.e., their shared culture. The culture was developed to allow a person to *have fun* medievally—not to actually *become* medieval. The "creative" within Society for *Creative* Anachronism allows people to enter this modern medieval world and explore it to the extent that their interest, time, money, and energy allow. Still there are many members within the SCA who strive to be as medievally accurate as possible and will not be seen drinking out of aluminum cans or wearing sunglasses at their medieval events.

The SCA was founded in 1966 in Berkeley, California when a group of students and friends with shared interests in the medieval period got together to give a friend a medieval-style going-away party. It consisted of a costumed medieval feast and a tournament. The revelers enjoyed themselves so much that they decided to hold more of these parties and tournaments in the following weeks and months. A few of the diehard regulars sat down and formally created an organization that eventually became incorporated as a non-profit educational society. As the members graduated or left school, they returned home forming groups of their own within this new organization. The SCA spread throughout California and nationally over the next several years. According to SCA's estimates, the society has grown since 1966 to include over 29,600 paying members (The SCA, Inc., 2003) in the United States and Canada with other affiliated groups and members found in Australia, Austria, Egypt, England, Finland, France, Germany, Greece, Iceland, Ireland, Israel, Italy, Japan, the Netherlands, New Zealand, Norway, Poland, Qatar, Romania, South Africa, Spain, Sweden, and Turkey. There are many more non-paying members and friends who participate in the Society's events so that the total amount of people engaged in the various activities of the kingdoms is closer to 50,000 people worldwide.

Most of the Society's activities take place in the context of a social structure adapted from the forms of the European Middle Ages, which allows participants to take a first-hand look at various aspects of the life, culture, and technology of the times under study. As a living history group, the Society provides an environment in which members can recreate various aspects of the culture and technology of the period, as well as doing more traditional historical research. (See the references at the end of this chapter.) They hold events such as tournaments and feasts where members dress in clothing styles worn during the Middle Ages and Renaissance, and participate in activities based on the civil and martial skills of the period. These activities recreate aspects of the life and culture of the landed nobility in Europe, beginning with the fall of the Western Roman Empire and ending in 1600 C.E. The members espouse the concepts of chivalry—honor in combat and in peace, while promoting the renaissance ideals of striving towards high accomplishments in the arts and sciences. The Society appeals to people of all generations, but the majority of the members are between 19 to 35 years of age, though it is not uncommon to find three generations of one family attending events. The Society serves two main functions for its members: (1) a place to socialize with like-minded people, and (2) an avenue for them to research and explore the world they are trying to emulate. The allure of this medieval world is such that members will drive an hour each week to strap on sixty pounds of leather and steel just to get whacked on the head and arms with weapons at a fighter practice with friends. Some come to learn the latest medieval dances, practice calligraphy, or how to design and create that new costume they saw in a book. The SCA is not your everyday social club.

The modern medieval world that members play in consists of seventeen Kingdoms that collectively comprise "The Known World." Each kingdom is headed by a King who has fought and won the throne for his Lady Queen at a Crown Tournament. Royalty in this organization is not by virtue of birth, but attained through martial prowess, which was how most of the European royal houses were originally founded. The King and Queen are not only figureheads in this organization. They actively rule their Kingdom creating and passing laws with the help of their Curia Regis which is made up of the principle officers of the Kingdom.

The responsibilities of administration of the kingdom do not rest solely on the shoulders of the monarchs. The King and Queen delegate the day-to-day running the kingdom and all the local groups to a well-organized civil service made up of volunteers. Each local group will usually hold monthly meetings. Larger groups will usually hold weekly fighter practices and arts & sciences workshops in addition to their monthly meetings. Members of the local groups decide to hold the various medieval events and volunteer to run the event. They go to great lengths to secure a site adequate for their purposes.

With a local group located in almost every major city and/or university in the United States, Canada, and Europe, you can usually find a medieval event being held each weekend within a three-to-four hour drive from your home and often much closer. Many of these medieval events have become large annual affairs. For example, members have been attending the great Pennsic War for over thirty years. It is held near Pittsburgh, PA each August and draws over 11,000 people. Estrella War is held near Phoenix, AZ each February draws over 6,000 people and has been attracting members for over 19 years. These "wars" began as a friendly way to demonstrate the martial prowess of the kingdoms involved giving the winner bragging rights over the others, not the subjugation of the loser's demesne.

A spectator at one of these large events would think they were walking through some medieval Crusader city with thousands of medievally dressed people acting *in persona*, with all of the pavilions and banners around them. As with most groups there is strong internal peer pressure to conform to the ideals of the Society as stated in the body of rules laid out by the Board of Directors (2004). Over the years the Society has matured and with that growth the Board has developed handbooks and guidelines for all the local groups to follow making it easier for volunteers in their administrative positions to carry out the smooth running of the group while having fun living "the Dream." Those who choose not to conform to the standards of behavior, who are disruptive, become dangerous to themselves or others at events are asked to leave by the local group's "constables," and are not invited or allowed back. If trouble persists, local law enforcement is called in.

Getting Involved

Society members work hard to recreate a feudal society that embodies the order, hierarchy, and pageantry of the period. Many newcomers are drawn to the SCA by the notion of chivalry and knighthood. A new person will usually come into contact with the SCA by watching a medieval tournament held in conjunction with, and as part of, a municipality's public celebration. They become intrigued by the Society's medieval ambiance seeing banners flying over pavilions, and fighters in armor with their swords and axes flailing about in a flurry of blows and parries. Drawn by pageantry of the formal ceremony of these martial contests in the tournament, new people witness knights in armor doing battle for the honor of their Ladies. They notice how the squires attend their knights and how the other medieval participants treat each other with deference. The experience kindles within the spectator thoughts that, "Maybe, I could someday be a knight, too." They see chivalric notions played out everywhere before their very eyes. It is this kind of romantic idealism that motivates the spectator to join the Society to learn how to fight in armor just like the knights of old and work diligently at their "dream" to become the equal of all those that bear the rank of knight within the kingdom.

Since the first SCA tournament back in 1965, the art of *heavy combat* (i.e., armored combat with heavy weapons) has developed into a true martial art with the knights and masters-of-arms being the "black belts" of this new martial art form. While the armor that the fighters wear is real, the swords and other weapons are not. The SCA decided that "live" steel broadswords were too dangerous to use for regular combat, though many members carry real swords and knives with them when medievally dressed at events. In heavy combat, fighters use swords made of rattan because it has the same weight and feel of a steel sword but bends on impact, dispersing some of the energy of the blow because of the nature of the wood. Each fighter is protected by wearing armor sufficient to withstand the sword blows safely.

A fight ends when one fighter receives, in *their* opinion, a *killing* blow—i.e., the blow struck a vital spot on the head or torso that would have killed the person had it been a real sword. It is on the honor of the fighter who received the blow to determine if it was good enough to "kill" him or her. Fighter practices are held regularly throughout the year in most of the baronies and shires. Knights and masters-of-arms will often hold special practices with their squires, teaching them both the fine points of armored combat and setting them tasks in learning the finer, more artistic, aspects of this modern medieval world. Brian Price, a Knight and Earl within the SCA writes in the introduction of a treatise on chivalry that, "One of the reasons that I continue to pursue the "chivalric arts" is for the pleasure of watching young squires and men-at-arms grow into their own. There is something priceless in being present as a combatant matures, moving from headstrong 'fighter' to competent swordsman to gentleman to master and knight" (Chamberlain, 1998).

The Society also provides ample opportunity to explore the many medieval Arts and Sciences such as: costuming and the various types of period costume design, needlepoint and embroidery, medieval recipes and cooking, brewing and wine making, candle making, medieval music and instruments, medieval poetry, medieval dance, calligraphy and illumination, heraldry, story-telling, juggling, ritual theatre, carpentry—e.g., the making of medieval furniture, metal-working such as jewelry making, coining money, the making of bows and arrows, and the forging and making armor, swords, and the making of medieval utensils.

Within the martial arts you can explore all facets of swordplay such as fighting in armor, classical fencing with rapiers and all their accouterments, and all facets of medieval archery. In relatively rural areas, you can find members pursuing the equestrian arts such as tilting at the rings or running at the *quintain* (i.e., a medieval practice target for jousting) on horseback. It is up to you to decide who you want to be and what you want to become. Members are more than willing to help you learn.

Over the years, members have engaged in research and developed quite a sophisticated level of expertise and competence. Dr. Helmut Nickel, former curator of Arms and Armor Exhibit for the Metropolitan Museum of Art in New York, calls much of the research and level of expertise of SCA members both "laudable" and "serious" (as cited in Fincher, 1981). Many members have published articles that would make many a thesis chairperson proud. These published articles add to the wealth of accumulated knowledge about these medieval pursuits and are available to members and the public.

Events

Most people enter the modern medieval world by attending a locally held *event*. These medieval events can take the form of a tournament, a feast or revel, a *schola* or university (i.e., where classes are taught on the various medieval arts and sciences), or any combination of each. You can find an event being held at a public park, at a campground, on a college campus, at a local school, at a church or civic organization's hall, or even in a farmer's field.

Outdoor events are like a minor Medieval fairs and will usually consist of a heavy tournament, possibly in conjunction with a "Rapier" tournament, and/or an archery tournament. Indoor events focus on the "finer" aspects of medieval life. The event may be a "schola" where people actually learn about various aspects of medieval life; it could be a revel, where the focus is on fun and games and there is a lot of music and dancing; or it may be a coronation of a new king and queen. Indoor events will usually conclude with a feast. Feasts are wonderful affairs consisting of many-courses meal that have been carefully researched and tested. As you sit eating, you are usually entertained by musicians, minstrels, poets, and jugglers in a candlelit atmosphere that really transforms the evening.

More detailed descriptions of tournaments and other outdoor and indoor events may be found on the supplementary webpage: <www.interactiveimprov. com/medievalwb.html>

Creating a Persona

So, who "else" can you be? Here are some ideas for warming-up to a character you might explore and possibly play out at some kind of medieval re-enactment event: Think back to when you were younger and pretending to be a fictional character or super hero, and spending hours playing in a world created totally out of your imagination. The SCA (and the other medieval groups) provides the alternate reality where adults can use those imaginative abilities honed as children. This imaginative process is very important in the creation of your medieval character. The SCA's medieval culture provides an excellent opportunity for would-be thespians to test their talents in a free-flowing improvisational way. Those who have acting experience can further hone their skills in this dynamic medium. Choosing a character to play for a sustained period of time is itself an elegant process, and modern clowns do it as part of their self-initiation process.

Within the SCA there is enough energy and enthusiasm to propel you to want to do well in your exploration of medieval life. When members gather at an event, they not only dress for the occasion in "period garb," but also don the personalities that fit their chosen time periods and the roles they will play within the social caste system of its medieval world. A few will develop more than one persona to best express their particular moods or whim, be it a mercenary or courtier. The persona they create becomes their medieval alter ego that gradually evolves, much as a child would develop into adulthood, wrought from the social and historical influences of living within this shared alternate reality.

Learning how to develop a persona will help you better understand the process needed to embellish a role for stage, screen, or real life, adding the nuances to enhance your presentation in front of others. You do not need to have studied "The Method" (Stanislavski, 1963) in order to develop a medieval persona for the SCA. Members develop their medieval characters not for the purpose of performing before an audience, but to be able to enter this world and share in its magic more fully.

When developing a persona, you will need to consider four factors: a name, a nationality, a time period, and the culture your persona will be living in. Members typically choose names for their medieval selves that reflect the flavor of an earlier age and culture from a point in time in history they find fascinating. (More about this process may be found on the web-page that supplements this chapter: <www.interactiveimprov.com/medievalwb.html>.)

Benefits and Pitfalls

Participating in medieval groups is a marvelous hobby for you to try. It is an excellent way to channel your creative energies in pursuits that will generally be recognized and rewarded. It can spark within you a passion that was not there before.

Besides becoming proficient in any number of the groups' activities cited earlier, participating in these groups could also enhance you psychological growth. Creating a persona and enacting that medieval alter-ego allows you to the opportunity to "stretch" yourself by developing new qualities or honing already established ones. Psychologically, the process of role playing your medieval persona in these groups provides you with the opportunity to "try out" new personality traits in a relatively safe and benign environment. For example, a shy person could develop a more engaging, extroverted persona by practicing those qualities that they would never *dare* test out in the real world. The mask of the persona creates a psychological buffer which can give them enough courage to slowly test being more "out there" with others. After successfully using these new behaviors and growing more confident and comfortable in applying these skills in this safe environment, they can generalize these new traits to their every day life.

Involvement in these medieval groups could also have a negative impact on people as well. Some people who are not very successful in their everyday lives who find new self-worth by receiving recognition from others, may start devoting more and more of their time, energy, and resources to their new hobby instead to their daily lives. There have been people who will spend much of their hard-earned wages on fabric to create a Tudor costume for the up-coming Twelfth Night Feast, but not have enough money to pay their telephone bill. As they become more involved in these groups, they may rise to positions and titles of power. Recognition "from above" and the wielding of "power" are addictive to some people and could cause problems in their lives both within the group, at home, and at work.

Role-playing through medieval re-creation and re-enactment groups is but one genre in a wide variety of historical living history groups. Whatever historical period your interest lies, you can find a historical role-playing group to satisfy that interest. For anyone who has an interest in medieval culture, they will find a whole new world to explore. Besides medieval groups, you can find groups that recreate the English Civil War, the American Revolutionary War, Black Powder groups that portray early American explorers and trappers, the Civil War, cowboys of the American West, World War I and II. Once you find a group, all it takes is imagination and effort.

Finally, role-playing is not only confined to historical periods. There are several groups called LARPs (Live Action Role Playing) that encompass science-fiction and fantasy genres where you may run across a whole community of vampires or even elves.

References

Further resources may be found near the bottom of the webpage supplement to this chapter <www.interactiveimprov.com/medievalwb.html>

The Society for Creative Anachronism, Inc. is a non-profit educational organization whose focus encompasses the general European medieval period 476–1600 C.E.) You can find out the group nearest you by calling the national office at (800) 789-7486 or by going to the SCA website at <www.sca.org> There you can also find links to the other medieval reenactment groups. (In Australia: <www.sca.org.au/lochac/

Chamberlain, John (1998). Of the Vertues that Apperteyne to Chyvalry. Retrieved January 17, 2004 from <www.chronique.com/Library/Chivalry/chivalry.htm> (The author writes about the chivalric qualities that make a knight—such as prowess, courage, honesty, loyalty, generosity, faith, courtesy, and franchise citing translations of period pieces in discussing each chivalric quality.)

Fincher, Jack. (1981, June). They 'joust' as if knighthood were in flower today. *The Smithsonian Magazine*, pp. 94–103. (The author writes about the SCA and provides a good overview of life at some of the medieval events they hold.)

Page, Tim. (1985, September 30). Medieval Festival: Fort Tryon Park and Cloisters Bedecked. *The New York Times*

The Society for Creative Anachronism. (2003). *The Seventeen Kingdoms of the SCA*. Retrieved January 10, 2004 from <www.sca.org/geography/welcome.html>

The Society for Creative Anachronism. (2004). *Society For Creative Anachronism, Inc. Organizational Handbook*. Milpitas, CA: The SCI, Inc.

Stanislavski, C. (1963). *The Actor Prepares*. (Hapgood, E. R., Trans.) NY: Routledge.

Chapter 30

INTERACTIVE CLOWN PRACTICES

Doyle Ott

Clowns working on the stage or circus ring, in hospitals or schools, often base their work on interaction with audience members. This chapter will examine that aspect of clowning that considers the improvisational and interactive dimensions of the dramatic process of clowning. Also emphasized is the way clowns can help others discover their own improvisational playfulness.

In a circus tent audience members become circus stars as a clown directs them in a silent film routine. In a school for the developmentally disabled, children put on make-up and practice a clown routine they have just learned. In a hospital, a child fighting cancer puts on a red nose and conducts an "orchestra" of two clowns in white doctor's coats playing slide whistles. Business executives discover mind-body connections and learning dynamics by learning to juggle. In a Zen center a group of people learn clown walks, while in a school an entire grade level transforms itself and the schoolyard into a circus.

These are just a few instances in which clowns, often in unexpected places, practice a form of interactive performance in which audience members tap into their own spontaneity and thus find a bit of clown in themselves. While circus clowns have often interacted with the audience to some extent as part of their acts, a growing number of clowns reach out into their communities and find ways in which they can empower others though the art of clowning.

What is a Clown?

Many people picture a clown as someone in baggy pants, white face make-up with a broad red smile, a funny hat, and, of course, a red nose. This is the icon of the clown that has developed from masterful circus clowns such as Lou Jacobs, and been cemented in our collective minds by the commercialization of Bozo, Ronald McDonald and other television clowns. These televised icons of the clown have contributed to the idea that clowns are only for children, an idle frivolity. On seeing a good circus or theatre clown perform in person for the first time, a contemporary audience may be surprised to find that the clown, while being watched, *watches back* and invites the audience to play, if only from the comfort of their seats. A good clown is every bit as interactive in performance as a child engaged in a game of make-believe.

Clowns have been around in one form or another in every civilization. Wherever there are humans, there is humor, and where there is humor, there are clowns. The clown has also been called the trickster, the fool, the jester, the zany, the comic, the eccentric, and many other names. In Sanskrit dramas in India, *vidusaka* (translated as "one given to abuse") and *vita* are clown roles. In Chinese theatre, the *ch'ou* clowns entertain with wit and acrobatics. Native American cultures, Arab cultures, the island cultures of Bali and Java, all have their own clown traditions.

While each clown tradition has idiosyncrasies, all have a few things in common. First, of course, clowns make us laugh. They do so with verbal wit and/or physical skill. In addition, clowns usually invert power structures and social norms. The more sacred the ground, the more likely some type of clown will be dancing on it. Finally, clowns transforms themselves through makeup, clothing, exaggerated mannerisms, and practiced performance. Clowns use this transformation in interactive performance.

One way clowns interact is that they may invite members of the audience to join them on stage or in the ring. Another approach is known as walk-around or "carpet-clowning," in which the clown goes into and interacts with the audience. A combination of these two is used in going beyond the theatre or circus and into various locales in the community, where they begin to mix in roles such as teacher and care-giver. While working as clowns, often in full make-up and costume, they focus on developing new perspectives, insights, and discoveries by those with whom they interact.

Traditional Clown Techniques

David Shiner, as a clown and part of the stage shows *Fool Moon* and *Cirque du Soleil*, brings three audience members on stage. He pre-selects these volunteers and preps them backstage, and then brings them onstage. Using mime and gesture he directs them in a melodramatic silent-movie style scene involving a jealous lover and culminating in a shoot-out. He creates a structure with enough direction so that his partners from the audience can play, and then steps back and acting as the cameraman lets them play the scene. The results are inevitably hysterical and three average audience members become stars in a performance for a thousand other people. Despite the amazing technical prowess of the professional performers, Shiner's pantomimed gunfight between audience members becomes a highlight of the show. This sort of work is integral to clowning. If one of the clown's jobs is to invert power structures, interacting with the audience in this way clearly does the job. The clown steps out of the ring and the spectators step in, transformed into clowns in their own right.

Walk-around, or "carpet" clowning depends heavily on such interaction. While some clowns in the ring or onstage may perform a routine without even a nod to the audience, in walk-around clowning they must interact directly with individual audience members. Walk-around clowning generally takes place before a performance or during intermission in a circus context. This kind of clowning also forms a large part of the work of many clowns who have never performed in a circus, but who may work at parties, store openings, street fairs and other events.

Master teacher Jeff Raz, founder and head of the San Francisco Clown Conservatory, conceptualizes three main elements to walk-around clowning: First, the clown has some activity or act that is highly visible and welcoming to an unfocused group of people. Second, the clown has an interactive bit, probably related to the no-focus act, in which the clown engages with a few individuals, finds a way to share and play with them, and then disengages to find others to involve. Third, the clown has a mini-act to perform for the small groups that are likely to form to watch the other parts of the walk-around act. For example, a clown might welcome the unfocused crowd by balancing a flower on her nose, then engage an individual with a bit in which the flower wilts and the clown enlists a spectator to revive it. Then, if a group forms around that play, she might bring out two more flowers and perform a short juggling act. The clown may employ several of each element of walk-around to fill an hour's play and be able to keep a group involved in fresh ways.

Most circus clowns use a combination of highly rehearsed performance pieces (often called *entrées*) and walk-around clowning techniques in their work. A clown who performs in the ring often does at least little bit of walk-around before the main entrée to warm up the audience. John Gilkey, who has worked extensively for Cirque du Soleil calls this as "animation," and notices a profound improvement in the audience's reaction to his entrée if they have had a chance to get to know him through walk-around before his performance.

Clowns working at parties and fairs may base their work on walk-around skills, but will likely have at least a short entrée to perform as needed.

Audience participation and walk-around are ways in which most clowns engage in interactive play. In fact, a skilled clown constantly partners with the audience in both overt and subtle ways, and improvises based on their reactions. This way of working lays the groundwork for more intensive, community-based interactions.

Clowns Out of the Ring

A growing number of clowns have begun to look for ways in which to extend their work beyond the traditional realms of the stage and circus. Beyond the obvious opportunities to perform in schools and at parties and street fairs, many have found ways to partner with various communities in ways that empower others to transform themselves with make-up, noses and clown skills. In the following pages, I will discuss ways in which clowns have identified needs for the clown and partnered with various communities and individuals to fill those needs. I have selected this short list to show the breadth ways in which clowns work. Many other individuals and groups are doing similar work in their own communities.

Clowns as Healers

In his book *Clowns*, clown historian John Towsen (1976) notes that in many cultures the clown serves as a shaman, a sacred healer. Many clowns have discovered this aspect of clowning and focus on exploring the healing aspects of clowning by empowering others to transform themselves. They seek to bring humor into hospitals and other, often humorless, medical institutions. Most clowns who work in such theraputic settings emphasize the need for a strong clown skills, supplemental training to learn how to interact effectively with the populations they clown for, and the importance of working in pairs or groups.

Clown Therapy. Paoli Lacy created techniques in which the clown, working with therapists and other staff at institutions for the developmentally disabled and severely emotionally disabled (SED), bring the transformational power of clowning to those populations. In Lacy's technique, clown therapists always work in pairs, and work in full costume and make-up. Staff working with the participants on a day-to-day basis are on hand for safety and security of the participants, and are consulted closely on the needs of each individual.

The structure of a clown therapy session allows participants to safely go far out to the edges of their identity and safely return at the end. Each session has six sections: the opening circle, warm-ups, technique, transformation, self-expression, and closing. The Opening Circle is a ritual in which each participant selects a clown name for the day and affirms their understanding of the ground rules. Warm-ups focus the mind and prepare the body for the work. Technique lessons offer tools and structure for clowning, and usually include both circus skills such as acrobatics and clown skills such as presentation. In transformation, each participant selects costume and make-up. Self-expression allows members of the group to perform their new skills. Closure provides a vehicle for the participants to remove make-up and costumes, and to practice relaxation and centering exercises to safely return from the clown world.

Clown therapy, like other expressive arts therapies, offers a unique combination of physical and psychological benefits. It provides, in Lacy's words "a safe way to explore issues of physical powerfulness, powerlessness, and self-acceptance." Clowning gives "method to madness," and allows participants "to go way out" and safely "come back," and empowers participants emotionally and physically. By learning clown walks, slaps and falls and practicing tumbling, participants both gain physical skills that may help them deal with the unique physical challenges they may face. Those with a history of abuse gain a new comic way to work through the violence they have suffered without acting out on others.

Clown therapy has served many special needs populations from children to adults, dealing with challenges including homelessness, HIV, physical and cognitive disabilities, as well as severe emotional disturbance and developmentally disability. Lacy stresses that clowns should not undertake this work lightly. A clown therapist must first have a solid grounding in the art of clowning, and then apprentice with experienced clown therapists and partner with receptive licensed therapists and social workers to develop the skills to work with special needs populations.

Clowning in Hospitals

Another type of therapeutic clown activity is hospital clowning. Many individuals and groups bring clowning into hospital settings. Some, such as Michael Christiansen and the Big Apple Circus' Clown Care Unit come from the circus and theatre, seeking to use their skills to heal. Others, such as Patch Adams, are medical professionals who have discovered the power of laughter in their medical practice. The Clown Care Unit consists of professional clowns specifically selected and trained for the sensitive work of entering hospitals to engage patients. They partner with the hospital staff to identify patients who most need their care and to help ease the fear and powerlessness many young patients experience. By parodying medical procedures and performing clown medicine using familiar objects in place of obscure medical equipment, they seek to put patients at ease.

As they may not know the mood of the patient when they enter a room, clowns must constantly interact and improvise. Additionally, as they attempt to empower the patient, clowns often give choices to each child they encounter. Such choices begin with simply asking permission to enter the room. The choices may then extend to what props the child wants to play with, whether and what music he or she would like a clown musician to play, and the extent to which the child wants to take part in the play. Taking cues from the child, or occasionally a parent or doctor, the clowns pick a routine or gag to start with and enter into play with the patient.

As noted earlier, most hospital clowns come to their work as either clowns or caregivers, and then develop their skills through apprenticeship and practice. Therapeutic clowning has become a worldwide phenomenon, with formal training programs offered at universities and through organizations dedicated to hospital clowning.

Clowns in Education

Educational settings provide another outlet for interactive clowning. In many schools and other organizations clowns teach their skills to youth and adults. A few organizations, such as the Great All American Youth Circus at the YMCA in Redlands, California, and the Sailor Circus in Sarasota, Florida, have been offering children instruction in circus arts for over fifty years. Over the last twenty years many more groups have started to offer instruction in clowning and other circus skills to young people.

American Youth Circus Organization

The youth circus movement has been gaining momentum for over a decade, and a surge of interest as well as the communication facilitated by the internet has resulted in the creation of the American Youth Circus Organization or AYCO. This program was founded in 2001 by Kevin Maile O'Keefe and Erin Maile, a husband and wife team; they, in turn, also run an organization called Circus Minimus, which conducts two-week residencies in schools. In those programs participants learn clowning and circus skills and produce a circus performance at the end of the residency. The Prescott Clowns in Oakland, California, provide another model, in which a classroom workshop by teacher Aileen Moffitt has expanded to a year-round program serving many schools in the Oakland district. These education programs represent a far end of the spectrum of interactive performance.

Whereas some professional clowns include very little interaction in their performance, others include little performance in their interaction, focusing on the interactions of teaching and directing. Wavy Gravy is one such clown, whose primary work is social interaction. Since 1974 Camp Winnarainbow, a brainchild of Wavy's wife Jahavara, has taught circus arts including clowning to children and adults, many from disadvantaged backgrounds. The camp focuses on using circus skills to foster cooperative working skills. "Camp teaches responsibility for one's own inner behavior and develops confidence, inner security and appropriate self expression," according to its website, <www. campwinnarainbow.org>. Wavy Gravy calls his approach intuitive clowning, and as the camp's curriculum indicates he is particularly interested in clowning's potential for personal transformation. He integrates his knowledge of non-European clown traditions, particularly Native American and Indian clowning into his work. In addition to the educational work he does at Winnarainbow, Wavy worked for years as a hospital clown, and has also used clowning as political art.

Clowning in Political and Social Activism

There is a rich history of political clowning. Dan Rice, perhaps the most famous American circus clown of the 19th century, included topical political commentary in his clowning, and is largely responsible for the image of the Uncle Sam character often used in political cartoons and as a War Bonds poster icon in the 1940s. In Europe during the first decade of the 20th century, Vladimir Durov was arrested in both Germany and his native Russia for the political content of his gags.

More recently Wavy Gravy has been involved in many political actions of various kinds. Wavy has been an icon of the sixties counter-culture since at least 1968, when he served as Master of Ceremonies for the original Woodstock festival. He began clowning as a spiritual practice of working with hospitalized children and discovered that the clown was also an effective persona for political activism. Having been severely beaten by police during anti-war protests, he experienced a revelation when he discovered that, in his words, "the clown is safe." The police and other institutional powers saw Wavy-the-clown as non-threatening, allowing him a measure of protection. Much as the medieval fool might have said things about and even directly to feudal rulers that others could not, Wavy Gravy found that he could do and say things as a clown that would have resulted in violent reaction if done by a non-clown. He has continued his life of political activism and his commitment to social activism in a numerous ways, and his example has inspired a generation of politically active clowns.

Clowns Without Borders is an international movement of clowns who bring their art into refugee camps and areas of conflict. Founded in Barcelona in 1993, the movement has spread internationally, and many clown missions have been launched by various Clowns Without Borders organizations. Key to the ideals of clowns without borders is that "the work starts in your own backyard," in the words of Moshe Cohen, the United States contact for CWB. Clowns are needed anywhere "where humor serves as a psychological recourse or support for individuals and communities that suffer some kind of crisis" according to clownswithoutborders.org>. The U.S. website spells out a strong code of ethics for clowns working under the Clowns Without Borders banner. In this code of ethics Clowns Without Borders carefully distances itself from any form of propaganda, and focuses on serving people in need.

Clowns and Spirituality

In many cultures, the clown has much in common with the shaman. As a trickster and transformer, the clown interacts with the world of spirit. A number of clowns have taken their cue from this aspect of the clown world, and engage in clowning for spiritual reasons. The paths of these clowns range from Zen Buddhist to Evangelical Christian, and their styles range just as far, but they all see clowning as a sacred activity, a way to be and bring others on a spiritual path.

The use of clowning as a tool for demonstrating Christian faith has become a widespread form of clowning. Clown ministers have developed their own adaptations of classic clown gags for use in promoting their faith. An entire set of theological precepts related to clowning has evolved, and clown ministers have found Christian symbolism in traditional clown iconography and in the transformative act of becoming a clown. Olive Drane structures the flow of her performances to be interactive in order to emphasize the importance of the personal nature of spiritual relationships and the accessability of the gospels. "In Clown Ministry the very act of becoming a Clown is a symbol of a person's decision to accept Christ," according to Floyd Schaffer and Penne

Sewall, authors of the book *Clown Ministry*. Christians of all denominations practice clown ministry, although the majority appear to belong to evangelical protestant sects.

The Faithful Fools of San Francisco have taken the idea of spiritual clowning to a deep level. Founded by Sister Carmen Barsody and Reverend Kay Jorgensen, a Catholic nun and a Unitarian minister, the fools focus on issues of homelessness, hunger and poverty in inner-city San Francisco and the barrios of Nicaragua. They celebrate fools as those "who see the world in all its glorious absurdity and act on what they see." Among their foolish exploits, they conduct regular street retreats in which they and any who will join them spend a day, a weekend, or longer living on the streets to bear witness to those who live there out of necessity. The Faithful Fools demonstrate spiritual clowning at its deepest level by allowing the fool to inform their day-to-day existence, living in the communities they serve.

The Spiritual side of clowning is not just recognized by Christian sects. The Order of Disorder, a "non-organization" envisioned by Roshi Bernie Glassman and Moshe Cohen, uses clowning as a form of engaged Buddhism. Cohen has taught workshops entitled "Humor Your Human" at a number of Zen centers. Egyoku Wendy Nakao, of the L.A. Zen Center said, "He is, in fact, helping you connect with your own humor, and that's a gift, really," (Yeung). The spirit of engaged, interactive play and spontaneity fostered by clowns resonates with the spirit of some aspects of zen, and is simultaneously an effective remedy to self-conscious or sanctimonious spirituality.

The individuals and organizations doing interactive clown work are far too numerous to list, and as this overview shows, every clown interacts in different ways. Whether working in city hospitals or the dirt roads of refugee camps they share some common threads. Most agree that aspiring clowns should learn as much as they can about the art of the clown. Many recommend working with partners or in groups, and working closely with medical professionals, social workers, or others trained to meet the special needs of the people with whom the clowns may interact. Common to all is a belief in the power of humor and the clown's unique perspective to do more than merely entertain. All share a willingness to take a chance, to appear foolish, and to step out of the ring and off the stage to engage with the world as fully as possible.

References

Other Training Centers, Organizations, Resources and References: may be found on the webpage supplement to this chapter: <www.interactiveimprov. com/clownwb.html>

Adams, Patch, M.D. and Mylander, Maureen. *Gesundheit!: Bringing Good Health to You, the Medical System, and Society Through Physician Service, Complementary Therapies, Humor, and Joy.* Rochester, VT: Healing Arts Press. 1993. This is the book that, along with his work, stimulated the making of the late 1990s movie, "Patch Adams," and presents his philosophy and vision of humor and health care.

Bolton, Reg. (1982) *Circus in a suitcase.* Bethel, CT: New Plays Incorporated. (A brief book outlining Bolton's early work in circus education. It provides basic information for teaching a circus workshop.)

Drane, Olive M. Fleming. (2004). *Clowns, storytellers, disciples: spirituality and creativity for today's church.* Oxford England: Augsburg Fortress Publishers. (Contains both theological backing and practical tips for clown ministry.)

Gravy, Wavy. (1993). *Something good for a change: random notes on peace through living.* New York: St. Martin's Press. This book presents the author's memoir and philosophy.

Sugarman, Robert. (2001). *Circus for everyone.* Shaftsbury, VT: Mountainside Press. (Overview and also a listing of training opportunities, ranging from community programs to college degrees.)

Towsen, John H. (1976). *Clowns.* New York: Hawthorn Books. (An essential historical overview of clowning. Out of print, but the text is available online, as noted below.)

Yeung, B. (2002). Clowns Without Borders: <www.sfweekly.com/issues/2002-12-04/feature.html>

Web Resources

<www.worldclownassociation.com> The site of the World Clown Association, including educational resources and clown insurance information.

<www.clownresourcedirectory.com> A broad listing of online resources about clowning, sorted by category.

<www.clownconservatory.com> The website of the United States premier clown training program.

<www.americanyouthcircus.org> The website of the American Youth Circus Organization. It features articles about circus education and has links to many schools and other clown training programs.

<www.bloomfield.edu/towsen/pc/pchome.htm> Site maintained by clown scholar John Towsen. It includes full text of his book, *Clowns*.

<www.faithfulfools.org> Site describing the Faithful Fools programs and philosophy.

<www.clowning4christ.com> Site with information, links, and bibliography of Christian clown ministry resources.

<www.clownswithoutborders.org>: Site of the U.S. Clowns Without Borders.

<www.hospitalclown.com>: Site of the *Hospital Clown Newsletter*, a quarterly newsletter dealing with clowning in hospitals and related service.

Chapter 31

THE MOVIEXPERIENCE

Daniel J. Wiener

The MOVIExperience (ME), an approach created by David Shepherd, is an intensive experience for a group of from ten to thirty-five people who come together to create a video movie. Like playmaking and other forms, this approach engages the group in dramatic interaction and creativity, exploring the roles of playwright, director, actor, and so forth. The entire ME is created within a short time period (typically over a single weekend, and sometimes only 24 hours), during which all of the following are accomplished: creating a scenario, casting, finding locations, operating equipment, acting in front of the camera, editing (often done in-camera), and holding a screening of the final product (usually running from twenty minutes to an hour).

David Shepherd has been a pioneering figure in improvisational theatre for fifty years. (Some of his work is mentioned in Chapter 27 on TheatreSports.) This is a slightly different venture. Noting that changes in technology have made it possible for people without expensive equipment or professional skills to participate in movie-making, Shepherd has brought his theatrical experience and enthusiasm to dozens of MEs throughout North America since 1994. He views the ME as a personally and socially transforming process which allows ordinary people to participate in what has until recently, been a professionally exclusive activity. Unlike Hollywood movies, which can cost upwards of $10,000 per minute of finished film and involve the coordinated efforts of hundreds of specialized professionals, the ME can be achieved by a small group of untrained people, over a weekend, on a budget of a few hundred dollars.

Shepherd has written a book on the ME, "… that Movie in Your Head: Guide to Improvising Stories on Video" (2004). This practical guide covers nearly everything that an interested amateur might need to know to create a successful ME, including: choosing interesting locations; screen-testing and casting; writing scenarios which form the basis for improvising; technical production information on using the video camcorder, sound, and lighting; Coaches Signals; project managing and coaching in the field; and numerous case studies of problems that were encountered and overcome in particular MEs.

A defining feature of the ME is that the movie itself is secondary to the participants' involvement with the project. As Shepherd puts it: "Is the final tape more important than the *experience* your group has? No! The way we designed it, our improv movie should be shaped by its players. They are in on every big decision—from scouting locations to choosing which footage to edit or dupe." (p. 22). This process is fun, absorbing, demanding, social, skills-building and expressive of what the group has to say. The ME has also occasionally been done with the creation of a parallel documentation movie about the making of the ME movie.

Any collective of people will be suitable to having a satisfying ME, provided they don't start out mistrusting one another. Participants have been guests at house parties, groups of friends, work colleagues, church members and youth groups. The ME works best with people who already know each other, or who get acquainted before the shoot. When one person or a small group invites other participants with the intention of having both a quality experience and a worthwhile movie, it is helpful to include those who have: known talents for improvising, debating and performing; tolerance for new games and activities; and playfulness and humor.

Once a group has been assembled, the leader organizes a Brainstorming process to develop a scenario. The leader need not have been involved in prior MEs, nor possess formal organizational skills, but has a clear vision of facilitating the process by which the group creates a ME. The leader is steering the process initially, though a palpable moment occurs in which responsibility for the project shifts from the leader to the group. As John Fucile, another director of improvisational movies notes, the ME is a collective, rather than an entrepreneurial venture.

The brainstorming process, which usually takes two to four hours, may center on: a generic topical theme (such as "employment"); a topic with social, political or moral impact for that particular group (such as "housing developers threatening our community"); or the creation of a unique story. In its early stages, brainstorming works better among smaller sub-groups of three or four members; once the subgroups have had some time to come up with promising, agreed-upon ideas the same process can be enlarged to a larger group of ten to fifteen people. Brainstorming increases both the buy-in for all participants individually and a "group mind" of collective ownership. Shepherd notes that very few people leave a ME once underway, other than for health reasons. Power struggles are unlikely, since the repeated voting on all important decisions creates consensus. Ideas are compiled and then voted on a number of times.

The tangible result of the brainstorming process is a written scenario of about 250 words (sometimes supplemented by quick-sketch story-boards) which sets forth the plot/premise and specifies characters and locations. (By contrast, professionally-made movies require hundreds of times more detail for a shooting script). A shorthand version of the scenario is the "spine," consisting of from one to three sentences and which summarizes "what it's about." [example: *A poor relative comes to live with a rich family. One by one, he converts them to beliefs, which gives the exact strength & peace each of them needs. One day he's gone. (p. 118)*].

As it may not be easy for the group to reach consensus on a scenario, Shepherd suggests a few exercises to facilitate the process: In *grabbing interest*, one player starts to tell a scenario story that s/he believes will grab the group's interest. Another player times the story with a watch while the rest of the players hold up a hand when they lose interest. If a majority of players have a hand raised before the story ends, it's the next player's turn to grab interest.

In *beginnings and ends*, Players stand in a circle, and select one sentence for the beginning and another for the end of a story. Going around the circle, players take turns fleshing out the middle of the story. Finally, if the group cannot agree on a scenario, the leader may ask the group to brainstorm themes (such as "love" or "fame" or "revenge"). After voting on a favorite theme the group comes up with a dozen short scenes linked by the theme. Once a scenario is chosen there is an opportunity to reconsider: "is this what we really want to do?" If there seems to be diluted enthusiasm, the group takes a short break and then returns to the brainstorming process.

The next part of the ME is the collective making of specific, realistic choices of locations (e.g., a nearby park, deserted at night), numbers and types of characters, and the key activities that will occur in scenes (e.g., a duel with water balloons). In this stage there is a fitting of stories to locations, characters to locations and actors to play characters. Not infrequently, it is discovered that the scenario must be modified or discarded because the group lacks the locations needed to tell the story, or lacks the number or type of characters called for in the scenario.

Unlike scripted movies, a ME relies on improvisation, as there isn't time to write, rewrite, memorize or rehearse a script. The scenario provides just enough structure for coherence and continuity, yet reflects the ideas of its many contributors. Moreover, lines that are improvised sound fresh; because ME characters are built from personal experience they often appear livelier than enactments of scripted characters by professional actors.

Shepherd stresses that neither individual scenes nor the entire scenario should completely specify an ending. Just as life is interesting because we don't know how things are going to come out, shooting without a known ending keeps players energized and interested. Instead, endings of scenes and the entire movie emerge during the shooting of the movie, or from an editorial choice of alternate endings shot during the making of the movie. Even where the scenario specifies an outcome, the choice of how it comes about is left open-ended. Overall, despite the necessity of some planning and structure, the spirit of a ME is chaotic—players discover what happens as they go through this creative, confusing, seat-of-the-pants experience.

After the scenario is decided, functional roles for each participant are selected by the group, although the person(s) organizing the ME may already have agreed to take the leadership role. The key leadership roles are: Project Manager, Coach, Experience Host and Camera Operator, roles which may be held by fewer than four separate persons in smaller MEs.

The Project Manager, who creates the group through inviting/recruiting participants, organizes the logistics of the production phase and handles the money, is typically the overall ME leader. As a skillful leader, the Project Manager oversees the entire operation, delegating/empowering participants to undertake specific tasks, leading the brainstorming sessions, and dealing with unhappy participants. The mission of the ME leader, remember, is to co-create a fun experience, so a balance has to be struck continually between attending to people's feelings and getting the job done.

The Coach functions somewhat as a theatrical Director, although with far less control over the acting on-stage. As Shepherd notes: "What's the difference between a theatre Director and an improv Coach? The Director thinks of an Actor as a very interesting lump of clay, to be carefully molded and shaped. The improv Coach treats a player like an energy that's been donated to the movie. It can't be changed but can be guided." (p. 53). The Coach is alert to bad acting, deciding whether another take is needed, gives props to provide focus and make characters more defined, offers warm-ups whenever energy flags and offers constructive feedback to bring out the best performances.

The Experience Host attends to the group's comfort, maintaining a strong, positive energy throughout the ME. The Experience Host fills in for others or supplies whatever is lacking or in need of improvement, whether that is a clean toilet, a needed prop or costume, help with makeup, freeing up a video camera so a participant can have the experience of shooting footage, answers to questions, or prizes awarded for "most vivid character."

The Camera Operator not only performs his/her title function but typically heads the Tech crew (camera-, lighting- and sound-persons, including various assistants) and continuity persons (monitoring for internal consistency).

All these roles, including that of Actor, can be shared or rotated during the production. A single participant may, in the course of a ME, act a speaking role, appear in a crowd scene, scout a location, bring props and potato chips, learn how to adjust sound levels, ask passers-by at an outdoor public location to keep out of the camera's line of sight, and vote on a movie ending. The process of coming up with these functional roles is a fluid one—some players come into the ME with strong expectations of how they will participate while others are more flexible. With large casts there may be more participants who want to stand out on camera than there are speaking parts in the scenario. Bridges (brief scenes that show some relevant action and which are interpolated between main scenes) provide opportunities to feature more players in smaller parts, as extras, or in crowd scenes. Once the scenario is chosen, there can be another, briefer brainstorming session to invent bridges. When bridges are filmed they will require as much coaching as main scenes.

When among the people gathered for a ME there are none possessing either the technical skills to operate equipment nor the desire to learn how, local tech talent can be hired; often students majoring in Communications, Broadcasting or Film from a nearby college will gladly work for a modest stipend in order to have the work experience. Resources are sought and identified—who will drive crew to and from locations, supply food, and provide props and costumes. By way of orientation, the leader or project manager asks players to imagine it's the end of the ME and to say what has happened during the past 36 hours. This helps players to attend to their expectations and clarify what the sequence of activities will be.

Casting is a group process in which players are invited to use the personality traits they have, though they are also encouraged to stretch themselves to be expressive beyond their everyday roles. Even when the actors are well-known to one another, Screen Tests are held since, as Shepherd explains, "... it's part of the process of making a movie. From childhood, people dream of the Hollywood audition. Now they can have one on their home turf." (p. 22)

During the "Coach's Signals" (improvisational warm-ups described further below) players explore the emotive and movement features of their characters. If someone can't play their character convincingly the role may be recast, although the threshold of acceptable performance is likely to be modest by professional standards. In general, people look good on camera when: they are playing a part close to what they do in real life; play the part with plenty of feeling; are warmed up before the shoot and keep breathing while on camera. Giving people a chance to try out for roles during the Screen Test will not always provide a fair test of their capacities; however, once a player warms up in character, mismatches are revealed—the actor playing a police captain is soft and doesn't project leadership—the actor playing the therapist appears frozen and inattentive. Players, it should be stated, are not being judged but fitted for a part; changes in actors' parts are made quickly, right from the beginning of the shooting or during the casting process.

One game useful to quickly explore actors' flexibility and range is called *shorties*. On each of several 3 x 5 index cards, an encounter between two conventional characters is sketched (e.g., a tourist who speaks no English asks directions from a local resident who speaks almost no English). In pairs, players choose a card and play the scene in about one minute. Their enactments are filmed so they can see "how they test." *Shorties* also give reliable indications of how actors "play off" one another which in turn can be used to select or modify scenes involving their characters.

Coach's signals are improvisational games, mostly for pairs of players, used to warm players up, both to character development and to on-camera acting. Some of these games are: *contact* (where, on each speech turn, players can't talk until they touch their partner in a new way that makes sense in terms of the scene already established); *fast mo/slow mo* (where players change the speed of their speech and movement at points which make sense); "5-second Delay" (where players are required to wait 5 seconds after another player finishes speaking before saying anything, while also making the silences make sense in the scene); and *mood swing* (where players gradually change their emotions from one extreme in the beginning to the opposite extreme at the end). *Coach's signals* are used right before shooting each scene to warm up players to the moment, offsetting their tendency to try to memorize lines and actions. (Coach's signals and other warm-ups are also opportunities for novice camera operators to learn how to shoot action). In addition to playing *coach's signals* with their ME scene partners, players develop a "back-story" for their characters through conversation which adds depth and realism to the filmed scenes.

One singular feature offered to prospective ME leaders is a typology of ME group members that Shepherd has encountered repeatedly, along with suggestions for handling different types and their impact on the ME group's dynamics. Among others, one encounters: *Stabilizers*, who take few risks in life and will usually play only themselves on-camera: *wafflers*, who hate to be counted on (Shepherd suggests that if you want one waffler to participate, invite five); *no-nos*, who are bent on being critical, yet who may offer valuable suggestions; *pros*, who are highly responsible but refuse to take chances that might result in them coming off badly; *sky jumpers*, who are conflicted about taking risks and will usually fill their risk-quota early on; *goofs*, who expect life to be wonderful and leave if they don't get to joke around continually; *gratefuls*, who have few expectations and are glad to be involved with a non-routine project; and *serious players*, who are desperately tired of being their conventional selves and welcome the opportunity to play unusual roles. Of these last, Shepherd writes: "Protect them even when they fail, because they grasp the essence of play." (p. 85)

Others who have led MEs are also interviewed in Shepherd's book: Nancy Fletcher, who has applied the ME to a program called ACT NOW! which empowers personal and group creativity for adolescent girls; Nikhil Melnechuk, a young filmmaker who starts with a rudimentary script and then encourages improvised action and dialogue; George Kuchar, a film professor who has been directing his students in the making of ultra-low-budget videos each semester for over twenty years; and John Fucile, an award-winning independent filmmaker whose works have been shown at numerous film festivals. The latter two contributors differ from David Shepherd in their use of scenarios; Kuchar sees scenarios as pointless, since for him the only reason to make a movie is to discover something that the group has inside itself, while for Fucile worthwhile scenarios arise from a movie-making process in which players are genuine and present, so that the choices made are inherently correct.

Throughout the entire ME, the spirit both of maximizing team participation and allowing for impromptu changes is followed. The camera is passed around so that everyone has a chance to do some filming. New suggestions for choices are continually encouraged, as improvised dialog and action often spark insights, creativity and discoveries. Unanticipated problems with locations, props, costumes, or on-camera performances lead to flexible (and often improved!) substitutions. The attitude remains playful, caring, competent and committed.

The editing of the raw ME footage (which usually consists of a few takes, at most) of each scene, can be done by one person (professionally, as in the work of Kuchar), by a group of outsiders or by the group itself through a polling/voting process. Editing may be done for viewing on local access cable TV, or entered in a local film festival.

The screening of the finished product (often on the following weekend) is done for the group, typically with invited friends and family members, further broadening the social experience. Shepherd also encourages groups to send their movies to his website (see below).from which they can be accessed on line by others. Some groups also make their movies available to the community through their local video stores.

As David Shepherd tells ME participants before the screening: "It doesn't really matter what happens to this footage. It's your experience that's important, and you had that before the screening" (p. xiv). The excitement, involvement, learning and satisfaction that is regularly generated by a ME will continue to attract participants increasingly as word gets out.

References

Shepherd, David (2004) ... *that Movie in Your Head: Guide to Improvising Stories on Video.* Shutesbury, MA: Gere Publishing.

Website: <www.groupcreativityproject.com>

Chapter 32

THEATER OF GAMES

Bernie DeKoven

In the development of children, there is little distinction made by them between make-believe dramatic play and many of the games they play. (This distinction becomes more defined in late childhood and the teen years.) Ordinary children's games offer opportunities for a range of role-taking and group-building activities, and in this respect they should be recognized as extensions of drama. Applied later in life, in addition to the various theatre games described elsewhere in this book, a variety of regular games may be used also in the service of reminding people how to play, how to explore spontaneity and the building of mutually supportive relationships. Though degrees and types of competition vary, from types in which everybody wins to some types that do have a win/lose dynamic, they're still games as long as "it's fun!"

Background

After receiving my Master's degree in Theatre, I was hired by the School District of Philadelphia to write a drama curriculum for elementary school teachers. I was working with inner-city children between the ages of 5–11, most of whom were sent to us because they were someone else's behavior problem. I very much wanted to help the kids create some kind of theatre experience that they found meaningful, relevant, and, most importantly, fun. My single criterion for success was that, if I walked out of the room for two minutes, the kids would be doing the same thing when I came back. It was really the only way I could think of to be sure that they were doing it for themselves, and not for a grade or for me. This was a very tough test for my understanding of what it meant to teach theatre.

Nothing I tried really worked. They didn't warm-up to the warm-ups. They were too skittish for the skits. Oh, they were polite, and they'd do what I asked, but nothing clicked. Eventually, I and tried some of Spolin's theatre games. They were enthusiastic about the game part, but the moment I stepped out of the room, chaos ensued. Finally, out of desperation, I asked them if there were anything at all that they actually wanted to play together. "Yes," they chorused, "a game."

A game!?! Not a theatre game, just a plain, silly kids' game. "You know," they appended, "like Duck-Duck-Goose." That's a game where everyone sits in a circle and one kid, the Fox, taps each kid on the head and says "Duck" until she reaches the one kid she wants to get chased by. She calls the kid "Goose." The Goose stands up and gives chase. If tagged by the Goose before getting to the Goose's vacated seat, the Fox has to start over again. If not tagged, the kid that got chosen is the new Fox. It struck me as a silly game, with really no relevance to the higher dramatic arts. But a deal is a deal. So we played. After a while, I walked out, and after another while, I came back in—and they were still playing!

They even invited me to play. I was honored, but hesitant. I gave in. I played their game, because it was theirs—and, yes, I had fun. And while I was having all that fun I began to be able to appreciate the game as *more than a game*—as, in fact, drama! For us potential Geese, it was all about acting like you wanted to get chosen (or not). Too enthusiastic or blasé, and you stay a Duck forever. For the Goose, it was about whom do you pick, and how hard do you run. Should you pick a friend who is faster than you? someone you don't like who is slower than you? someone you want to like? someone you want to like you?

And once the Goose is chosen, the game achieves something like high drama. The Goose jumps up and gives chase. Can the Fox make it back to the Goose's home place and free herself of the curse of Foxhood? Will the Goose tag the Fox and damn it to yet another cycle of Foxiness? Unless, of course, the Goose doesn't really want to catch the Fox. Unless the Goose actually wants to become Fox herself. But what if the Fox wants to remain Fox? What if she doesn't run so fast, or stumbles, or has other sly strategies for maintaining her Foxiness yet another round? As the drama unfolds, the rest of us Ducks, temporarily relieved of any further involvement, observe in relieved delight. Will the Fox make it? Is it a good chase? Do they run as if being Fox or Goose were as important as life itself? Or as if it were just plain silly?

The Dramaturgy of Games

I had to play it first. And when I did, I realized that the clearly silly game of Duck-Duck-Goose fully satisfied my criteria for a meaningful, kid-produced, kid-acted, kid-directed, theatrical experience. It was highly dramatic. It was something they actually wanted to do, actually could organize and become engaged with. Thus I began work on my "theatre" curriculum and my lifelong exploration of that intriguing sub-field of applied theatre or the way games can be drama that I've called "Theater of Games." I soon discovered I was working within a global theatre. Searching for more and more games, I found books of games from all over the world. The Games that are played out in the Theater of Games are in fact a form of literature—not written, maybe, not even oral, perhaps, but "enacted"—and thus handed down, from generation to generation, brother to brother, culture to culture. The literature of games can convey complex relationships, roles and consequences, issues of conflict and heroism.

The comic-tragedy of Duck-Duck-Goose holds a great fascination for young audiences, and is one of many variations on a theme of what one can only call the "Game of Tag:"

1. Somebody is "*It*." One person is singled out and assigned a role different from the undifferentiated many. This makes his actions so monstrously predictable that we call him *It*, because in order to do what he is supposed to, he *always* has to do *It*. 2. *It* Doesn't Want to Be *It*. In fact, *It*'s goal is to make somebody else *It*. 3. If *It* Tags You (all *It* takes is contact), you're *It*! There's an instantaneous reversal of roles.

Before most children play Tag, they find themselves fascinated into sheer delight by a group of tag-like "games" called "Monster." Played by very small children—almost as soon as they are old enough to waddle—and large adults. Somebody is Monster—usually *It* is type-cast. That person, *It*-like, chases everybody else. Everybody else runs and runs until the Monster catches them and eats, or tickles, them up. Then, everybody runs away again, and the Monster does his thing. The kids play the Monster to laughing exhaustion. Then they wait to continue the drama the moment the Monster shows signs of readiness.

As a theatre piece, Tag is as profound as it is entertaining. It describes a relationship between fear and its victims. Tag is an irreversible relationship. The role of *It* is enforced equally by the pursued as well as the pursuer. By the time children begin playing tag, they are more interested in games where the role of authority is reversible, where the drama resides as much in the relationship as it does in the roles. Like any good drama, the game only works as long as there is conflict and as long as we are interested in that conflict. If *It* never catches anyone, if the same person is always *It*, the game is no fun.

Another way to think about Tag as drama is that it is also a contest for position, even though the position is, in itself, untenable. The person in the role of *It* is the Labeled One. The conflict centers on who gets to be what, how, and for how long. In some games, everyone wants to be the Labeled One. Everyone. At the same time, no one really wants to be labeled for very long. The drama reaches its peak and, once having become identified as *It*, the whole game depends on transferring the role of *It* to someone else.

And then there are variations of Tag: In "Red Light", *It* is given the power to decide when people can try to get him. In "Captain, May I?" *It* gets to tell the other players *how* they can move. In "What's the time, Mr. Wolf?" *It* has the power to decide when the tag-chase is going to start, and in "Johnny, May I Cross the River?" *It* has to publicly declare his intended victims. The aforementioned "Duck Duck Goose" falls in this category, also. In "British Bulldog," *It* is able to get the other players to help him. In "Circle Tag," *It* is restricted in its territory, or, as in "Freeze Tag" *It* doesn't have as much territory as everybody else. In that game, the other players also can escape more easily, while in "Squirrel in the Tree," they can substitute other players.

Sometimes, such as in the tag game "Cat and Mouse," there are people who are neither *It* or NOT-*It*, but rather are there just to make it harder for *It*. The tag may be with something other than *It*'s hand, as in "Ball Tag," or, in "Steal the Bacon" or "Football," *It* has an object that he is trying to put somewhere. (More detailed descriptions of many of these games may be found on websites such as: <www.gameskidsplay.net> or wikipedia.)

Then there are the versions of Tag when there is more than one *It*, when there's "us" and "them:" In "Guard the King" if one of us gets tagged, we lose the whole game, while in "Lemonade" or "Crows 'n Cranes," when one of us gets tagged, we join the other team. In "Prisoner's Base" or "5-10-Ringo," we and they both have the power of tagging, and if we get tagged by the wrong guys (them), we are out of the game until we get tagged by the right guys. The ingenuity of variation is impressive.

Though there is conflict between *It* and NOT-*It*, no score is being kept. Though you may really not want to be *It*, and though you might find yourself being *It* much longer than you bargained for, you never actually lose. Or, for that matter, win. After spending so much time on Tag, *It* almost comes as a shock to discover how different those very familiar games are from the games we have come to think of as "real,"that is, the contests that make up the world of educationally and commercially-supported sports. These are generally what in game theory are called "zero-sum" games, which means that they are a type of game in which, for one side to win, the other has to "lose."

In the dramaturgy of play, Tag is one type in a continuum of games. I have identified four different game types, looking at games not so much in terms of competition and cooperation, winning or losing, but rather in terms of the relationships they depicted. Tug-of-war, for example, went in the same volume as "Pit-a-Pat" (Pattycake) where nobody's *It* and everybody ultimately loses because both games are really hard to quit. The players in this game category are in a relationship to each other and have to somehow work it out to its conclusion.

Tag and Hide and Seek are categorized as "Locating" games, because the focus is on finding oneself in relationship to the group. There's a category I call "Expressing" games that are most like traditional theatre games, and, finally, a category of Adjusting" games, that involve changing the rules or goals. The games can be further classified according to how "active" the game is, and how the role of *It* is configured (i.e., individual, individual-group, individual-team, team-group, and team-team). Finally, another classification of games is distributed according to who seems to be in control of the major actions of the game.

However, despite the practicality of these classifications for some purposes, almost as soon as the curriculum was printed I was forced to admit that there was a still more enjoyable and in some ways effective approach: Play a game— any game will do. And then, when you have the opportunity, play a different game. The game that turns out to be the most fun for everyone will also prove to be the most healing, so play *that* one again!

The Way of Games

For the next two years I explored this game/theatre literature in depth, playing children's games, researching them, and ultimately compiled five volumes of over a thousand children's games. As I began to teach teachers, and discovered that they were so fascinated by the first game I taught Duck-Duck-Goose, and it was so much fun for them that it was difficult to stop! Finally, I was able to illustrate eight different games, each one demonstrating a different aspect of the "way of games:" team and individual, cooperative and competitive, active and quiet. The more I played with adults, and the more groups I played with, the more deeply I appreciated the power of children's games. I learned that, in less than a day, I could take a group of strangers, from virtually any background, and, playing children's games, create a community, a responsive, supportive, open, attentive, fun community. And in five days, these total strangers would be all over each other like kittens!

I discovered that in the great variety of children games, certain games could help people explore different ways of relating to each other. My repertoire of children's games gave me a kind of language of relationships, one I could easily share; these games and the language that identifies different types could prove instrumental in helping people create truly supportive, mutually empowering relationships. Over thirty-five years later, I'm doing the same thing, using the Theater of Games to help adults rediscover the experience of fun and community. Of course, given the vast dramaturgy of games, most of the games I play are the fun and community building kind. And, for the people I play with, the whole thing is a kind of healing, a kind of affirmation of the transforming power of the collective imagination.

For the part of me that is still a theatre artist, bringing the Theater of Games back to the field of drama, being included in this anthology, is like bringing my project back home. Every game becomes an invitation to energize mind and body, to observe each other more carefully, to focus spontaneity, to respond more quickly. A drama coach or director who has a wide-enough repertoire of children's games can use the Theater of Games not only to help build the actors' abilities to work together, but also as a tool to help actors develop a kind of language for exploring the relationships between characters as demanded by the script. Hide and Seek is one kind of relationship, Tag, quite another. Tug-of-War, Patty Cake, each a path towards better defining the connections between characters and the words they are saying to each other.

For the practitioner of applied theatre, the Theater of Games can become a living, multi-functional tool for developing healthy and healing relationships between individual and community, actor and company. As an invitation to participation, the Theater of Games offers a multitude of delightfully safe ways for people to interact with each other, physically, socially, and intellectually. When "fun's the thing," barriers between genders or ages, abilities or origins can be overcome almost instantly.

Having faith in the fun of it all is an important first step towards the effective use of children's games in almost any setting—professional, therapeutic or recreational. Here are some further steps:

1. *Voluntary*. Make and keep participation voluntary. The success of any game depends on the psychological and physical safety of its players. By keeping participation voluntary at all times, participants can safely regulate their level of involvement, almost regardless of level of trust. Sometimes, you can do this by establishing a "safe area"—an "out-of-bounds" place for people to retreat

to as needed. Often, I find myself having to devote maybe a whole session to "quitting practice." If people know it's really all right to quit (well, maybe you have to give a warning before you opt out of being say the base of a human pyramid), then they know that everyone is playing *only* because they want to.

2. *Focus on the game.* Recognizing that when either kids or adults play children's games, the issues evoked can reach very deep into the individual and collective adult psyche. Their dynamics never fail to bring up lessons about attitude, tendencies to take certain types of roles, and of lessons to be learned. When a game doesn't work (a.k.a. isn't fun), the lessons can all too easily become personal. The temptation to "process" begins to overpower the opportunity to enjoy each other. Resist this temptation, don't try to be an amateur therapist. Remember that it is a lot easier to change the game than the people who are playing it. If a game doesn't work, change it. Or play something else. As they say, "play on."

3. *Vary the play.* Don't get stuck playing only one game. Even if people really like playing Duck-Duck-Goose, and are finding the drama so relevant that it becomes, in fact, the only game they play, having a choice of games is as important to the participant as it is to the group. It's the difference between a "game community" and a "fun community." In a game community, it is the game that ultimately decides who is good enough to play. In the fun community, the *players* decide if the *game* is good enough. Start something else going with the people in the safe area, even if you're the only one there.

4. *Invite invention.* No game is as fun as the one the players are making up. No game is as well-adapted to the people you happen to be with, or where you happen to be, or what you happen to have to play with. The larger the shared game repertoire, the easier it is to find new ways to play together. It is a delicious circle.

The "best" games for creating this kind of collective sense of safety and openness tend to be those that are most intentionally designed to be fun. These games are often not even scored. Often there isn't even a winner. These games are generally fun, and often make people laugh. I call them "pointless games" not only because no one keeps score, but also because we play them for purpose other than the fun they bring us.

I've used "fun" three times in the last paragraph. It is impossible to overstate how central the fun connection is to the healing quality of the game—as it is played and experienced. In fact, as you widen the group's repertoire of games, fun turns out to be the best and most reliable criterion for finding just the right game for bringing the group to just the right place.

Most children's games, and any of my Pointless Games can be welcome tools, any time you need to set the stage for almost any kind of theatrical or role-playing relationship people want to explore. But it is important to remember that when you play for "fun" games not only set the stage, but also become the stage—a stage where even the most fundamental of conflicts and the deepest of dramas can be played, with delight.

Resources

The webpage supplement for further additions or links: <www.interactiveimprov. com/gameswb.html>

DeKoven, Bernie. (2000). *The well-played game: a playful path to wholeness* (2nd ed). Lincoln, NE: iUniverse. (The first edition of this book, in 1978, framed the core philosophy of the New Games training program.)

DeKoven, Bernie. (2004). *Junkyard sports.* Champaign, IL: Human Kinetics. (This book describes a more improvisational approach to games, and hence a more relevant tool for developing the skills and teamwork needed for improvisation. See <www.junkyardsports.com>)

LeFevre, Dale. (2002). *Best new games.* Champaign, IL: Human Kinetics. (Although the New Games Foundation no longer exists and the New Games books are out of print, Dale has done worked and played hard to keep the "spirit" and concept alive. Many of these games can be found online in my collection of "Pointless Games"—pointless, because no one keeps score, and the only real point is having fun—<www.deepfun.com/ pointless.html>)

Michaelis, Bill, & O'Connell, John M. (2000). *The game and play leader's handbook: facilitating fun and positive interaction.* State College, PA: Venture. (This is the best book on facilitating New Games, and, as a matter of fact, any invitation to play.)

Online

When it comes to exploring the Theater of Games, my DeepFUN website: <deepfun.com> offers probably the most diverse and extensive collection of links, articles and resources related to fun and games. All of the books and organizations recommended here can be found, amidst maybe 50 more, on: <www.deepfun.com/resources.htm>

As mentioned above, point-less (score-less) games are at deepfun.com/pointless.html>

Articles about the therapeutic dimensions of fun are at deepfun.com/health.htm>

Games Kids Play: <www.gameskidsplay.net/"> a collection of a couple hundred actual children's games.

Children's Folk Games <<digilander.iol.it/cfgames2000/>: a welcome, extensive, remarkable resource of folk games from around the world!

Eldrbarry's Group Games <<www.eldrbarry.net/vbs/gamedex.htm>>: a youth group leader's collection of traditional active games for children

Game Finder <<family.go.com/features/family_0000_01/famf/gamefinder_ tlp/>: find kids' games by age, number of players, indoor our outdoor, and by occasion.

Games for Groups <<www.gamesforgroups.com/>: don't be fooled by the purported therapeutic values, these games are genuinely fun!

Street Games <<www.streetplay.com/thegames/>: real games from real street play by real kids, really—documented, illustrated, filmed

Simulation games take the Theater of Games to the educational stage. One of the most prolific proponents and teachers is Sivasailam Thiagarajan ("Thiagi")—a wonderfully playful teacher whose games, books and courses are inspirational. His website is <www.thiagi.com>

When you're ready to get deeper in to the meaning of it all, TASP, The Association for the Study of Play, offers a well of research and theory about play and culture. You can find them online at <www.csuchico.edu/phed/tasp

For equally playworthy resources, try Youthwork Links and Activities http

Chapter 33

RELATED FIELDS

Adam Blatner

The underlying dynamism in drama should be recognized as a powerful social and psychological tool that can be used in a variety of ways—education, business, therapy, social action, personal development, and re-creation. The term, "applied theatre," has come to be used to describe the adaptations of improvisational and interactive drama for these practical purposes. However, interactivity and improvisational approaches are also being used in related fields beyond the theatre, and their use informs or overlaps with the general spirit of this book.

Performance Studies

In academic settings, efforts to construct a theoretical framework for applied theatre and performance is expressed through the relatively new field calld "performance studies." Scholars are exploring ways to evolve concepts and develop ways to investigate the underlying dynamics of anthropology, social psychology, literature and the arts, semiotics, critical theory, postmodernist philosophy, theatre arts, and other disciplines. It recognizes that drama offers not only a method, but also a kind of intellectual lens for better understanding many aspects of the social sciences (Carlson, 2004). The work of Richard Schechner (2003) is seminal in Performance Studies, and many articles expressing this field's perspectives may be found in the journal *TDR: The Drama Review*. (On the webpage supplement to this chapter, my observations on the nature of performance may be considered, and further additions will be added as research progresses.)

Creativity Studies

A related interdisciplinary field brings in thinkers in neuroscience, psychology, business and organizational development, education, and other fields. A few hundred years ago traditionalism was a foundation of morality, but increasingly, the idea of freedom—political, economic, spiritual, and social—requires a re-evaluation of earlier fixed norms and beliefs. This trend is accelerating as global competition requires continuing innovation, so there are economic incentives that support the intellectual challenge of better understanding what may be the most sublime edge of our human potential. There are now organizations devoted to exploring and promoting creativity, such as the American Creativity Association.

Moreno was perhaps the first (and perhaps also the least recognized) critic who noted the connection between improvisation and creativity. While some new ideas emerge in times of quiet reflection or contemplation, more often the do so in the process of actively experimenting, moving body as well as mind, allowing for an influx of energy and intuitions from the subconscious mind. (While Freud tended to see the subconscious as merely a repository of that which the ego disowned, Jung, acknowledged this function and astutely noted that a far greater part of the subconscious mind operated as a source of constructive intuitions, humor, inner guidance, and creative imagery!)

Beginning more vigorously in the 1960s, various psychologists, artists, writers, and others considered the nature of creativity and spontaneity—often coming to conclusions similar to those of Moreno (Blatner, 2000, pp. 80–88.). Mihalyi Csikszentmihalyi's (1990) concept of "flow" is an example of this re-thinking of the nature of certain more complex psychodynamics, and his writings elucidate the value of improvisation for its own sake.

Play

Another field related to creativity and performance is that of play, referring to a number of associated dynamics. In our culture, much of play is associated with organized sports, passive entertainment, travel, while imaginative, make-believe play tends to be thought of as only being appropriate for children. More recently, though, there have been trends towards live-action role playing and other forms of helping adults to enjoy types of imaginative play (King, 1998; Noxon 2006).

As with performance studies, serious academic consideration has begun to be given to the dynamics of play, again involving ethology (the comparative behavior of animals), anthropology, child development, sociology, the "entertainment industry" (e.g., the emergence of increasing numbers of "theme parks" such as Disneyland), and other phenomena. The Association for the Study of Play (TASP) offers a general umbrella organization for considering this field.

Deriving from this, the related fields of "leisure studies" and "recreation" also address aspects of play. They are concerned with, among other endeavors, the more effective design of playgrounds and parks (overlapping with other fields such as city planning and landscape design), recreational facilities and programs, summer camps, and lifelong learning programs. Far from being restricted to the domain of childhood, a re-thinking of the nature of play now is relevant in planning facilities for the retired. Play is more than mere frittering away of time; it can involve serious work that is not subject to many of the demands of organizations, and thus overlaps with volunteerism, lifelong learning, and opportunities for personal integration and deeper meaning-making.

Humor Studies

This is a growing field that is emerging as businesses and other organizations are recognizing the need for promoting morale at a grass-roots level. Three-quarters of a century ago much of work and study was motivated more by fear than the lure of intrinsic motivation. However, creativity wilts as anxiety increases; alternatively, creativity tends to emerge more in contexts that are considered safe. Play and humor tend to communicate greater safety and free up improvisation and interactivity.

Simulations

A more grown-up form of children's play is the use of more elaborate tools and procedures to set up situations for experimentation. As systems and situations become more complex, their designers cannot anticipate all possible problems. Programs need to be developed through a process of trial and error. While a bullet can be aimed, a space ship, traveling many magnitudes of distance further, must of necessity re-check and be able to adjust its course as it flies. So, too, the capacity to adjust a course of action requires a process of acting, obtaining feedback, and creative adjustment.

Certain kinds of simulations can be aided by using computerized and complex technology, so flight simulators and the like may be used to train certain technical skills in pilots and astronauts. A more complex simulation may require even further technology, but also has the added challenge of dealing with human interactions, verbal and non-verbal communications, styles of communication, cultural differences, and the like. These may or may not involve some technical aids, but also become a kind of group role playing—i.e., a sub-set of applied theatre.

Role playing also has the benefit of being able to be used in many situations in which there are no technical aids, which makes the procedure a kind of user-friendly "mind tool." It recognizes that a person's technical skill acquisition must often be integrated with the more elusive challenge of "people-skills." For example, there are some military exercises now being conducted that use paid actors to play the parts of the natives of a country in which there are also insurgents. Soldiers are being trained in the art of diplomacy, too.

Medical schools are beginning to use actors to role play problem patients, so as to train students to develop a better bedside manner, interviewing technique, and ways of encouraging patients to accept and practice a healthful regimen of prevention or treatment. Even hotels are using actors to play problem guests in order to train staff in ways of dealing with such problems.

Role Playing for Role Expansion

In addition to role playing in education or the training of vocational skills, there is also value to be found in more playful role playing, as described in Chapters 26–29. Although it's a new idea to some folks, for those who have picked up on the idea, there is a natural enrichment that comes with developing a repertoire of alter egos. These may be characters one takes on a live action role playing (LARP) activity, on an internet role playing game (e.g., Sims, Warquest, etc.), at a Star Trek or some other social association that explores fantasy and science fiction characters, and so forth.

The role playing that goes with major cultural holidays should be recognized as a core element. Halloween seems to be becoming ever more elaborate, the variety and vividness of costuming and accessories less expensive and more available, and the creation and staffing of the haunted house is now big business. Mardi Gras and communities that celebrate costume parties and dress up likewise offer opportunities not only to show off a clever or sexy costume, but to get into character, perhaps even develop a "backstory" or fabricated history of that role. (The whole activity of enjoying, designing, and elaborating uniforms of various types is described by Fussell [2002], and informs this activity as well as complements writings in performance theory.)

Other ways people enjoy role taking include celebrity impersonation, getting into character and costume at a community parade, etc. I discuss the psychological value of role expansion in an essay that is a webpage supplement to this book, "The More We Can Be": <www.interactiveimprov.com/morewecanbe.html>

The Arts

In spite of the tendencies towards separating the arts in different departments and social compartments, interdisciplinary efforts and syntheses are common. Opera mixes music, drama, singing, and various degrees of art (in stage design), costume design, dance and movement, and so forth. The dialogue may be variably poetic in nature. Similarly, some of the methods in this book weave in other arts, such as the way playback theatre uses a musician accompanist. The variable of *improvisation* is similarly expanding in these forms and throughout the arts, replacing the cultural dominance of the fully scripted and rehearsed production. (Interestingly, some of Shakespeare's early plays were more improvised than generally recognized, drawing both on the general structure provided by the playwright, but enjoying also some of the tone of the commedia dell'arte still prevalent in Europe.)

The Creative Arts Therapies

Influenced in part by Moreno's emphasis on the vitalizing power of spontaneity, art therapists, dance-movement therapists, poetry and music therapists as well as drama therapists begin to build in increasing amounts of improvisational activities in the mid-20th century. These trends, in turn, stimulated mainstream arts practice to also take on elements of improvisation. Indeed, some artists, using videotape, capture events that cannot be fully rehearsed, as they draw on elements of nature, the spontaneity of an interactive audience (as in the "happenings" of the late 1960s), and so forth. Thus, these parallel efforts in other fields influence and are influenced by improvisational drama.

Dance-Movement Improvisation. This sub-set is especially noteworthy as having significant relevance to improvisational and interactive drama. While not having as much of the theme of dialog, this modality does engage the body—indeed, may do so even more fully. Alluded to in Chapters 18 and 23, certain forms are worthy of being mentioned here. More about them may be found on the webpage supplement to this chapter: Ruth Zaporah's Action Theatre; Nina Wise's work; Contact Improvisation; Interplay. The reader will doubtless encounter other innovators, and we welcome hearing about and linking to them on the webpage supplement.

(Indeed, we were impressed enough by the near-drama work of these pioneers that we considered giving them chapters in the book—but then realized that there was some degree of scope to this book, some boundary to be exercised. This problem came up with some of the other related fields mentioned in this chapter, also.)

Improvisational Theatre and Comedy ("Improv")

Only minimally interactive, mainly performed by professionals as entertainment for paying audiences, this field is growing and represents a significant intermediate arena which, like dance-improvisation, almost fits within the scope of this book—but not quite. Its emphasis on performance makes it a bit closer to traditional theatre. On the other hand, many improv theatre artists are also teaching improv classes, using it in business, and so the fields blur. Improv should be recognized as a significant development in theatre that overlaps to some degree with TheatreSports (Chapter 27).

Play Therapy

There is a mixture of varying degrees of drama in play therapy for children, using puppets, toys, weaving in varying degrees of mutual story-telling. Drama therapists and psychodramatists who work with younger children do activities that overlap with other more traditional play therapy approaches. Some of the benefits of play therapy can also be enjoyed by adults who are invited to participate with or without their children (Schaefer, 2003).

Action in Psychotherapy

Another related group of approaches involve types of psychotherapy that, like psychodrama, have moved the client off the couch or chair and into physical action. In addition to the way Gestalt therapy and family therapy (i.e. in the form of family sculpture) have integrated psychodramatic methods, others have independently or with little acknowledgment of the contributions of Moreno also begun to use dramatic elements: Hal and Sidra Stone's "Voice Dialogue" elaborates on the role playing technique of having one part of the mind talk to another part in two different chairs. Richard Schwartz' Internal Family Systems Therapy uses similar techniques, as do some others. Derived from dance-movement therapy, Al Pesso's Pesso-Boyden System Psychomotor sets up "structures" (like tableaux or sculptures) and works with these as ways to more vividly re-experience the stress and the corrective emotional experience of what in psychodrama has been called the *reformed auxiliary ego* technique.

The Human Potential Movement

Drama, play, imagination, spontaneity, these and the active therapy approaches mentioned above have all been adapted for moving beyond the clinical context (i.e., treating diagnosed psychiatric disorders) and applied also to help healthy people become even healthier. The psychologist Will Schutz (1967, 1971) described ways these various "encounter techniques" could be woven together to build a more complex personal growth experience. Over the subsequent three decades, the idea of designing an experiential workshop for various more focused purposes as become more refined, and examples of this may be found in this present book in Chapters 4, 18, and 23.

Story-Telling

Beyond the artistic elements and opportunities for personal expressiveness and intergenerational socializing, the art of storytelling can offer opportunities for oral history, the construction of memoirs or the bringing alive of stories constructed from genealogy and family traditions. Relating again to the emerging leisure activities for the elderly (as discussed in Chapter 3), helping people to write, read, and with some animation, enact their stories, all deepens the sense of personal meaning in life for actors and audience alike.

(Telling tall tales, liars' club performances, and reveling in the performance of thrasonical bombast—a fancy way of talking about b.s.—these humor forms, like near-improvisational "pun-offs," poetry slams, and other contests also celebrate improvisation in an indirect fashion.)

Reader's theatre is another form of drama that can include more people and yet demand less in the way of memorization and rehearsal than traditional scripted theatre. While not improvisational or interactive, it stands as a related field.

On-Line Internet Drama

In a webpage supplement to this chapter <www.interactiveimprov.com/onlinedr.html>>, Toni Sant and Kim Flintoff describe a field at the edge of drama and the theatre arts. There are those who are taking role playing on the internet and developing a wide range of ways to interact, create other dramatic structures. It's a bit complex, but suffice it to say that millions of people are playing multi-user adventure games, or create a world-type games (such as the Sims), and these have been featured in major news magazines. Is it drama? Time will tell.

The Applied and Interactive Theatre Guide (AITG)

To begin with, there is the rich scope of methods noted on Toni Sant's internet website, *Applied & Interactive Theatre Guide.* This is an online resource for (in Sant's words), "… those who use theatre techniques for *other* or *more than* arts or entertainment purposes, and for those whose theatre styles incorporate other than traditional presentation styles. It serves mainly as a directory of websites related to alternative and applied theatre. Through a small number of general categories, the AITG groups online resources into manageable clusters of otherwise eclectic listings."

Sant further writes, "The AITG is primarily designed to help those who are exploring some of the niches being filled by theatre practitioners who seek to use their skills in ways not represented on a traditional stage. The website is not only a directory but also a networking resource for anyone who felt, as Bertolt Brecht did, that theatre is a tool to make a better life by helping people explore their communities.

Theatre professionals throughout the world are working to bring their skills as change agents, as awareness builders, and as empathy masters to the personal and social needs of a world hungry for connection. Still, the differing forms of applied theatre and interactive drama are varied enough that even terminology remains a difficulty. Theatre-in-Education, Drama-in-Education, Non-Scripted Theatre, Sociodrama, Forum Theatre, Community Theatre are all descriptors that can be found in the various scholarly indices. The Applied and Interactive Theatre Guide was created on a web server at the State University of New York's Institute of Technology in Utica by Joel Plotkin in 1995 to provide an online forum for exploring the means to arrive at more widely accepted terminology for the various branches of this growing field."

(Toni Sant continues.) "In September 1998 Joel Plotkin asked me to move the website to a web server at New York University, and, in the process, I redesigned the guide to incorporate a modest message board, search facilities, and other enhancements. A further upgrade has taken place since then, thanks to the technical support of the MaltaMedia Online Network, automating the database on the web server.

The current version of the AITG covers eleven major areas of interest. They are (in alphabetical order): Boal Techniques, Drama Therapy, Hacktivism, History of Theatre, Playback Theatre, Psychodrama, Radical Theatre, Sociodrama, Theatre in Education, Training and Development, and WorldWideWeb Resources and Links."

Summary

This chapter notes the variety of cultural developments and psycho-social "technologies" that operate at the edge of interactive and improvisational drama, using some elements and in turn contributing influences and ideas. This cross-fertilization is occurring globally in many and varied contexts. I was impressed with the ways theatrical methods were being applied in combinations and variations demonstrated abundantly at the International Drama and Theatre in Education (IDEA) conference in 2004 in Ottawa, Canada,.

One of the benefits of the webpage supplement and the associated website for this book is that it makes the book interactive. If you see something that needs to be corrected, or if you would like to suggest some additions—a program, link, anecdote, or new references—, please write to me. This way, the overall "book-website" complex continues to be updated and refreshed, opening to the needs of the moment and the spontaneity of the readers.

Finally, I envision the related fields mentioned above serving synergistically with the various types of applied theatre to provide a richer cultural infrastructure. They are all tools for the mind, for consciousness raising, community-building, empowerment, mind-expanding recreation, education, and other constructive purposes. The boundaries of applied theatre continually expand and the role of drama in our lives promises to become more and more relevant.

References

Further references and notes may be found on the webpage supplement to this chapter: <www.interactiveimprov.com/relatedfieldswb.html>.

Blatner, Adam. (2000). *Foundations of psychodrama: History, theory and practice.* New York: Springer.

Carlson, Marvin A. (2004). *Performance: A critical introduction* (2nd ed.). New York: Routledge.

Csikszentmihaly, Mihalyi. (1990). *Flow: The psychology of optimal experience.* New York: Harper & Row.

Fussell, Paul. (2002). *Uniforms: Why we are what we wear.* Boston: Houghton Mifflin.

King, Vivian. (1998). *Soul play: Turning your daily dramas into divine comedies.* Georgetown, MA: Ant Hill Press.

Kipper, David. (1986). Therapeutic principles of behavior simulation. In *Psychotherapy through clinical role playing.* New York: Brunner/Mazel.

Noxon, Chris. (2006). *Rejuvenile: Kickball, cartoons, cupcakes and the reinvention of the American grown-up.* New York: Crown.

Schaefer, Charles (Ed.). (2003). *Play therapy with adults.* Hoboken, NJ: John Wiley & Sons.

Schutz, Will. (1967). *Joy: Expanding human awareness.* New York: Grove. (This and the reference below were key books in the mid-period of the "human potential movement," and mention a number of techniques.)

Schutz, Will. (1971). *Here comes everybody: Bodymind and encounter culture.* New York: Harrow/Harper & Row.

Wise, Nina. (2002). *A big, new, free, happy, unusual life: Self-expression and spiritual practice for those who have time for neither.* New York: Broadway Books/Random House. (Also, see on her website, good articles: <www.ninawise.com/body_tells.html> Stories the body tells. And <www.ninawise.com/exercises.html>)

Zaporah, Ruth. (1995). *Action theater: the improvisation of presence.* Berkeley, CA: North Atlantic Books.

Zaporah, Ruth. (2006). *Action theater: The manual.* (Publisher: Author). <www.actiontheater.com>

Appendix A

GENERAL BIBLIOGRAPHY
(Annotated)

Adam Blatner

A certain number of books have been referred to by a significant number of the chapter contributors, and, since these refer to the general themes of this whole book, instead of listing them repeatedly in each chapter, we chose to list them all together here. These books are also general comments on the nature of drama. Please note that books that deal with warm-up exercises, improv techniques, or structured experiences are listed separately in Appendix B.

As new books are published, I'll put them along with other references that may be a little more peripheral onto a webpage supplement to this Appendix.

Some other books commonly mentioned, such as the ones by Spolin and Boal, address both techniques and also principles.

Especially notable is Toni Sant's website: **Applied and Interactive Theatre Guide**. This is being updated periodically, so can offer sources that emerge after the actual publication of this book. It is the richest source of material, with sections on Boal Techniques, Drama Therapy, Playback Theatre, Psychodrama, Sociodrama, Theatre-in-Education, Training and Development, and other resources and links. <www.tonisant.com/aitg>

Barton, Robert. (2006). *Acting: Onstage and off* (4th ed.). Belmont, CA: Thomson Wadsworth. (Although aimed at actors-in-training, there is some here that can speak to the general public in building the skills of spontaneity. It complements Blatner's "*Creating Your Living*" (2nd edition, revised, in preparation)—about how to use these methods in everyday life. An further revision of this book will be titled "Theatre in Your Life.")

Bergren, Mark, Cox, Molly, & Detmar, Jim. (2002) *Improvise this! How to think on your feet so you don't fall on your face.* Hyperion Press, NY. 2002. Generally useful in appreciating the value of improvisation.

Blatner, Adam. (2000). *Foundations of psychodrama: History, theory, and practice.* (4th ed.). New York: Springer. (Has discussions of values of improvisation, spontaneity, self-expression, and related issues that apply equally well to thinking about using drama in everyday life, business, community building, etc.—not just psychodrama, and not just for therapy.)

Blatner, Adam & Blatner, Allee. (1997). *The Art of Play: Helping adults to reclaim imagination and spontaneity.* New York: Brunner/Mazel. Has chapters on cultural factors that inhibit improvisational and imaginative play, as well as methods, good references for applications in education, therapy, and other contexts.

Boal, Augusto. (1979). *Theatre of the oppressed.* (Boal's seminal work in the 1970s has continued to spread and influenced and merged with other approaches to applied drama, theatre of development, etc. See more specific references at the end of the Chapter 21, and there are further references on his warm-ups and techniques in Appendix B.)

Boal, Augusto. (1995). *The Rainbow of desire: The Boal method of theatre and therapy.* New York: Routledge. (Explores a philosophical approach to theatre as a tool for empowerment.)

Bolton, Gavin. (1986). *Selected writings on drama in education.* London: Longman.

Booth, David & Martin-Smith, Alistair. (1988). *Re-cognizing Richard Courtney: Selected writings on drama and education.* Markham, Ontario, Canada: Pembroke. (Courtney is a profound theoretician of the dynamics of drama, psychologically, educationally, culturally.)

Booth, Eric. (2001). *The everyday work of art: Awakening the extraordinary in your daily life.* Lincoln, NE: iUniverse. Captures the spirit of creativity that is associated with many forms of improvised and interactive drama.

Boyd, Neva. (1975). *Hanbook of recreational games.* New York: Dover. (Earlier published in Chicago: H. T. Fitzsimons). This pioneer stimulated Viola Spolin (1906–1994), whose work on Theatre Games (see Appendix B) continues to be a major source of inspiration to those promoting the cause of improvisation.

Cameron, Julia. (2002). *Walking in this world: The practiced art of creativity.* New York: Penguin Putnam. <www.penguinputnam.com> (And also her other books, *The Artist's Way, The Golden Thread*, etc.)

Cook, H.Caldwell. (1917). *The Play Way.* London: Heinemann. One of the early writings that laid the foundation for drama in education.

Courtney, Richard. (1974). *Play, drama and thought: The intellectual background to drama in education* (3rd revised edition). New York: Drama Book Specialists. (This is a classic, for appreciating not only drama in education, but informs and supports the other approaches in this book. His many other writings further elaborate on and deepen the argument of the way drama can promote fundamental skills needed in today's world. (See Booth and Martin-Smith)

Courtney, Richard. (1980). *The dramatic curriculum.* New York: Drama Book Specialists.

Courtney, Richard. (1990). *Drama and intelligence: A cognitive theory.* Montreal: McGill-Queen's University Press. (This book offers a more in-depth, philosophical, psychological, and intellectual foundation for the many possible applications of drama, especially in education. Not only is the subject matter learned more deeply, but the other skills of dramatizing are also valuable in life.)

Courtney, Richard. (1995). *Drama and feeling: An aesthetic theory.* Montreal: McGill-Queen's University Press. (As with his earlier book, Courtney presented ideas that can be studied and pondered deeply.)

Dewey, John. (1916/1966). *Democracy and education.* New York: The Free Press (The MacMillan Company). (This is a major contribution by an eminent American philosopher, speaking to the value of learning by doing.)

Emunah, Renée. (1994). *Acting for Real: Drama Therapy Process, Technique, and Performance.* New York: Brunner/Mazel. (Documents the power of drama therapy and provides a useful manual for developing, selecting, and sequencing activities to reach a given population or group. See other books in the chapter on drama therapy, also.)

Evreinov, Nikolai. (1927, 1970). *The theatre in life.* (Ed. and translated by Alexander Nazaroff). New York: Benjamin Blom. (Essays on the basic impulse towards drama, what the author calls "theatricality," beyond the social institution of traditional theatre.)

Gressler, Thomas H. (2002). *Theatre as the essential liberal art in the American university*. Lewiston, NY: Edwin Mellen Press.

Halpern, Charna;, Close, Del; & Johnson, Kim. (1994). *Truth in comedy: the manual of improvisation*. Colorado Springs, CO: Meriwether. (Beyond warm-up games, this explores longer forms of improv drama.)

Hodgson, John & Richards, Ernest. (1966). *Improvisation*. London: Methuen. (Explores the values and other aspects of this primal dynamic.)

Izzo, Gary. (1997). *The art of play: the new genre of interactive theatre*. Portsmouth, NH: Heinemann. (In spite of this book having the same initial title as Blatner's *Art of Play* book, and a fair amount of shared vision, it has become more widely known, and as the subtitle suggests, addresses the dynamics of interactive theatre. See Appendix B for his related book).

Johnston, Chris. (1998). *House of games: Making theatre from everyday life*. New York: Routledge (Taylor & Francis). (In addition to presenting principles in useful ways, the book also offers a number of games and exercises.)

Johnston, Chris. (2006). *The improvisation game: discovering the secrets of spontaneous performance*. London: Nick Hern. (<www.nickhernbooks. co.uk) The book explores improvisation practice as it is used in a range of contexts, in theatres, community centers, sites of conflict, prisons and hospitals. How do improvisers work together? What are the protocols, conventions and practices? The book considers primarily theatre but in looking at improvisation as a core discipline, also considers its use in dance and music.

Johnstone, Keith. (1979). *Impro: Improvisation and the theatre*. New York: Routledge.

Johnstone, Keith. (1999). *Impro for Storytellers*. New York: Routledge/Theatre Arts Books.

Jones, Brie. (1993). *Improve with improv: a guide to improvisation*. Colorado Springs, CO: Meriwether. (These publishers have a variety of books on aspects of Improvisation!)

Kerrigan, Sheila. (2001). *The performer's guide to the collaborative process*. Portsmouth, NH: Heinemann. Many ideas for team-building, for anyone working with a troupe.

Klein, Maxine. (1978). *Theatre for the 98%*. Boston: South End Press. (The author promotes this present book's vision of a more popular use of drama methods.)

Koppett, Kat. (2001). *Training to imagine: Practical improvisational theatre techniques to enhance creativity, teamwork, leadership and learning.* Sterling, VA: Stylus.

Lowe, Robert. (2000). *Improvisation, Inc.: Harnessing spontaneity to engage people and groups.* San Francisco: Jossey-Bass.

Nelson, Linda & Finneran, Lanell. (2006). *Drama and the adolescent journey: Warm-ups and activities to address teen issues.* Portsmouth, NH: Heinemann.

Nicholson, Helen. (2005). *Applied drama: Theatre and performance practices.* London: Palgrave McMillan.

Pine, B. J. & Gilmore, J. H. (1999). *The experience economy: Work is theatre and every business a stage.* Boston: Harvard Business School Press. (Building on Disneyworld, notes how many businesses now integrate an increasing trend towards transforming mere products or services into experiences designed with a dramaturgical sensibility.)

Polsky, Marvin. (1998). *Let's Improvise: becoming creative, expressive and spontaneous through drama* (3rd ed.). New York: Applause Theatre Books. Has some reflections on the values of improvisation above and beyond the techniques presented.

Rohd, Michael. (1998). *Hope is Vital: Theater for community, conflict, and dialogue.* Portsmouth, NH: Heinemann. (This is an especially important book! Speaks to many aspects of applied theatre, and provides strategies to help young people open up and explore their feelings through theatre, offering a safe place for them to air their views with dignity, respect, and freedom.)

Spolin, Viola: See in Appendix B. Though most of her books describe theatre games and warm-up techniques, she also presents some useful philosophical and psychological reflections. She is one of the more essential people to know about.

Stanislavski, Constantin. (1949). *Building a Character.* (trans. Hapgood, E.R.) New York: Theatre Arts Books. (These two classics of "method acting" have become foundations of drama training in many classes.)

Stanislavski, Constantin. (1948) *An Actor Prepares.* (trans. Hapgood, E.R.) New York: Theatre Arts Books.

Sternberg, Pat. (1998). *Theatre for conflict resolution: In the classroom and beyond.* Portsmouth, NH: Heinemann. (Offers practical examples for applying theatre as a problem-solving approach in a range of settings that can be adapted for use with people with disabilities.)

Sternberg, Pat & Garcia, Antonina. (2000). *Sociodrama: Who's in your shoes?* (2nd ed.). Westport, CT: Praeger. (1st ed., 1989, 1994.) (Presents effective tools for engaging groups in role-play and enactment.)

Taylor, Philip (Ed.). (1996). *Researching drama and arts education*. London: Faliner.

Taylor, Philip. (2000). *The drama classroom: Action, reflection, transformation*. London: Routledge/Faliner.

Taylor, Philip. (2003) *Applied theatre: creating transformative encounters in the community*. Portsmouth, NH. Heinemann. <www.heinemanndrama. com> (This book is one of the first about this emerging field, though its scope is narrower.)

Taylor, Philip, & Warner, Cris (Eds). (2006). Structure and spontaneity: the drama in education of Cecily O'Neill. Sterling, VA: Stylus. <www. styluspub.com>

Thompson, James. (2003). *Applied theatre: Bewilderment and beyond*. Bern: Peter Lang AG.

Warren, Bernie. (Ed.) (1984). *Using the creative arts in therapy*. Cambridge, MA: Brookline Books.

Wirth, Jeff. (1994). *Interactive acting: Acting, improvisation, and interacting for audience participatory theatre*. Fall Creek, OR: Fall Creek Press. (This is also a classic.)

Appendix B

WARM-UPS, THEATRE GAMES, EXPERIENTIAL EXERCISES, IMPROVISATION METHODS AND ACTION TECHNIQUES

Adam Blatner

Many of the approaches in this book involve the use of activities referred to by putting words like "warm-up," "action," "theatre," "drama," "experiential," and "structured" together with other words such as "techniques," "methods," "exercises," "experiences," or "games" in various combinations. For a limited time, in a workshop, class, or program, group members all engage in a similar endeavor, each giving the task his or her own creative expression. These activities have a number of different sources:

- psychodrama, sociodrama, and drama therapy
- creative drama, theatre games, and "Improv" or improvisational theatre
- encounter groups and programs for personal development
- organizational development, team building
- children's play and games

Psychodrama gave rise to role playing, sociodrama, bibliodrama, and the like, and the warm-up techniques have proliferated since Moreno developed the method in the mid 1930s (Blatner, 2000). Many of these action techniques were then incorporated into the other approaches mentioned. Moreno believed that the most creative work derives from an improvisational dramatic process, and Moreno noted that improv—the spontaneity process—required a gradual process of warming-up. One couldn't be expected to start cold and proceed with creatively exploring a situation in action.

Theatre Games are most associated with the writings of Viola Spolin, and since then, further variations and new techniques were developed. Most of these have come to be used by adult improv groups, teen-aged groups, and to some extent, teachers of drama in elementary schools.

Creative Drama came out of the early work of a number of innovators, such as Nellie McCaslin. (Spolin, too, wrote her first book for younger children.) By the later 1960s, many drama teachers were beginning to use Spolin's and other people's warm-up activities as ways of engaging their classes and developing the flexibility of the would-be actors.

Encounter Groups began as a group therapy-like approach adapted by Humanistic Psychologists as a form of personal development for healthy people who are seeking to become even more mentally flexible and interpersonally sensitive and skilled. Beginning around the mid-1960s, these groups also began to integrate action methods and experiential exercises drawn from a wide range of approaches: Moreno's psychodrama was a significant source, but techniques were also adapted from Fritz Perls' Gestalt therapy; Alexander Lowen's Bioenergetic Analysis; Roberto Assagioli's Psychosynthesis; guided fantasy; sensory awakening; simple martial arts-related exercises (such as those associated with Tai Chi); various spiritual practices; and other active approaches in psychotherapy. The psychologist, Will Schutz, was especially important in the way he integrated many of the aforementioned modalities, making these groups not just opportunities for interpersonal encounter, but weaving in more opportunities for multi-dimensional personal development, self-awareness, and vitality.

Training Games have emerged in the fields of business and organizational development. Some of this has roots in role playing and sensitivity training in the 1950s. By the late 1960s, these were more focused forms than the encounter group. These were aimed at building creativity, initiative, and team spirit.

Drama Therapy emerged in the 1970s and, in addition to absorbing techniques from psychodrama and other sources, has developed a number of original techniques that added to those available.

Play Therapy became more recognized as the idea of structured experiences and active intervention began to supplant the previously dominant approach of the therapist as relatively passive. Responding to this, a host of innovators developed board games, with cards that suggest that the player enact some simple feeling or talk about some aspect of life. Catalogues of play therapy and child psychotherapy materials now are replete with these role-playing games.

Others have been exploring ways to help adults develop their childlikeness and spontaneity.

Social and Emotional Skill Learning: The use of the aforementioned board games and classroom exercise now are applied in various educational contexts, aside from therapy. The goal of helping young people to develop their psychological resiliency, in addition to the content of the basic traditional curriculum, has expanded the use of these kinds of approaches. Now these are also applied in religious schools.

A Caution

These techniques are best used within a planned program adapted to the needs of the client population, and that program should include a number of components besides the use of action techniques. Dr. Irvin Yalom, in his classic texts on group psychotherapy, revised from the mid-70s through the mid-90s, both acknowledged the possible place of such techniques and warned against their mindless use. He suggested that group leaders understand a thinking through of which techniques are indicated, and questioned their use if the group is proceeding nicely.

The point here is to recognize that you may find ideas about warm-ups and experiential techniques in any of the aforementioned fields, and so you shouldn't limit yourself to just looking at references in your own field. Drama therapists can get ideas from teachers of improv, or from psychodramatists, and vice versa. As for which techniques are truly "original," we should note that these techniques have been passed along and modified so that it is difficult if not impossible to trace back the originators of this or that technique and give them credit.

Websites

A few of the more important sources will be noted here as well as in the web-page supplements. There are scores of these books, chapters, articles in professional journals, and so forth. Because the field continues to grow, the supplements can be updated periodically. To begin with, this chapter has a webpage supplement of more references:

<www.interactiveimprov.com/apxbwarmups.html> It notes numerous websites on improvisation—and there are many others. The following websites, though, seem to be especially rich, serving in part as clearing houses that link to others and offer articles, lists of improv games, etc:

<www.spolin.com> (In addition to noting some theatre games, Gary Schwartz also has interesting articles about improv and related activities, as well as other useful links.)
  <www.lowrent.net/improv/>
  <www.fuzzyco.com/improv/games.html>
  <www.creativedrama.com>
  <www.byu.edu/tma/arts-ed>
  <www.svsu.edu/theatre/summercamps/theatregames.htm>
  <www.improv.ca/Official website for the Canadian Improv Games>
  <www.humanpingpongball.com/improv_games.html>
  <www.sheeridiocy.net/games.html>
  <www.unexpectedproductions.org/new/playbook/playbook.html>
  booklist at <www.edta.org/thespian_store>

Books

The following have been a bit more impressive as resources, and others will be added to the webpage supplement to this chapter mentioned above.

Baim, Clark; Brookes, Sally; & Mountford, Alun. (Eds.). (2002). The *Geese Theatre handbook: Drama with offenders and people at risk*. Winchester: Waterside Press. (www.watersidepress.co.uk)

Basom, Jonas. (2005). The Drama Game File—A CD-ROM for Arts and Literacy, Pre-K through 12th Grade. (Free tour, sample pages, ordering: <www.DramaEd.net>) (Includes school system theatre arts standards, printable posters, integration ideas, etc.)

Bergman, John & Hewish, Saul. (2003). *Challenging experience: An experiential approach to the treatment of serious offenders*. Oklahoma City: Wood n' Barnes.

Blatner, Adam. (2000). A compendium of psychodramatic terms and techniques (pp. 235–257), in *Foundations of psychodrama: history, theory & practice* (4th ed.). New York: Springer.

Cossa, Mario., et al. (2000). Acting Out: the workbook. (See references in Chapter 25). Many games.

Gwinn, Peter and Charna Halpern. (2003). *Group improvisation: the manual of ensemble improv games*. Colorado Springs, CO: Meriwether Publishing. (This publisher is notable for offering numerous books about improvisational drama: <www.meriwetherpublishing.com>)

Izzo, Gary. (1998). *Acting interactive theatre: A handbook*. Portsmouth, NH: Heinemann. This book offers 150 workshop exercises, a valuable source for building a troupe.

Jones, Justine & Kelley, Mary Ann. (2006). *Improv ideas: a book of games and lists*. Colorado Springs: Meriwether. (This book is a plentiful resource, especially for drama teachers in secondary schools, community colleges, and recreation programs. Over 80 games described in a fair amount of detail with lists of examples.)

Jennings, Sue. (1986). *Creative drama in group work*. London: Winslow Press.

Polsky, Milton. (1997). *Let's improvise: Becoming creative, expressive and spontaneous through drama*. (2nd ed.). Englewood Cliffs, NJ: Prentice-Hall.

Schafer, Max. (2003). *Viola Spolin's Theater games for the classroom CD-ROM*. Evanston, IL: Northwestern University Press. <www.nupress.northwestern. edu All ages, 130 games, examples, lesson planning.

Spolin, Viola: This pioneer has written a number of classic books about theatre games! also see above item under Schafer for the CD-ROM of Spolin games

Spolin, Viola. (1999). *Improvisations for the theater: a handbook of teaching and directing techniques*. (3rd ed.) 412 pg. (1st ed. 1963, 2nd ed. 1985). Evanston, IL: Northwestern University Press. Edited by Paul Sills, her son, and includes new exercises. DeKoven notes: An excellent introduction to the use of theatre games with children, and for me the foundation of my exploration of the Theater of Games. Her "Seven Aspects of Spontaneity" in the theoretical part of the book is a most insightful introduction to play and creativity, and worth the price of the book alone.

Spolin, Viola. (1985). *Theater games for rehearsal: a director's handbook of improvisation for the teacher*. Evanston, IL: Northwestern University Press. (Paperback reprint 1995.) Useful handbook of games and activities that can be easily adapted for use with groups of varying skill levels

Spolin, Viola. (1986). *Theater games for the classroom: a teacher's handbook*. Evanston, IL: Northwestern University Press.

Spolin, Viola. (1989). *Theatre game file*. (200 color-coded cards). Evanston, IL: Northwestern University Press.

Swados, Elizabeth. (2006). *At play: Teaching teenagers theatre*. New York: Faber & Faber. (Many action warm-ups.)

Warren, Bernie & Dunne, Tim. (1996). *Drama games*: drama and group activities for leaders working with people of all ages and abilities. Studio City, CA: Players Press.

White, Liz. (2002). *The action manual: Techniques for enlivening group process and individual counselling*. Toronto, Canada: Author. Available from: www. lizwhiteinaction.com Many psychodramatic methods.

Zimmerman, Suzi. (2004). *More theatre games for young performers*. Colorado Springs: Meriwether.

Appendix C
GLOSSARY
Adam Blatner

Act hunger: Moreno coined this term to recognize that people have a need to not just talk about their feelings, but rather to actually express themselves physically, to speak directly to the "other," or better, to get up and employ the full body in facial expression, gesture, and action. People need to feel themselves actively engaging a situation in order to experience mastery.

Affect: In addition to its more conventional meaning as a verb (i.e., to influence someone or something), the term has another meaning as a noun (i.e., a basic emotional state). Emotions are more complex, often including attitudes associated with affects. According to the psychologist Sylvan Tomkins, basic affects include shame, fear, interest, disgust/dis-smell, enjoyment, sadness. They're built into our neuro-physiological functioning.

Antagonist: A term occasionally used to designate the person in the reciprocal relation to the protagonist. Daughter to father, customer to salesperson, supervisor to employee, etc.

Auxiliary ego (or, often, simply '*auxiliary*'): Moreno's term for anyone who takes a significant role in supporting (acting as an auxiliary to) the protagonist (q.v.) in a psychodrama. It's like "supporting player," but auxiliary roles can include standing in for the protagonist (q.v.), acting as a double (q.v.), and so forth. The task of the auxiliary is to be guided by the director in facilitating the protagonist's exploration of a problem.

Catharsis: The full expression of emotion associated with a thought, attitude, or predicament, often associated with some relief, and at times, a shift of that emotion (e.g., from anger to laughter, from anger to sobbing grief, from fear to anger).

Choice point: A moment in an enactment when a director can decide to stage a scene in either of at least two ways.

Culminating enactment: The scene that most fully expresses the key issues in a psychodrama or sociodrama. This term contrasts with warming up or scenes that are developing the issues, or the cooling-down, scenes that extend the working through of the key feelings. Often this enactment is the most likely to result in a catharsis.

De-roling (also may be spelled as *de-role-ing*): At the end of an enactment, the director or the auxiliaries initiate an clear behavior that indicates to the audience or group that one is no longer in role. This also helps for the person playing an intense or absorbing role to let go of elements of the character just played, to segue back into being his more authentic self, to collapse role distance.) In process drama, the teacher may take off or put on a token piece of costume, a hand prop or special chair to indicate those moments when the teacher leaves the role, while reversing it indicates stepping back into role.

Developmental Transformations: In this method created by David Read Johnson, a noted drama therapist, the client improvises a movement and/or action and, within moments, the therapist responds with a subtle shift in the meaning of the action, the implied context, or other creative association. In turn, the client improvises a response and the two people interact in this fashion for five to fifty minutes. Variations of this type of embodied encounter may occur also among group members in therapy or personal development classes.

Director: In drama, this is the person who facilitates the enactment. In psychodrama, this role also includes being not only the producer, but also therapist, group process manager, and analyst both of the protagonist in the enactment and the group dynamics.

Distancing: This is an approach used to balance emotional and cognitive engagement in an enactment. Some people are *overdistanced* (somewhat too emotionally detached) while others may be *underdistanced* (easily enmeshed in emotional content; overwhelmed by emotion). The distancing needs of a participant can fluctuate, so a drama activity or approach can be adjusted based on the group or individual's distancing needs.

Double: Moreno used this term to designate the auxiliary (q.v.) who portrays the inner voice or role of either the protagonist or antagonist in a psychodrama or sociodrama or role play.

(See "shotgun doubling.")

Fluid sculpture: A term taken from playback theatre, in which a tableau (q.v.) is presented in a moving form. (Also related to the psychodramatic technique of the action sociogram, which evolved in some settings as family sculpture.)

Forum Theatre: One of the main approaches within the complex that comprise Augusto Boal's Theatre of the Oppressed (Chapter 21). A scene, usually indicating some kind of oppression, is shown twice. During the replay, any member of the audience ("spect-actor") is allowed to shout, "Stop!" and then come forward and take the place of one of the oppressed characters, showing how they could change the situation to enable a different outcome. Several alternatives may be explored by different spect-actors. The other actors remain in character, improvising their responses.

Hot Seating: One of the players in an enactment can be interrogated by the audience as to his motivations, underlying attitudes, and other thoughts not expressed in roles. In a sense, it draws out "asides" and deepens the psychological understanding of the role. The responses are given by the player "in role," but being more disclosing than that role might be in actuality. This technique is used in theatre-in-education (TIE), Theatre of the Oppressed, and other methods. Sometimes characters may be hot-seated in pairs or small groups. This technique also helps the audience to develop their critical thinking and questioning skills.

Interactive Drama: There's a spectrum of inter-activity ranging from a discussion of audience members with actors and director, through audience members getting on stage and re-playing a scene with the actors (as sometimes happens in the Theatre of the Oppressed), to the main players and supporting players being the group members.

Joker: The term used by Augusto Boal as a key player in the Theatre of the Oppressed. Taken from the Brazilian word referring to the wild card, capable of in effect playing many roles, referring to the role roughly corresponding to that of the director in psychodrama. In Boal's work, though, this role has many functions. For example, not only in some ways does the joker facilitate, but sometimes "difficult-ates" or works the situation to bring out its complexities and moral ambiguities. Generally, though, the joker acts as a intermediary, facilitates communication between the players and the audience.

Mandala: A circular figure, created as a drawing, sand painting, with scarves, or other elements, suggests a center and a somewhat symmetrical inner design. Mandala is a Sanskrit word, from the culture of India. Carl Jung noted the power of this figure as a resonant symbol for the dynamic in the mind that seeks a balanced center. As a symbol, it suggests wholeness or completion.

Mantle of the Expert: Another term in process drama in education (Chapter 9), this technique, developed by British pioneer Dorothy Heathcote, involves imagining that the students are experts in a particular field, while the teacher is relatively ignorant. This presses the students to investigate more actively, since they are expected to know the "answers." More about this technique may be found on: <www.mantleoftheexpert.com>

(More about Dorothy Heathcote: <www.partnership.mmu.ac.uk/drama/archive.html>)

Playback theatre: An approach developed in the mid-1970s by Jonathan Fox and Jo Salas, described in Chapter 1, in which a troupe of actors re-enacts a story told by someone in the audience. It is becoming increasingly more popular and represents an important example of the improvisational and interactive approaches described in this book. In addition, many of its component techniques have been integrated into many of the other methods described in these pages.

Playmaking: In theatre, it may involve the whole process of developing a product-oriented play, but as part of an interactive process, it refers more to an approach that draws on the creativity of all the actors as co-playwrights and co-directors.

Protagonist: In psychodrama, the person whose experience is being explored during the enactment. Auxiliaries (q.v.) are used to help fill out the characters in the scene.

Psychodrama: Described more fully in Chapter 15, the term refers to a role playing enactment in which the focus is on the individual's experience, related to the particulars of the people involved. (See contrast with sociodrama.)

Psychodramatic methods: Also known as action techniques, experiential exercises, these directed activities may be applied in other group settings, apart from the full sequences of classical psychodrama. (See Appendix B.)

Rant (the): A technique in which four or five participants create one spontaneous, intense monologue. One speaks at a time, then drops out immediately when interrupted. The objective is to represent the experience of the group as a whole. (Related to "soliloquy.")

Role reversal. This psychodramatic technique can involve either: (1) two people exchanging roles at a certain point in their interaction; they try to imagine what the situation seems to be from that other viewpoint, to empathize and speak from that perspective; (2) in spite of the other "real" person may not be present, the protagonist takes that absent other's role for the purposes of understanding, and then speaks and continues the interaction. Or the other person is played by an auxiliary. Role reversal is a way to temporarily relinquishing egocentricity and developing empathy, sometimes as a way to explore a situation with greater understanding and wider perspective.

Shotgun Doubling: A variation of doubling in which anyone in the group is free to get up and take the role of the unspoken voice or "voice over" of one of the main players in a psychodramatic or sociodramatic interaction.

Sociodrama: The role playing of situations or conflicts between role types or sub-groups.

In contrast to psychodrama, which addresses the particulars of a person's life, sociodrama examines those elements that are part of a role and thus may be shared with others who play the same role. The exploration examines the general cultural definitions and implied expectations, attitudes, backgrounds, competencies, and demands of these roles, and how they play out in relation to each other—such as police and member of a minority, teenaged boys and girls, etc.

Soliloquy: In drama, a person, usually the protagonist, speaks as if expressing inner thoughts.

Tapping In: A technique in which, during an enactment, the director or teacher may tap on the shoulder of one of the people playing a role in the scene to ask to hear what the group member is thinking. It evokes asides or the equivalent of a voice over.

Teacher in Role: A technique in process drama (Chapter 9), in which the teacher becomes on of the characters in a dramatic predicament. In role, the teacher asks questions of the students who are also in role, playing other parts in the situation. These tend to reinforce the role-taking and elicit thinking and enquiry from them.

Theatre games: Group activities designed to warm people up, develop the capacity for spontaneity and improvisation. (See Appendix B.)

Theatre of the Oppressed: This is a theatre approach that uses a variety of methods, ranging from workshops to interactive performance. Described more fully in Chapter 21, it is becoming increasingly influential.

Warm-up: The process of building the readiness of a group to engage in improvised activity. It includes helping people to feel more trust in others in the group, building group cohesion, an interest in certain common concerns, an increasing willingness for self-disclosure, and a heightened level of spontaneity.

Glossary of "improv" terms: <www.humanpingpongball.com/improv_glossary.html>

CONTRIBUTORS'
BIOGRAPHICAL SUMMARIES
(Alphabetically Arranged)

Sally Bailey, MFA, MSW, RDT/BCT is associate professor of theatre at Kansas State University in Manhattan, Kansas where she directs the drama therapy program and graduate studies in theatre. She is past president of the National Association for Drama Therapy and current treasurer of The Drama Therapy Fund. She is also the author of *Wings to Fly: Bringing Theatre Arts to Students with Special Needs*, and *Dreams to Sign*.

Clark Baim, M.Ed., Dip. Psychodrama Psychotherapy (UKCP), is an independent psychodramatist, trainer and theatre director/teacher. He was the founder and first Director of Geese Theatre UK, which focuses on work with offenders. He is a trainer for the UK Probation Service and continues to specialize in working with offenders.

Adam Blatner, M.D., is doubly Board Certified in Adult and also Child & Adolescent Psychiatry, a Certified Trainer, Educator, & Practitioner of Psychodrama, and the author of several major books and many chapters and articles about psychodrama and related subjects. Retired from practice and living in Georgetown, Texas, he continues to write, teach and seeks to promote mental flexibility and psychological literacy. <www.blatner.com/adam/

Allee Blatner co-authored with Adam Blatner *The Art of Play: An Adult's Guide to Reclaiming Imagination and Spontaneity*. She is a creative artist who was trained at The University of Texas at Austin and Carnegie-Mellon University.

Staci Block, MSW, LCSW, is Director of the Reflections program and also of Creative Interventions in Hackensack, New Jersey. She is an Adjunct Professor at William Paterson University and an instructor for the Arts in Prevention Certificate Program through Rutgers University School of Social Work Continuing Education Program. Her expertise involves using action methods in team building, developing peer leaders, addressing adolescent substance abuse and creating interactive training for staff development.

Kim Burden, MA, LCMHC, ADTR, RDT/BCT, CP, Certified Practitioner of Body-Mind Centering™, is an adjunct faculty member at Antioch University New England. She has extensive experience as a performer, choreographer and director and worked for ten years with ActingOut, a youth theatre drama therapy program in Keene, New Hampshire. She has presented extensively at psychodrama, drama therapy, and dance-movement therapy conferences and maintains a private psychotherapy and healing arts practice in Keene, NH.

Mecca Burns is a Registered Drama Therapist and Board-Certified Trainer in Charlottesville, Virginia. After years of working in inpatient settings, she began to apply theatre to social issues. She currently co-directs PRESENCE Center for Applied Theatre Arts, has a private drama therapy practice serving children with developmental issues, and is project director for the Charlottesville Living History Initiative.

Linda Condon, LMHC, PAT, is a Licensed Mental Health Counselor and Certified Psychodramatist with a private practice in Largo, Florida. She has a special interest in integrating mental health and spiritual growth. She conducts psychodrama training workshops, directs retreat experiences, and is the author of *The Warm-Up Ring: Keys for Energizing Your Group.*

Mario Cossa, MA, RDT/MT, TEP, CAWT is a psychodramatist, drama therapist, and theatre educator who specializes in work with adolescent groups and trauma survivors. He is also an actor, director, choreographer and playwright. He travels globally, offering trainings in the USA, Canada, the UK, South Africa, Australia, and New Zealand. His book, *Rebels with a Cause: Working with Adolescents Using Action Techniques,* was published in 2006 by Jessica Kingsley Press. <www.dramario.com>

Anne M. Curtis MA, RDT, CTSS is a Drama Therapist, Actress and Theatre Instructor, active in mystery theatre for many years. She specializes in trauma work using improvisational theatre and humor to assist people of all ages in healthcare settings. Author of *Circles of Life: A Creative Curriculum for Healing*

Traumatized Children, Anne presents professional workshops on "Trauma Drama" for community agencies, conferences and universities.

Bernie DeKoven, M.A., is an educator, drama therapist, and the author of *The Well-Played Game, Junkyard Sports*, and many articles about the connections between games and fun. He promotes the use of more constructive recreation, lectures and travels widely. He has taught his "Deep Fun" approach at the Esalen Institute in Big Sur, California.

Allison Downey, M.F.A., is an Assistant Professor of Creative Arts Education, and former Director of Theatre Education at Western Michigan University. She is the co-founder of Theatre Action Project in Austin, Texas' only TIE company. Allison earned her MFA in Creative Drama and Theatre for Youth from the University of Texas at Austin. She is a professional performing songwriter and storyteller as well: <www.allisondowney.com>

Hannah Fox, MA, is Assistant Professor of Dance and Theatre, Manhattanville College, and the artistic director of Big Apple Playback Theatre. She is a lead trainer with the International School of Playback Theatre. Hannah also devises original theatre with teenagers, most recently at the 92nd Street Y (an Eve Ensler project.) She is the daughter of the founders of Playback Theatre.

Joel Gluck, MEd, RDT, is a dramatherapist and creator of Insight Improvisation. As Senior Affiliate with The Ariel Group, Joel has offered theatre-based leadership training through Harvard Executive Education and major organizations internationally since 1994. He's brought drama for personal growth to schoolteachers in India, tsunami survivors in Thailand, and ex-prisoners in Boston's inner city. Joel uses his background in theatre, meditation, and education in Insight Improvisation workshops, dramatherapy training programs, and private practice.

Muriel Gold, Ph.D., is former Artistic Director of the Saidye Bronfman Centre Theatre in Montreal, Quebec and has taught at McGill University, Concordia University and Dawson College. She has written three books about the Fictional Family technique.

Mary K. Grigsby, MEd, LPC, is licensed as a professional counselor in North Carolina and nationally certified as a group psychotherapist. She has provided counseling and training since 1983 with families, couples, individuals, and groups.

Gordon Hensley, BS, MFA, is an Assistant Professor of Theatre at Appalachian State University in North Carolina, and is a member of AATE. The founder of <www.cre8tivedrama.com>, he has acted and directed many places across the country, as well as presented at multiple national conferences.

Catherine Hughes wrote *Museum Theatre: Communicating with Visitors through Drama* (1998). For many years, she coordinated the Theatre Program at the Museum of Science, Boston, and was the founding executive director of the International Museum Theatre Alliance. She is finishing a Ph.D. in education at Ohio State University's School of Teaching and Learning. Her research focuses on how performance affects memory and learning.

Daniel A. Kelin, II, MFA, is Director of Drama Education for Honolulu Theatre for Youth and Director of Theatre Training for an American Samoa company. He authored To Feel as our Ancestors Did, a book on oral history with young people. In 2006 he received a fellowship from the International Children's Theatre Association supporting work in India. He is working on a book on Drama with English Language Learners.

Abigail Leeder, MA is the advisor of the Sexual Wellness Advocacy Team, a peer education group that uses theatre to engage students about healthy sexual relationships at the University of Oregon. She was formerly a Primary Counselor at Project Pride in Oakland, California and graduated from the Counseling Psychology/Drama Therapy program at the California Institute of Integral Studies. She is a founding member of the Emerald Valley Playback Theatre troupe in Eugene, Oregon.

Ronald Miller, Ph.D is an Associate Professor of Theatre Arts at McDaniel College, where he directs the focus area in interactive theatre within the Theatre Arts major. He teaches courses in interactive and therapeutic theatre, in acting, and in performance theory. He is the director of McDaniel Playback, an undergraduate playback theatre company. He also leads workshops in sociometry for staff development, and in using drama to work with interpersonal conflict.

Doyle Ott, Ph.D, is the artistic director of Splash Circus Theatre in Emeryville, California and lecturer in theatre at Sonoma State University. A clown and arts educator, he has performed and taught with numerous circuses and theatre companies, and chairs the research committee of the American Youth Circus Organization. He trained at the Dell'Arte School and is a graduate of the San Francisco Clown Conservatory.

Doug Paterson, Ph.D., is Professor of Theatre at the University of Nebraska at Omaha. He has hosted international conferences on the Theatre of the Oppressed since 1995; offered over 250 TO workshops and presentations regionally, nationally and internationally; co-founded four theaters; and published on numerous topics. His passion remains theatre and social change and he continues to work actively to promote the work of Augusto Boal and Paulo Freire.

Jade Raybin, M.A. in Women's Spirituality, MFA in Theatre, has studied and facilitated transformational theatre with youth and adults throughout since 2002. Jade has acted as an educational theatre consultant for Planned Parenthood Golden Gate, University of Oregon, New Conservatory Theater Center, and Revelation Law Firm. Currently, Jade is a faculty member at New College in San Francisco, California, where she teaches courses on theatre arts and adolescent rites of passage.

Ted Rubenstein, MFA, MA, RDT, Psy. D. Candidate Vice President Expressive Arts Therapy Music Institute of Chicago Clinical Director Institute for Therapy through the Arts in Chicago; writing about applications of role playing in business.

Sheila Rubin, MA, LMFT, RDT/BCT, is a Licensed Marriage and Family Therapist in private practice in San Francisco. She is an adjunct professor and graduate of the California Institute of Integral Studies (CIIS) Drama Therapy Program, and offers Life Stories Self-Revelatory Performance workshops and alternative track drama therapy training in her Berkeley studio. She directed The Heart-to-Heart Intergenerational theatre troupe. <www.thehealingstory.com>

Thomas M. Stallone, Psy.D., is a psychologist and director of the Attention Disorders Clinic of Vancouver, Washington. He has authored several clinical articles and has an avocational interest in psychodrama, adult and children's theatre, Celtic and medieval cultures. He has taught children's theatre, performed in Off-Broadway plays and has played numerous roles as part of his involvement with medieval re-creation groups.

John Sullivan, M.A. is a drama therapist on the faculty of the University of Texas Medical Branch, affiliated with the Sealy Center for Environmental Health & Medicine, the National Institute of Environmental Health Sciences, and the Department of Preventive Medicine & Community Health. This role involves many outreach programs in environmental toxicology, risk communication, medical ethics, ecology, and other socially relevant issues. He has an extensive background in this work.

Armand Volkas, MFA, MA, MFT, RDT/BCT, Associate Professor in the Drama Therapy Program of California Institute of Integral Studies in San Francisco, Clinical Director of The Living Arts Counseling Center and Director of The Living Arts Playback Theatre Ensemble in Oakland California, conducts a private practice in psychotherapy, and travels widely fostering workshops that address inter-cultural and international tensions through his Healing the Wounds of History program.

Gustave J. Weltsek-Medina, Ph.D., is an Assistant Professor at the University of Puerto Rico, Cayey, in the Departmento De Ingles. His research explores the way words are used in cultures, challenges subtle assumptions embedded in dominant ways of talking and writing, and weaves in feminism, aspects of postmodernism, and considers how drama and other performance activities deal with them. His activist work includes La Obra Del Curaje in Indianapolis.

Daniel J. Wiener, Ph.D., RDT/BCT, is a licensed psychologist and a Professor in the Department of Counseling and Family Therapy at Central Connecticut State University. In addition to authoring the book, Rehearsals for Growth, he is also the editor of two recently published anthologies about the creative arts therapies. Board-certified in Family Psychology, an AAMFT Approved Supervisor, he has written and presented extensively on the therapeutic applications of dramatic methods.

Rosilyn Wilder, Ed.D., RDT/BCT, died in early 2006. She was the author of several books on using drama with elders, creative drama, and intergenerational theatre. Holding a doctorate Gerontology and Creative Arts, she had over 25 years experience as professional actress/director, and applied drama in many other settings, in addition to being on the Board of Directors of the National Association of Drama Therapy.

David L. Young, Ph.D., is the Organizing Chair of the 2007 conference of the American Alliance for Theatre and Education (AATE) and the editor of their *Stage of the Art* (SOTA) journal. He has published numerous articles on drama education theory and is a playwright and theatre director. He teaches drama at the Blacklock Fine Arts Elementary School in Langley, a suburb of Vancouver, BC (Canada).

Deborah J. Zuver, MA, LMFT, RDT/BCT, is coordinator for Project STIR (Steps Toward Independence and Responsibility) at the University of North Carolina Center for Development and Learning in Chapel Hill. Ms Zuver has developed a range of projects that address clinical issues and use enactment as a training tool with all ages and ability levels.

INDEX

978-0-595-41750-6
0-595-41750-7

CPSIA information can be obtained
at www.ICGtesting.com
Printed in the USA
LVHW051115051221
705331LV00010B/1453

9 780595 417506